TURNING POINTS
in the
EDUCATION OF DEAF PEOPLE

TURNING POINTS
in the
EDUCATION OF DEAF PEOPLE

by

Edward L. Scouten

National Technical Institute for the Deaf
Rochester Institute of Technology
Rochester, New York

The Interstate Printers & Publishers, Inc.
Danville, Illinois

Library of Congress Catalog Card No. 83-80062

1 2 3
4 5 6
7 8 9

ISBN 0-8134-2293-0

DEDICATION

Each of the following educators of the deaf represents a "turning point" in the author's personal career as a teacher of the deaf. To each of them, this history is dedicated in gratitude for their instruction, assistance, and friendship over many years.

Dr. Frank W. Booth
Mr. Harvey T. Christian
Mrs. Mary Elizabeth Hill
Dr. Elwood A. Stevenson
Dr. Thomas C. Forrester
Dr. Percival Hall
Dr. Sam B. Craig
Dr. Powrie V. Doctor
Dr. Lloyd V. Funchess
Dr. William J. McClure
Dr. D. Robert Frisina
Dr. William E. Castle

Be ashamed to die until
you have won some victory
for humanity.

FOREWORD

Throughout the centuries, the men and women who have pioneered developments in the field of education of the deaf have been obsessed with a singleness of purpose: teaching deaf children to process spoken and written language accurately, thereby permitting them to master learning and to interact successfully with the world around them. Over the years, those dedicated individuals developed a repertoire of approaches that sometimes bewilders those encountering the profession for the first time. Educational philosophies and methodologies have grown up around the singular beliefs of their initiators, often injecting controversy into the process of development and implementation. The stories of these various beliefs, artfully assembled in this volume, reveal an inspiring pattern of fervent dedication and hard work. Whether or not one chooses to accept these beliefs as appropriately oriented, they serve to memorialize those who devoted their lives and intellectual energies to these efforts.

As one reads through this book, it is obvious that under different guises the same basic objectives have guided, and more or less eluded, educators of the deaf over the years. What is striking is not so much the repetition of those approaches but their diversity. This book will be useful to historians and educators with an interest in deafness, and particularly to those with a deep appreciation for the human spirit that perseveres when the cause is just. This is a book about giants and their times.

Within the past few decades, developments have occurred in the United States that have altered and expanded the methods of providing services to deaf children and youth. Parent education programs have been developed and stressed to help parents assume vital roles in the education of their children. At the same time, early childhood and continuing education have come into greater prominence, offering services for deaf persons earlier and later in their lives. Since World War II, state and federal agencies and programs have provided valuable support for the training of deaf individuals in a variety of new careers by increasing the accessibility of educational opportunities. Organizations of and for the deaf have drawn closer together, not so much because philosophical differences have been resolved, but because the threats inherent in emerging public attitudes and educational trends require that they explore positive areas of mutual concern and support. Finally, the numbers of institutions providing services to the deaf at the post-secondary level have multiplied tremendously in recent times. Those and other developments take their places in this account of historic turning points in the education of deaf individuals.

To sum up, Ed Scouten's chronology becomes an important addition to the literature that recounts the history of a very special area of special education. It is a view of events from the perspective of a teacher of the deaf who is driven by the same tireless energy, dedication, and sense of purpose that characterize the pioneers whose works are documented in this book.

Robert R. Davila

Washington, D.C.
January, 1983

PREFACE

Education of the deaf through the ages has been marked by a great number of significant turning points. Each of these has proven to be a testimony to the determination of the human spirit in its efforts to free and to be freed from the shackles of ignorance and prejudice. These "turning points" and their lines of influence are the concern of this presentation.

The format of this study is a chronological series of narratives describing those historical occurrences which have had, each in its own way, a specific impact on the direction and progress of education for the deaf. While the historical backdrop of each episode is developed and linked to the occurrence depicted, interpretations of the event described are suggested in the light of our present-day understanding.

If this book can serve two purposes, the author's mission will have been fulfilled: first, to preserve the substantive thought of past educators of the deaf and second, to inspire those educators of the present and those of the future to an ever-growing dedication and diligence in their teaching of deaf children and youth.

E.L.S.

ACKNOWLEDGEMENTS

While authorship is a personal and solitary activity, it should also be remembered that such work is also frequently attended by a host of helpful people. They are those who lend the author support through their providing him with particulars of information and those who provide him with physical assistance toward bringing his efforts into reality.

Consequently, this author is indebted to a number of people who through their interest and concern have made this book possible. Their activities range from the patient ferreting out of details from the pupil records of the Illinois School for the Deaf to the translating of text materials from the French. Without such varied assistances this author's work would have been impossible to complete.

Hopefully, forgetting no one who has been directly associated with the production of this work, the author would like to acknowledge the kind assistance of the following persons: Mr. Jan Afzelius, artist/illustrator, Stockholm, Sweden; Dr. Richard G. Brill, supt. (ret.), California School for the Deaf, Riverside; Mr. Henry Buzzard, librarian, New York School for the Deaf, White Plains; Ms. Vi Cadieux, curator, Loy Golladay Museum, American School for the Deaf, Hartford, Conn.; Ms. Sara Durman, specialist in Yiddish, Rochester, N.Y.; Father Tom Erdle, chaplain, NTID/RIT, Rochester, N.Y.; Ms. Sue Finster, research specialist, CAID National Office, Washington, D.C.; Ms. Joan T. Foreman, English specialist, NTID/RIT; Mr. Peter Haggerty, English specialist, NTID/RIT; Dr.

Marshall Hester, supt. (ret.), New Mexico School for the Deaf, Santa Fe; Dr. Ralph Hoag, supt. (ret.), Arizona School for the Deaf, Tucson; Mr. Robert F. Iannazzi, media specialist, NTID/RIT; Ms. Jean Ingham, marketing assistant, Public Information Office, NTID/RIT; Ms. Lorraine L. Kline, supervising teacher, Illinois School for the Deaf, Jacksonville; Ms. Nanette F. Knight, director, Information Service, Alexander Graham Bell Association for the Deaf, Washington, D.C.; Mr. Kendall D. Litchfield, supt., New York School for the Deaf, White Plains; Ms. Eloise M. Lyman, Research Library, Perkins School for the Blind, Watertown, Mass.; Ms. Dominique Mallory, communication specialist, NTID/RIT; Ms. Alice Morton, archivist, U.S. Institute of Education, Washington, D.C.; Dr. William J. McClure, president (ret.), Florida School for the Deaf and Blind; Mr. Jean Guy Naud, associate professor, Applied Photo/Media Production, NTID/RIT; Ms. Lorna O'Brien, coordinator, and the NTID/RIT Word Processing Staff; Ms. Barbara Phillips, executive secretary, NTID/RIT; Mr. William Repp, manager, publicity and marketing, NTID/RIT; Mrs. Audrey Ritter, Resource Center, NTID/RIT; Mr. Edward Scott, assistant supt., Illinois School for the Deaf, Jacksonville; Dr. S. Richard Silverman, director (ret.), Central Institute for the Deaf, St. Louis; Mr. Jack Slutzky, education specialist, NTID/RIT; Ms. Gladys Taylor, archivist, RIT Wallace Library, Rochester, N.Y.; Ms. Diane West, librarian, Texas School for the Deaf, Austin; and Mr. Roch Whitman, marketing specialist, NTID/RIT.

I should especially like to express my appreciation to Dr. William E. Castle, Vice-President of RIT and Director of NTID, who suggested this historical project to me and who fully supported my efforts in its production.

Finally, I wish to give my heartfelt thanks to my dear wife, Eleanor Powell Scouten, an outstanding educator of the deaf in her own right, for her professional advice and assistance through the composition of this work.

TABLE OF CONTENTS

TURNING POINTS
in the
EDUCATION OF DEAF PEOPLE

Chapter One
Deaf People in Antiquity

1

Herodotus on Deafness
and the Deaf
in the 6th Century B.C.

"Man, do not kill Croesus!" These were the horrified words which burst out above the metallic din of clashing swords and crashing shields. With that desperate warning the Lydian king reeled about and cleaved the skull of his Persian adversary. Then over his foe, he stood doubly shocked, first because of his narrow brush with death and second because of the fortuitous, and at the same time, miraculous warning which had broken from the lips of his son.

This occurrence was, indeed, miraculous because the son had never before spoken in his life. He had been a deaf-mute from birth, yet with the terror of seeing his father about to be slain, the lad somehow screamed his words of warning and Croesus, the King of Lydia, was saved. From that day forth the son's power of speech remained with him. (Herodotus, *Persian Wars*, Book I, pp. 47-48.)

This is the first account relative to deafness and the deaf in recorded history and for it we are indebted to Herodotus of Halicarnassus (c. 484 B.C. - c. 425 B.C.), the "Father of History."

To be sure, many of the occurrences described by Herodotus in his classic *The Persian Wars* strain the imagination, because the sources of this first historian were often veiled in the mists of an even more ancient past. Nevertheless, it may be said that at the heart of the most fantastic of legends may rest a solid kernel of fact which time has evolved into a fantasy.

Roots of attitude regarding deaf people:

Herodotus, in other references to Croesus and his deaf son, give us some insights into the attitudes of ancient society toward deafness and the deaf. This first historian wrote,

> For Croesus had two sons, one blasted by a natural defect, being deaf and dumb; the other distinguished far above all his mates in every pursuit. The name of the last was Atys. (*Ibid.*, pp. 19-20.)

Strangely, nowhere in Herodotus' entire story of Croesus and his two sons does the name of the deaf son ever appear. The reason for this curious oversight becomes clear when we read the words of Croesus as he addresses his hearing son, Atys, "For you are the one and only son that I possess; the other whose hearing is destroyed, I regard as if he were not." (*Ibid.*, p. 22.)

Despite Croesus' apparent verbal disregard for his deaf son, Herodotus writes:

> He [Croesus] had a son, of whom I made mention above, a worthy youth, whose only defect was that he was deaf and dumb. In the days of his prosperity Croesus had done the utmost that he could for him, and among other plans which he had devised, had sent to Delphi to consult the oracle on his behalf. (*Ibid.*, p. 47.)

The priestess at Delphi, however, spoke a very modern Catch 22–like warning to Croesus. It was that he should never listen to the hoped-for speech of his deaf son. If the boy did speak, disaster would surely follow. As we know, the lad broke his muteness and miraculously warned Croesus. To be sure, the King of the Lydians was saved, but only to lose his war with the Persians and to be thrust into captivity. To pin a date on this event, the year was 546 B.C.

Croesus' attitude toward his deaf son, according to Herodotus, was that he regarded him "as if he were not." The lad was in what would be called today a non-person status. Remembering the long established practice of the ancient Greeks, who were said to place their handicapped infants on a hillside to die, makes one wonder how Croesus' son survived to maturity in the presence of a father for whom only perfection was acceptable.

Infanticide and deafness:

It may be that in actuality this harsh rule of infant destruction did not always apply to deaf children as it did to those children with other more obvious physical handicaps. The reason for this assumption is that deafness was not an immediately discernible handicap. Consequently, deaf children may have survived long enough to prove their potential value in terms of physical strength and manual dexterity. Thus they were permitted to live. Croesus' son and others like him, being fair of face and strong in body, could well have survived and served unnamed as weapon bearers, sheep herders, and wall builders. The possible reasoning of the ancient Greeks for sparing deaf children may have been that, after all, neither can the oxen speak, yet they serve well.

Surely Herodotus' account of Croesus and his son unquestionably nurtured the roots of superstition in the minds of generations of people. The result was that a low and primitive attitude concerning deaf-mutes dominated the thinking of kings, philosophers, and priests for the next 2000 years. (See Appendix 1.)

2

Legal Perspectives Concerning the Deaf in Biblical Times

Primitive people:

Early societies probably made few distinctions between people as long as they were physically whole and were able to function in the activities of household, hunting, and warfare. The work requirements for existence in a primitive community were perhaps relatively simple and sufficiently routine that a perceptive deaf youth, boy or girl, could through imitation learn those skills necessary for his or her survival.

Physical strength and manual dexterity, both of which carry high material premiums in today's society, were probably even more acceptable to the earliest people who gathered together for their mutual protection and welfare.

The Hebrews:

It was not until the ascendancy of the Hebrews and their formulation of a written moral code that we encounter the strict Mosaic order, "Thou shalt not curse the deaf. . . ." (Leviticus 19.14.) This command bespeaks a respect and a concern for those individuals who could not orally defend themselves.

While the ancient Hebrews obviously had no such clarifying terminology as *prelingually* and *postlingually* deaf, it was still possible for them to discern the distinction. This is clearly reflected in their legal concern, which was directed toward the protective needs of the prelingually deaf as opposed to those who were postlingually deaf.

It was clearly recognized that, being unable to speak, the prelingually deaf could not assume those responsibilities expected of hearing people. Hence, such deaf persons were denied the right of property ownership. This situation probably stemmed from the danger of their becoming possible targets of the unscrupulous. Thus owning little, these individuals were spared the necessity of perpetual alertness and concern. In truth, it appears that the general regard for them by the community was like that toward children. This provided them, of course, with the same rights of protection.

On the other hand, it may be observed that postlingually deaf persons, those who had speech and obviously language, were accorded a variety of rights. Individuals who lacked speech, but who could hear and understand language, were similarly given certain rights.

Thus we see that speech and its integral element, language, together formed the common denominator for social acceptance. Today, these same two elements are no less important and form or should form the primary thrust and direction for modern education of the deaf.

3

Social and Legal Status
of the Deaf in Ancient Rome

Wealth and position as survival factors for the deaf:

The deaf-mutes of antiquity appear to have been largely disregarded by society in terms of their genuine potential and usefulness. The common belief creating this predicament was succinctly expressed in the lines of the early Roman poet and philosopher Titus Lucretius Carus (96? - 55 B.C.), who wrote:

> To instruct the deaf, no art could ever reach,
> No care improve, and no wisdom teach.

There were occasionally, however, individual instances of compassion and understanding. Most of these were generated by financially and politically well-placed parents who sought some assistance for their deaf children. As an aside, the offspring so favored always appear to have been sons. This was true at least down to the 18th Century and its school-attempt for educating deaf children.

Pliny the Elder in his *Natural History* describes one such case of parental interest and assistance. Quintus Pedius, a Roman deaf youth in the 1st Century A.D., was indebted to his father for interceding on his behalf with the emperor, Augustus. The father, a man of influence and position, requested the emperor's permission to allow the son to study to become an artist. While there is no word extant as to the young man's ultimate success in his chosen field, we may surmise that his good fortune in receiving the emperor's approval may have inspired the high-born parents of similarly handicapped youngsters to seek imperial assistance for their offspring.

The fact of intercession in the case of young Quintus Pedius might substantiate to some degree the idea that the deaf children of other favored parents might similarly have received opportunities which, unfortunately, were not recorded. Deaf children, however, from families in the lower echelons of the Roman social scale were obviously forced to live by their own silent wits.

The Justinian Code:

In A.D. 528 the Roman emperor Justinian appointed a commission which identified, collected, and organized the mass of Roman laws which had accrued over the previous four centuries. This tremendous compilation of statutes became known as the Justinian Code.

Deaf-mutes were recognized in the Code as a group which required special attention and protection under Roman law. To clarify the position of those persons who were to receive this regard, five categories were designated:

1. The Deaf and Dumb with whom this double infirmity is from birth;
2. The Deaf and Dumb with whom this double infirmity is *not* from birth, but the effect of an accident supervened in the course of life;
3. The Deaf person who is not dumb, but whose deafness is from birth;
4. The person who is simply deaf, and that from accident;
5. Finally, he who is simply dumb, whether this infirmity be in him congenital or the effect of an accident.

In referring to the Code, Harvey Prindle Peet, a pioneer in American education of the deaf, wrote, ". . . the Deaf and Dumb from birth are without exception and without regard to degree of intelligence, condemned to a perpetual legal infancy." (*Legal Rights*, p. 7.) This statement was certainly true in its reference to congenitally or prelingually deaf persons. It was further substantiated in the Code, which stated that while the rights of property acquisition and inheritance were granted to the "Deaf and Dumb" in the First Classification, they were forbidden the right to control their property. All purchases and sales which they might wish to make had to be arranged through a *curator* or guardian. Neither were such deaf people allowed to make wills, create estates, or free slaves.

Those deaf persons who belonged in the Second Classification, i.e., those whose deafness had occurred as the result of accident or disease, could have all of their privileges returned to them, if they were able to communicate in writing. This group was also believed to be educable. The only evidences in this direction are relative to the instruction of deaf persons in art or painting. There is nothing extant regarding the pursuit of academic studies.

The Third Classification posed a problem for Dr. Peet, because it seemed to him to be so wholly erroneous that a person could be born deaf and at the same time acquire speech. A possible answer to this question in the light of today's knowledge lies in the generic term *deaf* which was and *still is loosely used* to include all degrees of auditory impairment. Obviously a Roman born hard-of-hearing or becoming hard-of-hearing in infancy or early childhood might very naturally have acquired speech. It would obviously have been imperfect speech, but speech nevertheless, hence the Third Classification. Quite likely such people functioned legally as hearing persons, depending, of course, on the extent of their hearing losses which again would be reflected in their quality of speech.

The Fourth Classification made no difference in a person's social or legal status for the simple reason of his speech retention.

The Fifth Classification concerned muteness *per se* as a single handicap. It allowed for the causes either congenital or adventitious. In the latter case, if the individual were capable of reading and writing, his status would probably have been similar to that of an individual in the Second Classification. If the muteness were of autistic or psychogenetic origins, the unfortunate was quite likely declared *non compos mentis* and relieved of all social privileges.

In that Roman law, specifically the Justinian Code, served as the foundation for the legal structure of the whole western world, we may appreciate the magnitude of the barriers faced by the subsequent early teachers of the deaf. Even today there are vestiges of these laws in some of the nations of Europe along with some deep-rooted prejudices born of ignorance. Occasionally even today in the United States these same prejudices are encountered by deaf people and those who work in their behalf.

4

St. John of Beverley as a
Teacher of the Deaf
A.D. 640-721

Deafness and Muteness, the subjects of philosophers:

Through the early centuries after the birth of Christ, western-world philosophers and physicians pondered the nature of deafness and its frequently accompanying affliction, muteness. None of them, however, gave any thought or time to the liberation of those intellectually imprisoned by silence.

It was not until the Middle Ages that interest in teaching deaf people was sporadically demonstrated and in a few instances recorded. The early medieval efforts at instructing the deaf, or, as they were commonly called, "the dumb," were always sparked by a religious zeal to provide salvation. Persons, however, who made such attempts were doing so in the face of St. Augustine's teaching, which indicated that handicaps in children were frequently the results of sins of the parents. Such sentiments may obviously have discouraged attempts to rectify those difficulties which were understood to be fore-ordained. Other persons, however, remembering Christ's own example relative to deafness and muteness, sought to eliminate these predicaments the best way they could, through faith, ingenuity, and determination.

St. John of Beverley:

One of these early medieval teachers of whom we know was St. John of Beverley, the story of whose instructional efforts on the behalf of a deaf youth was told to the Venerable Bede by the Reverend Mr. Bethun, "a man of undoubted veracity." Bede later recorded the story of Beverley's work in his great Anglo-Saxon chronicle, *The Ecclesiastical History of the English Nation.*

The year was A.D. 685 and the season was Lent. The Bishop of Hagulstad, subsequently known as St. John of Beverley, requested his people to seek out "some poor person labouring under any grievous infirmity or want." This unfortunate was to be brought to the Bishop's compound to receive both shelter and alms. Finally a young mute whom the Bishop had occasionally seen before and to whom he had given pecuniary assistance was brought from a nearby village.

The youth's predicament was bad because not only was he without speech, but he also bore "scurf and scabs on his head, that no hair ever grew on the top of it, but only some scattered hairs in a circle round about." The miserable lad was allowed to live in a small cottage which had been especially built for him.

After the first week of Lent, the kindly Bishop asked that the young man be brought to him. To be sure, the youth was afraid, but without reason, excepting that born of ignorance. As the young mute knelt, the Bishop urged him gently to draw forth his tongue, which he did. The Bishop, "then laying hold of his chin, made the sign of the cross" on the lad's tongue and then told him to draw it back. The Bishop then directed him to speak the words *yea* or *yes* in the speech of the Angles. "The youth's tongue was immediately loosed, and he said what he was ordered."

Thereafter the Bishop distinctly pronounced the individual letters of the alphabet and encouraged the young man to do likewise. After the lad was able to speak the letters satisfactorily, the Bishop then logically proceeded to put the letters of elements into syllables which were again imitated by the boy. Next came whole words, and finally the Bishop commanded him to speak whole sentences, which he did.

According to the account given to the Venerable Bede, the whole instruction and practice process continued "all that day and the next night" as long as the young man could keep awake. During this time he was said to have "expressed his private thoughts and will to others which he could never do before."

The Bishop was so pleased at the young man's acquisition of

speech that he ordered a physician to treat the lad's severe scalp condition. "Thus the youth obtained a good aspect, and a beautiful head of hair, whereas before he was deformed, poor, and dumb." Divine Intervention on the behalf of this young medieval mute was concretely manifest in the genuine interest and effort made in his behalf by the good Bishop.

St. John's achievement in a modern light:

Today, of course, we have many questions regarding Bede's account. Was the lad truly deaf? Was his deafness of psychogenetic origin? Was he a cured aphasic? Historians have suggested that the time frame described for such a mastery of speech is grossly exaggerated, and this is obvious. Even the confusion between speech and language given in Bede's account is understandable in a medieval mind; however, that such a confusion has continued practically through our 20th Century is patently incomprehensible.

Disregarding the time element, the Bishop's procedure of instruction shows an uncanny analytical sense of speech development and application. It is little wonder that the Bishop, St. John of Beverley, is today the Patron Saint of Teachers of the Deaf. We teachers need all the help we can get!

As an aside, it should be observed that a period of 800 years was to elapse before any further thought was given to deaf people and their education. (See Appendix 2.)

Chapter Two
Education of the Deaf in the 16th and 17th Centuries

5

Education of the Deaf
During the Renaissance

Rudolphus Agricola 1443-1485:

In the Netherlands one Rudolphus Agricola described a deaf-mute who was taught to read and write. No mention, however, was made as to who actually taught him. Such an achievement was, of course, thought to be phenomenal in the light of what was commonly believed. Curiously, Agricola's work *De Inventione Dialectica*, which included the above-mentioned account, was not published until 1528, a full 43 years after his death.

Ludovic Vives, a Spanish intellectual, after reading Agricola's account of the deaf-mute's successful education, greeted the Dutchman's story with a dubiousness which was politely intended to put the story to rest as a probable case of misunderstanding. Of course, by this time Agricola was long departed and unable to speak on his own behalf.

It was during this same period that the conquering Spanish forces of Philip II dominated the Netherlands culturally as well as militarily. The Spaniards, as a consequence, looked upon the achievements of the Dutch as being several cuts below those of their own variety. From Vives' point of view certainly such a feat as educating a deaf-mute in the Netherlands bordered on the impossible, hence his dismissal of it.

Girolamo Cardano 1501-1576:

The negative judgment of Vives would quite likely have concluded the whole matter regarding Agricola had not a more eminent scholar, Dr. Girolamo Cardano (Jerome Cardan) of Italy, discovered the Dutchman's remarkable story. Instead of skeptically closing his mind to the achievement described by Agricola, Cardano began to give the story his most analytical attention.

Cardano came to reason that written words were really independent of the sounds of speech. Symbols or words set on paper could, therefore, be understood, taught, and studied without aural reference to the sounds which they represented. This, as Dr. Ruth Bender indicates in her book *The Conquest of Deafness*, was the initial concept upon which the genuine educability of the deaf was first predicated.

Although this tremendously important concept is described in Cardano's autobiography, *De Vita Propria Liber*, it is nowhere mentioned in the prodigiously detailed two-volume *Life of Girolamo Cardano* (1584) by the Englishman Henry Morley. Perhaps the omission indicates the general indifference of the British intelligentsia toward the plight of the hearing-handicapped during the 16th Century.

Ponce de Leon 1520-1584:

While Cardano was thus engaged in educational theory concerning the possibilities of teaching reading and writing to the deaf, a Spanish Benedictine monk, Ponce de Leon at the Monastery of San Salvador, was effectively doing this very thing.

To understand and appreciate the circumstances of Ponce de Leon's work as a teacher of the deaf, it would be helpful to understand the period during which he lived. Spain was in its ascendancy as an empire. Under the leadership of Philip II the nation was expanding its influence across Europe and extending it into the New World. Wealth abounded and the great Spanish dynasties were consolidating their holdings at home and searching for new sources of wealth abroad.

These tightly knit families of the nobility and the upper middle class, in addition to their securing more riches, were particularly interested in holding on to what they had. Experience indicated to them that intermarriage provided them the strongest protective alliances possible. This effort to achieve security by uniting families for the sake of holdings became a common practice. These families learned, however, after a few generations of such a custom, that where they materially gained in one way they substantially lost in another. The effects of intermarriage began to manifest themselves in an increase of deaf offspring. The male heirs among these, because of their inability to hear and speak, were consequently deprived of their right of primogeniture. (Wright, *Deafness*, p. 140).

In the dark hour of such a discovery, that a handsome young son was in truth a deaf-mute, there was no place for a family to turn except in supplication to the Church. This was the plight and the action of the family de Velasco, which turned to the local Monastery of San Salvador. This family had not one son but two, Pedro and Francisco. With both of their futures apparently blighted by the inability to hear and speak, the two youths were expected to achieve little either materially or spiritually.

Fortunately, there resided at a nearby monastery the aforementioned monk, Fra Ponce de Leon, who had earned a substantial reputation in the region for having successfully taught a deaf-mute, one Gaspard Burges, both to read and to write. The monk's first concern for the two de Velasco youths was spiritual, for without words confession was impossible, likewise absolution and obviously salvation. In short, without words, the ultimate Word would be lost to them. As an aside, through several of the following centuries, spiritual salvation was the prime motivating factor for educating the deaf.

Under the instruction of Ponce de Leon, Pedro and Francisco de Velasco made extraordinary progress. In addition to their acquiring the basic language skills of reading and writing, they also learned to speak. The educational progress of the two lads appears to have been phenomenal because both boys eventually assumed their full responsibilities as members of the Spanish landed gentry.

Thomas Arnold, the classic historian in education of the deaf, relates that Ponce de Leon quite likely recorded his teaching procedures; however, the documents are presumed to have been lost in the library fire at San Salvador. As to Ponce de Leon's specific procedures for teaching the deaf, there is an account by his former student Pedro de Velasco. It states that Ponce de Leon first taught the written names of objects, then their oral pronunciation. These two aspects of the words were then practiced in association. The chief mode of instruction appears to have been writing, with no indication whatsoever of speechreading or the manual alphabet ever having been used. In terms of history it is clearly established that Ponce de Leon was the first *bona fide* teacher of the deaf.

6

Bonet and Carrión of Spain in the Early 17th Century

Prince Charles of England goes to Spain:

The year was 1623 and the place was the palace of Spain's Philip IV. The chatter of noble small talk suddenly ceased as the clarion sound of trumpets rang through the Grand Salon. Immediately all eyes turned toward the great doors which slowly opened. Through the entrance strode His Excellency the Vice-Chancellor, who with well-practiced voice proclaimed, "Your Highness, Prince Charles of Britain; my lords, esteemed clergy, and ladies of the Court. He comes, Philip, the Sovereign of Spain and the Ruler of our dominions in the New World. Greet our King!"

At this point, Philip IV, a slight figure and elegantly attired, came to the doorway and acknowledged with a nod the full bows and curtsies of his noble subjects and also the nod of his royal English guest.

Among those assembled were some top dignitaries of the royal entourage of Prince Charles, who had as his prime objective in coming to Spain the fair hand of the Infanta. A possible match seemed dimmer each day; however, the warm Spanish sun and the golden oranges were something special for Charles. He did not really count the sojourn a total loss.

Sir Kenelme Digby, the observer:

Among those in the royal English party was one young gentleman, Sir Kenelme Digby, a keen observer who drank in the entire scene of Spanish gold and lace. He took note of every detail of person, dress, and manner of those about him. Not surprising was it, therefore, that his attention was captured by the striking appearance and manner of one of the Spanish courtiers, a 13-year-old prodigy.

This youth's uniqueness lay not in the fact that he was extraordinarily handsome and gracious, but, as the people said, he had miraculously transcended the enormous handicaps of deafness and muteness. A miracle, indeed, it was, but one wrought only through the lad's determination and hard work combined with the instructional efforts of his teacher.

The prodigy, Luis de Velasco:

Charles, the English prince, was awed by the charm of the young grandee and no less was Sir Kenelme. Indeed, the lad despite his extreme youth was a favorite with the entire Court, especially His Highness, Philip himself. The boy was of the old family de Velasco and was known to all as Luis. Everyone wondered at his achievements in learning and decorum. Upon a first meeting with him, he would announce emphatically, "I am not mute, only deaf."

Most certainly Luis was far from being mute; on the contrary, he was quite loquacious. A probable reason for this was that he had discovered that in his talking he could usually control the topic. As long as the adults about him permitted this, he was secure. Once losing the subject, however, Luis' dark eyes would search the countenance and body movement of the dominant speaker in an effort to ascertain the conversation's topic once again. One would presume to find such a child rather obnoxious, but instead everyone looked upon him with fascination.

Sir Kenelme Digby, for his own information as much as for that of his Prince, made inquiries regarding the boy's background and upbringing, for such a prodigy could evolve only through a considerable expenditure of time and effort on the part of someone. How was it possible? At the age of two years little Luis de Velasco was stricken ill and lay fretfully in the hold of a high fever. After a couple of days this fever suddenly broke and it was obvious that the little boy would recover. As the child gradually gained in strength his nursemaid noticed that he talked considerably less than he had prior to his illness. He also appeared to be somewhat preoccupied and content to roam quietly about the nursery.

It was this behavior that concerned the child's mother, the young and noble Doña Juana de Cordoba. Prior to his illness, Luis had been a veritable little magpie, but now he was silent and appeared attentive to some inner sound which held him fast. Even the yelping hounds being readied for the hunt in the courtyard failed to bring him to his nursery window.

After some weeks the young duchess was finally forced to admit not only to herself but to the entire household that little Luis was, indeed, deaf. Over the days and weeks that passed the child spoke less and less. When he was particularly fatigued, he indicated hearing some phantom chords or voices which arose and fell in repeated crescendos within his head.

Bonet's compassion:

Juan Pablo Bonet (1579-1620), a long-time secretary to the family de Velasco, was deeply saddened by the plight of the child, Luis, and his distraught young mother. Bonet determined to find help. He recalled there had long been a story in the family de Velasco of two brothers, both of whom had been deaf and both of whom had become educated through the offices of one Ponce de Leon, a Benedictine friar. These two brothers were actually the granduncles of little Luis. If these two deaf brothers were so educable, most certainly the child, Luis, would be also. With this thought in mind, Juan Bonet set out to locate someone who could instruct the little boy. After some weeks Bonet finally found the name of Ramirez de Carrión, a teacher of articulation, who was serving as both a tutor and a secretary to a deaf man, the Marquis de Priego in Montilla.

Carrión comes to the family de Velasco:

Bonet, a persuasive fellow, wept, cajoled, smiled, and promised that only good things would result if only the Marquis de Priego would release Carrión for awhile to serve as the teacher of the child, Luis de Velasco. The Marquis at last relented. Carrión could go to the family de Velasco for three years but certainly not for more than four. Triumphantly, Bonet returned home to Madrid with the newly found teacher.

Once installed in the household de Velasco, Carrión began his instruction of Luis. Before the master could hope to teach the child, it was necessary for him to become acquainted with his young charge and to establish a rapport between them. Carrión was immediately struck by the winning manner of the boy and his amazingly mature desire to learn.

While little Luis' infant speech had all but vanished after months of disuse, Carrión may have conjectured that as young as the child was, a vestige or two of his inner language may have remained. His call for "Pepito" would turn his dog's ears and make its tail wag. Perhaps the child might understand that other things had names, too. If this were true, it would obviously facilitate the child's learning.

Bonet, the ever-present observer:

As Carrión worked with Luis, the teacher may or may not have been aware of an almost ever-present observer in the person of Juan Bonet. It was clearly not an obtrusive manner of observation, but quiet and subtle. Above all, Bonet was anxious for Carrión to succeed with Luis. After all, Bonet was responsible for bringing the teacher into the household. Carrión's success would unquestionably be Bonet's own. Intrigued with Carrión's technique for developing the letters of the alphabet and their corresponding sounds, and his methods for developing words, phrases, and sentences, Bonet began to set down notes. He similarly recorded Carrión's procedure for teaching speech. Bonet then began to theorize and formulate an instructional method based on Ramirez de Carrión's successfully demonstrated procedures with young Luis. For all of this material he accrued, Bonet had a definite plan.

Carrión meanwhile continued his teaching of the lad until the boy was nine years of age. A period of four years (1615-1619) had finally passed, and a firm foundation had been provided Luis in the reading, writing, and speaking of Spanish. With this all-essential key of language, Luis' subsequent education was to be a relatively simple matter.

Carrión, the unrecognized contributor:

Bonet clearly perceived Carrión's genius as a teacher and set about to write a book incorporating his instructional procedures. As Bonet wrote, he interlaced Carrión's practices with his own theories relative to the teaching of deaf children. It was not until a year after Carrión's departure that Bonet in 1620 published his book under the protracted title *Simplification of the Letters of the Alphabet and Method of Teaching Deaf-Mutes to Speak.*

Readers of the book would, of course, be unable to discern which of the two men, Bonet or Carrión, had conceived which ideas, because nowhere in Bonet's text did he give Ramirez de Carrión a word of recognition or credit. Ironically, this omission today subtly magnifies Carrión's importance in the early history of education of the deaf. Without Carrión and his work, there surely would be no Bonet to be honored today.

The pragmatic approach:

In considering Bonet's book there is one very significant passage which may reflect Carrión's pragmatic approach to the teaching of deaf children. We read:

> The deaf are both most quick to comprehend the gestures made to them, because they attempt thus to supply the loss of hearing, and very clever at making use of them themselves . . . to take the place of speech. And so the instrument to be chosen should be one to which they are habituated, and the sounds of the letters must be made known to them by signs.

Continuing the quotation:

> It is necessary that in a house where there is a deaf mute, all who can read should know this alphabet, in order to converse with him by its means, and not by other signs, which will be less beneficial to him, whether it be writing or manual gestures; nor should they permit him to make use of them, but he should reply by word of mouth to the questions put to him.

Comprehensive language environment as a key principle:

As an aside, this statement embodies the concept of the *comprehensive language environment,* one of the vital principles essential to the successful education of deaf children. Since its original appearance in Bonet's book in 1620, however, the idea has disappeared and reappeared numerous times in the thinking of educators

Old Spanish Alphabet - Bonet 1620

Reproduced by Dept. of Photography Ohio State University

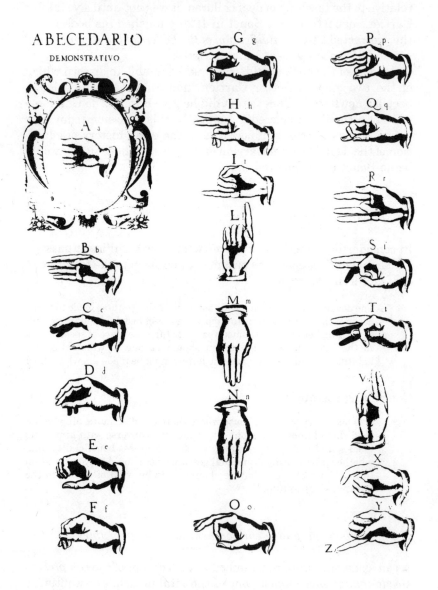

of the deaf. Persistently the concept resurfaces and each time its common-sense validity is demonstrated. Subsequently, however, it is then inexplicably pushed aside to be rediscovered at some future date.

A reflection:

Reflecting once again upon the story of Luis de Velasco, it was Sir Kenelme Digby who in his letters and subsequently in a book described the young grandee, his education, and his accomplishments. In the year 1628, at the age of eighteen, Luis received at the hand of his monarch the title of Marquis de Fresno.

Juan Pablo Bonet and his generally unheralded collaborator, Ramirez de Carrión, stand together with the Benedictine, Ponce de Leon, as Spain's great contributors to the early education of deaf people.

7

The Beginnings of Education
for the Deaf in England:
Digby, the Recorder, and
Bulwer, the Theorist

Sir Kenelme Digby goes abroad:

Because of the rising unpopularity of England's Charles I and his
Cavaliers in the early 1640's, a number of the latter, foreseeing an
increase in personal inconvenience and a possibility of danger, chose
to visit the Continent. Among those sojourners abroad was Sir
Kenelme Digby. Sir Kenelme, it will be remembered, had served the
young Charles in his earlier days and had even accompanied his
highness on his unsuccessful mission to Spain to woo the Infanta.
This time, however, Sir Kenelme traveled under less elegant
circumstances. His stay in Paris was not to be a holiday exactly, but
simply a period of waiting. It was to be a dull time during which
everyone, noble Englishmen, that is, would be forced to economize
as much as possible.

Sir Kenelme's contribution to education of the deaf:

Sir Kenelme, seeing some good in the worst of situations, decided
to utilize his days in the inexpensive pastime of reflection, reflection
upon his past and upon various topics which he felt obligated to
record for posterity. The result of his efforts eventually found its way
between the leather bindings of a pretty book entitled *Treatise on
the Nature of Bodies*. The year was 1644.

It was in this volume that he wrote of his contact with Bonet and the Spanish prodigy, Luis de Velasco. Indeed, it was this account that was instrumental in eventually stirring some of England's sharpest thinkers into action regarding the predicament of deafness.

One such thinker was Dr. John Bulwer, a physician. Bulwer had long been intrigued by the various forms of hand and gesticular communication such as that employed by actors and orators. His study and thinking led him to the writing of a book. The work, *Chirologia; or The Natural Language of the Hand*, was published in 1644.

In this volume Bulwer mentions a deaf man named Babbington whose wife was able to talk to him by taking his hand and pointing to the various finger joints, each of which represented a letter. Thus she could converse with him quite readily even in total darkness! With such an interest in manual communication, Bulwer was naturally taken by Digby's account of the Spaniard Bonet and the young deaf nobleman de Velasco.

Dr. Bulwer on deafness:

After further study and cogitation, Bulwer in 1648 produced another book entitled *Philocophus* (The Deaf Man's Friend). In this volume, he reproduced completely Digby's account of Luis de Velasco. In setting forth his own philosophy, Bulwer strongly advocated the use of the "hand ABC" as a preliminary step toward the eventual teaching of "Lip-Grammar" or speechreading. Instruction in speech he considered to be the final phase. Eventually this sequence was determined by many educators to be the most practical in teaching those children who are congenitally or prelingually deaf. This sequence was also to become the chief distinction between the *oral method* and the *pure oral method*, the latter of which was to be introduced some 40 years later by John Conrad Amman. (See Appendix 3.)

Bulwer, indeed, proved himself to be tremendously perceptive relative to the basic approaches in teaching the deaf. Despite his extensive interest in speechreading and speech, he never moved beyond his theorizing. Through this, however, his contributions to early British thinking in education of the deaf were substantial.

8

Dr. William Holder and
Dr. John Wallis,
England's First Teachers of the Deaf

Two Englishmen, neither of whom could abide the other, have ironically been inseparable down through the centuries because of their intense interest in teaching the deaf and because of their deep professional antipathy for one another. The two principals in this story are Dr. William Holder (1616-1698) and Dr. John Wallis (1616-1703).

Dr. Holder takes a pupil:

In 1659 Admiral Popham and Lady Wharton sought a teacher for their deaf-mute son, Alexander. It was at Blexington in Oxfordshire that they located a person for the task. Dr. William Holder, an Anglican clergyman and member of the Royal Society, agreed to assume the responsibility, and young Alex was committed to his tutelage. The child's being congenitally deaf presented a genuine challenge to Dr. Holder.

It should also be said that the problem of instruction must have been further complicated by the fact that the boy had a malformed head which included congenital atresia. The former condition might well indicate the possibility of the child's having had learning difficulties in addition to those posed by his deafness. In any event, Dr. Holder, with interest and zeal, tackled the problem of teaching his young charge.

Over the next three years the boy was provided instruction in speech. In an effort to depict the various tongue positions, Holder was said to have used a small leather strap which he could bend and shape according to the form which he wished the child to imitate with his tongue.

First, Holder taught the elements or "sounds." These were then combined into syllables, and finally whole words were taught. Writing accompanied all of the speech work. Dr. Holder also employed a manual alphabet as a means of developing pronunciation. David Wright hints that Holder's manual alphabet may have been the one invented by his brother-in-law, the famous Christopher Wren. (Wright, *Deafness*, p. 148.)

Dr. Wallis takes Dr. Holder's pupil:

In 1662 Lady Wharton, perhaps the impatient parent prototype, became dissatisfied with her son's progress and unceremoniously withdrew him from Dr. Holder's instruction and placed him in the charge of Dr. John Wallis. Wallis, a man of high reputation and numerous interests, received young Popham gladly and proceeded to teach him.

Holder's chagrin at this switch grew into a genuine bitterness which manifested itself in a continuing but futile castigation of Dr. Wallis. Between potshots at his adversary, Holder was eventually able to describe his own instructional procedures in a book entitled *Elements of Speech &. with an Appendix Concerning Persons Deaf and Dumb*. The publication year was 1669.

This book set forth a unique analysis of sounds and their application to the teaching of speech to the deaf. In reality, for all his cantankerousness toward Dr. Wallis, Holder was, indeed, a creative and dedicated teacher of the deaf.

A closer view of Dr. Wallis:

Dr. John Wallis, comfortable and secure in his numerous academic successes as an Oxonian professor of mathematics, was also sustained by his reputation of having been one of the founders of the Royal Society. Problems, obtuse and irregular, invariably succumbed to his intellect. Therefore, in 1661 there was little surprise when he accepted the seemingly impossible task of teaching a young deaf man, one Daniel Whalley.

Wallis appears to have been particularly well fitted for this task because of his long-standing fascination with language and its anatomy. In 1653 he had written a book with the extended title translated from the Latin to read *Grammar of English for Foreigners with an Essay on Speech or the Formulation of Sounds*. With such a background in that day, Wallis appears to have been eminently qualified to teach a deaf person.

Whalley, the pupil, was just 25 at the time Wallis accepted the task of teaching him. After a bit more than one year's instruction, the young man was able to read orally from the Bible and to understand its narrative portions without difficulty.

When this achievement was aired through the scholastic community, Wallis was prevailed upon to bring his pupil in for a demonstration before the Royal Society. To be sure, the presentation was most impressive. It may be parenthetically observed that in that day Wallis and most certainly his confreres of the Royal Society probably little knew the significance of the fact that Daniel Whalley was postlingually deaf at the age of five.

Dr. Wallis' expanding reputation:

Nevertheless, word of Wallis' educational triumph was soon circulated across London and to the ear of Lady Wharton, whose prelingually deaf son, Alex Popham, was, as previously mentioned, making arduous progress under the instruction of Dr. William Holder at Blexington. With the over-simplification of a naive parent, Lady Wharton possibly reasoned that if one teacher could labor for three years with her son with but slow progress while another teacher with another deaf scholar could achieve the near-absolute in only one year's time, the latter master must obviously be the superior one.

Dr. Wallis ultimately did not debate this logic and accordingly accepted Alex Popham with warm assurances to Lady Wharton that her son would soon be on the road to success. Actually, little is known of Alex's educational progress under the instruction of Dr. Wallis, excepting that the lad's abilities were never presented to the Royal Society. Dr. Wallis' reports of progress, on the other hand, were always favorable.

The Holder-Wallis feud:

Dr. William Holder at home in Blexington nurtured his contempt for Wallis by labeling him a fraud. Not to be topped, Wallis replied in the fashion of the day with a pamphlet entitled "A Defence of the Royal Society &., in Answer to the Cavils of Dr. W. Holder 1678."

Their quarrel ultimately narrowed down as to which one was England's first teacher of the deaf. Considering Dr. William Holder and Dr. John Wallis and their unsettled differences, perhaps their greatest service to the education of the deaf in 17th-Century England was the public attention which their bickering brought to this little-known area of human need.

They both were, indeed, England's first teachers of the deaf.

9

George Dalgarno's
Didascalocophus
1680

An idea lost and found:

George Dalgarno in the year 1680 published *Didascalocophus* (The Deaf and Dumb Man's Tutor), one of the most significant books in the history of education of the deaf. The small volume was, however, lost to the public for over 150 years. Finally, Dalgarno and his works were saved from oblivion through the efforts of one Mr. Dugald Stewart, a member of Edinburgh's prestigious Maitland Club. This club was a scholarly organization dedicated to philosophical and literary discussions.

Mr. Stewart in the early 1830's had fortuitously come upon Dalgarno's essays, had read them, and was exceedingly impressed by their philosophical and educational import. In consequence, Mr. Stewart proposed to the Club members that the Club underwrite the cost of republishing Dalgarno's collected works and thus save the evidence of his genius for posterity.

Dalgarno's background:

Dalgarno, a Scot, served for many years as a master in one of Oxford's private grammar schools. He was locally known as an armchair philosopher, a man of many intellectual interests, the chief one of which centered on language and its various aspects. There was consequently little surprise among his friends when in 1661 he produced a book entitled *Ars Signorum* (The Art of Signs).

This book presented a graphic system for depicting concepts without any dependency upon language. Despite this published work being eventually recognized by the renowned German philosopher Leibnitz, Dalgarno continued to remain relatively unknown outside Oxford Town. Similarly, he was hardly known even in Aberdeen, the city of his birth.

Dalgarno's interest in deafness and the deaf:

Thanks to the Holder-Wallis brouhaha, Dalgarno became gradually knowledgeable and then fascinated with the educational problem posed by congenital deafness and specifically the problem of language acquisition for a person so afflicted. While the acrimonious exchange between Holder and Wallis was, indeed, a useless exercise, the conflict did serve to pique Dalgarno's interest and to shape a challenge for his intellect. Dalgarno's many years as a Latinist and a grammar school teacher gave him some valuable insights into the constructions of language and the learning process as applied to language acquisition and mastery.

Blindness vs. deafness:

Initially, the afflictions of blindness and deafness posed in Dalgarno's mind two of mankind's most insurmountable intellectual barriers. However, as he contemplated these two conditions, it became apparent to him that blindness, horrendous as it is, is much less restricting in an intellectual sense because it in no way limits an individual's capacity for linguistic growth. As a blind individual's speech and language skills evolve, likewise does his ability to recognize and appreciate the abstract.

A person, however, stricken with deafness in infancy must bear also the accompanying handicap of muteness. Such an individual being without either speech or language may thus grow into maturity with no concept whatsoever of the abstract. Indeed, the intellectual predicament of the congenitally deaf person is considerably greater than that of the congenitally blind. The barrier of deafness, therefore, represents the supreme educational challenge for both the person so afflicted and his teacher.

Dalgarno thus formulated his thoughts on the learning processes as they relate to blindness and deafness. A comparative study of the two handicaps evolved into an effort to determine their surmountability through education. It was his thinking on this subject that enabled George Dalgarno to write his classic *Didascalocophus*. This essay sets forth for teachers of the deaf some basic psychological and pedagogical principles, many of which might have fallen through the cracks of time had it not been for a few discerning individuals down through history who have revived them with considerable success.

Dalgarno's "Tabula Rasa":

Dalgarno begins his *Didascalocophus* with the sentence "Though the soul of man come into the world, *Tabula Rasa*, yet it is withal, *Tabula Cerata*, capable thro study and discipline, of having many fair and goodly images stampt upon it." As an aside and at the risk of being accused of academic nit-picking, it might be observed that Dalgarno introduced the *Tabula Rasa* concept a full decade before John Locke used it in his renowned classic *An Essay on Human Understanding*. While Dalgarno's thoughts were philosophically oriented, they were also eminently practical.

Dalgarno on early childhood education for the deaf:

Dalgarno, centuries ahead of his time, was the first proponent of early childhood education, and in this instance it related specifically to the deaf. He wrote,

> ...there might be successful addresses made to a dumb child, even in his cradle, when he begins – *risu cognoscere matrem* [i.e., to recognize his mother by her laugh], if the mother or nurse had but as nimble a hand, as commonly they have a tongue. (*Didascalocophus*, p. 121.)

Subsequently he states,

> And tho I persuade myself that, some time or other, there may be a mother found who, by her own care, and such directions as I am treating of, will lay a good foundation in her deaf child, even in the first stage of his minority; yet, seeing this is like to be but a *rara avis*; I will advance our blind and deaf scholars to a higher form, and place them in a severer discipline than that of the nursery, which I suppose none will deny them now able to bear; for I will suppose them entered in the seventh year of their age. (*Ibid.*, p. 124.)

Dalgarno, in his efforts to compensate for the auditory and resultant language limitations imposed upon a deaf child, suggests an effective instrument of communication.

> This powerful and successful engine is not the tongue of the learned, but the hand of the diligent. The hand of a diligent tutor will not fail to make a rich scholar, if *copia verborum* [i.e., great numbers of words] may deserve the name of riches. . . . Let the deaf child then have for his nurses, not the nine muses, but the nine magpies. (*Ibid.*, p. 136.)

"Diligence" required for success:

Thus it is apparent that Dalgarno advocates that the deaf child be constantly inundated in simple child-English centered on simple child-interests. The key, however, is *diligence*. For Dalgarno, diligence is the fulcrum upon which the lever of teaching must rest in order to lift the deaf child from his predicament of ignorance into understanding and communication.

Dalgarno's implicit faith in the educability of the deaf is manifest in his following words which reflect again his belief in *diligence* as the imperative for the successful teaching of the deaf.

> The only point of art here is, how to make an application to your deaf scholar, by the same distinction of letters and words to his eye, which appear to the ears of others from words spoken; that is, to know his letters and to write them readily; diligence will do the rest. For example; let the same words be seen and written by the deaf man, as they are heard and spoken by the blind; if their faculties of memory and understanding are equal, the measure of knowledge will also be equal. (*Ibid.*)

Analysis of Dalgarno's theory:

An analysis of Dalgarno's theory of diligence in language instruction reveals that he is referring to the consistent, persistent, and repetitive exposure to and use of meaningful English as the means for providing the deaf child with language acquisition.

Dalgarno then sets forth the following principles for teaching the deaf:

> 1. Here the first piece of diligence must be . . . using the pen and fingers [fingerspelling] much. . . . Great care, therefore must be taken, to keep your scholar close to the practice of writing; for, until he can not only write, but also have got a quick hand, you must not think to make any considerable progress with him.

2. And because of the conveniency of writing cannot always be in readiness, another great help will be to have *tabulae deletiles* [i.e., smoothed tablets] of stone or black wood hanging up for expedition in several convenient places.

3. . . . have some common forms written on these tables, there to continue, and to be filled up as occasion requires, . . .such as, *Where is? I pray, give me! Who? When? What?* etc. These may serve not only for expedition, but by them your scholar may be taught to vary. Pocket table books [writing tablets] may sometimes be more ready than these [wall tablets].

4. When neither of these is in a readiness, then practice by an alphabet upon the fingers; which by frequent practice, as it is the readiest, so it may be the quickest way of intercourse and communication with dumb persons.

5. Another piece of useful care will be, to keep him from any other way of signing, than by letters.

6. Add to this, that his familiars about him be officious [obliging] in nothing, but by the intercourse of letters, that is, either by grammatology [writing/printing] or Dactylology. (*Ibid*, pp. 137-138.)

Further in his essay Dalgarno provides some significant ideas which relate not only to the teaching of English to the deaf, but to the introduction of a breadth of concepts relative to nature and society. This is the freight to be borne by language. Without such concepts, language *per se* is purposeless. Dalgarno writes:

I will make way for particulars by observing, first, in general, that the way of teaching here, must be something mixt, and as it were middle between the grammatical way of the school, and the more rude [less formal] discipline of the nursery.

The first initiation [to language] must be purely grammatical; but when your scholar is got over this difficulty, of knowing and writing his letters readily, then imitate the way of the nursery. Let *utile* [usefulness] and *jucundum* [pleasantness], variety and necessity, invite and spur him on specially if he be young or of a lache [cowardly] temper.

You must not be too grammatical in teaching till you find his capacity will bear it: he must not be dealt with as school-boys, who are often punished for not learning what is above their capacity. It is enough for him to understand the word or sentence proposed, without parsing every word and syllable; for this is all the use of language that not only children but even people of age that are illiterate have; they understand the meaning of what is spoken, but can neither tell how many words, syllables, or letters came from the speaker's mouth. So that the hearing the vulgar use of a language, and the understanding it grammatically are very different things. And this preposterous way of learning the learned languages, first the Grammar and then the language, is the cause of so slow progress in those that apply themselves to the study of them.

The first exercise you must put your scholar upon, is to know his letters written or printed, and upon his fingers, and to write them himself; and when he comes to join, let his copies be of such words as he may be taught to understand; so at once he may be learning both to write, and understand the meaning of what he writes. When you have got him to write fair, keep him to constant practice, that you may bring him to write a quick hand, which his condition requires.

Let him begin to learn the names of things best known to him, how heterogeneous soever; such as the *elements, minerals, plants, animals, parts, utensils, garments, meats*, etc. and generally the names of all such corporeal substances, natural or artificial; not only absolute, but relative as *father, brother, master, servant; groom, tailor, barber*, etc. for all these will be as easily apprehended as the most distinct species of natural bodies. Let his nomenclature be written down fair, and carefully preserved, not only in a book, but on one side of a sheet of paper, that it may be affixed over against his eye in convenient places. (*Ibid.*, pp. 140-141.)

While some of Dalgarno's ideas reflect a particular antiquity in the light of our modern understanding and grasp of the business of teaching deaf children, others of his ideas could be well reconsidered for their genuine merit as practical approaches to some of our continuing problems.

Dalgarno's manual alphabet:

Throughout Dalgarno's material thus far, one encounters frequent references to *dactylology, finger-alphabet, fingerspelling*, and *handlanguage*. In each of these references he is alluding to a manual alphabet of his own creation. It is markedly different from that advocated by the Spaniard, Juan Pablo Bonet, whose work was reproduced in England by Digby. Dalgarno presents his alphabet in his Chapter VIII under the title "Of an Alphabet upon the Fingers." This alphabet is unique, because it was the first hand alphabet devised specifically for the deaf. (Wright, *Deafness*, p. 149.) Bonet's alphabet, while used in communicating with the deaf, was originated presumably by medieval monks who found it handy in circumventing their vow of silence.

In Dalgarno's alphabet, instead of the fingers forming a distinct configuration for each of the 26 letters, one designates the letters by pointing to 26 separate points on the open palm, with the fingertips representing the vowels *a, e, i, o,* and *u*. This procedure may bring to mind Bulwer's account published in 1644 of Babbington's wife, who was able to communicate with him by "pointing to the various finger joints, each of which represented a letter." In any event, history has credited Dalgarno with originating this particular concept of fingerspelling.

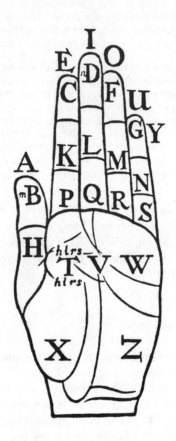

Dalgarno further suggests an idea

> for enabling young beginners to practice more easily and readily; let a pair of gloves be made, one for the master and one for the scholar, with the letters written upon them in such order as appears in the foregoing scheme. To practice with these will be easy for any that do but know their letters and can spell; and a short time will so fix the places of the letters in the memory that the gloves may be thrown away as useless. (Dalgarno, *Didascalocophus*, p. 157.)

Dalgarno's pedagogical advice:

Dalgarno also provides a bit of pedagogical advice which may prove traumatic to the 20th- and 21st-Century special educator, because of its 17th-Century bluntness. Its pertinence as opposed to its impertinence, however, will become abundantly clear if some time is given it for interpretation.

> ... the principal point of art in teaching a slow scholar, is to use no other art but that of diligence; and if so, a second inference will be, that there is none so fit to teach a slow scholar as a slow master; that is, one dunce to teach another. This I know will seem ridiculous and absurd to many, yet I declare, that I am much of this mind in earnest, in our present case, where Grammar is excluded. For an acute man will be impatient, and not able to stoop so much as the other. And to clear this further, I think it will be easily assent to, that a prattling nurse is a better tutrix to her foster-child, than the most profoundly learned doctor in the university.

> My last instance, therefore, shall be – Take master and scholar, qualified as before, adding diligence as I have described it, and let a liberal reward be proposed to the master; if the work be not effectually done, let me be the dunce for them both. (*Ibid.*, pp. 138-139.)

For all of George Dalgarno's 17th-Century quaintness of expression and his intolerable male chauvinism, which no more than reflects the age in which he lived, he may be credited with having had more impact upon the subsequent centuries of education of deaf than any other single writer. Much of what he espoused may well hold a key to some of the major problems confronting our modern educators of the deaf.

10

John Conrad Amman and the Beginnings of Pure Oralism in the 17th Century

When Dr. John Conrad Amman left his native Switzerland to take up his medical practice in the Dutch city of Haarlem, he little knew the circumstances which awaited him and which would in turn set him on a wholly new career. Long interested in the mysterious power of speech with which man had been endowed, Amman devoutly believed speech to be a gift from God.

Amman's belief in speech for the deaf.

Amman believed that the fact that a deaf person could issue forth voice in laughter, crying, or surprise was, indeed, a certain indication that such a person could be taught to speak. Thus it was this belief that set him to work to prove that deaf people could learn to talk.

A Haarlem businessman, Pietar Koolaert, was much impressed with his observations of a deaf child whom Amman had taught to speak. Having a deaf child of his own, Koolaert urged Amman to assume the task of teaching his child. Koolaert even offered him residency in his own home in order to do the teaching. Amman finally agreed and began his task of instructing little Hester Koolaert.

As the child was gradually brought into speech, Amman's confidence in himself as a teacher obviously increased. After a period

Amman decided to share his knowledge and skill with others; thus in 1692 he wrote in Latin a book entitled *Surdus Loquens* (The Talking Deaf Man). The little volume was subsequently rendered into English by a British physician and scholar, Dr. Dan Foot.

In his book Amman gives a detailed description of the "letters" or speech elements, and their formation and blending. He divides the elements into three basic categories: consonants, vowels, and semi-vowels. The consonants he classifies as *simple breath* or *explosives*, i.e., "with the voice conjoyned." (Amman, *Surdus Loquens*, p. 39.)

Amman, the Father of Pure Oralism:

After a deaf pupil had learned to render a specific element, a combination of elements, or a word, Amman advocated writing the form and requiring the pupil to do so, too. This act of writing, he believed, aided in fixing the form in the pupil's mind. If a pupil erred in articulating an element and consequently sounded another, Amman would nod approvingly and provide the pupil with the corresponding written form of the element spoken and drill on it until it was perfected. He would then return to the original element for formation, practice, and writing.

Curiously, Amman's interest and attention were directed almost entirely toward the mechanics of articulation rather than to language *per se*. It was only after a child could *read*, that is, orally speak written words, that Amman would teach "Nouns which are obvious, as well as Substantives and Adjectives, so also the most necessary Verbs and Adverbs, than [sic] Declinations and Conjugations." (*Ibid.*, pp. 85-86.)

Amman's insistence, however, upon the sequence of speech *first* and writing *second* is the basic instructional concept which today differentiates the *pure* oral method from the less restrictive oral method.

Chapter Three
Education of the Deaf in the 18th Century

11

Henry Baker,
Teacher of the Deaf
1698-1774

In 1720, young Henry Baker completed his apprenticeship as a bookseller, which field of endeavor he found sufficient for a living, but minimal in excitement. He therefore looked forward to a long holiday with his relatives in Enfield. He was quietly hopeful that the trip would offer him some new perspectives beyond the bookstalls of London, as indeed it did.

Henry Baker meets a challenge:

One of Baker's Enfield relatives, John Forster, a lawyer in the community, had a problem with his young daughter, Jane. While most children provide their parents with problems of one kind or another, eight-year-old Jane was unique, at least in Enfield: she was a deaf-mute.

Little Jane Forster's plight immediately seized 22-year-old Baker's imagination, and he began to determine ways and means for educating her. To be sure, the child's father was elated to find someone who would give his young daughter something more than a second thought. Consequently, he enthusiastically encouraged young Baker's interest in the possibilities of teaching her. This was the beginning of a nine-year association of Henry Baker and the Forster household.

An unexpected source of information:

Book-oriented Baker began to search for some literature which would provide him with ideas for tackling the problem. While there was, indeed, a dearth of such literature, coincidence came through as she so often does, with a documentary novel entitled *The Life and Adventures of Duncan Campbell* by the author of *Robinson Crusoe* fame, Mr. Daniel Defoe.

Duncan Campbell, a real-life person, had achieved considerable fame throughout England because of his psychic abilities. In addition to this, he was a deaf-mute. Defoe, probably with an eye to the book market and the public's great interest in psychic phenomena, produced the Campbell novel in 1720, shortly after the publication of his classic-to-be, *Robinson Crusoe*.

In the development of Campbell's story, Defoe in Chapter III described his subject's education, which had been guided along the precepts of the late Dr. John Wallis. Wallis was remembered by a few old-timers for his verbal encounters with his arch-rival in education of the deaf, Dr. William Holder.

Defoe's Duncan Campbell:

Henry Baker, however, interested in neither psychic stuff nor old feuds, focused his attention on Defoe's Chapter III of *Duncan Campbell*. One can easily guess the enthusiasm with which young Baker read and reread the following excerpt on teaching deaf children (pp. 38-40):

> It is, I must confess, in some Measure amazing to me, that Men (of any moderate Share of Learning) should not naturally conceive of themselves a plain Reason for this Art, and know how to account for the Practicability of it, the Moment they hear the Proposition advanced; the Reasons for it are so obvious to the very first Consideration we can make about it. It will be likewise amazing to me, that the most ignorant should not conceive it, after so plain a Reason is given them for it, as I am now going to set down.

> To begin: How are Children at first taught a Language that can hear? Are they not taught by Sounds? And what are Sounds, but Tokens and Signs to the Ear, importing and signifying such and such a Thing? If then there can be Signs made to the Eye, agreed by the Party teaching the Child, that they signify such and such a Thing; will not the Eye of the Child convey them to the Mind, as well as the Ear? They are indeed different Marks to different Senses; but both the one and the other do equally signify the same Things or Notions according to the Will

of the Teacher, and consequently, must have an equal Effect with the Person who is to be instructed: For tho' the Manners signifying are different, the Things signified are the same.

For example: If, after having invented an Alphabet upon the Fingers, a Master always keeps Company with a Deaf Child, and teaches it to call for whatsoever it wants, by such Motions of the Fingers, which if put down by Letters, (according to each invented Motion of each Finger) would form in Writing a Word of a Thing which it wanted; might not he, by these regular Motions, teach its Eye the same Notions of Things, as Sounds do to the Ears of Children that hear? The Manner of Teaching the *Alphabet* by Fingers, is plainly described in this Plate.

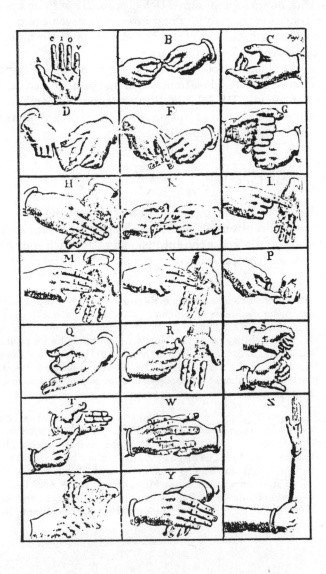

When the Deaf Child learned by these Motions a good Stock of Words; as Children that hear, first learn by Sounds; we may methinks call (not improperly) the Fingers of such a dumb Infant its *Mouth*, and the Eye of such a Deaf Child its *Ear*. When he has learn'd thus far, he must be taught the *Alphabet*, according as it was adapted to the Motions of his Fingers. As for instance, the Five Vowels, *a, e, i, o, u,* by pointing to the Top of the Five Fingers; and the other Letters, *b, c, d,* etc. by such other Place or Posture of a Finger as in the Plate represented; or otherwise as shall be agreed upon. When this is done, the Marks B, R, E, A, D, (and so of all other Words) corresponding with such Finger, conveys thro his Eyes unto his Head the same Notion, *viz.* the Thing signified, as the Sound we give to these same Letters, making the Word *Bread* go into our Heads thro' the Ears.

This once done, he may be easily taught to understand the Parts of Speech; as the *Verb*, the *Noun, Pronoun, etc.* And so by Rules of *Grammar* and *Syntax* to compound Ideas, and connect Words into a Language. The Method of which, since it is plainly set forth in Dr. *Wallis'* Letter to Mr. *Beverly*, I shall set it down by way of Extract; that People in the same Circumstances with the Person we treat of, and of the like Genius, may not have their Talents lost for want of the like Assistance.

Continuing in his reading of Defoe's Chapter III, young Baker encountered Dr. John Wallis' detailed account "concerning the Method of Teaching the Deaf and Dumb to Read" (pp. 41-52). Thus armed with some concrete procedures for teaching his first pupil, Henry Baker began his career in education of the deaf. He remained Jane Forster's teacher for a period of nine years.

During this period, Baker established an acquaintance with the celebrated Defoe, and in 1729 married the author's daughter, Sophia. It was at this time that Baker left the employ of the Forster family.

Baker recognized as a teacher of the deaf:

While contemporaries, Samuel Johnson among them, confirmed Baker's success as a teacher of the deaf, he unfortunately chose to keep his procedures secret because they represented his main source of livelihood. In any event, we know of his initial dependency upon Dr. John Wallis and of his twofold debt to Daniel Defoe. While Baker continued as a bookseller all his life, his chief occupation and interest was teaching the deaf.

12

Jacob Rodrigues Pereira, the First Teacher of the Deaf in France 1715-1780

Pereira and his "heart interest":

The greatest motivating force to bring a person into the education of deaf children is what might be called a "heart interest." Such an interest stems from a familial association: the love for one's deaf parents, a deaf son or daughter, a deaf brother or sister. Such love has quite naturally enough produced some of the most dedicated and outstanding educators of the deaf, and not the least of these was Jacob Rodrigues Pereira.

Pereira, a Spanish Jew, was because of his faith driven with his family from Spain westward into Portugal. The family's unsettled state continued until their ultimate arrival in Bordeaux in 1741. Through the previous years of hardship Jacob Rodrigues Pereira had but one grave concern, and that was regarding the well-being and intellectual development of his deaf-mute sister, whom he was endeavoring to teach.

As early as 1734, young Pereira had sought books on the subject of deaf-mutes and their education. Consequently upon his arrival in Bordeaux at the age of 26, he was fairly well steeped in theory relative to the teaching of language and speech for the deaf. By this time, too, Pereira's sister was a marvelous example of the educational results achieved through his unique instructional talents.

Pereira's success:

Without especially advertising his willingness to teach deaf pupils, Pereira's skills in this art became known. In 1746 a prelingually deaf lad of 16 was brought to him. The boy, d'Azy d'Etavigny, had received some previous instruction in Amiens without having made too much progress. After two years of Pereira's dedicated instruction, however, the youth's intellectual and educational progress was sufficient to merit the attention of the Academy of Caen. Finally in 1749 Pereira was invited to present young d'Etavigny to the French Academy of Science.

Despite the lad's nervousness in appearing before the prestigious Academy, he was able to impress its members with his intellectual perceptiveness and skill in answering their questions. It must be remembered that in the eyes of the Academy a deaf-mute's *speaking*, *reading*, and *writing* bordered on the miraculous. Arnold, the British historian, quotes the Academy's memoir of the event as follows:

> the objects of Pereire in the education of the deaf included teaching them not only to pronounce all the words of the French or any other language, but also, what is essential, to understand their meaning, and to express, both verbally and by writing, their thoughts like other people; rendering them, therefore, capable of learning and practising any art or science, except those for which hearing is necessary. (Farrar, *Arnold's Education*, p. 33).

Subsequently the Academy appointed a group of scholars among whom was the famous French naturalist, Buffon. This commission prepared an account of its observations, which states:

> this young deaf-mute reads and pronounces distinctly all sorts of phrases; gives sensible replies, both verbally and by writing, to familiar questions made by writing or signs; understands and executes whatever he is required to do by writing or the manual alphabet; recites prayers by heart . . . and in all respects shows a competent knowledge of grammar and syntax . . . and is fairly correct in his articulation. . . .

> We find that the progress made by d'Azy d'Etavigny justifies Pereire in hoping that, by his method, congenital deaf-mutes can not only learn to read, pronounce, and understand common words, but also acquire abstract notions, and become capable of reasoning and acting like others. . . . We have no difficulty in believing that the art of lip-reading, with its necessary limitations, will be useful to other deaf-mutes of the same class . . . as well as the manual alphabet which Pereire uses. (*Ibid.*, pp. 33-34.)

Pereira meets his pupil, de Fontenay:

Such recognition by the French Academy of Science was tantamount to national recogniton. Consequently, that Pereira's work had caught the eye of the Duc de Chaulnes is not surprising. The Duc de Chaulnes, a singular light in the Court of Louis XV, had some years previously assumed the spiritual and moral development responsibilities as the godfather of an acquaintance's child. After a few years it became clear that the child, a little boy, one Saboureux de Fontenay, was a deaf-mute. In the year 1750, when the boy was 13 years of age, the Duc de Chaulnes placed him under the instruction of the renowned Pereira.

Although the lad had had some previous teaching, his progress had been but minimal. After one year's instruction following Pereira's method, however, the boy's progress was phenomenal, and Pereira was invited to appear before the French Academy for the second time with young de Fontenay accompanying him. After Pereira's presentation of the lad and his newly acquired academic skills, the secretary of the Academy recorded a statement reaffirming the excellence of Pereira's procedures in the teaching of reading, writing, articulation, the manual alphabet, and speechreading.

Although Saboureux was under Pereira's instruction for only a period of five years, this was a sufficient time for the master to inculcate in the lad not only the subjects for successful living, but also a deep love for intellectual self-improvement. Young de Fontenay, therefore, continued his pursuit of education long after his association with his mentor. It is stated that the young deaf man subsequently mastered a foreign language with the help of dictionaries. Arnold writes, "M. de Fontenay himself became a teacher and succeeded surprisingly." As an aside, while this achievement on the part of a prelingually deaf person was surprising in the day of its occurrence, it was similarly surprising to Arnold even 110 years later. Curiously enough, such intellectual achievements, although relatively common among American deaf people today, still continue to be a surprise to many European educators of the deaf.

Pereira, of course, continued in his work; however, he unfortunately documented almost nothing of his instructional procedures. The reason for this was that teaching the deaf was his means of livelihood, and to him it seemed to be bad sense to share his "trade secrets" with any possible competition. Needless to say, deaf children of the poor went unschooled; however, it must be remembered that indigent hearing children went unschooled as well, for such were the times. Poverty, not deafness, was the common denominator.

De Fontenay describes Pereira's methods:

The only extensive account of Pereira's thinking on education of the deaf is that given in a letter written in 1764 by his remarkable student, de Fontenay.

Arnold provides the following summary:

(1) The most distinctive feature of Pereire's method was his manual alphabet. He had adopted the Spanish manual alphabet, but considering it to be inadequate to his purpose, he greatly simplified and augmented it. It served both as a means of communication and of indicating the pronunciation. M. de Fontenay tells us that it "is contained in the fingers of one hand, and is composed of twenty-five signs of written letters and of the signs which M. Pereire invented for conforming this manual alphabet exactly to the laws of pronunciation and of French orthography. Thus there are as many sounds – 33 or 34 – and written combinations *(liaisons)* – over 32 – each making one sound in pronunciation, as there are signs in the manual alphabet; which for this reason, I named *Dactylology*, a word Pereire adopted. Moreover, the different sounds which the same letters and combinations had in different words were distinguished, so that the dactylology comprised in all more than eighty signs;" and Pereire says, "each particular position of the fingers indicates not only the form of one or several characters, but the arrangement and action of the organs of speech necessary to produce the value of the vowel or consonant which these characters indicate. . . . My dactylology is also expeditious in indicating at once several letters by one sign. . . . It prevents ambiguities in pronunciation and writing. . . . [I]n reading it saves my pupils the disheartening trouble of spelling."

(2) This manual alphabet closely associated with speech formed the fundamental basis of Pereire's method of teaching. In addition he made use of signs, reading and writing. Of pantomimic gestures, however, he never seems to have had any great opinion, as one of his pupils, Mdlle. Marois, tells that when his pupils had made some progress in speech, he interdicted their use, and only resorted to them as a means of explanation to be dispensed with whenever he could do without them.

(3) Pereire does not appear to have given lip-reading so prominent a place in his method as Amman did.

(4) He divided his course of instruction into two periods; the first, of

twelve or fifteen months, devoted to mechanical exercises in pronunciation, and the second to intellectual exercises in language and its meaning, and to the acquistion of some elementary knowledge; this latter course necessarily taking a much longer time.

(5) As to his method of teaching language, M. de Fontenay describes his primary lessons in language as founded on action. "In the same manner," says he, "in which an infant learns French, so Pereire applied himself at first to give me a knowledge of words in daily use and of the commonest phrases, such as *open the window, close the window, open the door, close the door.* Finding me sufficiently acquainted with the dialogues of everyday life, he abandoned the use of gestures in my presence, but at the same time he employed the Spanish manual alphabet which he had enlarged and perfected. ... And in order to exercise me still more in the meaning of familiar phrases, he made me take part in doing everything according to the import suggested to my mind by the language which anyone would employ who wished to command me; reply to all questions, easy or difficult; and reproduce my own thoughts. He also obliged me to give a daily report of everything that had occurred, to repeat whatever had been said, to converse, to dispute with himself or others about everything of ordinary interest which we might think of; to write letters in my own way to my acquaintances, and to reply to their's [*sic*]." (*Ibid.*, pp. 35-37.)

M. de Fontenay sums up his personal acquisition of the vernacular under Pereira's method with the words, "I can say, without much doubt, that it was by usage I learned French, and that my education was not mechanical. ... This usage was nothing else than a constant repetition of the same words, phrases, and modes of speech, applied in all sorts of ways and on all occasions." (*Ibid.*, p. 37.)

Pereira's high expectations for his students:

While it was generally supposed that deaf-mutes were wholly incapable of grasping abstract concepts, Pereira entertained no such limiting ideas. With a "ladder-like" procedure he would lift his students one rung at a time from the concrete into the abstract. M. de Fontenay's example of the technique reads, "One day it would be raining. Pereire would take the opportunity to explain that tomorrow it might be fine; that he *expected* and *hoped* it would be so, from which he would proceed to deduce the word *hope*." (*Ibid.*, pp. 37-38.)

Thus we are indebted to M. Saboureux de Fontenay's brief account of his mentor's art. What the description lacks in detail, it compensates for in revealing Pereira's thoughts relative to language development, the *alpha* and *omega* of education for deaf children.

13

Thomas Braidwood of Scotland
1715-1806

When Thomas Braidwood established his school of mathematics in Edinburgh in the middle of the 18th Century, he was reasonably certain of success in his enterprise, because being located in the University city, he could always be assured of a number of collegiate aspirants in need of preparation for their college entrances. In addition, there were always those university students, too, who were in need of perpetual tutoring.

Braidwood enrolls his first deaf pupil:

In the fall of 1760, Braidwood, being a specialist in the field of numbers, surprised his colleagues when he accepted the tuition of a 15-year-old pupil for "writing." The surprise was doubled when they learned that this lad, one Robert Shirreff, was also deaf and on the verge of muteness, having lost his hearing when he was but three years old. Young Shirreff's obvious intelligence, although caged in deafness, indicated itself clearly in a natural curiosity for the world around him and in a genuine desire to communicate. The lad and his needs both inspired and challenged Braidwood. Consequently, the teacher determined early to take his pupil educationally beyond their original goal of "writing."

Braidwood's enthusiasm for his educational endeavor was fueled by his reading of Bulwer's *Philocophus* (The Deaf Man's Friend), which advocated "the hand ABC." This was suggested as a basis for the introduction of "Lip-Grammar" or speechreading and was to be followed by instruction in speech. Braidwood also read the works of Wallis (Digby's account of Bonet-Carrión) and Holder. Thus, he was well fortified in the theory of his day, relative to teaching the deaf, and consequently, he was anxious to try his hand at the art.

We may surmise that early in the association of Braidwood and Shirreff as teacher and pupil, Braidwood discovered the lad's vestiges of infant speech and language. This was more than likely, because the child's onset of deafness, as previously indicated, occurred at the age of three. This, of course, might well account for his high degree of receptiveness to language: reading and writing. At any rate, success marked the school experience for both pupil and teacher. Progress with young Shirreff was sufficiently satisfactory that Braidwood soon opted to teach him speech as well.

In 1766, Braidwood decided to take another pupil. The second child was a 13-year-old congenitally deaf boy from London, the son of a physician, a Dr. John Douglas. After four short months under Mr. Braidwood's instruction, young Douglas made outstanding progress.

Braidwood's Academy expands:

By 1767, Braidwood's Academy, as it was called, had several pupils, both boys and girls. Mr. Braidwood announced that he could teach any deaf pupil to speak, read, write, and cypher within a period of three years. The only preliminary requirement for a pupil was that he be of average intelligence.

With the idealism and enthusiasm which has traditionally characterized teachers of the deaf, Braidwood was motivated to serve not only the children of those parents who could afford to pay him well, but also the children of those parents who could not afford to pay at all. In order to achieve this ideal, however, Braidwood recognized the need for a public subsidy. He consequently appealed to the philanthropic citizens of Edinburgh for money which would enable him to extend his instructional efforts to the children of the indigent.

Braidwood's disillusionment and resort to secrecy:

One might suppose that such a request would certainly have

touched the hearts of those gentlemen who comprised "the power structure" of the city. However much Braidwood's appeal may have touched their hearts, it most certainly never touched their purses. After a couple of such unsuccessful ventures into the field of fund-raising, Braidwood retreated into his academy. Disillusioned and embittered by his experience, he matched the callousness of his city with a personal policy that only the children of moneyed people would thereafter be able to derive the benefits of his instruction. Thus came about what has been referred to as the "Braidwood monopoly." Actually, the monopoly aspect of Braidwood's policy was that he kept his instructional procedures secret. This move, however, in no way prevented a possible competitor from setting up a similar shop, although no one did. The Braidwood Academy flourished in its reputation, in its pupil population, and in its financial success. Eventually, in 1783, the school was moved southward to the more remunerative field of Hackney, London.

To assist with the increasing responsibilities of his school, Braidwood had sometime before enlisted the efforts of his nephew, John Braidwood, who joined him and loyally maintained the secret of the Braidwood method. Incidentally, this loyalty to the family confidence was kept by succeeding nephews and finally ended in 1809, three years after old Thomas Braidwood's demise. Dr. Joseph Watson, a Braidwood nephew and an established educator of the deaf in his own right, published in 1809 two volumes which released, he claimed, the Braidwood "secrets." To these were added some of Watson's own developments of the procedure. The most complete account, however, revealing the original instructional philosophy and procedure as practiced by Thomas Braidwood was assembled and written by a contempory, an American colonial named Francis Green. The volume, entitled *Vox Oculus Subjecta* "or (as it *may* be englished) Voice made visible," appeared in London in the year 1783. Green's identity as the book's author was covered by the enigmatic pseudonym "A Parent."

Green's account of Braidwood's work:

The most likely reason for this disguised authorship might be best explained by the fact that the American Revolution, having been recently concluded, placed things American in bad odor. To be sure, the reception given to a Boston colonial at that particular time would probably have been less than cordial. Therefore, to mollify the British readership of his day, Green opened the Preface of his essay with the words,

Politicks and party views, which, at this day, occupy and engross the minds of so many, have no place or share in this unambitious publication; of course prejudices and resentments, on that ground cannot be provoked. (Green, *Vox Oculus Subjecta*, p. v.)

Green's interest in Thomas Braidwood's Academy commenced when he determined upon it as a school for his eight-year-old son, Charles, who was either born deaf or rendered so "by sickness from earliest infancy." Green's nonpareil enthusiasm for Braidwood and his Academy is reflected throughout the book. In addition to Green's own observations of the school, he includes in the Appendix of his volume several reputable contemporary sources. The first of these concerning Braidwood's method is a descriptive piece taken from Argot's *History of Edinburgh*.

He [Braidwood] begins with learning [*sic*] the deaf, articulation, or the use of their vocal organs, and at the same time teaches them to write the characters, and compose *words* of them. He next shows them the use of words in expressing *visible objects* and their *qualities*: after this, he proceeds to instruct them in the proper *arrangement* of words, or grammatical *construction* of language. . . . The connexion between our ideas and written language being purely arbitrary, it is very hard to give the deaf any notion of that mode of conversing, theirs being only hieroglyphical; another still greater difficulty is to enable them to comprehend the meaning of the figurative part of language: for instance, they soon understand *high, low, hard, tender, clear, cloudy etc.* when applied to *matter*, but have not the smallest conception of these qualities when applied to the *mind*. – Notwithstanding these difficulties, the deaf attain a perfect knowledge of written language, and become capable both of speaking and writing their sentiments in the most distinct manner, and of understanding what they read: being thus advanced, they are capable to learn any art or science (music excepted), and to translate one language into another; – Mr. Braidwood's pupils are under his tuition from three to six years, according to their age, capacity, and conveniency. – When we visited this Academy, we found that the boys could not only converse by the help of the artificial alphabet they learnt, by putting their fingers into certain positions, but that they understood us, altho' perfect strangers to them, by the motions of our lips. In this manner they actually conversed with us, returning an answer distinctly, yet slowly, *viva voce*.

A layman in matters of teaching the deaf, but a professional in portraying matters of fact, Argot gives sufficient information to formulate at least a broad picture of Braidwood's grasp of deafness and its implications, his philosophy, and his mode for attacking the problems of speech and language. Also revealed was the fact of Braidwood's being one of the first speech pathologists.

Particularly clear and important in Argot's account is Braidwood's dedicated confidence in himself as a teacher of the deaf.

Clear also is his unflagging faith in the complete educability of the deaf. In these respects, he reflects his English predecessors, Holder and Wallis.

The next Braidwood Academy visitor quoted in Green's *Vox Oculus Subjecta* is the renowned British conversationalist and lexicographer, Dr. Samuel Johnson. Johnson, accompanied by his close friend and admirer, James Boswell, went on a tour of the north country, Boswell's native Scotland. Their itinerary naturally included Caledonia's chief city, Edinburgh. In his *Journey to the Western Islands of Scotland* (1775), Johnson wrote,

> There is one subject of philosophical curiosity to be found in *Edinburgh*, which no other city has to show; a college of the deaf and dumb, who are taught to *speak*, to *read*, to *write*, and to practice *arithmetic*, by a gentleman whose name is Braidwood: the number which attends him is, I think, about twelve; which he brings together in a little school, and instructs according to their several degrees of proficiency. . . .
>
> The improvement of *Mr. Braidwood's pupils is wonderful:* they not only *speak*, *write*, and understand what is written, but if he that speaks looks towards them, and modifies his organs by distinct and full utterance, they know so well what is spoken, that is an expression *scarcely figurative* to say, *They hear with the eye*. . . . It will readily be supposed by those that consider this subject, that Mr. Braidwood's scholars spell accurately. . . . [T]o those students every character is of equal importance; for letters are to them *not* symbols of names, but of things; when they write they do not represent a *sound*, but delineate a *form:* – this school I visited, and found some of the scholars waiting for their master, whom they are said to receive at his entrance with smiling countenances and sparkling eyes, *delighted* with the hope of new ideas.

Johnson also describes his observations of a young girl to whom he had given a multiplication problem. "She looked upon it, and quivering her fingers in a manner which I thought very pretty," she set about to resolve it. After revealing a depth of understanding relative to the child's victory over her deafness, Johnson concludes with one of his typically Johnsonian barbs for the Scots: "After seeing the deaf taught arithmetic, who would be afraid to cultivate the Hebrides?"

The final reference in the Appendix is an excerpt from *Pennant's Tour Through Scotland* (1772, Vol. 3, p. 256), in which Thomas Pennant provides the earliest account of Braidwood's instructional mode and sequence.

> Mr. Braidwood first teaches them the letters and their powers, and the ideas of words written, beginning with the most simple; the art of

speaking is taken from the motion of his lips, his words being uttered *slowly* and *distinctly*.

Of a 13-year-old girl, Pennant writes,

> . . . she readily apprehended *all* I said, and *returned answers with the utmost facility.* She *read* and *wrote* well. Her reading was *not* by rote. She *could cloath the same thoughts in a new set of words, and never vary from the original sense.*

The ability to paraphrase is, of course, the most obvious and accurate measure of reading comprehension.

These foregoing accounts from *Vox Oculus Subjecta* give a kind of background for Green's own highly personal observations of Braidwood's work. Green, it should be remembered, wrote not as a casual visitor, but as a deeply interested parent. By the time his eight-year-old son, Charles, arrived at the Braidwood Academy in 1780 the institution had been in operation for 20 years. By this time, too, the instructional procedures appear to have been well developed and quite successful. The most striking evidence of this fact is revealed in Francis Green's touching story of his small son's progress in Braidwood's program. Green writes,

> . . . I thought it my duty, however, to send my son across the Atlantic, upon Mr. Braidwood's agreeing to undertake the tuition of him, who accordingly received in February, 1780. He was then *eight* years old: although sprightly, sensible, and *quick of apprehension*, yet having been either born *deaf*, or having lost his hearing by sickness in earliest infancy, he could not *at that time* produce or distinguish *vocal* sounds, nor *articulate* at all, neither had he any idea of the meaning of words, either when spoken, in writing, or in print; and for *want of* hearing, should doubtless have remained as speechless as he was born. – I soon received the pleasing intelligence that he was beginning to articulate, and soon after that he could plainly express (upon seeing the form in characters) any word in the English language. My first visit to him was in May, 1781. It exceeds the power of words to convey any idea of the sensations experienced at the interview. – The child, ambitious to manifest his acquisition, eagerly advanced and addressed me, with a distinct salutation of *speech*. He also made several inquiries in *short* sentences. – I then delivered him a letter from his sister (couched in the *simplest* terms) which he read so as to be understood; he accompanied many of the words, *as he pronounced them*, with proper gestures, significative of their meaning, such as in the sentence, "*write a letter* by papa:" on *uttering* the *first* word, he described the action of writing, by the motion of his right-hand; the *second*, by tapping the letter he held; the *third* by pointing to me. – He could at that time repeat the Lord's Prayer very properly, and some other forms, one of which in particular (*which I had never heard before*) I then took down in writing from his repetition; a convincing proof of his speaking intelligibly. – I found that he could in that short time read distinctly,

in a *slow manner*, any English Book, although it cannot be supposed he had as yet learned *the meaning* of many words: he, however, made daily progress in that knowledge. As to writing, there can be no reason why deaf persons may not, by imitation, learn that art as well as any other persons; accordingly I was not surprised, that he could write *very plainly:* this he did with *uncommon readiness* and dexterity, and seemed not a little proud of all of his new attainments. – I had also the satisfaction to see such specimens, at that time, *in the proficiency of others* who had been longer at this Academy, as left no doubt in my mind of his acquiring, in due season, a perfect acquaintance with *language* both oral and written. . . .

On my next visit, in September, 1782, his improvements were very perceptible in speech, the construction of language, and in writing: he had made a good beginning in *arithmetic*, and *surprising* progress in the arts of drawing and *painting*. – I found him capable of not only comparing ideas, and drawing inferences, but expressing his sentiments with judgement. – On my desiring him to attempt something he thought himself unequal to, I set him the example by doing it myself upon which, he shook his head, and, with a smile, replied (distinctly, *viva voce*) "You are a man, Sir, I am a boy." – Observing, that he was inclined in company to converse with one of his school-fellows by the tacit finger-language, I asked him, why he did not speak to him with *his mouth*? – To this, his answer was as pertinent as it was concise, "He is deaf." Many other instances I could mention of expressions of mind, as proper as could be made by *any boy* of his age, who had *not* the disadvantage of deafness.

Following this passage are a couple of letters from Braidwood and his nephew, John. They describe young Charles' progress and set forth also his educational potentialities in the areas of mathematics, "the *sciences*, the *French* and as much *Latin* as may give him a competent knowledge of the derivation of words. This all, of course, bears upon young Charles' mastery of English."

Subsequently, Green reflects upon Thomas Braidwood's philosophy. The education of deaf children

must be the work of time, and unremitted perseverance, for years, under the constant eye of the teacher, who gives "*line upon line, and precept upon precept, here a little, and there a little;*" not only in school, but at meals, in walking, playing, etc. And upon all occasions making a lesson out of every suitable occurrence: – but what *time* or *expense* can be *too much* to bestow for acquisitions of such *infinite* consequence to the individual?

The import of this passage is of such consequence that one can little wonder at the reasons for Braidwood's success. Even had these principles been fulfilled to a moderate degree, their results would have been considerable. While a light sprinkle of questioning salt may be distributed over the fantastically glowing accounts provided by Green and his fellow observers, withal one may sense that Braidwood may have had "something." Perhaps in his story there is even a possible solution to some of the confusions confronting our late-20th-Century education of the deaf. (See Appendix 4.)

14

Samuel Heinicke,
the Father of German Oralism
1729-1790

The year was 1750. Twenty-one-year-old Samuel Heinicke, upon first joining the Elector of Saxony's Guard, found his military life considerably more appealing to his youthful and imaginative spirit than life on his father's farm. Also it was more acceptable than the thought of a lifetime with the stout young thing his father had chosen for him to marry. He was determined, obviously, to marry in his own time and to his own choice.

At once stationed in Dresden, Heinicke, the young soldier, was completely occupied with his training duties. He was certain he had found his place in the world. With pride he wore his forest-green military tunic and was well aware of its magnetic influence on *brauhaus* maidens. All went well for the young man until the routines of endless drilling and the countless guardmounts finally became second nature to him. It was then that Heinicke began to seek the intellectual stimulation afforded by study. The Guard's chaplain, becoming acquainted with the young man, found in him a willing scholar and consequently supplied him with plenty of books and good discussion.

Heinicke, the soldier-teacher:

After a few months of meshing his studies with his military responsibilities, Heinicke began to tutor the children of his officers.

60

So successful was he in this endeavor that after awhile he began to think of himself as a teacher first and a soldier second. The instruction of youth afforded him not only some extra pocket *pfennigs,* but a diversion which he thoroughly enjoyed.

As Heinicke's success as a teacher increased, so did his number of pupils. Obviously, making his military formations on time and fulfilling his teaching commitments kept the young guardsman extremely busy. One wonders how on earth he ever found the time to court, propose to, and marry "his own choice," Johanne Elizabeth Kracht, but this he did. That year, 1754, was a busy one for him, indeed.

Heinicke becomes a teacher of the deaf:

It was also at this time that his professional attention as a teacher was to move in a new and challenging direction. Heinicke's latest pupil, a young boy, was a deaf-mute. The lad's plight presented the soldier-teacher with a fascinating challenge. Accounts indicate that the lad's instruction in writing met no great difficulty, nor did his acquisition of arithmetic. Despite these achievements Heinicke was particularly anxious that the boy should learn to speak. Therefore the young teacher set himself to the study of Amman's Latin work, *Surdus Loquens,* and also the work of a proponent of Amman's methods, Georg Raphel.

Thus fortified with some specific procedures and with his own inventiveness, Heinicke taught the boy speech. His success in this endeavor inspired him to choose the education of deaf children as his life's vocation. Consequently, he decided to discontinue his career in the military.

Heinicke's subsequent military experience:

The intercession of politics, however, determined for Heinicke that he would remain a soldier at least for awhile longer. His subsequent experiences provided him with sufficient adventure to satisfy a professional adventurer a whole lifetime.

Dresden, the Saxon capital, was buzzing through the whole of July in 1756, for the obvious reason that the Prussian legions led by Frederick the Great were slowly moving inexorably in the direction of the Saxon border. This was but one of hundreds of military moves in a conflict which historians eventually designated as the Seven Years' War.

To be sure, all military leaves were cancelled within the Elector's Guard, and only a few passes were issued and those only to married men. Quite naturally the restrictions were keenly felt by Heinicke, not only because they interfered with his teaching activities, but more importantly because they limited his family life. As Frederick's juggernaut moved closer to the Saxon border, Heinicke sought to free himself from the Elector's service on grounds of personal family obligations. Failing in this, he painfully swallowed his personal feelings and accompanied his detachment to Pirna.

On August 29, 1756, some 70,000 Prussians moved across the Saxon border. Little resistance was offered by the Elector's 20,000 men. After the capital city of Dresden was taken, the garrison at Pirna soon succumbed to Frederick's obviously superior force. Among the many captured was the once-aspiring teacher of the deaf, Samuel Heinicke.

As a prisoner, Heinicke was shunted back to Dresden, where his greatest concern was the possibility of his being forced into the Prussian military service. To avoid this possibility, Heinicke relied on his histrionic talents and accordingly disguised himself as a vagabond fiddler, complete with hump and whiskers. Thus equipped and guised, he successfully fiddled his way past the guards and on to the road toward Jena.

Once in Jena, Heinicke was reunited with his family. His hope was to become a student at the university; however, it was not long before he suspected that he was recognized by the Saxon military authorities. Rather than risk being nabbed and possibly imprisoned for desertion, Heinicke took to the road once again. It was in Hamburg that he settled and quietly set himself up as a tutor. The year was 1757.

Three years later, through the assistance of some professional friends, Heinicke received an appointment as a secretary to a nobleman, one Count Schimmelman. (Bender, *Conquest,* p. 100.) Heinicke remained in the Count's employ until 1768, when he sought greater independence and secured a position as a teacher and choir director in the town of Eppendorf, near Hamburg.

Heinicke's renewed interest in the deaf.

So many years had passed since Heinicke's initial contacts with deaf youngsters, one might suppose that his interest in the problems of the deaf had certainly waned if not disappeared entirely. His interest, however, was quickly rekindled one fall with the presence of a bright 13-year-old deaf-mute boy among his new pupils.

With the revival of his former enthusiasm, Heinicke concentrated on his new deaf pupil and in a relatively short time was able to bring him to a demonstrable level of achievement. Word as to Heinicke's success as a teacher of the deaf soon spread throughout the city, and thoughts of a more extensive school program began to occupy his mind. Unfortunately, in 1775 Heinicke's beloved Johanne died, and he felt a strong compulsion to leave Eppendorf. The opportunity to make the move finally came in 1778, when he was invited to Leipzig for the purpose of starting a school for the deaf in that city.

Shortly after his arrival, a comely young widow, Catherine Elizabeth Morin, became the center of his attention and eventually his love. Catherine, being the sister of one of Heinicke's pupils, held a "heart interest" for deaf youngsters, and this was quite likely one of the many compelling facets of her nature that persuaded him to "pop the question." After their wedding Heinicke enthusiastically went back to work in his new school. The results of his dedication were such that the interest of the Elector Frederick August was captured, and His Highness provided Heinicke with a substantial annual grant. The plan of school operation was that the deaf children of the moneyed families paid tuition, while the children of the indigent were enrolled without cost.

Heinicke, like Thomas Braidwood, his Scottish contemporary, succeded in establishing through his sons-in-law a dynasty in German education of the deaf, the influence of which continues in modern West Germany. (It should be observed that this dynasty phenomenon appears again and again in the history of education of the deaf, and it becomes clearly an important factor in determining philosophical directions relative to instructional method.)

Heinicke and pure oralism:

In terms of influence, certainly Heinicke exerted a considerable amount. It will be recalled that his own mentor was John Conrad Amman, whose *Surdus Loquens* became his guidebook for instruction. This volume was also substantiated by the accounts of Raphel's instruction of his three deaf daughters. From all of this and his own personal experience, Heinicke formulated an unshakeable belief in what is today termed the *pure oral* method.

Heinicke planned to write extensively about his methodology;

however, he was never actually able to do this. The simple reason for this apparent scholarly dereliction was one of which countless master teachers are guilty. He was just too busy teaching deaf children to take time for writing, which he considered a less vital activity. Heinicke did, however, produce one significant work in 1778. This he entitled *Beobachtungen uber Stumme* (Observations on the Deaf and Dumb).

An often quoted statement from Heinicke bears quoting again because it epitomizes his total commitment to the oral approach.

> In my method of instructing the deaf, spoken language is the fundamental point – the hinge upon which everything turns. By means of this, to which various classes of ideas are united, they require conceptions and proceed from the sensible to the intellectual. In a word, they think in sensations acquired by art, and by representations cohering with these sensations, which conjointly and separately influence their faculty of affecting and repugning, and produce the arbitrary cause of their thinking and acting.

In this passage one may see in application an ingenious psychological insight or perception a full 100 years before William James and the advent of psychology as a recognized science.

Heinicke's principles of instruction:

Arnold provides us with the summation of Heinicke's principles which clearly sets forth his philosophy:

1. The knowledge of a thing precedes its naming. The education of the deaf must, therefore, proceed from intuitive instruction.

2. Clear thought is possible only by speech, and, therefore, the deaf ought to be taught to speak.

3. Learning speech, which depends on hearing, is only possible by substituting another sense for hearing, and this can be no other than *taste*, which serves chiefly to fix the vowel sounds.

4. Although the deaf can think in signs and pictures, this is confusing and indefinite, so that the ideas thus acquired are not enduring.

5. They can also receive ideas by writing, but these can only be retained by the frequent repetition of the written words; and by the help of the conceptions thus acquired they are capable of a certain degree of thought, but the progress is slow, and the ideas thus formed are of a fleeting character.

6. The manual alphabet is useful, but, contrary to its ordinary use, it only serves to combine ideas.

7. The deaf can understand the speech of another from the speech motions of the lips.

8. As soon as they have learned to speak they should converse either with one another or with the hearing and not use signs. (Farrar, *Arnold's Education*, pp. 54-55.)

Probably the most extraordinary of Heinicke's ideas was his use of the sense of taste as an avenue for facilitating a pupil's mastery of the vowels. In applying this idea, Heinicke associated a specific flavor with a specific vowel. The consistent application of this given flavor, as its particular vowel was articulated by the pupil, would theoretically reinforce in the pupil's mind the element's formation and movement. In effect, taste was presumbably a substitute for hearing.

For the curious, Arnold's German source, Walther, lists the vowels and their corresponding taste substances as *a*, pure water; *e*, wormwood; *i*, vinegar; and *u*, olive oil. Unquestionably the pupils with the strongest stomachs were the best equipped to master the vowels; all others probably settled for the schwa.

During Heinicke's long career, which ended in 1790, he was recognized across Germany as the founder of the pure oral movement. This procedure he staunchly defended against the newly conceived phenomenon of sign language, which was finding its origins in contemporary France. For all of this, pure oralism was eventually to dominate increasingly the European scene of education of the deaf.

15

De l'Epee and His
"True Manner" Contested
1712-1789

A quick review of the history of education for the deaf will reveal that all of the significant instructional efforts up to the time of the Abbé de l'Epee had been oral, with the frequent advocacy of fingerspelling and writing as the supplementary and complementary modes for speech. Consequently, when de l'Epee in his new Parisian school came forth with signs as a medium not only for social communication but for instructional communication as well, one may readily see why this obviously unorthodox approach eventually stood as a challenge to the German educator Samuel Heinicke. It will be recalled that Heinicke was an adamant supporter of pure oralism, the roots of which were found in the early work of John Conrad Amman.

As to signs *per se*, it has been generally believed down through the years that de l'Epee actually originated the sign language. Harlan Lane, however, in his fascinating book *The Wild Boy of Aveyron*, states that de l'Epee did not invent the sign mode of communication (pp. 79-80), but instead adopted and adapted the gestures used by the deaf children and adults with whom he was associated. Thus from a completely unstandardized mass of natural gestures, de l'Epee began to systematize the natural signs and add to them his own "invented" methodical signs, which were to be used for instructional purposes.

De l'Epee meets with opposition:

This new thrust in the direction of manual signs stirred opposition not only from Samuel Heinicke in Germany, but also from Jacob Rodrigues Pereira, de l'Epee's Parisian competitor, who looked upon the good Abbé's sign making with a particularly "jaundiced eye." Pereira's penchant for professional secrecy prevented him from engaging de l'Epee in any extensive debate. Heinicke, however, while as secretive as Pereira, felt he could launch into the business of exchanging letters with de l'Epee and perhaps even dissuade him from his peculiar philosophy.

If ever the concept of "being at loggerheads" were personified, it was so in these two aging authorities, de l'Epee and Heinicke, each of whom possessed a remarkable contempt for the thought and work of the other. The correspondence between these two Titans, neither of whose language was comprehensible to the other, began in their respective languages, French and German. Both being educated men, however, they set aside their national prides and circumvented the problem by writing in Latin. With such a precedent set for communication among educators of the deaf, the modern scholar may readily understand why, even today, the makers of signs and the advocates of speech are still not really able to understand one another. Perhaps after almost two centuries, both factions are still missing the point.

The Abbé de l'Epee, not accustomed to being "put down" in any language, French, German, or Latin, happily believed that he had the last word in his 1789 publication which bore the be-all-end-all title of *The True Manner of Instructing the Deaf and Dumb, Confirmed by Long Experience*. This volume obviously set education of the deaf moving in a new direction.

De l'Epee's educational goal — "language comprehension":

To understand the new direction, however, one must first grasp the significance of one statement which served as the generally unadvertised basis for de l'Epee's instructional philosophy. In a letter to his successor, the Abbé Sicard, he wrote, "Do not hope that they [the deaf] will ever be able to communicate their own ideas by writing." (Bartlett, "Family Education," p. 31.) De l'Epee believed that it was enough for the deaf to be able to understand ideas expressed in written language or in speechreading and then to translate either medium into signs. Similarly, it was essential, he believed, for a deaf pupil to be able from dictation to translate methodical signs into acceptable written language.

De l'Epee's major emphasis was, therefore, upon the *comprehension of receptive language* rendered through signs or the "labial alphabet" (speechreading). The medium, whichever, was then translated movement-by-movement by the pupil into word-for-word written French.

In the instructor's use of speechreading, there was no voice, only lip movement. (De l'Epee, *True Manner*, p. 128.) As to use of signs, de l'Epee in a letter to Heinicke wrote,

> But Methodical Signs are of no language. They express no words, nor yet letters: they signify Ideas, which the scholar apprehending expresses in his own language, whatever that be, and in his own words; nor can he possibly do otherwise than understand the sense of a word chosen by himself to be written. (*Ibid.*, p. 171.)

The methodical signs referred to were de l'Epee's arbitrarily devised gestures which were frequently compound in nature. An example of such signs might be the sign designation for the concepts *male-small*. These two signs, in turn, might variously be translated to mean *boy*, *lad*, *little fellow*, *male-midget*, or any one of a number of similar interpretations. Thus, it becomes clear that the preciseness of meaning rests with the extensiveness of the established vocabulary of the individual making the interpretation.

De l'Epee on "Speech":

Lest one believe that the Abbé de l'Epee was wrapped up solely in his methodical signs, it should be understood that he did have a considerable interest in teaching speech to the deaf. This fact is clearly manifest in his book *The True Manner*, Part Second, in which he devotes two chapters to the subject of speech instruction. In "Preliminary Observations" which precede these chapters, he acknowledges his gratefulness to the Spaniard, Bonet, and the Swiss-Dutchman, Amman, for their influence upon his work.

During de l'Epee's detailed explanation relative to the manner of developing various elements and syllables, he stresses the need for patience in the teaching of deaf children. "No man of quick temper, subject to starts of impatience, is fit for the office of their teacher." (*Ibid.*, p. 117.) While de l'Epee was interested in speech development, he was unable to pursue it with his pupils because

> the lesson given a Deaf and Dumb scholar on the art of speaking is necessarily personal and serves for him alone. Now having sixty

scholars to instruct, if I allotted ten minutes to each, for the purpose of pronunciation and reading, it would take me up ten whole hours. And where is the man whose constitution is able to undergo this continually? And then, how could I continue to carry on the mental part of their education, that part which is the principal object of my concern? (*Ibid.*, p. 121.)

The Abbé continues with what might be considered today a temple-shaking statement when he writes,

The number of Deaf and Dumb children in a seminary cannot be brought to read and pronounce, with accurate distinctness, without masters devoted solely to this branch of instruction, to exercise them in it daily. People of high talents are by no means wanted for the office; whoever brings to it good nature and zeal, and will faithfully put in practice what we have exposed, is amply qualified. The employment being purely mechanical, men of talents are rather to be feared than desired, as they would soon revolt at it. But in stooping to the level of common schoolmasters, we shall have a better chance of finding such as will give into it with good will and assiduity [Dalgarno called it *diligence*]; provided, what is indeed essential to secure success, that the avocation form a permanent livelihood for them. (*Ibid.*, pp. 121-122.)

The contending thoughts of Heinicke and de l'Epee:

To be sure, Samuel Heinicke must have been in agreement on some aspects of these statements relative to speech. His unrelenting opposition to de l'Epee's philosophy was, of course, in regard to the latter's adherence to goals other than speech. Heinicke, being a pure oralist, objected even to the introduction of language through either printing or writing. This objection was vividly expressed in one of his letters to de l'Epee.

Words whether printed or written resemble heaps of flies' or spiders' legs; they have no form or figure which, while absent, the faculty of our imagination can represent to itself: hardly can we exhibit to our mind any fixed and determinate shape, a single separate letter, much less an entire word. (*Ibid.*, p. 163.)

De l'Epee, however, countered with the argument that the written word *Paris* could conjure up images of the city based upon an individual's experience.

Contrarily, it was Heinicke's belief that in order for a pupil to think, he first had to speak. (*Ibid.*, p. 178.) This idea was apparently based upon the self-observable fact of any hearing or postlingually deaf person, that inner speech appears to be a fundamental requirement of much of the thinking process. As an aside, the absence of speech or even language does not preclude thinking along concrete lines, but it does obviously preclude thinking relative to the abstract which is conveyed by spoken, written, or fingerspelled words and/or numbers. This concept, however, has yet to be proven correct or incorrect by our modern scientists of thought in their thinking laboratories.

De l'Epee calls on the Academy of Zurich:

De l'Epee, dissatisfied with the arguments of his German colleague, elected to set both of their theses before an impartial tribunal. In doing this, he chose the Academy of Zurich; before this body of scholars, he placed the issue of the education of deaf children and the arguments "pro and con" of the two opposing philosophies.

After a time, de l'Epee received an extensive reply dated February 2, 1783. It was entitled "Decision of the Academy of Zurick, in an Assembly of Its Members on the Controversy Arisen Between the Teachers of the Deaf and Dumb." (*Ibid.*, pp. 185-202.)

The content of the decision was an objective and dispassionate reply which reviewed the evidences of Heinicke's philosophy and work. These were then contrasted with the philosophy, evidences, and testimonies of de l'Epee. The ultimate decision as to the more efficacious system was in favor of that of the Abbé de l'Epee. Indeed, the Academy was politely critical of Samuel Heinicke's failure to understand de l'Epee's techniques, and it was of the opinion that he had never really read de l'Epee's work. At the same time, the Academy found some of Heinicke's writings untranslatable, even though they were written in his native German. (*Ibid.*, p. 199.)

Despite the Academy of Zurich's "put-down" of Samuel Heinicke, his work and influence continued to grow and have a significant impact on the education of the deaf throughout Germany. This influence continues to the present.

De l'Epee's methodical signs similarly flourished throughout France and continued until his demise in 1789. His kindly and generous spirit evolved in teachers of the deaf a strong missionary attitude toward their work. This deep sense of dedication and personal sacrifice prevailed in the profession well into the 20th Century.

16

Sicard's Revolutionary Encounters 1792

Sicard's debt to Louis XVI:

Probably one of the most significant episodes in the whole history of education of the deaf turns on the harrowing Revolutionary experiences of de l'Epee's successor, the Abbé Sicard, director and principal of the National Institute for the Deaf of France. Having received his position through the grace and auspices of the Bourbon monarch, Louis XVI, Sicard was logically beholden to the king and his regime, which debt also obviously explains his subsequent status as a nonjurant priest.

While the Institute had been a center of attraction for scientists and intellectuals from its earliest days, Sicard and his instructional innovations increased the interest particularly among the capital city's elite. The spectacle of deaf-mute youngsters communicating in the esoteric mode of sign language was in that day a phenomenon to behold. Hence the Institute was generally swamped with visitors. The cicerone for high prelates and visitors of royal or noble blood was always, of course, none other than the director, the Abbé Sicard himself. For persons of lesser degrees of churchly standing or social status, a lay brother was delegated to conduct the tour.

Thus it was considerable limelight which the Institute enjoyed, and with it all came the beneficences of many philanthropic people who were charmed by the good being done there. This work was personified by the Abbé Sicard, who labored incessantly for the betterment of all the deaf children under his spiritual care and educational guidance.

Enter the Blue Guards:

In August, 1792, the limelight which had been persistently shed upon royalty, nobility, and nonjurant churchmen alike also brought these same people to the attention of the revolutionary Tricolor Commissioner and his Blue Guards. This force was ordered by Danton, the Minister of Justice, to arrest and incarcerate all aristocrats or persons of royalist inclinations who might be suspected of plotting to foil the Great Revolution. Thus it was in the name of the Republic of France that the Abbé Sicard was seized at his Institute for the Deaf and placed in confinement.

Obviously, the Abbé's pupils were distraught at the arrest of their benefactor, and in response they moved *en masse* to the National Assembly to plead the cause of their teacher. Startled, quite possibly, were the members of the Tribunal when they spotted a thin line of agitated deaf people led by a large, gesticulating man in a black greatcoat. Effectively he elbowed his way forward through the noisy crowd of representatives and onlookers. His followers, similarly gesticulating, advanced in his wake. The big fellow stopped immediately below the high desk of the Tribunal, while his companions surged in support around him.

The petition:

The man, Jean Massieu by name, was not speaking but was nonetheless emphatically vocal as he reached up and placed a document on the desk of the Tribunal. The Tribunal, oriented to the popular informalities of the period, slid the document along the high desk to a secretary at the far end, who took it up and commenced to read it aloud. At that moment the normally noisy and unruly representatives fell into an inexplicable silence to listen.

August 26, 1792

Mr. President:

> They have taken from the deaf and dumb their fosterer, their guardian, and their father. They have shut him up in prison as if he were a thief and a murderer. But he has not killed, he has not stolen. He is not a bad citizen. His whole time is spent in teaching us to love virtue and our country. He is good, just, and pure. We ask of you his liberty. Restore him to his children, for we are his children. He loves us as if he were our father. It is he who has taught us all we know. Without him we should be like beasts. Since he was taken away, we have been full of sorrow and distress. Return him to us and you will make us happy. (Bender, *Conquest*, p. 78.)

With the last word of the petition spoken, the representatives and gallery burst into a crashing applause of approval, and the Tribunal conferred hurriedly.

Luzerne Rae, the first editor of the *American Annals of the Deaf*, writes in his essay "The Great Peril of Sicard" that

> an order was immediately issued, directing the Minister of Interior to render to the Assembly the reasons of Sicard's arrest; but among the confusions of the time this order was either forgotten or neglected, and the Abbé derived no benefit from the prompt and generous interference of his pupils. Days passed away and he still remained in the *Hotel de la Mairie* with his doomed companions. (Rae, "Great Peril," p. 18.)

Thomas Carlyle, in his epic volume *The French Revolution*, Part II, Chapter II, describes some of the typical persons who were arrested and hurried off to prison: an elderly pensioned soldier, a crippled newspaper editor, and an officer of the "effervescent *Regiment du Roi.*"

> Saddest of all: Abbé Sicard goes; a Priest who could not take the Oath, but who could teach the Deaf and Dumb: in his Section one man, he says, had a grudge at him; one man at the fit hour, launches an arrest against him; which hits. In the Arsenal quarter, there are dumb hearts making wail, with signs, with wild gestures; he their miraculous healer and speech-bringer is rapt away. (*French Revolution*, p. 484.)

Thus it was that Sicard and the others found themselves hustled off to "preliminary Houses of Detention, and hurled in thither as into cattle-pens."

On Sunday, September 2, after three days in a temporary lockup, Sicard and his confreres were unceremoniously pulled from their cells and pushed out into the Townhall courtyard, where several carriages were awaiting them. Carlyle describes the sequence of action as follows:

The tocsin is pealing its loudest, the clocks inaudibly striking *Three*,
when poor Abbé Sicard, with some thirty nonjurant priests, in six carriages, fare along the streets, from their preliminary House of Detention at the Townhall, westward toward the Prison of Abbaye. Carriages
enough stand deserted on the streets; these six move on, – through
angry multitudes, cursing as they move. "Accursed Aristocrat Tar-
tuffes, this is the pass ye have brought us to! And now ye will break
the prisons . . . ? Out upon you, Priests of Beelzebub and Moloch; of Tar-
tuffery, Mammon and the Prussian Gallows, – which ye name Mother-
Church and God!" – Such reproaches have the poor Nonjurants to endure and worse spoken in on them by frantic Patriots, who mount even
on the carriage-steps; the very Guards hardly refraining. "Pull your
carriage-blinds?" – "No!" answers Patriotism, clapping its horny paw
on the carriage-blind, and crushing it down again. Patience in oppres-
sion has limits: we are close on the Abbaye, it has lasted long: a poor
Nonjurant, of quicker temper, smites the horny paw with his cane; nay
finding solacement in it, smites the unkempt head, sharply and again
more sharply, twice over, seen clearly of us and the world. It is the last
that we see clearly. Alas, next moment the carriages are locked and
blocked in endless raging tumults; in yells deaf to the cry of mercy,
which answer the cry for mercy with sabre-thrusts through the heart.
The thirty Priests are torn out, are massacred about the Prison-Gate,
one after one, – only the poor Abbé Sicard, whom one Moton a watchmaker, knowing him, heroically tried to save and secrete in the Prison,
escapes to tell; – and it is Night and Orcus, and Murder's snaky-
sparkling head *has* risen in the murk! (*French Revolution*, pp. 492-493.)

Thus rescued from the mob by Moton, the watchmaker, Sicard was
secured in the dubious safety of the Prison Abbaye.

Sicard again endangered:

Two days later, on September 4, a number of "patriots" broke into
the prison with the determined spirit to slay all of those in-
carcerated. As an aside, some prison officials were unconcernedly
conducting business in a room adjoining the chamber in which
Sicard and two fellow prisoners were locked. Carlyle writes and
subsequently quotes the words of Sicard regarding his predicament:

> I tapped gently, trembling lest the murderers might hear on the op-
> posite door, where the Section Committee was sitting: they answered
> gruffly, that they had no key. There were three of us in this *violon*; my
> companions thought they perceived a kind of loft overhead. But it was
> very high; only one of us could reach it by mounting on the shoulders
> of both the others. One of them said to me that my life was usefuller
> than theirs: I resisted, they insisted: no denial! I fling myself on the
> neck of the two deliverers; never was scene more touching. I mount on
> the shoulders of the first, then on those of the second, finally on the

loft; and address to my two comrades the expression of a soul over-whelmed with natural emotions. (*Ibid.*, p. 499.)

Carlyle then adds, "The two generous companions, we rejoice to find, did not perish." As to the final subsequent action and release of the Abbé Sicard, Carlyle strangely says little.

The "Great Peril" account by Luzerne Rae, however, goes further with the story. Rae describes one or two more of the Abbé's harrowing escapes from death and his final legal absolution of any guilt against the Republic. Despite all of his "close calls," the Abbé returned to his duties as principal and director of the National Institute for the Deaf.

During the Revolutionary period, had the Abbé Sicard been removed from the scene by any one of his several encounters with Fate, the evolution and direction of American education of the deaf would be considerably or perhaps even wholly different from that which we know today. (See Appendix 5.)

Chapter Four
Education for the Deaf Begins in the United States

17. Gallaudet and Clerc Open the Hartford School, April 15, 1817

17

Gallaudet and Clerc
Open the Hartford School
April 15, 1817

England was perhaps not the most cordial nation in the world for a young American to visit in the year 1815. The reason, of course, was that the previous year a war with the United States had been concluded with the defeat of His Majesty's forces. The young American here considered was Thomas Hopkins Gallaudet, a 28-year-old theological student from Hartford, Connecticut.

Gallaudet was wholly unconcerned with international politics but was instead absorbed with a strange zeal to teach the deaf and dumb. At least it was a strange zeal to his fellow passengers on shipboard when they learned of it. The peculiar awe with which they regarded Gallaudet, indeed, made him feel as though he were perhaps "something." It was, however, his endless praying for Divine guidance and an ever-increasing assurance within himself that he was about to do God's work that enabled him to disembark confidently at Liverpool.

Gallaudet meets the Braidwoods:

In England Gallaudet first went to Birmingham, where he encountered one Thomas Braidwood who was no less than the grandson of the original. It was only upon convincing Braidwood of the sincerity of his desire to teach the deaf that Gallaudet was able to begin his negotiations for being accepted as a normal student.

It was Gallaudet's acknowledgement, however, of having read something of the Frenchman Sicard's work, and also the fact that he found the material interesting, that planted misgivings in Braidwood's mind as to Gallaudet's suitability for acceptance as a recipient of the Braidwood secrets. Leaving Thomas Braidwood to ponder his suitability, Gallaudet went on to London to visit the "Asylum for the Deaf and Dumb," where he met the school's headmaster, Dr. Joseph Watson.

Dr. Watson, a nephew of the first Thomas Braidwood, shared the family antipathy toward the Abbé Sicard and his adherence to methodical signs. Consequently, Watson, too, had to ponder the problem of Gallaudet's worthiness to learn the Braidwood secrets. All the while Gallaudet struggled with the idea of the practicability of keeping the Braidwood procedures secret in a public school such as he planned to found in the United States; such a place would hardly be the milieu for keeping instructional procedures "under wraps."

With misgivings relative to the Braidwoods, Gallaudet went on up to Edinburgh to visit the original Braidwood school; there, too, he received the same, what might be termed, "runaround" with the secrecy bit. Thus, Gallaudet's involvement with the members of the Braidwood dynasty, their strict adherence to the oral method, their strong opposition to the procedures of Sicard, and their reluctance to share freely their instructional procedures all left the young American a bit discouraged. Time was a precious element for Gallaudet, because Dr. Mason Cogswell and the other gentlemen of Hartford, his sponsors, had provided him with limited funds, *ergo* a limited time for achieving his objective. With a tentative and unenthusiastic agreement to become a teacher-trainee with the Braidwoods, Gallaudet headed southward to London.

Gallaudet meets the Abbé Sicard:

Shortly after his arrival in the great City, Gallaudet learned of a demonstration of the French Method being conducted by none other than the renowned Abbé Sicard of the National Institute for the Deaf. The circumstance which brought the Abbé to England was Napoleon's "100 Days" sojourn in Paris. This occasion practically emptied the city of all its former Bourbon sympathizers. Sicard, having experienced enough excitement during the Revolution, was not of a mind to tempt Fate again. After all, who needs excitement at 73?

In the Abbé's company during his London visit were two of his former pupils, Jean Massieu and Laurent Clerc, both of whom were now his outstanding teachers. Needless to say, the uniqueness of the French Method with its fascinating system of gestures, along with high order of responses from Massieu and Clerc to the most intellectual of questions, captivated the British public. Not the least of those captivated, however, was the young American who saw for the first time the charming, elderly Abbé communicate through facile signs with his deaf colleagues.

At the conclusion of Sicard's program, Gallaudet hastened to meet the Abbé and to make his interests known to the venerable man. We do not know, of course, but presumably a rapport was established and an invitation was extended to the young American to come to the French National Institute to study Sicard's methods. All of this was contingent, naturally, upon the Emperor's departure. When that event finally occurred, all of the emigres, including the Abbé Sicard and his two deaf colleagues, happily returned to Paris. Consequently, on March 9, 1816, Gallaudet bade farewell to England, the Braidwoods, and all of his frustrations, and sailed for Havre, some 20 miles across the Channel.

Gallaudet arrives at the Paris Institute:

The National Institute for the Deaf in Paris stood as a protective fortress around what was an evolving miniature society composed wholly of deaf people. (Lane, *Wild Boy*, p. 209.) This new deaf community, a prototype, was replete with its own language, its own growing heritage, and eventually its own near-ethnic pride. Within the Institute a sociological phenomenon was, indeed, in the making, the evolution of which continues to this day, particularly in the United States, as manifested in the modern expressions of "Deaf Pride," "Deaf Culture," and "Deaf Power."

The graduates of the Paris Institute looked upon their school and its beloved director, Sicard, with a deep affection born of the dedicated service which had been so generously rendered to them. Naturally, young Gallaudet caught the growing spirit and the challenge during his stay at the Institute. In the weeks and months that followed he learned signs under the tutelage of the great Massieu. Observations of Clerc at work in the classroom taught him vital instructional procedures and techniques.

Gallaudet finds a colleague in Laurent Clerc:

Obviously, in such a stimulating environment, the young American with his newly found knowledge began to "chomp at the bit" and to have thoughts of home and the great task that awaited him. Needless to say, Gallaudet was humbly awed by the responsibility which awaited him in America. Thus, he wisely looked for assistance from the one man who could help him the most, Mr. Laurent Clerc. It has been suggested that Clerc asked Gallaudet first about the possibilities of joining him in the American mission. In any event there was a tacit agreement between the two young men regarding the Hartford project. A final step, however, had to be taken: that of seeking Clerc's release from his teaching obligations. This meant securing the Abbé Sicard's permission and his blessing for the suggested arrangement.

Gallaudet found that asking the Abbé to release his best teacher was no small sacrifice for the old schoolman. After considerable thought, Sicard finally agreed to let Clerc go with Gallaudet, provided there would be no attempt to separate the young Frenchman from his Catholic faith. This request was readily agreed to, and plans were made for the departure of the two young men for America.

Clerc's mastery of English on shipboard:

Gallaudet and Clerc spent 52 days on shipboard, during which time they were occupied with matters related to the teaching of deaf children. Clerc naturally continued to tutor Gallaudet in sign language. The amazing development of the entire voyage, however, was Clerc's phenomenal *mastery of expressive English*. Unlike Gallaudet's learning sign language, which was a relatively simple feat, Clerc's mastery of written English in 52 days marked him as one having a particularly superior intellect and an amazing capacity for language learning.

Clerc in "the land of opportunity":

Unquestionably young Clerc felt a great sense of mission in making this voyage to America, and even though "the land of opportunity" concept had not yet burgeoned, the young deaf Frenchman sensed the potentialities and opportunities which lay ahead. He resolutely prepared himself to take full advantage of them, not only for his own sake, but for the sake of all the deaf people in America who, in a sense, were awaiting him.

Arriving in New York on August 9, 1816, Gallaudet and his French colleague made a "beeline" for Hartford to report to Dr. Cogswell and to take the initial steps for opening the proposed school. The first obvious objective for Gallaudet and Clerc was to raise sufficient money to open the school.

Gallaudet and Clerc "sell" education of the deaf:

Henry Barnard, reminiscing in his "Elegy to Gallaudet," states that Gallaudet and Clerc devoted the next eight months to traversing the Atlantic seaboard, addressing state legislatures and various groups of interested citizens. In these sessions Gallaudet would make the introductory remarks and then invite from the audience written questions which were put to his colleague. Mr. Clerc, in turn, would write his responses in *English* on a slateboard. The questions ranged through the areas of history, philosophy, and general information. Without faltering Clerc answered each question satisfactorily. His impressive responses, indeed, convinced the American public on the educability of the deaf. Upon the conclusion of this fund-raising drive, Thomas Hopkins Gallaudet and his deaf colleague, Laurent Clerc, on April 15, 1817, opened their school under the now horrendous name, "American Asylum for the Deaf and Dumb." They began with 7 pupils and by the end of year, they had 33.

The instructional procedures of this first public school for the deaf included to a large degree those employing the methodical signs of the Abbé Sicard. There were, of course, modifications to accommodate the idiosyncrasies of the English language. It should be understood that Sicard's procedures differed considerably from those of his predecessor, the Abbé de l'Epee. While Sicard had always evinced the highest respect and reverence for the founder of the Paris institute, he was by no means in philosophical agreement with him.

Clerc's expectancies set the standard for deaf Americans:

It was Sicard's strong belief in the intellectual potentialities of the deaf that enabled him to educate Massieu and Clerc so completely. His faith in them was subsequently transmitted through them to all of the deaf with whom they came in contact. Consequently, it was this subtle force of success-expectancy which Clerc brought to the first American school for the deaf, to his pupils, and to all of the hearing and deaf teachers whom he trained. With such a beginning, Clerc and Gallaudet together were bound to succeed in the launching of American education of the deaf.

Chapter Five
The French Intuitive Approach to Language Acquisition

18

Marie Joseph, Baron De Gerando
1772-1842

The Baron De Gerando, having served the Emperor Napoleon as His Highness' Secretary General, was also noted in his youth for his personal bravery as a common soldier. In fact, it appeared that De Gerando would, indeed, make the military his life's career. It was, however, his insatiable curiosity for matters of the intellect that saved him for greater things.

The contest:

In the spring of 1798 the French Institute conducted an essay contest and invited scholars throughout the nation to write competitively for a prize on the following topic: "To determine what has been the influence of signs upon the formation of ideas." Young De Gerando, but 26, was late in learning of the contest; however, the topic captured his interest and immediately he set to work on his essay. Writing night and day, De Gerando finally completed his manuscript and sent it "just under the wire" to the Institute's board of judges. Relative to this essay, Edward Peet, in his translation of Edward Morel's biographical sketch of De Gerando, states:

> So much ability was shown in its preparation, that the astonishment of the judges was very great when they broke the seal of the successful

essay and found that it was the production of a simple soldier in the garrison in Colmar. ("De Gerando," p. 181.)

Winning this contest was a veritable "open sesame" for the young soldier. Vistas beyond the military became clear to De Gerando, and he began to aspire to a career of intellectual service. Upon his final separation from the army, he was immediately chosen by the Minister of the Interior, Lucien Bonaparte, to serve in a government capacity as the Secretary of the Consulting Bureau of Arts and Sciences. While in this position De Gerando was able to expand on his prize-winning essay. Ultimately it became his four-volume classic, *On Signs and on the Art of Thinking in Their Relation to Each Other.*

De Gerando discovers the National Institute:

De Gerando's interest in human thought and communication brought him eventually to the National Institute for the Deaf and Dumb. Intermittently through the years of his numerous assignments in the service of the Emperor, the now Baron De Gerando was able to visit with the Abbé Sicard. Obviously, the Baron's understanding of the problems of deaf children grew as did his ideas relative to their education, and not always did his ideas concur with those of the methodical-signs advocate, Sicard. As a result, De Gerando determined to write a comprehensive study and history of education of the deaf. Thereby he could objectively present his findings and perhaps benefit this great area of educational need. Some time was to lapse, however, before he could bring such a book together.

De Gerando's opportunity:

The year 1815 was personally significant to De Gerando because the political winds which had swept Napoleon out of the Capital City also returned him for the period which history has called the 100 Days. It will be remembered that the aging one-time Bourbon sympathizer Sicard found it meet at Napoleon's return to seek refuge across the Channel. As may also be remembered, this move was to prove vital to the cause of American education of the deaf, which was seeking its roots through the efforts of young Thomas Hopkins Gallaudet.

The Abbé Sicard's sudden departure from Paris with the Institute's two outstanding teachers, Massieu and Clerc, left the school in a near-chaotic state. This, of course, was De Gerando's opportunity to step into the breach as the Institute's acting head and to bring it under control. Unquestionably, the Baron's brief tenure as the school's superintendent provided him with considerable time for observation and reflection upon the instructional procedures employed. His own ideas relative to the natural evolution of language in a young deaf child were in no way compatible with what he saw demonstrated in the classrooms. It was then that he determined to move forward with his planned comprehensive study of education of the deaf. As an aside, some time after the conclusion of Napoleon's 100 Days, the Baron relinquished his principalship to the venerable Abbé Sicard, who upon his return subsequently invited the American Gallaudet to the National Institute.

De Gerando writes on the education of the deaf.

It was finally in 1827 the Baron produced his long-planned study and history entitled *Education of the Deaf and Dumb*. In this work De Gerando set forth what he termed the five instruments of instruction used in teaching the deaf.

1. Design, with its conversion into symbolic or ideographic writing. This cannot be used out of the school-room on account of its narrow scope. [This is Sicard's transitional procedure from object to picture to written word.]

2. The language of action, embracing pantomime and methodical signs, which, however, cannot be used generally.

3. Alphabetic writing. In this method of instruction, the pupil will, according to De Gerando, attach to the word, "the image of the thought itself," without a translation into signs.

4. The manual alphabet or dactylology, intimately connected with writing. This is available in circumstances where writing is not convenient, or when addressing a number of persons.

5. The labial alphabet or reading on the lips and the gutteral alphabet, or the sensation in the throat and mouth by which the pupil recognizes and regulates the words he speaks. (*Ibid.*, pp. 184-185.)

While expressing no brief for one method or another, De Gerando did allow himself one personal opinion, the logic of which eventually served to point French education of the deaf in a new direction.

> The probable circumstances in which the pupil will find himself placed after leaving school should be regarded in the course of instruction, with a view fully to qualify him for the post which he is expected to fill. (*Ibid.*, p. 185.)

De Gerando divided the procedures for teaching the deaf into two categories:

a. Those in which articulation is thought to be essential and
b. Those in which articulation is thought to be unessential.

Of these two classifications De Gerando preferred the first. In that muteness is the result of deafness, he believed that speech should be taught in every instance because "through the aid of artificial articulation the deaf and dumb may be restored to society and influence." (*Ibid.*)

New direction for French education of the deaf:

Unquestionably the Baron De Gerando's prestige as a national figure and as an intellectual gave him considerable influence both politically and socially. In education of the deaf, however, it was his pragmatic and direct approach to language and speech *sans* methodical signs, and his realistic recognition of the communication demands of the workaday world, which eventually gave credence to his ideas among many French educators of the deaf.

19

Auguste Bebian
1789-1839

Auguste Bebian, a French colonial, was a particularly favored young man because his mentor had been none other than the renowned Abbé Sicard. The Abbé recognized in him a tremendous potential and as a consequence became his patron. Bebian, a teacher in training at the National Institute for the Deaf and Dumb, was an apt and perceptive student. Indeed, Sicard had marked him for a winner and specifically as his own possible successor. In 1816, when Laurent Clerc accompanied the American, Gallaudet, to the United States, it was Bebian who replaced him.

The new direction further indicated:

Bebian early demonstrated his understanding of the deaf and their instruction in an 1817 article entitled "Essay on Deaf-Mutes and Natural Language." This essay was quite thought-provoking for French educators of the deaf. The Abbé Sicard, although pleased with his protege's success, was slightly concerned about the touch of difference it manifested relative to the established Sicard procedure for language instruction. This essay, however, was but a precursor of ideas to come.

Nevertheless, in 1819, Bebian, with Sicard's blessing, was appointed the Institute's principal of studies. In 1820, however, Bebian found himself in a growing disagreement with the Council of Administration. Finally, in January, 1821, he tendered his resignation from the Institute. Despite his disagreement, Bebian retained the high regard of the Council. (Fourgon, *Historique,* Vol. 2, p. 531.)

Out of deference to the aging Sicard, Bebian thoughtfully refrained from extensive writing and awaited a more propitious time for expounding his educational convictions regarding language for the deaf. Finally, upon the demise of the Abbé Sicard in 1822, Bebian began work on his *magnum opus* entitled *Manual of Practical Instruction for Deaf-Mutes.* In 1826, he succeeded in establishing, according to his own philosophy, his Boulevard du Montparnasse school. The following year, 1827, he published his *Manual* in two volumes. Despite his previous disagreements, the Council of Administration adopted his *Manual* as the official instructional guide for the National Institute.

It is interesting that the content of Bebian's course contained no systematic classification of grammatical principles nor vocabulary program. (*Ibid.,* p. 153.) The procedure stressed, instead, a natural approach in contrast to Sicard's strictly structured one. Sicard, of course, knew only the traditional French system in which he had been raised. It was, therefore, logical for him to plan his language program for the deaf in the same way. The result was a plethora of signs which tended to obfuscate the meaning of thought rather than to clarify it. During his lifetime, the impressiveness of his labors and the extent of his personal sacrifices all seemed to raise him and his method above criticism.

Bebian's constraints removed:

After the old Abbé's passing, however, Bebian felt no longer the constraints of his former loyalty and proceeded to reveal his own views relative to the predicament imposed upon prelingually deaf children. The French historian in education of the deaf, Fernand Fourgon, writes that, while the Abbé de l'Epee had a strangely exaggerated idea that young deaf people had knowledge "just about equal to that of young hearing people," Sicard had a contrary view "comparing the mind of the deaf and dumb person who was not instructed or taught in any way as being a *tabula rasa.*" (*Ibid.,* p. 532.) Bebian's view of prelingual deafness, however, shows a considerably more explicit understanding. Fourgon quotes from Bebian's *Manual* (Vol. 2, p. 1):

> Deafness which occurs at an early age always begets mutism. It does not detract, as has long been believed, from intellectual faculties. It does exclude the child who is a victim of deafness, from the sphere of normal social relationships. Deafness restricts the acquisition of concepts relative to the realm of personal experience and deprives the child of a powerful instrument which is language and to which the human spirit owes a great part of the development of its abilities.

With this realistic view of prelingual deafness as a basis for his thinking, Bebian adds,

> It is not that the deaf and dumb do not have a natural language, a means through which they make themselves understood by people in their immediate environment, but this language is as crude as its spirit, is limited to the concepts of which it is an illustration. It is understood only by those people who are intimately familiar with the language. If we wish to mainstream the deaf person into society, he must live by the law of the majority, and learn the language of his country. (*Ibid.*, pp. 1, 2.)

Two parameters always to be considered:

In referring to "the law of the majority" and "the language of his country," Bebian states the two parameters which must be unequivocally faced by educators of the deaf, if they are to achieve their goals for prelingually deaf children. While the former parameter is obviously achievable, the latter eternally poses the question as to how "the language of his country" is to be taught. In reply, Bebian states:

> We can replace hearing by sight and the spoken language by a written language. If we can succeed in giving the deaf and dumb an understanding of written language, their education can then enter into the main stream. Written language can then to a certain point take the place of oral instruction, thus making accessible to him all knowledge which can be acquired through lectures or reading. Thus instructors must address their first efforts to teaching the language. This is the specific objective of the teacher of the deaf and dumb. (*Ibid.*, Vol. 1, pp. IJ, IIJ.)

Relative to the teaching of speech and speechreading, Bebian had some very definite ideas. For him, these two oral modes did not hold very high priorities as instructional objectives. Following are his reasons:

> One can explain to the deaf and dumb person the mechanism of speech. One can teach him to articulate sounds, to read words on the lips, to understand the play of organs used in voicing, but the movements he sees on the face and lips are nothing more than parallel of the written word. Speech for him can be no more than a group of fleeting characters written on the lips. (*Ibid.*, Vol. 2, p. 2.)

The following statement, italicized in part by this author, emphasizes the basic rule of the oral method as opposed to the pure oral method.

> Therefore although we would like to use speech as the basis of instruction for the deaf and dumb, *it is always the written language which we must teach them.* This is the total means and goal of this type of education.
>
> *In order to be able to read on the lips, they must be able to read on paper.* (*Ibid.*)

In other words, there can be little accurate comprehension through speechreading by the average prelingually deaf person if he does not have an adequately working knowledge of written English syntax. It has been the disregard of many oral educators relative to this basic oral principle which has largely led to the deterioration of oral instruction in the 20th Century.

In his language instruction, Bebian stressed practical, simple sentence structures without emphasis upon grammar *per se.* Unlike Sicard, Bebian was always concerned with linking the concept with its word or label. He was careful not to compound the learning problem by introducing more than one difficulty at a time, and "this difficulty should never be above the actual intelligence development of the deaf and dumb student." (*Ibid.*, p. 39.) Obviously, he stressed the importance of sequencing concepts from simple to complex.

One of the marked differences in Bebian's approach and that of his predecessor, Sicard, was in the area of communication. Fourgon writes,

> Bebian, on this point, is very eclectic. He uses every means of communication fingerspelling, mime, and the written word. The only exception is the spoken word. (*Historique*, Vol. 2, p. 539.)

The mime utilized was what might be termed today *body language.* Speech as previously indicated found no place in Bebian's procedure.

Intuition as a tool for learning:

The great innovation in Bebian's instructional system was his reliance upon the pupil's intuition for grasping meanings. He appears to be the first to exercise the pupil's intellect for deduction, for "putting two and two together," or for drawing logical conclusions. In the beginning steps, the procedure involved *mediated intuition*, i.e., the use of drawings and illustrations. The function of a picture was to provide a more concrete and accurate concept of the thing to be taught than could ever be conveyed through a gesture or sign. For Bebian, forming a clear mental image of the question or problem was the first step toward its solution.

> No matter what the difficulty, it is at least half resolved when one has well grasped the knot. It is completely dissolved if one knows how to divide and reattach it to a specific notion or concept which has already been understood and explained. It is when one skips steps that one encounters difficulties. There are no difficulties for the instructor who knows how to build and demonstrate a chain of grammatical structure: it is similar to climbing a very gradual slope which climbs so gently that you reach the top without any effort or fatigue. (*Ibid.*, p. 153.)

In conjunction with pictures, printed words identifying the objects or animals portrayed could be placed under or beside them. A variety of practice strategies were suggested to teach concepts. To give the idea of gender, Bebian would place a variety of animal pictures in two columns, males and females with their young, according to species. The males would form one vertical column and the females with their offspring another. By discussing the pictured animals with the pupils and by asking them questions, Bebian could lead the class into an understanding of gender. De l'Epee and Sicard would have found it much simpler, of course, to make signs for *bull* and *cow*, and so it would be. Through Bebian's *intuitive method*, however, pupils were required first to reason and second to establish a concept for which the teacher would provide the appropriate orthographic word written and fingerspelled.

Bebian also used what he termed *Exercises in Assimilation*. These exercises were arranged in a "pyramid type of hierarchy of learning, one step leading to the next and so on." After a new step or lesson had been taught, it was followed by a series of assimilation exercises which would help to fix the form or principle firmly in the pupil's mind.

While Bebian did divorce himself from Sicard's methodical signs, his emphasis upon mime or natural signs still required translation. Nevertheless, the introduction of his *intuitive method* as a means of grasping individual and textual meanings set French education of the deaf on a new and constructive course.

20

Jean Marc Itard
1774-1838

In 1800, at the time of his appointment as resident physician at the National Institute for the Deaf and Dumb, young Jean Marc Itard never dreamed that his new association with the school would become a lifelong commitment to deaf children. Shortly thereafter, an additional challenge was added to his responsibilities at the Institute. This second challenge came in the form of a feral child who had been captured in the forest of Aveyron.

Itard's special pupil:

The "wild boy" was sent to the Institute because of his total lack of speech or language. The Abbé Sicard, although frankly not enthusiastic about accepting the little "savage," did so because of public pressure. Sicard's staff had ample work to do without this additional burden; hence it was not altogether surprising that he was happy to assign the new pupil to his newly appointed school physician. Too, the young doctor had evinced immediate interest in the lad and his predicament.

The child, something literally "out of the trees," had no name and was forthwith named "Victor" by Itard, his newly designated teacher. The story of "The Wild Boy of Aveyron" has been thoroughly and ably explored in Harlan Lane's 1976 book by that name. To be sure, Jean Marc Itard's "claim to fame" lies in this singular story of personal dedication; however, unknown generally is his contribution to the education of the deaf, a field to which his life and interest were wholly devoted.

While never a teacher of the deaf *per se*, Itard developed a tremendous knowledge of that profession over his 38 years of observation and association with deaf children. During this very long period a personal philosophy evolved which reflected largely that of his contemporary, the Baron De Gerando.

Professor Edward Morel's "Biographical Sketch of Dr. Itard," translated by Edward Peet, states:

> Dr. Itard appreciated the utility of sign language in the instruction of the deaf and dumb, though himself ignorant of it, but he was of the opinion that its use should be restricted in proportion as the pupil acquires the ability to comprehend our language, and should be, at last, entirely discontinued, thus forcing the deaf mute to think and express himself in the idiom of the society in which he is destined to live. Dr. Itard himself, applied these correct principles in the instruction of several private pupils. He never instructed more than one pupil at a time; and as this pupil was one who had already received his primary instruction in the classes of the institution, he explained language by the aid of language, by asking upon what the pupil had read, by accustoming him to analyze and give the substance of the written text, to translate verse into prose, and to express the thought into different forms. He thus assisted him by synonym, contrast and paraphrases, in order to familiarize him with the structure and genius of our language. The efficacy of this method has a number of times been demonstrated by the happiest results. ("Itard," p. 118.)

Itard's legacy to French education of the deaf:

Through a such a piecemeal kind of experience over a period of almost 40 years Itard accrued a considerable experience and understanding of deaf people, their learning idiosyncrasies, and their intellectual potentialities. It was his belief that they could learn considerably more if provided sufficient opportunity. Advanced in years by 1837, Itard drew up his will, which placed the deaf and their education high among those good causes which were to benefit from his eventual estate. The following will sets forth a number of requirements which were to have their impact on education of the deaf. Two of these were a higher level of academic instruction and a stricter adherence to the language-centered philosophy of De Gerando and Bebian.

> I bequeath to the Royal Institution for the Deaf and Dumb, in trust to its Board of Directors, and subject to the authorization and

responsibility of the government, the yearly income of eight thousand francs, being the greater part of my subscription to the five percent stock on the Grand-livre.

To establish, in the aforesaid Institution, a new class to be called *classe d'instruction complementaire*, and six triennial free scholarships, for six deaf mutes, to be elected from among those pupils who shall have completed the ordinary period of instruction; and that this motive of emulation may suffer no interruption, the renewal of the class shall be partially made each year, by means of two elections. In order to establish a succession of admissions and dismissions, and to have, at the beginning, the requisite number of persons to fill the scholarships, six nominations will be made for the first year; two only of these first six pupils shall complete the term, and the four others shall leave, two at the end of the first year and two others at the expiration of the second year. The board of administration, after the professors shall have been consulted, shall decide what studies to pursue in the complementary class.

If my observations and experiments for forty years are of any weight, this remarkable fact will be deduced from them, which has for me all the character of a demonstrated truth, that nearly all our deaf mutes at the end of the six years allowed for their instruction, find it beyond their ability to read with a perfect understanding the greater part of the works of our language. It results from this, that wanting the ability to draw at pleasure on this great storehouse of the productions of the intellect and heart, the deaf mute, dismissed from the Institution, must remain all his life at the same degree of instruction at which his teachers have left him; and in consequence, that the most useful study for him will be that which shall lead him to read *understandingly* and without fatigue, all the most important works of our language. Such should be the result of the class of complemental instruction. But that this end may be attained, a rigorous condition of its organization should be the exclusion of pantomime and the requiring the pupils and the professor to communicate with each other only by language, whether by speaking orally, or by writing. It is of the utmost importance that the deaf mute, arrived at this final degree of instruction, should cease to think in his [sign] language, naturally imperfect and elliptical, translating as he does from it his ideas into our [French] language, and that he should think and express himself originally in the language of the speaking world, whether by the voice (if taught to articulate) or by writing. Without this condition, I repeat it, there would be one class more, but not a class of special instruction. (*Ibid.*, pp. 120-123.)

The biographer, Morel, adds that "The learned and generous testator concluded this very remarkable provision, by directing that the class of *complemental instruction* should be under the charge of a *speaking professor*, assisted by a deaf mute." (*Ibid.*, p. 123.)

This last provision relative to the instructional staffing of the *classe d'instruction complementaire* might upon first consideration be thought to be markedly prejudicial toward the "deaf-mute" by placing him in an assisting capacity rather than in his being the *professeur* of the class. Itard's *speaking* requirement, however, emphasized his desire for deaf students to use speech and speechreading, which objectives he thought could be best encouraged in them by a speaking, hearing person. While this idea offended practically none of the French deaf, it did much to offend some American educators of the deaf, both hearing and deaf, who were eventually to visit the National Institute. The significant aspect of Itard's proposed plan was that the pupil *should think and express himself originally in the language of the speaking world, whether by the voice (if taught to articulate) or by writing.* Itard could have been writing, perhaps, the educational objectives for the 21st Century.

21

J. J. Valade-Gabel
1801-1879

By the year 1855 Jean Jacques Valade-Gabel was a seasoned teacher of the deaf; hence when the Central Society for the Education and Aid of Deaf Mutes announced an essay contest on the subject of deaf education, Valade-Gabel was, indeed, prepared for it. Having begun his career in 1825 in Paris at the Royal Institute for the Deaf and Dumb, he was privileged to teach under the guidance and influence of the respected Bebian, and he continued his work in that school until 1838.

Valade-Gabel gets his opportunity:

Finally, in 1839 Valade-Gabel was named Director of the National Institute for the Deaf in Bordeaux. To this school the new director brought his zeal and all of his numerous ideas for correcting the ills which he believed dominated the whole of French education of the deaf. The ills, as he saw them, were centered in the extremely low reading ability and language usage of the deaf. Graduates of the various schools throughout France could communicate impressively in the sign language but had little grasp of the vernacular. Filled with a natural indignation at what he believed were correctable deficiencies, Valade-Gabel was determined to correct them. The Bordeaux school offered him this opportunity.

As a young teacher in Paris, Valade-Gabel, in addition to having been imbued with the educational philosophy of Bebian, had, of course, come to know the work of the Baron De Gerando and that of the old physician, Itard; hence when he finally studied Pestalozzi's *Mother Method*, his own philosophy of teaching deaf children was definitely determined. The thinking of each of these savants had pointed Valade-Gabel in one direction, that of teaching language through the use of language. To this, perhaps through the promptings of Pereira's shade, he added speech.

For all of his efforts to bring the Bordeaux Institute into a new perspective of education of the deaf, Valade-Gabel found the traditional forces of methodical signs too deeply entrenched to be dislodged completely. Nevertheless, he held steadfastly to his beliefs.

Valade-Gabel presents his philosophy:

Now by the year 1855 and with some 30 years' experience Valade-Gabel was, indeed, prepared to enter the Central Society's competition. This he saw as an excellent opportunity to solidify his thinking and to bring it before the national public. The final product of his efforts was entitled "Method Within Reach of Primary Instructors to Teach the French Language to Deaf-Mutes Without the Intervention of Sign Language." The essay, indeed, proved to be the prize winner and a contribution to educational thought.

Of this essay Professor Joseph C. Gordon wrote:

> Following the lead of Bebian in rejecting an artificial sign language, Valade-Gabel goes further and attempts to restrict natural signs to narrow limits, and to teach the deaf to associate ideas directly with written language. In the primary course there are five degrees. In the first the pupil obeys directions by actions, in the second he gives orders, in the third he answers questions, in the fourth he transmits the thought of the teacher, and in the fifth he asks questions in his turn or engages in dialogue. ("Valade-Gabel," pp. 130-131.)

Valade-Gabel's ideas for improving education of the deaf gained increasing recognition across the nation and within the Ministry of the Interior. As a result, he was finally appointed by the French government to make a nationwide study of all the schools for the deaf excepting those in Paris, Bordeaux, and Chambrey. Therefore, over a period of six years from 1862 to 1868, Valade-Gabel devoted himself to a comprehensive study of every aspect of French education for the deaf. Throughout the study the author reinforced his own advocated recommendations which he hoped would correct the major educational problems as he saw them.

Valade-Gabel's most significant and most often repeated recommendation, of course, dealt with the central theme of his 1855 essay, the elimination of methodical signs in favor of French through the use of French or the "intuitive method." Of this approach, he wrote in his national study:

> The intuitive method repudiates both methodical signs and grammatical theories and processes; it makes writing its principal instrument; instead of teaching the French language by translation, it teaches by intutition as mothers do. It aims to produce on the eye of the deaf-mute by writing effects similar to those produced on the ear of the hearing person by speech. Although forced to admit the language of natural signs for children who are wholly deaf and have never spoken, it places that in a secondary rank, and thus succeeds in putting them in a position to think with written words as we think with spoken words. This method, which makes the written language of the country not only the object of study, but the chief means of instruction for deaf-mutes, is a kind of neutral ground – a bridge connecting the German and French schools. Almost everywhere in France it is associated with or takes the place of the old methods. . . . ("Valade-Gabel," p. 245.)

While the growing impact of Valade-Gabel's intuitive method continued throughout France well into the 19th Century, it is interesting to note that the first influence of its logic was manifested in the United States as early as 1830.

Chapter Six
The Intuitive Approach to Language Acquisition Comes to the United States

22

Leon Vaisse
1807-1884

In 1830 M. Leon Vaisse, a young teacher from the National Institute for the Deaf and Dumb in Paris, was invited to come to the United States by Dr. James Milnor, president of the New York Institution. The purpose of the young Frenchman's mission was to introduce the famous Valade-Gabel system into the New York school. A more dedicated proponent of the "intuitive method" could never have been found. Vaisse's Gallic enthusiasm quietly permeated the school. Consequently, in February, 1831, when Harvey Prindle Peet came down from Hartford to take over as principal of the New York Institution, he found the school in a high state of ferment. It was ready for a change.

Vaisse implements the "intuitive method":

Peet, the new prinicipal, was aware of the changes which were taking place in the Parisian school, and what he knew of Valade-Gabel's approach to language instruction seemed most logical. Therefore, once he was settled in his new position, Peet and his young assistants, D. E. Bartlett and F. A. M. Barnard, along with Vaisse, went to work. Under Vaisse's direction they

> studied with eagerness and ever increasing fascination the captivating theories of De Gerando and the masterly manual of Bebian.

Irresistibly were they led to confess that hitherto the work had proceeded on no fixed principles. The theory had been imperfectly explored, the results but partially collated. In the method they had first received, they discerned grave defects.

Holding that the mind of the mute naturally associated ideas with visible representatives, Sicard had been content with finding such visible representatives in gestures, and had devoted his energies to creating a close and unnatural correspondence between them and words. Even his acute mind had overlooked the propositions that a visible ideographic language could be constructed of alphabetic constituents, written or given by manual alphabet; and that the language of gestures had an order, or syntax of its own, differing widely from that of the French language, still more the English. . . . Even in the institution over which Sicard himself had so lately presided, the practice was not in favor of articulation, of using signs always in their natural colloquial order and of training the mind to think directly in words without the intervention of signs. At New York it was resolved to follow the same course. (Syle, "Harvey Prindle Peet," p. 150.)

Emphasis upon the vernacular:

Thus it was from the traditional Sicard mode of methodical signs that Peet and his colleagues sought to free the New York Institution. Methodical signs were consequently discouraged by many of the teachers, particularly those who were less locked into tradition and who realized that such signs impaired both instruction and learning. Natural signs and pantomime for general communication among pupils, they found acceptable. From this evolved what is known today as the American Sign Language (ASL), an economical free-sign-mode which conveys concepts unburdened by English grammar. This gesture language was originally confined for the most part to pupils in their playground and dormitory communication. Untaught, this sign language spread from pupil to pupil and from generation to generation through our American state residential schools and continued until the reintroduction of methodical signs or "Signed English" in the latter part of the 20th Century. The new educational thrust in the New York Institution during the early 1830's was not in the direction of sign language, because Peet, like Vaisse, recognized the need for emphasis upon the vernacular.

Vaisse returns to France:

Although Leon Vaisse returned to France in 1834, the impact of his intuitive method on the New York school and on the whole of American education of the deaf was significant. To be sure, some older teachers held to their methodical signs which eventually died with them, but the concept of learning English through the use of English was established as a viable way to give language to deaf children.

During his long career in France, Leon Vaisse, like many teachers of the deaf, was too busy teaching to write as much as he would have liked. As he approached retirement, however, he wrote "Some Practical Suggestions" for the benefit of his colleagues and future teachers of the deaf. (While no one of the following sentences in translation from the French can be read in a single breath, each contains a thought sufficiently significant to make the effort worthwhile.)

> Our method is essentially that of intuition, the object or fact to be expressed being in the earlier lessons actually placed under eyes of the pupil, and the simple representation of this object or fact, by drawing or pantomime serving to render it still present to the mind when no longer before the eyes. This method, however, does not forbid, even in the presence of the object, the use of some signs, enabling pantomime (which has been justly denominated the psychological language of the deaf-mute) to perform its part as an instrument of analysis, giving to thought its necessary support as long as the pupil has not at his command a more perfect means. But this part of the instrument of analysis is assumed by the very language which is made the object of instruction, just as fast as the development of the pupil permits, and as soon as the form of expression which constitutes the subject of a new lesson can be explained by its decomposition into such forms as have already been taught.

> Thus the teacher causes the development of language to follow in an uninterrupted manner the development of ideas, relying on the success of instruction given not less on the native soundness of mind of the child than on the accuracy of his memory, and being able to rest with confidence on the second as soon as the first has performed its needful office. (Vaisse, "Practical Suggestions," pp. 13-14.)

To teach a deaf child successfully, it was Vaisse's belief that the teacher must have a comprehensive understanding of that child's family history, his family life, and his previous education. (*Ibid.*, p. 14.) This concept, of course, was many years in advance of its time. Today, however, the idea is recognized as being basic to any satisfactory pupil-teacher relationship, as evidenced in the U.S. Public Law 94-142 and its "individualized education program" (IEP). (Bishop, *Mainstreaming*, pp. 26-27.)

Re: The milieu reinforcement factor:

While the actual teaching of language was of prime concern for
Vaisse, he recognized as equally important the *milieu reinforcement factor* as a requirement for making the teaching "stick." In
modern education of the deaf this principle might be reconsidered
for greater emphasis and application. Like many other principles,
it has apparently slipped through the cracks of time. Relative to
reinforcement, Vaisse suggests:

> Just as the hearing person becomes acquainted with the language of
> his country by appropriating terms and forms of expression from those
> speaking around him, so the deaf-mute must acquire it by appropriating
> words in their visible form, and by imitating models placed before his
> eyes. . . . In order to multiply models of language, and render them
> permanent, it is important to introduce our pupils as soon as possible
> to the use of books, which some instructors commit the error of defer-
> ring to a later period in the course of study. ("Practical Suggestions,"
> pp. 14-15.)

In a report on Dr. H. P. Peet's 1851 European tour, the following was recorded regarding his observations of the famous Itard
classe de perfectionnement, taught by the then long-experienced
Professor Vaisse:

> Itard agreed with De Gerando that the "too constant use which the
> deaf and dumb make of gestures among themselves is the great
> hinderance to their progress in language." One of the conditions of
> Vaisse's class is that "the pupils and professor could communicate only
> by language, whether by speaking orally or by writing" and the pro-
> hibition of signs, says Dr. Peet, Mr. Vaisse "conscientiously obeys" in
> the explanation of his lesson. (Rae, "European Tour," p. 247.)

Gleaned from such experience, the venerable Professor Vaisse
was able to accrue the following information which he affectionate-
ly gave to his colleagues:

> Among the improvements with respect to the pupils may be noticed
> the present general practice in employing in progressive manner in
> their relations with those around them, from the beginning of the
> course of instruction, their acquirements in language, endeavoring to
> find in their vocabulary as it becomes richer and their syntax as it
> becomes more fully developed, expression for what they wish to ask
> of or make known to their teacher, who, on his own side, is anxious
> to encourage this disposition to social intercourse, whether it is car-
> ried on by the help of slate and pencil, or by the manual alphabet, which
> is the representative of writing.

It is true that a certain effort is necessary on the part of the teacher in his communication with the pupils not to have recourse to pantomime on account of the greater ease and rapidity with which a few gestures convey to their minds ideas which they would receive through words only slowly and painfully.

In communicating with the deaf, the manual alphabet has the advantage over writing of a greater degree of convenience, in as much as it dispenses with all material aid. The manual alphabet, however, may be advantageously replaced in its turn by the labial alphabet (speechreading), which is far more useful in the ordinary conditions of life and the acquisition of which is not attended with the difficulties that some teachers imagine. Should the pupil arrive at no other result than the power of recognizing the element of speech on the lips of others, remaining unskilled in reproducing them himself in a satisfactory manner, a great benefit would have been gained in the ability to recieve a lesson from the mouth of the teacher, even though the latter, to render his speech more easy to follow, must constantly resort to certain signs indicating the action of the organs not visible. (Vaisse, "Practical Suggestions," p. 18.)

Vaisse and speech for the deaf.

While the Abbé de l'Epee and the Abbé Sicard were interested in speech instruction, their experiences were largely negative in its application to large groups of pupils. Similar thinking also influenced Bebian's attitudes toward speech for the deaf. His interests were always centered on the reading and writing aspects of language instruction. As for Vaisse, the previously mentioned shade of Pereira along with the persuasive example of his phenomenal pupil, Saboreux de Fontenay, unquestionably confirmed his belief in the practicability of speech for the deaf. Hence over the years, Vaisse grew in his philosophy as an oral advocate.

> . . . I am firmly convinced that for the practice of articulation and lipreading to produce the desired result it must not be made exceptional, either on the part of teachers or pupils. That this teaching may have the legitimate chances of real and permanent success, it must not be kept in a state of inferiority or of singularity, it must not be opposed by what may be called the public opinion of the little world of fellow students among whom the pupil lives.
>
> In this branch of the child's education, as in others, we cannot expect uniformity of results; but in different degrees of perfection, or, if you will, of imperfection, the results show in most cases considerable success. Differences in the aptness of individuals for acquiring speech are often seen, but it is my profound conviction that spoken language can boast definite useful results in no fewer cases than written language. (*Ibid.*, p. 19.)

Vaisse's advocacy of the intuitive approach to language acquisition through its visible orthographic forms, writing and fingerspelling, along with his equal emphasis upon speechreading and oral language, pointed a new direction not only for French education of the deaf but for that of the United States as well.

23

Samuel Gridley Howe
and the Dark Silence
1801-1876

One of the most influential persons in early American education of the deaf was not a teacher of the deaf but a teacher of the blind. Dr. Samuel Gridley Howe, superintendent of Perkins Institute of the the Blind, had a long and varied list of credits as a physician, as a soldier of fortune, as an engineer, and, of course, as an educator of the blind.

Howe, the adventurer:

In 1823 Howe, a young physician, found his way to Greece to assist that nation in its war for independence from the Turks. Among the other young volunteers so engaged was one George Noel Gordon, Lord Byron, the surfeited British poet, who after some months in the Grecian Isles succumbed to malaria. Howe, considerably more fortunate, survived a six-year adventure in Greece and returned to his beloved Boston in 1829.

Howe, the humanitarian:

In that Samuel Gridley Howe's yearning to serve mankind was not satiated by his Grecian experience, he found the handicap of blindness in children a worthy obstacle to combat. Thus it was he began to take blind children into his home and to experiment in their instruction. This, of course, was the beginning of the now famous Perkins School for the Blind.

While the education of blind children provided Howe with a genuine challenge, he contemplated the problem of educating a blind child who might also be deaf and without speech. The predicament of such a child represented to him the supreme challenge, and, as he later wrote, "I resolved to make the attempt to teach the first one I should hear of." (Howe, "Laura Bridgman," p. 101.)

Howe meets Laura Bridgman:

Finally, in the year 1837, Howe received word of a little deaf-blind girl in New Hampshire. Her name was Laura Bridgman and she was not quite eight years old. This child at the age of 26 months had lost through scarlet fever both her sight and hearing. Her senses of taste and smell were also impaired. With such an early onset of deafness and the result of having been in total intellectual isolation for a period of five years, Laura was devoid of any language. This child was the challenge which Howe had been awaiting.

It should be understood that Samuel Gridley Howe moved into his endeavor to teach Laura Bridgman without any precedence or criteria to which he could refer. Hence it was necessary for him to rely wholly upon his own ingenuity and inventiveness. The procedure which he developed reveals a high degree of insight into the innate logic of the human mind. Of this logic he took advantage and gradually inched young Laura forward into an ever-widening understanding of herself and the world around her.

In retrospective, Howe's account:

The drama of this educational feat is revealed in a retrospective account written by Howe many years after his achievement. In subsequent years it served to guide the thinking of numbers of educators of the deaf. An aging Samuel Gridley Howe wrote as follows of his initial efforts in the education of Laura Bridgman.

> I shall not here anticipate what I intend to write about her, further than to say that I required her, by signs which she soon came to understand to devote several hours a day to learning to use her hands and to acquiring command of her muscles and limbs. But the principal aim

and hope was to enable her to recognize the twenty-six signs which represent the letters of the alphabet. She submitted to the process patiently, though without understanding its process.

I will give a rough sketch of the means which I contrived for her mental development. I first selected short monosyllables, so that the sign she was to learn might be as simple as possible. I placed before her on the table a pen and a pin, and then making her take notice of the fingers of my hands, placed them in three positions used as signs of the manual alphabet of deaf-mutes for the letters *p-e-n*, and made her feel of them over and over again many times, so that they might be associated together in her mind. I did the same with the pin, and repeated it scores of times. She at last perceived that the signs were complex, and that the middle sign of the one – that is, the *e*–, differed from the middle sign of the other, that is, *i*. This was the first step gained. This process was repeated over and over hundreds of times, until, finally, the association was established in her mind between the sign composed of three signs and expressed by three positions of my fingers, and the article itself, so that when I held up the pen to her she would herself make the complex sign; and when I made the complex sign on my fingers she would triumphantly pick up the pen and hold it up before me, as much as to say, "This is what you want".

Then the same process was gone over with the pin, until the association in her mind was intimate and complete between the two articles and the complex positions of the fingers. She had thus learned two arbitrary signs, or the names of different things. She seemed conscious of having understood and done what I wanted, for she smiled, while I exclaimed inwardly and triumphantly, "Eureka! Eureka!" I now felt that the first step had been taken successfully, and that this was the only really difficult one, because, by continuing the same process, by which she had become enabled to distinguish two articles by two arbitrary signs, she could go on learning to express in signs two thousand, and, finally, the forty and odd thousand signs or words in the English language.

Having learned that the sign for these two articles, *pin* and *pen* was composed of three signs, she would perceive that in order to learn the names of other things she had got to learn other signs. I went on with monosyllables as being the simplest, and she learned gradually one sign of a letter from another, until she knew all the arbitrary, tangible twenty-six letters of the alphabet, and how to arrange them to express various objects: knife, fork, spoon, thread, and the like. Afterwards she learned the names of the ten numerals or digits; of the punctuation and exclamation and interrogation points, some forty-six in all. With these she could express the name of everything, of every thought, of every feeling, and all of numberless shades thereof. She had thus got the "*open sesame*" to the whole treasury of the English language. She seemed aware of the importance of the process and worked at it eagerly and incessantly, taking up various articles, and inquiring by gestures and looks what signs upon her fingers were to be put together in order to express their names. At times she was too radiant with delight to be able to conceal her emotions ... and thus she instinctively and unconsciously aided in her happy deliverance. After she had mastered the system of arbitrary signs made by the various positions of the fingers used by deaf-mutes, and called dactylology, the next process was to teach her the same signs in types with the outlines of the letters embossed upon their ends. Thus with types, two embossed with *p*, two with *n*, one with *e*, and another with *i*, she could by setting them side by side in the quadrilateral holes in the blind man's slate, make the sign of *pen* or *pin*, as she wished and so with other signs.

The next process was to teach her that when a certain kind of paper was pressed firmly upon the ends of these types, held close together and side by side, there would be a tangible sign on the reverse of the paper, as *pin* or *pen*, according to the position of the three types; that she could feel of this paper, distinguish the letters and so read; and the signs could be varied and multiplied and put together in order and so make a book.

... Success came of faith and patience, and reliance upon her having the native desire and capacity for acquiring a complete arbitrary language, which desire had now become quickened to a passion for learning new signs. Moreover, I was greatly aided from the start by young lady teachers, who became in love with the work, and devoted themselves to it with saintly patience and perseverance. (*Ibid.*, pp. 101-104.)

Here Howe gives a singular emphasis upon the teacher qualities of faith, patience, and reliance and their positive relation to his pupil and her ability to succeed. To be sure, these qualities are statistically unmeasurable; however, their power and influence are immeasurable. In accounting for his success, Howe also credits his young lady teachers for their love of work, their devotion, and their "saintly patience and perseverance." While a modern teacher evaluation or competency study might minimize or wholly ignore such subjective elements, they continue to remain innate in the makeup of successful teachers of the deaf.

The essentiality of reinforcement:

Dr. Howe then recognizes a basic requirement essential to any successful language program, the *milieu reinforcement principle*. In describing Laura's learning environment, he writes:

Then great assistance was given by the blind pupils, many of whom learned the manual alphabet and took every opportunity of using it and conversing with Laura. Thus early in the process the material and moral advantages of learning began to show themselves. Without it the girls could only manifest their interest in Laura, and their affection for her, as one does with a baby, by caresses, sugar-plums, and other

> gifts, and by leading her up and down, and helping her in various ways. With it they began human intercourse through regular language. (*Ibid.*, p. 105.)

Obviously there could have been little or no language acquisition for Laura had her environment not provided her the essential receptive and reinforcement experience. In this direction it may be observed that today if the language acquisition and achievement levels of a given school population are low, the milieu reinforcement principle and its degree of application should be investigated. Dr. Howe finally summarizes:

> The method of instruction was, of course, novel, and the process long and tedious, extending over several years, until she was able to read and understand books in raised letters; to mark down various shaped signs upon a grooved paper, and so write legible by the eye; to attain a pretty wide command of the words of the English language, to spell them rapidly and correctly, and so express her thoughts in visible signs and good English. . . . I confine myself now merely to saying that in the course of twenty years she was enabled to do it all. She attained such a facility for talking in the manual alphabet that I regret that I did not try also to teach her to speak by the vocal organs or regular speech. The few words which she has learned to pronounce audibly prove that she could have learned more. (*Ibid.*, p. 106.)

It was probably Samuel Gridley Howe's feelings of regret for not having provided Laura with greater opportunities for speech that ultimately led to his interest in speech and speechreading for deaf children. It was in this direction that Howe eventually channeled considerable time and influence, thereby becoming an early leader in the American movement for the oral education of the deaf. (See Appendix 6.)

24

David Ely Bartlett
and His Family School
1852-1860

Upon graduating from Yale in June, 1828, David Ely Bartlett was hoping to secure a teaching position in or around New Haven. It was shortly thereafter that he was offered an opportunity to serve as a teacher in Hartford's Asylum for the Deaf and Dumb. Such a strange and little-known field of endeavor seemed to him to hold little promise for the future. The persuasiveness, however, of the Asylum's principal, Mr. Thomas Hopkins Gallaudet, soon won for the profession a man whose contributions were eventually to become most significant. For his normal training which included the learning of the sign language, young Bartlett paid Mr. Laurent Clerc $50. Bartlett evinced such natural aptitudes for teaching the deaf that both Gallaudet and Clerc agreed to retain him as a permanent member of the Hartford faculty.

Finally, after four years of teaching at the Asylum, Bartlett was lured by Principal Harvey Prindle Peet to accept a position in the New York Institution for the Deaf and Dumb. Peet, having become principal of the New York school the previous year, was well acquainted with Bartlett, for he had taught with him in Hartford. When an opening for an assistant teacher was available, Bartlett was a natural choice for the position. Thus were the circumstances of Bartlett's joining the New York Institution.

It may be recalled that Leon Vaisse, the young Frenchman, had already been at the New York school for two years, enthusiastically expounding the intuitive method. Bartlett, through Peet's influence, quickly became imbued with the procedure and its logic. It will be remembered, however, that this new intuitive approach required the complete elimination of methodical signs; consequently, to Bartlett the whole idea seemed to smack of heresy and betrayal of all that Mr. Gallaudet and Mr. Clerc had taught him. Nevertheless the young man conceded to himself the error of his former mentors. By the time Vaisse returned to France in 1834 the intuitive method had thoroughly established itself in Bartlett's evolving educational philosophy.

A master of the natural sign language and in constant demand as a lecturer and interpreter, Bartlett taught and served both his deaf pupils at the New York Institute and the adult deaf community of the city. Ever studying and ever observing, he pursued the intuitive approach in his classroom. Unlike many of his teaching colleagues, he began to minimize to a greater and greater extent his reliance upon the use of natural signs and to rely more and more upon what he called "alphabetic language," that is, fingerspelling.

Mr. Bartlett sets forth his ideas:

Like many other outstanding teachers of the deaf, Bartlett passed his years instructing children, formulating ideas, and discussing education at length with colleagues. Very little time did he find for recording his observations and theories. When he finally was moved to write, his subject fortunately dealt with "The Acquisition of Language." This essay was, in fact, a distillation of 20 years' experience in the area of English instruction for the deaf.

The major ideas set forth in the article deal with two principles which Bartlett had confirmed through his own long experience. The first is, "To educate the deaf and dumb is to teach them language." ("Acquisition," p. 84.) The second is, "The law of progress which governs us in the acquisition of language is habit." (*Ibid.*, p. 91.) In expanding on these two principles, Bartlett writes,

> In learning language, as in learning every thing else, it is practice only that makes us perfect. Theories and rules are good in their place; but without practice, and without *much practice*, they are comparatively of but little use. It is habit, the result of practice intentional or unintentional that impels us slowly or fast, as the case may be, after we have learned to move in any given course. . . . That which is first and oftenest done becomes easiest to do. (*Ibid.*)

This, as an aside, brings to mind the *milieu reinforcement* principle which has been previously stated as being one of the most frequently overlooked and yet one of the greatest essentials for any successful language instruction program.

> To the teachers of the deaf and dumb whose province it is to awaken, develop and instruct minds so peculiarly circumscribed in their condition, it becomes an important problem to solve, – how they can best avail themselves of the law of habit – how they can most advantageously follow the course of nature – how they can best and earliest present written alphabetic language to the minds of their pupils so as to turn the current of their mental action into this channel in which it is the chief object of their education to cause it to flow. (*Ibid.*, pp. 91-92.)

A revolutionary move:

For many years Bartlett had observed the distress of parents who would travel many miles in order to bring their young deaf children to be enrolled in the New York Institute, only to have them rejected because they were too young. The age of admission into the New York School, as in all other schools in the United States, was between 12 and 14 years of age.

Children of five, six, or seven years of age were consequently forced to return home and to grow in their ignorance to become recalcitrant, languageless beings. This situation preyed upon Bartlett's mind for a number of years, and in retrospection after a long career, he wrote:

> I became convinced that the exclusion of deaf-mutes from instruction from six to twelve years of age was attended with great loss, an injury to the children, thus deprived of education during those years best adapted to elementary education. I resolved that I could not and would not live and die a teacher of the deaf and dumb without at least experimenting upon the practicability of instructing little deaf-mutes from five years of age and upwards in the elements of verbal language. ("Family School," p. 273.)

One year after Bartlett's article on "The Acquisition of Language," two circulars were reprinted in the *American Annals of the Deaf*, under the heading "Family Education for Young Deaf-Mute Children." After a very complimentary introduction by the *Annals* editor, Mr. Luzerne Rae, the texts of the circulars appear. The first was dated February 16, 1852:

The result of an experiment he has been making with some little deaf-mutes, from six to ten years of age, for a few months past, has greatly strengthened and increased his belief in the practicability and advantage of beginning early the education of the deaf and dumb.

The plan of training he proposes is one adapted to the physical, mental and moral wants of children of an early and tender age, and to their advancing years.

D. E. Bartlett

("Family Education," p. 32.)

A second revolutionary move:

Thus was first recognized in American education of the deaf the need for early instructional intervention thereby making possible the utilization of the natural and inherent intellectual receptivity of young deaf children just as was done with their hearing counterparts. While this innovation was startling enough, Bartlett's second circular, published on August 10, 1852, contained an even more surprising idea for "the establishment."

Since the above [the first circular] was written and issued, applications have, in two or three instances, been made to the undersigned, from families having a deaf-mute child, for the admission into his family school, of a speaking and hearing child from the same family to be educated in company with the deaf-mute, each attending to his own appropriate studies, and at the same time opportunity being afforded for the cultivation and improvement of a free medium of communication between the two. This measure may be considered a most admirable and useful one for the deaf and hearing ones of a family. The hearing and speaking child, while pursuing the ordinary elementary studies that he (or she) would attend to if at school with children of equal aid and condition, being in the family with the deaf-mute brother or sister and associated with other little deaf-mutes in the process of education, will acquire a perfect knowledge of language of signs used by the deaf-mute, and also with alphabetic language expressed by the manual alphabet, (which is but a convenient form of writing) and will thus become a most interesting and advantageous of communication, as interpreter between the little deaf-mute brother or sister and the other members of the family. The deaf-mute pupil in the mean while, besides the pleasure and the advantage of being able freely to exchange his thoughts with, will derive great benefit in his progressive education by being led into the practice of receiving and expressing in *words*, – just the form of language that constitutes the leading and most important part of his education.

Intelligent and affectionate parents, brothers and sisters of families, having a deaf-mute child will readily understand and appreciate the advantage of this measure. (*Ibid.*, p. 33.)

The integration of hearing and deaf children at this period was, indeed, an educational move heretofore wholly inconceivable in the United States. Bartlett, however, perceived both the implications and the possibilities and went forward with it. Consequently, he was the first to attempt a kind of "reverse mainstreaming," an idea which has received some attention as an innovation in our late 20th Century education of the deaf.

In the last paragraph of Bartlett's circular, he describes something of his philosophy and its implementation.

> . . . We propose in this course of education, at first, not so much to confine the little ones to a regular routine of exercises in school hours, as to teach them and accustom them at the table, in their little plays, walks and amusements, and in the ordinary every-day occurring incidents of juvenile life, to express their thoughts and *learn to think in alphabetic language*, thus making the acquisition of language a matter of *early imitation, practice* and *habit*, as nature plainly indicates it should be.
>
> *Begin early.* Education in all cases, especially that of the deaf and dumb, in order to be successful, must be commenced early.
>
> Address, D. E. Bartlett
Late Senior Professor of the New York Institution
for the Deaf and Dumb
50th Street, New York.
>
> (*Ibid.*, p. 34.)

In a concluding statement relative to Professor Bartlett's circular, the *American Annals* editor, Mr. Luzerne Rae, acknowledges the significance of Bartlett's move to lower the age of school admission.

> It is greatly gratifying to know the progress which the education of the deaf and dumb is now making in this country. Not many years ago, a residence of four years, or at the longest, five years at some one of our public institutions, comprised the whole period of instruction for deaf-mutes. No provision was made for carrying the education such as had completed their regular course, and none for those who were below the proper age for admission. Both of these deficiencies are now supplied. . . . [T]he plan of Professor Bartlett leaves nothing to be desired for the profit of deaf-mute children; at least for such as have the pecuniary power to avail themselves of it. (*Ibid.*, p. 35.)

Bartlett and his wife soon realized that the 50th Street address of their school in New York City was not a particularly choice location for such a program because it lacked suitable play and running areas for their little deaf and hearing pupils. They were, therefore, on the lookout for a more suitable location. Finally one was found along the Hudson in the picturesque village of Fishkill, New York, to which community the little school was moved in 1853.

Bartlett's contributions recognized:

The parents of the pupils were most laudatory regarding the work of the Bartletts. The school, successful in its educational mission, was woefully weak financially. Finally, because of ever-increasing debts, Bartlett, one year later in 1854, was forced to move his school to Poughkeepsie. There he heroically managed to keep his program afloat for another six years. Had Bartlett been as successful a businessman as he was an educator, his school would have grown and continued indefinitely. Nevertheless, Bartlett's contributions were recognized. He had succeeded in demonstrating that young deaf children were educable, with the result that the age for school admission was lowered in many schools to six years. He also demonstrated specifically the young deaf child's potential for acquiring acceptable written English and reading skills. Such achievement, of course, was wholly contingent upon a comprehensive visually oriented English environment. At this point in history, speech as an educational objective had not yet generally manifested itself in the United States. Unbeknown to Bartlett at this time, he was eventually to become involved in the issue of speech for the deaf, too.

In 1860 the Bartletts gave up their school in Poughkeepsie and moved to Hartford, where they taught once again at the American Asylum.

By 1880 David E. Bartlett had finally come full circle and was content in having proved to himself the English learning potentials and capacity of young deaf children, provided they were given the opportunities for instruction, exposure, and usage. This was what he had hoped to do. (See Appendix 7.)

Chapter Seven
The German Roots of
American Oralism

25

Dr. Johann Baptist Graser
and German Oralism
1829

Samuel Heinicke in 18th-Century Germany, it will be recalled, came early under the influence of John Conrad Amman, the acknowledged Father of Pure Oralism. Heinicke, in turn, was acclaimed as the Father of Pure Oralism in Germany. Eventually this educational philosophy was to be further developed and refined by future German educators of the deaf.

Rising French dominance and German opposition:

With the rising dominance of the French and French culture across Europe during the early 19th Century, the conventional sign philosophy of the Abbé Sicard was carried into Germany. Not unnaturally, German cultural pride resisted the tide of French thought in many quarters. In terms of education of the deaf, the older pure oral philosophy continued to hold on doggedly although the use of conventional signs was gradually becoming recognized as the instructional mode for a number of German schools for the deaf. The Gallic rationale for using signs, nevertheless, persistently continued to distress certain German educators as being wholly illogical. One of the most outstanding of these educators was Dr. Johann Baptist Graser.

Education of the hearing as a model:

While Dr. Graser of Bayreuth enjoyed success and a considerable reputation as a teacher of the deaf, it was his writings that carried his name throughout Germany. Graser's chief literary contribution was a book entitled *The Deaf Mute Restored to Humanity by Visible and Spoken Speech*, which he published in 1829. This volume set forth the idea that the education of deaf children should follow as closely as possible the model of education for hearing children. The primary goal in doing this was to prepare deaf children for their eventual integration into public schools for hearing children. Thus we see an early application of the idea of *mainstreaming*.

Expectations help to determine achievement:

In his own practice, Dr. Graser would work with deaf children for 1½ years, providing them with both speech and speechreading closely allied to the structures of grammar. Upon their completing this program, he would move them into a hearing school milieu. Needless to say, however, in pursuing his system, Dr. Graser resorted neither to sign language (conventional nor natural) nor to fingerspelling. How such an instructional procedure could ever have had even a suggestion of success is probably an enigma to many a late-20th-Century mind. It was, however, Graser's high expectations of his pupils that inspired them to achieve his standards. For him, a teacher's expectations and a pupil's achievements were inextricably bonded. Interestingly enough, Graser's contemporary observers appear to have been more than satisfied with what they saw in his work. Through his insistence upon pure oralism, German education of the deaf became once again an entity and a model in its own right rather than a "carbon copy" of the French.

Graser willingly and eagerly shared his educational philosophy with many young future teachers of the deaf, among whom was the eventual notable, Friedrich Moritz Hill. With such a disciple, old Dr. Johann Graser could rest assured that his ideas would be most certainly preserved and even further expanded.

26

Friedrich Moritz Hill
and the "German System"
1838

Young Friedrich Moritz Hill was reared in a world of music. His father, a military musician, provided a sufficiently cultured environment for him that he grew up aspiring to become a teacher. An outstanding scholar with an urge to help humanity on its way, young Hill was accepted as a student by the renowned Pestalozzi at his normal school.

A career begins:

Upon the completion of his work with Pestalozzi, Hill was happily honored, along with a number of other students, by being named in 1828 to Dr. Graser's teacher education program at the Institution for the Deaf in Berlin. Graser's highly structured procedure for teaching deaf children quickly fired young Hill's imagination, and he became well aware that he had found his vocation.

It was with the Weissenfels seminary, an affiliate of the Berlin Institute for the Deaf, that Hill in 1830 accepted a teaching position, and there he was to remain for the balance of his career. At this seminary, Hill not only pursued the oral principles of Graser, but developed them more completely as well. It will be recalled that the hearing school model had served to guide Graser in his work with the deaf and so it did.

Hill's educational writings:

Hill's growing understanding of the deaf child, and his grasp of psychology and the phases of educational development were soon reflected in a series of books. The first of these was a *Guide to Deaf-Mute Instruction*, which was published in 1838. A year later, he wrote a *Complete Guide to the Instruction of Deaf-Mute Children in Mechanical Speech, Lipreading, Reading, and Writing for Public Teachers*. In keeping with Graser's mainstreaming concept, Hill, through his manual, prepared teachers of hearing children to teach deaf children as well. In 1840 a third volume appeared, entitled *Guide to the Instruction of the Deaf and Dumb, for Pastors and Teachers*. Thomas Arnold, a British educator of the deaf and historian, termed this book "one of the most valuable works in our special literature." (Farrar, *Arnold's Education*, p. 59.)

Natural signs in early education:

Unlike his mentor, Dr. Graser, Hill found natural signs, i.e., natural gestures and pantomime, to be important in the education of *beginning* deaf children. Of Hill's thinking on the subject of natural signs, Arnold wrote:

> As to natural signs, Hill was firmly convinced of their necessity, but used them at the lowest stage of instruction only, making no attempt to give them an artificial development, and gradually replacing them by spoken language. (*Ibid.*)

Relative to conventional signs, however, Hill was as strictly opposed to them as Graser. He also forbade the use of fingerspelling, because, again, like conventional signs, he believed that such spelling was a deterrent to the acquisiton of speech.

Three basic language propositions:

Accordingly, to Arnold, Hill's principles of language instruction may be summarized in three basic propositions (*Ibid.*, p. 60):

> I The deaf have to learn language in the same manner in which hearing children acquire it.

With this concept, the acquisition of grammar must be deferred. Experiences and objects become the center of instructional attention, with each being clothed in its own vocabulary and syntax. To implement this procedure, Hill produced 16 colored pictures depicting true-to-life experiences along with appropriately descriptive language. The pictures, of course, were designed to generate child interest and thought. These then served as a basis for natural speech instruction and usage.

> II   As with the hearing so with the deaf, articulate speech must form the basis of language; writing, however, has to be treated as a secondary mode of expressing thought, wholly dependent upon the former.

This sequence, of course, establishes Hill's procedure as being *pure* oral; i.e., speech instruction *before* writing. This follows in the traditional steps of Amman, Heinicke, and Graser. It was Hill's idea for speech to become an integral part of the thought processes as well as becoming the primary mode for thought expression. With speech as the expressive mode, closely allied was the receptive medium of speechreading.

> III   Almost from the first we must use speech as a means of instruction and intercommunication with our scholars.

In this concept is manifest the fact that speech, to become a working tool of communication, must be utilized in *every* situation.

The "German System" summarized:

The whole of the "German System" was effectively depicted in 47 principles by the German historian, Walther, in his book entitled *Geschichte des Taubstummen-Bildingswesen* (History of Deaf-Mute Educational Procedures), published in 1882. Following are the principles summarized by Thomas Arnold:

> 1. Oral language is the principal subject of instruction from the beginning to the end of the course, and to this all other branches are subordinate.
>
> 2. In language teaching four stages are to be distinguished: (a.) Preparatory language teaching – having for its aim the development of oral utterance and the fixing of elementary ideas. (b.) Fundamental language teaching – establishing a sure basis for further instruction and accordingly providing the pupils with suitable objects for observation and language, and with simple forms of speech. (c.) The amplification of language teaching – treating language as a subject of instruction, extending the principles of object teaching, and arousing the self-activity of the pupil in speaking. (d.) The conclusion of language teaching – by continued grammatical exercises rendering speech more

and more a conscious mental activity, leading the pupils to the comprehension of conversational forms and of simple popular literature, and enabling them to express in connected language and in writing their ideas of what they see, experience and feel.

3. In the language teaching of the deaf are distinguished: (a.) A mechanical language teaching having to do with its technical side. (b.) An object language teaching – providing the pupils with language materials. (c.) A formal language teaching – imparting the forms of speech. (d.) Free exercises in language – affording application and practice of colloquial language.

4. Simultaneously with language teaching are begun four exercises which constantly go hand in hand, viz., exercises in speech, lip-reading, writing and reading.

5. Since oral speech is at the same time the end and the means of instruction, it must receive the most solicitous care and practice throughout the whole course.

6. The clear and distinct utterance of single sounds and of the various combinations of sounds, the natural movements and positions of the vocal organs, the correct lengthening and shortening of sounds, the right emphasis of syllables and words, and the proper economy of the breath – the aim of mechanical speech – can be attained only by constant and conscientious effort.

7. Since it is not only essential that the deaf shall be able to make themselves understood but it is of equal importance that they shall understand others, the exercises in lip-reading should receive no less attention than those in mechanical speech.

8. The principles generally followed in the acquisition of language by hearing persons are applicable to the instruction of the deaf in language.

9. Language should therefore be associated directly with the objects, phenomena, and circumstances environing the pupils. In this way alone can an intimate union of the word and thing be effected, and language be rendered for the deaf-mute what it is for the hearing person – an organic mental activity.

10. In order to accustom the pupils to an independent use of language the need of oral speech must be awakened within them.

11. The need of oral speech is not awakened in the deaf if those associating with them employ the sign language. The use of this language also produces the following injurious results: the deaf children use speech unwillingly, do not learn to read from the lips of others, do not acquire colloquial language satisfactorily, gain only a limited range of language, do not fully grasp the forms of spoken language, and do not learn to think in this language.

12. The sign language must therefore be excluded from the instruction of the deaf and from intercourse with them.

13. As a means of explaining language and imparting ideas, only the direct perception of the object or its representative in language should be employed.

14. With the first instruction in language should be associated a regular course of object teaching, which should be carried on either in connection with the instruction in reading and language or as an independent branch. It should continue throughout the whole school period.

15. The aims of object teaching are: the quickening of the attention, the exercise and development of the faculties of observation and reflection, the acquisition of ideas and facts, the use of significant words, practice in the employment of language already acquired, and its further development by oral conversation and written exercises.

16. Object teaching is: (a.) Preparatory – going hand in hand with articulation teaching. (b.) Fundamental – furnishing material to the pupils. (c.) Descriptive – by descriptions of various objects aiming at the enrichment of language materials, and the comprehension and correct use of the forms of language. (d) Practical – seeking, in connection with progress in language, to acquaint the pupils with the practical relations of life.

17. The order in which the succession of objects is to be presented is determined by the circumstances of time and place.

18. Since the deaf-mute receives language under limited conditions and is slow in reaching accuracy in its use, the laws of language, to be comprehended and mastered, must be acquired partly by practice and partly by observation.

19. Although the need of language on the part of the pupil continues the leading motive in the development of his language, yet there must be a systematic progress in the presentation and practice of the forms of speech at every stage of the course of instruction.

20. In the later stage a regular course of instruction in grammar begins, for which the pupil has been prepared during the middle stage, making language itself the subject of treatment.

21. The forms of language are taught in connection with the reading book, but there may also be special lessons for this branch.

22. This branch of instruction can produce fruitful results only when it follows the maxim: Deduce the rule from the example.

23. In order that the deaf may acquire the power of expressing themselves correctly and freely in writing, they should be led to keep a diary, from which in the later years of school may be developed exercises in composition, imparting facility in letter writing. Moreover, every subject of instruction, so far as it has to do with the succession of ideas, must be made to contribute to the expression of ideas in writing. Written exercises must therefore be duly associated with oral instruction.

24. The free language exercises introduce colloquial language as it is used in the every day intercourse of life.

25. These exercises are connected with the immediate wants of the pupils, and seek to provide therefor. Occurrences at home and school, during walks and mutual intercourse, are made the subject of conversation, and afford practice in colloquial language, especially in its peculiar forms and idioms.

26. These exercises constantly give the pupil complete forms of language, without always considering whether the form employed has been prepared for and is fully understood.

27. Since it is of high importance for the deaf to learn colloquial language as comprehensively as possible, this aim must be considered in every branch of study whenever opportunity offers. What has been learned should also be applied in intercourse out of school.

28. Every subject of instruction must teach the language peculiar to itself; it enters, therefore, into the service of language teaching.

29. The entire course is based on speech. The written form is added as needed.

30. From the beginning of the middle stage the method of deaf-mute instruction resembles more and more closely that of the ordinary schools for the hearing, so that in the higher stage it does not differ from it at all. (*Ibid.*, pp. 62-64. For the complete list see Walther, *History*, pp. 240-244.)

While the national trend of German education of the deaf was pure oral, there was some opposition to it as will be subsequently considered in the efforts of J. Heidsiek and his visit to America. The impact, however, of German pure oralism was shortly to have a tremendous effect on the educational direction for deaf children in the United States.

27

Bernhard Engelsmann Brings Oralism to America
1863

In 1863 Bernhard Engelsmann, a German Jewish immigrant, was imbued with awe and enthusiasm at what he saw as he slowly sailed into New York Harbor. Deeply he shared in the strong sense of opportunity which prevailed among his fellow immigrants as they disembarked.

Engelsmann was not an artisan or craftsman with a marketable trade, but a teacher with very special talents. During the crossing he had quietly revealed to some of his fellow passengers that he could teach the *taubstummen* (deaf and dumb) to speak. In response most of them shrugged and looked dubiously at one another. To be sure, this man Engelsmann would have little competition in such a business, for who on earth could possibly want to pursue such a strange work? Little did they realize that in their midst was a genuine pioneer, one who would help push back boundaries, boundaries of which they had little knowledge.

Mr. Engelsmann had early estimated and even planned accordingly that the metropolis of New York would most certainly have numbers of deaf and dumb children sequestered within it. Such was, indeed, the case of several who were secreted away in the newly constructed tenements which lined the eastern side of the City. With this thought he began his search and the realization of his dream – to bring speech and learning to the deaf children of America. No better place could he imagine to begin his work than right there in New York City.

As Engelsmann attended his synagogue regularly, it was not long before the word of his unique mission was circulated throughout the congregation. Soon he was confronted by an anxious and sad-faced young father who had in tow a large-eyed and bewildered child. "*Er is toib!* Please teach him!" So then it was that Engelsmann began his historic work in American education of the deaf, and the year was 1864. Soon other youngsters of Jewish and German backgrounds were brought for his tuition.

Engelsmann's consummate skill as an oral teacher of deaf children had been keenly honed through his years of instructional experience in the Vienna Hebrew School for Deaf Children. All of this he brought to focus in producing speech in his young deaf pupils. While eager parents brought little money, they did bring great moral support to Engelsmann in his work, and it was not long before the more economically established of the City began to assist him financially.

On February 27, 1867, several Jewish leaders of the City were brought together by the parents of Engelsmann's pupils. They met at the home of Mr. Issac Rosenfeld to discuss the possibilities of making Mr. Engelsmann's school available to those deaf children whose parents were financially unable to meet the expense. Through this and other efforts money was soon raised to provide full support for Mr. Engelsmann's Hebrew School for the Deaf. With the establishment of a "formal organization," a full-fledged school at 134 West Twenty-Seventh Street opened its doors to 10 pupils. The date was March 1, 1867. Thus was established "the first exclusively oral school for the deaf in America that achieved permanent success." (Fay, "New York Institution," p. 415.)

Mr. Engelsmann continued as principal of the New York City Hebrew School until 1869, when he became the director of articulation at the New York Institution for the Deaf at Washington Heights. Subsequently in 1873 he studied medicine and became a physician, which profession he followed until his death in 1897.

Engelsmann's contribution, of course, was his successful introduction of the German pure oral system into American education of the deaf.

28

Mr. Francis Rising and the New York Institute for the Improved Instruction of Deaf-Mutes 1869-1873

Dr. Engelsmann's successor at the New York Hebrew School for the Deaf was a Mr. Francis A. Rising, an educator of considerable experience. Mr. Rising, with the help of the New York State legislature, brought about a reorganization of the school, which accordingly became known as the New York Institution for the Improved Instruction of Deaf-Mutes.

A consideration of reality:

Mr. Rising, although an oralist, was a bit more liberal in his educational philosophy than his predecessor. While writing understandingly of sign language in his "Institutional Report" for 1871, he did point out that despite the beauty, grace, and force of signs,

> the hard undeniable fact is that hearing and speaking people will not learn them; they will not even learn to spell with their fingers, and mutes so generally find it irksome and difficult to commuicate even with their parents, that home loses its distinctive charms; they feel like exiles there, the institution has become a home, their only native place.

> The question then presses itself upon thinking men, why teach this foreign language of signs at all? Why not teach English idioms directly and not compel him [*sic*] to a translation in order to a comprehension of their direct use? * * * Words and phrases are the signs used

by society, hence these should be persistently taught the mute. But signs are used as a means, it is alleged, "as a test of his comprehension of words." Therefore it would seem to follow that the more elaborate and extended the means, the more perfect could be the mute's mastery of language. The facts, unfortunately, are precisely the reverse of this. Those pupils who have been trained to spell words and phrases with their fingers, and to write them, rarely using signs, are the only ones who have ever acquired a fair knowledge of language. The accomplished, graceful sign-makers are notoriously incapable of correct composition even upon familiar subjects, and the printed page is to them a hidden mystery. The ablest instructors of the deaf and dumb now freely admit that, after fifty years of trial in this country, the system has been found wanting. It has failed to accomplish the ends desired, and the demands of parents and guardians for better methods can no longer be disregarded. (Fay, "Improved Instruction," pp. 262-263.)

The "articulate method":

Mr. Rising, in the "Report," then describes the "articulate method." The deaf child upon learning to pronounce short syllables is given the sentence, "What is that?" This covers his questions regarding the objects or pictures of objects which he sees. Next provided is the question, "What is the color, shape, etc., of this?" After this follows the question, "What is he doing?" Thus are given the key-questions to both *qualities* and *actions.* Signs are avoided in all explanations. In their stead objects and pictures are used extensively. Sentences and phrases must be repeated again and again until they are "ineffaceably impressed" on the child's memory. (*Ibid.*, p. 264.)

More optimism required, perhaps:

Mr. Rising's next statement in his "Report" quite possibly bore that seed of thought which ultimately led to the terminating of his career at his newly organized New York Institute for the Improved Instruction of Deaf-Mutes.

It is probable that only about half of the so-called deaf and dumb can be taught articulation. This includes the semi-mutes, the semi-deaf, and bright congenital mutes, not too far advanced in years. The remaining mutes by substituting the manual alphabet for speech, can, it is believed, acquire the ability to write and spell, and hence to understand English idioms, by this method of word and phrase building interpreted by objects, pictures and actions; and only when other resources fail by natural gestures; never by arbitrary, methodical signs. (*Ibid.*)

A resignation accepted:

While Mr. Rising was certainly progressive and, perhaps, even correct in his philosophy, his statement relative to the idea "that only about half" of the school's population could be taught speech, was certainly not in accordance with the thinking of the school's founder, Dr. Bernhard Engelsmann. While "comparisons are odious," unquestionably comparisons were made, and two years later, in 1873, Mr. Rising "resigned from the profession to engage in business." (Fay, "Changes," p. 211.) The principalship was again open.

29

Mr. Greenberger (Greene) Reinforces the German Oral Approach 1873-1898

Mr. Rising's successor as principal at the New York Institute for Improved Instruction was an extraordinary man named David Greenberger, who, like the earlier Bernhard Engelsmann, had been trained to teach the deaf in the famous Jewish Institute for the Deaf in Vienna. It was Greenberger's opportunity while there to work under the supervision and influence of the Institute's principal, Dr. Joel Deutsch. Deutsch inspired young Greenberger with a nonpareil enthusiasm for German oralism.

It was this intense spirit coupled with the confidence of a master teacher which David Greenberger ultimately brought in 1871 to his first job in America, and specifically to Chicago. In that city the public school system provided him with a classroom and thus was established the Chicago Day School for the Deaf. (Fay, "Day School," p. 204.)

Greenberger's success in Chicago soon marked him as an innovator, and it also marked him as a likely successor for the retired Mr. Rising at the New York Institute for Improved Instruction. Mr. Greenberger in his letters to the trustees emphasized the thoroughness of his Vienna oral training, and this, in turn, brought to their minds the dedication and philosophy of the school's founder Bernhard Engelsmann. David Greenberger was the man for the principalship and the year was 1873.

From the beginning the new principal set a determined course for the school and its program. Although a strict oralist and wholly opposed to the use of conventional or methodical signs, Greenberger did recognize and encourage the use of *natural* signs and gestures with deaf children in their *beginning* years. Concerning this subject Greenberger wrote:

> ... we have adopted the following rules for the use of natural gestures and motions as a means of instruction:
>
> I. At the lowest stage of the instruction they are the only means of intercommunication between teachers and pupils.
>
> II. As the scholar advances in language they are gradually set aside and superceded by spoken words, but even at the higher and highest states of his education they are tolerated and applied, though even more and more restricted, until they are at last reduced to mere facial expressions and gesticulation.
>
> III. Since we learn to understand a foreign language long before we are able to apply it, it is judicious that the teacher express himself oftener in his vernacular, but allow his pupil a more extensive use of the language of signs.
>
> These principles have been arrived at by instructors of deaf-mutes who had started from diametrically opposed stand-points and systems, and they will probably hold good for all time to come. ("Natural Method," p. 64.)

Greenberger's approach to speech development for deaf children was unique in that he advocated a *whole-word* approach as opposed to the analytical. (Greenberger, "Word Method," p. 296.) This was a full 40 years before Max Wertheim conceived his revolutionary psychology and gave it the *Gestalt* label.

In Greenberger's whole-word method, specific words were selected which included the most common speech combinations occurring in oral English. Mastering these, a deaf child would have the oral keys for all subsequent words which he might encounter.

In the teaching sequence, speech always preceeded writing, i.e., the written form would not be given to a child until he had first become familiar with the oral form. Reading the printed form was similarly postponed for two years or even longer, thus providing a greater amount of time for speech instruction and usage-practice.

It was Greenberger's belief that this maximum emphasis upon speech with deaf children would result in their having more accurate pronunciation, a better skill in speechreading, and a more certain grasp of oral language as a mode of thought. (*Ibid.*)

In the area of language development, Greenberger espoused the *natural method:*

> From the very outset of the instruction in language, the teacher should supply the proper words for everything the pupils express in signs. All their requests, complaints, questions, desires, etc., should at once be rendered into written or spoken language according to the system in use. If, for example, the class is in the midst of a lesson, and one of the children motions to the teacher that he is tired and wishes to sit down, the exercise should at once be interrupted and the child taught to say, "I am tired. Please may I take my seat and rest for awhile?" No artificial exercise can be devised which will be so beneficial as such natural practice in the use of language. ("Natural Method II," pp. 33-34.)

As indicated, this approach depends heavily upon the actual language needs of the children involved. They are consequently provided with that stock of vocabulary which the moment demands for the immediate expression of their ideas relative to their current experience. Relying on the spontaneity of children in their interests and activities, the instructor must be constantly alert to the opportunities for language as their thinking and activities may require.

> Strict dogmatists object to such indiscriminate introduction of words, tenses, etc., without any order or system. But experience has demonstrated that the best and most efficient plan of teaching language to a deaf mute is to supply the proper words whenever he has an idea in his mind and is going to express it. He can learn (phrases and short sentences) through frequent use, in the same manner as children in the possession of all faculties, acquire them. There is no reason why he should not be taught to use them till he has learned to distinguish them between the different parts of speech, the present and past tenses, etc. It is necessary that he should comprehend the meanings of each word in a phrase if taken separately. It is quite sufficient if he connects the right idea with the sentence as a whole. If complete sentences are constantly emphasized, he will soon find out the individual meaning of the words composing them. Besides our language contains a great many little words which are like ciphers in arithmetic. They derive their value or meaning from the place where they stand in a sentence. Taken by themselves, they mean nothing, and it would be a waste of time and labor to attempt to explain them separately. Such application of language, without any regard to grammatical orders, as is recommended here, does not interfere with any plan that may be in use for the arrangement of regular school exercises. On the contrary, the frequent use of one and the same word in different forms familiarizes the pupil with the various changes which some parts of speech undergo in the construction of sentences, and prepares him for that which we have to present to him in grammatical instruction. (*Ibid.*, pp. 34-35.)

This natural method of language instruction described by Greenberger was consistently and successfully followed and improved upon down through the years.

Greenberger from the beginning of his tenure exhibited an extraordinary zeal for the oral education of deaf children, particularly those who were classified as semi-mute, i.e., those who had post-lingual hearing impairments. It was his observation that great numbers of such youngsters, despite their having strong speech recollections, had been placed into schools for the deaf which were largely sign-oriented. As a result, such children were rendered mute, or practically so, not by reason of their initial affliction of deafness, but by the limited opportunities provided them for oral language reinforcement and development. Hence, Greenberger saw his mission as being clearly defined, and this he pursued unequivocally despite some amazing opposition and criticism.

The New York Institute for the Improved Instruction of Deaf-Mutes under State legislative action came to enjoy the same financial assistance as the "old" New York Institute under Isaac Lewis Peet's administration. Competition and rivalry between the two schools was a natural development. Consequently, Greenberger came in occasionally for some "heavy shelling" which was, indeed, not always justified. He was not, however, a man to back away from an unpleasant situation, but was known instead for standing strong and giving as good as he received.

According to the *American Annals of the Deaf* for October, 1892, David Greenberger legally changed his name to David Greene, and thereafter all of his work and writings were so identified. In 1898, after 25 years of invaluable service to deaf children, David Greene tendered his resignation as principal of the New York Institute for the Improved Instruction of Deaf-Mutes. It was his wish to become a teacher of speech unencumbered by the duties of administration.

Although Greene had severed relations with the Institute, the impact of his tenure was to carry well into the 20th Century. This fact is reflected today in the Institute's modern descendant facility, the Lexington School for the Deaf in Jackson Heights. The natural method of language instruction described by Greene has been successfully followed and improved upon down through the years. The most notable modern contributions to the system were made first in 1958 by Dr. Mildred Groht in her now classic *Natural Language for Deaf Children*, and then in 1962 with Mrs. Beatrice Ostern Hart's informative work entitled *Teaching Reading to Deaf Children*.

Chapter Eight
Expanding the Educational Horizons for Deaf Americans

30

E.M. Gallaudet and His
National Deaf-Mute College
1857

Washington, D.C., was virtually a sea of mud in the spring of 1857. At least this was the way it appeared to 20-year-old Edward Miner Gallaudet. He felt a bit self-conscious as he sat beside his host, Mr. Amos Kendall. The conveyance in which they rode from the depot was a magnificient black phaeton, drawn by two spirited horses and expertly reined by a liveried driver. Skillfully the phaeton was threaded through the street vendors to K Street and east to Fifth Street and then north to Boundary.

Young Gallaudet, accustomed to his hometown of Hartford, found the Capital City a disappointment. While the far-from-finished Capitol Building held great promise for the future, it did little, at that time, for its present. Mud was everywhere.

En route, Mr. Kendall studied Mr. Gallaudet as they trundled along. He observed to himself that Gallaudet was in reality only a boy, hardly one to assume the responsibility of a school superintendency. Gallaudet, however, had come highly recommended by the illustrious Dr. Harvey Prindle Peet, superintendent of the New York Institute for the Deaf and Dumb. Actually, Kendall had initally sought Peet's son, Isaac Lewis Peet, for the position, but that young man was being carefully groomed to become his father's successor. The senior Peet, however, having recently seen Edward, the son of his late mentor, Thomas Hopkins Gallaudet, was impressed by the young man and with a moment's inspiration recommended him for the position.

Young Gallaudet had a tremendous background and upbringing as the son of the late founder of the American Asylum in Hartford. To the senior Peet, there was no greater service that he could render his own great teacher than to see that man's son well placed in the profession.

As young Gallaudet overcame his initial shyness, he began to ask for some detailed particulars relative to the proposed school, the children to be served, and his own responsibilities. Mr. Kendall was happily impressed by the young man's forthrightness, his maturity of manner, and his obviously dedicated interest in the deaf, their education, and their welfare. The old man calmly assured the young fellow that all of his questions would be duly answered. He then suggested that Gallaudet rest after his long journey, get acquainted, and generally enjoy himself.

In his portmanteau, Gallaudet carried the letters which he had received from Kendall regarding the position, and it all sounded very promising. While their correspondence had been fine, getting answers *vis-à-vis* was ever so much better. Meeting Kendall was, indeed, an experience in itself, and he was most anxious to make a good impression on his host.

As the pair rode along, young Gallaudet observed Mr. Kendall to be a veritable Methuselah. White-haired and luxuriantly sideburned, this man had actually served Andrew Jackson as Postmaster General. He also had accrued sufficient wealth to own a phaeton and a large estate, which they appeared to be rapidly approaching.

The phaeton rolled along Boundary Street, and turned through the gates and up along a perimeter road which passed a few white frame houses. The driver slowed down a bit as they passed one of the houses. Several romping and chortling children skipped about outside under the approving eye of their housemother. Young Gallaudet was eager to stop at that moment, but the older man nodded to the driver to go on, because there would be time enough later to visit. For the young teacher, 40 years awaited him. The phaeton moved briskly along a lane which led across some meadowland and then up a hill toward the woods. Circling through the trees, the phaeton drew up to a mansion set up on a terraced lawn and completely surrounded by huge oaks and maples. On arriving, Mr. Kendall turned to his guest and announced warmly, "Welcome to Kendall Green!"

In the evening, Mr. Gallaudet learned that some months before "a man of the cloth," one P. H. Skinner, had come to the Capital City and had gathered together a group of children, some of whom were blind, and the rest of whom were deaf and dumb. With this pathetic entourage, the Reverend Mr. Skinner traversed the city asking for donations for his obviously Christian effort to feed, to clothe, and to house his handicapped waifs. The good man then rented as soon as possible a large house on G Street and set up his charitable home.

Certainly Mr. Skinner could not have hit on a more certain scheme for wringing the shekels from the Washington elite. Thus, it was that Amos Kendall became involved, along with a number of other philanthropically inclined individuals. When the bad news came that the Reverend Mr. Skinner was less than trustworthy in dealing with the children or with the money he had collected, he was forthwith relieved of his responsibilities, leaving Kendall and his colleagues with the entire menage.

Kendall, never one to shirk his duty, assumed full responsibility for the children and magnanimously had them moved to one of his houses on his estate. He then placed them under the able care of some of the ladies of his church. It was then, of course, that he began his correspondence with Harvey Prindle Peet and then later with young Gallaudet.

The first day after Gallaudet's arrival, Kendall knew that he was his man for the job. The youthful aspect of Gallaudet had caused a bit of doubt, which was allayed when the young man suggested that he could bring his mother, who might serve as matron. Kendall instantly agreed.

Mrs. Sophia Fowler Gallaudet, a deaf woman of considerable ability, had successfully raised five hearing young ones, three boys and two girls. She had been educated at the American Asylum and had continued in her education as the wife of Thomas Hopkins Gallaudet. She was, indeed, eminently qualified for the matron's position.

When the final agreement was drawn up between Kendall and Gallaudet, the latter included a vital stipulation which signaled one of the most significant turning points in the history of American education of the deaf. Gallaudet, for all of his youth, had seriously dreamed of and discussed for a number of years the possibility of establishing someday a college exclusively for the deaf. Now that the opportunity had arrived for putting in a word for such an undertaking, Gallaudet included it as a possibility for the future. Thus, when the little school for the deaf and blind was created, the seed for its ultimate evolution into a national institution of higher learning for the deaf was securely embedded.

The Columbia Institution for the Deaf, Dumb and Blind was

incorporated by Congress in February, 1857; E. M. Gallaudet was appointed its superintendent on May 30 of that year. Thus, with the administration for the school determined, the new superintendent could move forward in the appointment of his teaching assistant and other personnel. In her biography of Edward Miner Gallaudet (*Voice of the Deaf*, p. 27), Maxine Tull Boatner writes,

> The school was opened with nine deaf-mutes and five blind pupils. Edward had three assistants and three servants, altogether a family of twenty-one persons. The assistant matron was Mrs. Maria M. Eddy—of Worcester, Massachusetts and James Denison of Royalton, Vermont was Edward's assistant. Edward later recalled how the presence of his dear mother—and of good Mrs. Eddy—gave to the establishment dignity and distinction "which were, for the time being, lacking in its youthful male officials."

During the next seven years, the little school began gradually to increase its deaf pupil population. The blind children, being discovered to be somewhat incompatible with the deaf because of conflicting social and recreational interests, were transferred to a Maryland school for the blind. Always in Gallaudet's mind, however, was his long-range ambition for the institution to begin its collegiate offerings. Such a curriculum was gradually assembled, but not without some contention between Kendall and Gallaudet. Finally, the old man conceded to Gallaudet's curricular plans, and the first graduating class was scheduled for June, 1867.

On April 8, 1864, President Abraham Lincoln signed the enactment "empowering this institution to confer collegiate degrees upon deaf-mutes." President Lincoln, however, was unable to attend the Inauguration of the College ceremony, although, as Patron, he did sign the first diploma. This diploma was for an honorary Master of Arts degree presented to an outstanding prelingually deaf man, Mr. John Carlin. Carlin was a gifted artist, writer, and worker on behalf of the rights of deaf people. An exemplary person in every way, Carlin had achieved his numerous accomplishments through great effort. His achievements, performed without the benefit of a college education, set a hallmark for all succeeding generations of deaf students who were to enjoy the advantages of the newly established National Deaf-Mute College. With this, the college's President, Edward Miner Gallaudet, began a new era in education of the deaf.

31

Harriet B. Rogers Moves
to Northampton
1867

While the German oral method had received considerable attention and praise in Horace Mann's 1843 report to the Massachusetts legislature, it was either politely minimized or ignored by established educators of the deaf. At that time Mann's document most "directly menaced" the American Asylum, its philosophy, and its instructional reputation. Harvey Prindle Peet's New York Institution, which had pursued speech instruction for 18 years, had come immediately to the aid of the American Asylum against Mann's "wild exaggerations." The New York School reported that articulation and speechreading had been given a fair test and "in a year proved a failure." (Syle, "Harvey Prindle Peet," p. 151.)

Three concerned families:

Such substantial pressures were sufficient to put the oral idea to rest for a score of years. Actually the oral issue did not become a point of concern among educators of the deaf until it was gradually revived in the Commonwealth of Massachusetts through the interest of three concerned families. The first of these were the Hubbards of Boston. Gardiner Green Hubbard was the father of a young daughter, Mabel, who had become deaf at the age of four. His greatest concern regarding his child was that her speech would slip away if she did not have proper instruction. He therefore took her to the American Asylum in Hartford with the hope of receiving advice and direction.

In Hartford, Mr. Hubbard discussed Mabel's problem with some of the teachers. In a subsequent testimony he stated:

> We consulted Mr. [Thomas] Gallaudet, the son of Dr. Gallaudet; we consulted with our good friend Prof. Bartlett, and with other gentlemen; and they told us the child could not keep her speech three months.
>
> . . . Mr. Bartlett told us to keep on, and he is the only teacher of deaf-mutes who gave us the slightest encouragement; and he told he was afraid her articulation would be so unpleasant, even if we preserved it, that we should not want to hear her talk. . . . The feeling of all persons who knew anything about deaf-mutes was to discourage us from undertaking to teach our little girl articulation. (*Deaf-Mute Education in Massachusetts*, pp. 201-202.)

Gardiner Green Hubbard, a determined parent, did not find himself in agreement with the gentlemen of Hartford. Hence, it was that be began to inform himself further on the subject of articulation and its possibilities for his young daughter.

At about the same time, Rhode Island's governor, M. A. Lippitt, had a young daughter, Jeanie, who had become deaf at four years and three months as a result of scarlet fever. After several months of convalescence for Jeanie, her mother began her instruction. The child "had lost all knowledge of forming sentences, although she remembered the names of some things." As to Jeanie's instruction the mother wrote, "We used no means except articulation from the commencement, being particularly directed in this by Dr. Howe." (*Ibid.*, pp. 229-230.)

The third family involved with deafness was the Cushings, whose little daughter, Fannie, lost her hearing at the age of 3½ years. The Cushings were fortunate in obtaining the teaching services of Miss Harriet Rogers, a sister of one of Dr. Howe's teachers. Miss Rogers worked with the child under Dr. Howe's direction, and consequently introduced her to speech along with the manual alphabet. However, fingerspelling was later dropped in favor of speechreading.

Thus, it was with these strongly pro-oral families, that Dr. Howe's efforts in behalf of speech for the deaf received a renewed emphasis. Dr. Howe and Gardiner Green Hubbard in 1864 had attempted to persuade the Massachusetts Legislature to approve of their establishing an oral school in Boston; however, the American Asylum exerted its influence in opposition, and the idea of such a school was defeated.

The Governor's call for a hearing:

It was not until January 24, 1867, at the request of Massachusetts' Governor Bullock that the first public hearing of the Joint Special Committee on the Education of the Deaf heard the evidences both in support of and in opposition to the proposal that the Commonwealth assume the responsibility for the education of its own deaf children. Heretofore all Massachusetts deaf children had been sent, at the expense of the State, to the American Asylum for the Deaf and Dumb in Hartford, Connecticut.

The Hartford school was at that time the only educational institution for the deaf in the whole of New England. Being an institution with 50 years of history and tradition, the administration did not welcome the idea of a new competitive school in the area, particularly one which would espouse articulation. The reasoning was that the procedures and philosophy of T. H. Gallaudet and Clerc relative to the efficacy of signs were "tried and true" and, being based on long practical experience, were obviously indisputable and immutable. Consequently, persons without such understanding, training, and experience and who presumed to make recommendations relative to the education of the deaf were looked upon as interlopers.

Governor Bullock's call for a public hearing had now brought all of the contenders together. The American Asylum was represented by the Reverend Collins Stone, principal, and the venerable Mr. W. W. Turner, principal emeritus. Both were, of course, staunch advocates of "manual signs" and "finger language." There were also, of course, a number of witnesses representing each of the two groups.

Dr. Howe's presentation on the behalf of oralism:

The first hearing was launched by Dr. Howe, who acknowledged Massachusetts' debt of gratitude to the American Asylum for its long service to the deaf children of the Commonwealth. He did, however, make very clear his disapproval of the methodology employed in that institution. He also objected strenuously to the congregating of "these children together in great numbers." He emphasized that

> the great law of nature in this class of unfortunates, as in all classes, demands that they be brought, as far as possible, under the ordinary influences of society. The whole object of their education is to counteract

the effects growing out their condition. How do we do this? By subject-
ing them to the ordinary social influences, so that they shall escape the
effects of their condition. (*Ibid.,* Appendix, p. 4.)

In modern parlance Howe advocated *mainstreaming.*

Howe also pointed out in his presentation that in Europe "in order
to train a deaf-mute child as he ought to be trained, you should
begin with him as early as he can leave the mother's apron-strings.
Even in Germany they begin at four years of age." (*Ibid.,* p. 5.) This
recommendation of early educational intervention should sound
familiar to our late-20th-Century ears. Of all of Howe's ideas,
however, those relative to speech and speechreading seemed the
most disturbing to the representatives of the American Asylum. In
Gardiner G. Hubbard's statement before the Committee, he described the success of his young daughter's oral training. This, too,
was received negatively by the Hartford contingent.

The Reverend Collins Stone speaks for Hartford:

In presenting the opposition's stand, the Reverend Collins Stone
reviewed for the Committee the 1844 Mann-Howe reports, in which
Mann critically stated "that the schools for deaf-mutes in this country are very far behind those of Germany." (*Ibid.,* p. 66.) Stone then
described the late Horace Mann as being "imperfectly acquainted
with the system of instruction pursued in American Asylums."
(*Ibid.*) He then quoted and remarked extensively on Prof. Day's 1844
and 1858 reports regarding his observations in German schools for
the deaf. These observations, as might be expected, were quite
negative as to the success of the German schools for the deaf and
served to counter-balance the glowing reports of Mann and Howe.
Day had at one time been a teacher of the deaf and was also skilled
in speaking, reading, and writing German. All of this obviously added to the credibility of his deprecating observations of the German
system. On the other hand, both Mann and Howe knew but little
German and were, consequently, at the mercy of their interpreter
during their entire tour. This point was a score for the gentlemen
of Hartford.

Probably the most difficult testimony for the Asylum's representatives to refute was that of a maiden lady, Miss Harriet B. Rogers.
Miss Rogers was looked upon as something of a threat because she
had entered the nearly all-male domain of education of the deaf,
had founded a school, and had presumed to teach young deaf
children orally. All of these things she had done most successfully.

In fact, Miss Rogers' achievement in her Chelmsford school was considered to be something of a then-modern phenomenon as is indicated in *Deaf-Mute Education in Massachusetts: Report of the Joint Special Committee of the Legislature of 1867*, pp. 11-12.

> Her success is another proof of a truth which our late war has developed, that woman has more energy, tact, perseverance and capacity than have heretofore been acknowledged.
>
> Nor is it strange that woman should have best success with lessons by the lips. Thousands of men, with every faculty perfect and intensified, have thus learned their happiest and their saddest lessons by a silent expression. . . . Nature will have it that woman shall somehow retain and enjoy the privilege of expressing more words in a given time than is vouchsafed to her brethren!

Despite this awkward and "hedgy" compliment to Miss Rogers and American womanhood, the gentlemen of the Massachusetts Special Legislative Committee did recognize her achievement.

As the oral forces gradually gained ground, Samuel Gridley Howe repeated his long-standing criticism that the Hartford Asylum had not improved its system in a half century. This statement at once brought a desperate reaction from the Reverend Collins Stone:

> It has been said that there is no progress in Hartford. . . . Now any person who makes such a remark is profoundly ignorant, I am very sorry to say, of what we have done and what we are doing. . . . We have the same purpose in view that we had at first, fifty years ago. The desire to enlighten the mind of the deaf-mute and relieve him of his misfortune. We take the same means. We take his natural language, what he does know, to teach him what he does not know. Aside from that, there is nothing there that was there fifty years ago. The process, the modes of instruction, are entirely different. The old French system of Sicard was methodical signs. The old system of teaching when we first started was teaching endless vocabularies – hundreds and hundreds of words, – isolated words, – without giving the children any language at all. We do not do that now. We teach the different classes of words. We teach a few nouns, a few verbs, a few adverbs, a few adjectives, and put them immediately into connected language, just as other children are taught; so that in that matter we are entirely removed from the old French style. . . . You may not be aware of the fact, that the great difficulty with the deaf and dumb is, that we do not think in the order in which we talk. We think of the objects before we think of their qualities. We do not think of a *black* horse – putting the "black" first; we think of the horse, and then of the quality or color. It is so with regard to actions. We do not think of the qualifying word and then the action. Well, this language lies in the minds of the deaf and dumb just as it does in our minds; but, as a matter of education, we have come to arrange language in an artificial way. Sicard thought the best method of teaching was to give the words just as they stand

in our speech. Take a phrase like this, "A strong man rows a small boat easily." (The speaker illustrated the method of teaching this phrase by signs, which, of course, cannot be exhibited on paper.) So you have given a sign for every word, you have told just what part of speech it is, and just where it stands in the sentence. You have taught the child all that; he writes it down; he knows it; and you have taught him just as much and no more than if you were to add up a column of figures, and tell him the sum. It is a matter of memory only. You have not taught him how to construct any sentence. We do not teach in that way at all now. How do we teach now? We teach a sentence in the order of construction; we teach it just as anybody ought to teach it, as we hold. We give the idea in the first place. I ask a boy, "What did I tell you about? Did I speak about a horse, dog, bird, man?" He says, "Man." That is the subject. "Did I qualify that at all? Did I say black man, white man, weak man, strong man?" He says, I said "strong man." I tell him we put the adjective before the noun because it does not sound well to put it after. "Did I say two men, three men, one man?" He says, "a man." "What did this man do, – run, shout, or what?" He says, "He rows." Well, that is an action. "What does he row? Does he row a ship, a wagon, or what?" He rows a boat. "That comes next. Did I qualify that in any way? Did I say small boat, little boat, iron boat, wooden boat?" "You said, small boat." "How does he row it – easily or in what way?" "He rows it easily." Simply by calling his attention to these points, he gets real instruction. Then I give him another sentence similar to that. I do not help him about that, but he suggests these questions himself, and puts the sentence into form. Thus you see the child learns something. That is not the way they used to teach, it is a new and better method. (*Ibid.,* Appendix, pp. 84-85.)

In the "new and better method" described by the Reverend Mr. Stone we see a variation of Vaisse's intuitive method. The weakness of the approach, however, as perceived by Howe, Hubbard, and Rogers was its dependence upon the deaf child's "natural language" which in the Hartford context meant *sign language.* Also perceived was what they believed to be the greatest negative aspect of the Hartford procedure, its total disregard for speech and speech-reading as viable educational goals.

Mr. John Carlin's letter of testimony:

Among the many testimonies presented to the Committee was a letter written by Mr. John Carlin. Mr. Carlin, a well-know prelingually deaf man, a graduate of "the Philadelphia deaf-mute school," and a recipient of a Master of Arts degree from the National Deaf-Mute College, set forth in his letter his reasons for advocating the establishment of a school in Massachusetts. These reasons largely concerned the American Asylum and its instructional procedures.

. . . At the school hardly over five out of the two hundred pupils are annually found familiar with the principles of English grammar, and the rest are more or less deficient in written languages. This is a stubborn fact, and one indeed far beyond dispute. Now it may be asked how this deficiency is caused, and I can safely answer, by *their excessive use of signs, always encouraged by their teachers,* who declare, no doubt honestly, that the sign language is the deaf-mute's natural mode of communication. Your attention is again called to the following observation: The pantomimic language, generally employed in the classroom as well as in the sitting-room and elsewhere, is not a language of words in written order. It is simply a jargon of gestures, each gesture representing a word or action, and all the gestures are thrown together, utterly without regard to the grammatical order. (*Ibid.,* Appendix, pp. 37-38.)

Here, Carlin's rather undiplomatic description of sign language might quite easily be used to describe the modern American Sign Language (ASL). He continues:

At school, bits of history and science are given *ad libitum* in attractive gestures. This course, in my opinion, is useless and often pernicious to the process of the pupil's mind in spoken language. But the objection might be removed were dactylology constantly employed, and *that even to excess,* (and there can be no excess,) with a few signs, if judged necessary, for the explanation of new words and phrases. The signs thus used should, by all means, be in written order. (*Ibid.,* p. 17.)

Carlin here describes and proposes something akin to our currently modern and innovative "Signed English," simultaneous method, or Total Communication (TC). Relative to the English instruction of deaf children specifically, Carlin concludes:

Gentlemen, you ask if another better *modus operandi* could be devised and brought into successful operation in the classroom, and I answer, *Yes.* How? By enforcing on the pupil the use of digital spelling and writing on the slate, the use of mischievous signs being strictly prohibited, and by the repetition of his lessons till the grammatical rules are deeply impressed upon his memory. You inquire whether this mode could be introduced into the old institutions, and I answer, *it could not,* because of their obstinate adherence to the old system. Thereupon you will see the necessity of a new institution, with a new system. (*Ibid.*)

Mr. John Clarke of Northampton:

Numerous other testimonies figured in the hearings; however, it was the weight of Dr. Howe and his forces who wrote or spoke in favor of speech, speechreading, reading, and writing that won over the Commonwealth's legislative body. Also, as is well known, money speaks with great persuasion, and so Mr. John Clarke, a gentleman of influence, contributed to the Commonwealth $50,000 for the establishment of a school for the deaf in his home town of Northampton and with this, the die was cast. After six days of hearings and 236 pages of evidence and testimony the Legislature passed "An Act Concerning the Education of Deaf-Mutes" which included the establishment of the Clarke Institution for Deaf-Mutes at Northampton. The year was 1867.

With this Miss Harriet B. Rogers packed three carpetbags with her personals and two saratogas with school supplies. She then moved her school from Chelmsford to Northampton, orally cautioning her pupils to keep their little heads inside the carriage. Oral education for the deaf was unquestionably underway in the United States.

32

A.G. Bell and Language Instruction for the Young Prelingually Deaf Child 1872

The story of Alexander Graham Bell and his invention of the telephone is common knowledge. Not so common, however, is the knowledge of his having been a genuinely superb teacher of the deaf. This fact was not fully revealed until the observations of a very perceptive deaf educator, Mr. James Denison, first brought Bell's early instructional experiences to light.

Denison, an alumnus of the National Deaf-Mute College, had served as a teacher and later as the principal of The Kendall School. Each fall, a new crop of pupils would arrive at Kendall with the hopes of being prepared for entrance into the National Deaf-Mute College.

George Sanders comes to Kendall Green:

During the first weeks and months of the fall semester in the year 1882, Denison became aware of a most interesting 15-year-old prelingually deaf pupil named George Sanders. Young Sanders, although not possessed of any extraordinary academic attainments, did have a phenomenal command of the English language, which he used "with a freedom and accuracy quite exceptional in a congenital deaf-mute." (Editor's note to Bell, "Upon a Method," p. 124.)

Denison was so impressed that he brought the lad's linguistic ability to the attention of Dr. Edward Allen Fay, Vice-President of the College and editor of the *American Annals*. Dr. Fay, upon learning that boy's first teacher was Alexander Graham Bell of telephone fame and fortunately a man with whom he was well acquainted, immediately made a contact and then a request.

Dr. Bell agrees to explain his instructional procedure:

The request specifically was that Dr. Bell recollect and record the instructional procedures which he had employed some 10 years previously in introducing a very young George Sanders to the English language. Whatever the procedure had been, it had, indeed, made the English language a natural and viable medium of communication for the young man. In compliance with Fay's request, Bell replied with the following paper, which was subsequently featured in the January, 1883, issue of the *American Annals of the Deaf*, Vol. 28, pp. 124-139:

UPON A METHOD OF TEACHING LANGUAGE TO A VERY YOUNG CONGENITALLY DEAF CHILD

To the Editor of the American Annals of the Deaf and Dumb:

SIR: You have been kind enough to express the opinion that the readers of the *Annals* would be interested in knowing the method I adopted in educating a very young congenitally deaf child, who became my pupil in 1872, and who has since acquired a vernacular knowledge of the English language in its spoken and written forms.

This boy was only about five years old when his education was commenced, and the results obtained in his case during the first two years indicate that the education of congenitally deaf children might profitably be commenced at home, and that they might even acquire a vernacular knowledge of English—at least in its written form—before being sent to school.

The value of early home training in language cannot be overestimated. Our pupils, as a rule, do not enter school until after the age when children most readily acquire language. If they could commence their school course with even an imperfect and rudimentary knowledge of English, the labor of the teacher would be enormously reduced and the progress of the pupil immensely accelerated.

In the autumn of 1872 I became interested in the boy whose education forms the subject of this paper, and the following extract from one of my note-books will give an idea of the general plan which guided my first steps:

"October 1, 1872

"Master George S----, aged 5 years, became my pupil this morning.

"He was born totally deaf, and has never spoken a word in his life. He has never been to school, but has received private instruction for three weeks from Miss Fuller, principal of the Boston School for the Deaf and Dumb.

"He seems a fine, bright, intelligent boy, and there is no apparent defect in his vocal organs.

"For my own guidance, and for the information of friends I shall briefly sketch out the course I intend to pursue with him.

"It is well for a teacher not to burden himself with too many rules, but rather to grasp *general principles*, and to leave the details of instruction to be worked out by experience.

"I propose to divide his education into two great branches – one relating to articulation, the other to mental development.

"The method of teaching articulation has been explained at length in the *American Annals of the Deaf and Dumb* for January, 1872.

"The general principle is this: *The pronunciation of words and sentences is not to be attempted until the vocal organs have been well drilled on elementary sounds and exercises.* (Experience and reflection have led me to modify this principle.)

"While, then, the mouth is being brought under control by the use of the visible speech symbols, the mind is to be educated by ordinary letters. The pupil must learn to read and write.

"I believe that George Dalgarno [in his work entitled 'Didascalocophus, or the Deaf and Dumb Man's Tutor,' published in 1680 – see the *American Annals*, Vol. 9, pp. 15-64] has given us the true principle to work upon when he asserts that *a deaf person should be taught to read and write in as nearly as possible the same way that young ones are taught to speak and understand their mother tongue.*

"We should talk to the deaf child just as we do to the hearing one, with the exception that our words are to be addressed to his eye instead of his ear.

"Indeed, George Dalgarno carries his theory so far as to assert that the deaf infant would as soon come to understand written language as a hearing child does speech, 'had the mother or nurse but as nimble a hand as commonly they have a tongue!'

"The principles inculcated by Prendergast (in his 'Mastery of Languages,' 1864) and by Marcel (in his 'Study of Languages, or the Art of Thinking in a Foreign Language,' 1869, reviewed in the *Annals*, Vol. 14, pp. 193-204) would, if applied to deaf-mutes, point to the same result and to the same method of teaching.

"The principles of Froebel's Kindergarten method of teaching are applicable to deaf-mutes.

"Froebel believes that *the natural instinct of the child to play should be utilized in his education.*

"His ideas would seem to indicate that the successful teacher must appeal to the faculties of *imagination and imitation*, and encourage *self-activity* in his pupil.

"*I propose, then, to blend the principles of Dalgarno and Froebel – to familiarize the child with written language by means of play.*"

In pursuance of this plan the school-room was converted into a play-room, and language lessons were given through the instrumentality of toys and games.

I was fortunate in securing the co-operation of a very excellent teacher – Miss Abbie Locke, now Mrs. Stone, of St. Louis – with whose assistance George's education was carried on.

Every toy was labeled with its proper name. The different parts of the room, the articles of furniture, and the various objects in the room were also all labeled, so far as possible. Each window had pasted upon it a piece of paper on which was written the word "window;" so with the doors, mantel-piece, table, blackboard, etc., etc.

The words were written in ordinary script characters, with the letters slightly separated. Against one wall was a card-rack arranged to display from one to two hundred little cards, each about one inch square.

Upon these cards were written from time to time the names of his toys, and of all the different objects for which he had invented sign-names. Most of his playthings were kept locked up, and were only produced one or two at a time, so as to afford constant variety.

Word Exercises

1. Our exercises would commence somewhat as follows: George would make his appearance in the morning anxious for play – making vigorous signs for some of his most valued toys. For instance, he would fold his arms and beat his shoulders rapidly with his hands. This was his sign for "doll." The doll was accordingly produced, and his attention was directed to the word "doll" pasted upon the forehead. We compared this word with the words written upon the cards, to see who would first find that card with the word "doll" upon it. Of course in the beginning – to his chagrin – I would generally be the successful searcher. Having found the proper card, we would play with it a sort of game of hide-and-seek, which interested him exceedingly. He would turn away or shut his eyes while I replaced the card in the rack in some place to him unknown. The game consisted in finding it again.

Doll in hand, he would search for the card, comparing each written word with the word on the doll's forehead. He would shake his head gravely at each wrong word, and nod vigorously when he thought he had found the correct one.

When he made a mistake I pointed out the proper card and made fun of him. He was very sensitive to ridicule, and was generally ambitious to try again and again until he succeeded without my assistance. He was also much interested in my (pretended) unsuccessful efforts to find a card placed by him in the rack while my back was turned.

George seemed to enjoy this game exceedingly, but we rarely continued it for more than a few minutes at a time, and even then we constantly varied the names sought for, so as to avoid monotony.

In the beginning the cards were all blank, and the first day I filled in about half a dozen names, but required him to find only one card. Next day we sought not only for that card, but for one or two of the others. After the lapse of a few days he became pretty familiar with all the names, and then each day two or three new names were added, until he had quite an extensive collection of words at command.

2. When he became familiar with a few names I would get him to seek for the proper card without first consulting the label upon the toy. He would pick out some card and then compare it with the word pasted upon the toy. Great was his mortification when the two did not correspond, and great also was his triumph when they did.

I made a mental note of the names he learned by heart in this way, and then pretended not to understand his signs for the corresponding objects.

For instance, I remember that one morning he came down stairs in high spirits, very anxious to play with his doll. He frantically beat his shoulders with his hands, but I could not understand what he meant. I produced a toy-horse; but that was not what he wanted. A table; still he was disappointed. He seemed quite perplexed to know what to do, and evidently considered me very stupid. At last, in desperation, he went to the card-rack, and, after a moment's consideration, pulled out the word "doll" and presented it to me. It is needless to say that the coveted toy was at once placed in his possession. I always pretended to have great difficulty in understanding his signs when we were anywhere near the card-rack, so he soon became accustomed to pick out the words for any objects he desired.

3. The same plan was pursued at meals. A little card-rack was prepared for the dinner-table, so that he might have written words at hand for everything he required to eat or drink.

4. Another word exercise, pursued for a few minutes each day, consisted in the recognition of such words as "stand," "sit," "walk," "run," "jump," etc., which were written upon the black-board and illustrated by standing, sitting, walking, running, and jumping.

Sentence Exercises

The greater portion of our time was taken up – even from the first day – with the recognition of complete sentences, instead of single words.

The exercises appeared under two forms: (1) impromptu written conversation, and (2) regular sentence exercises.

1. The impromptu conversation was going on all the time. I constantly asked myself the question, "If George could hear, what would I say to him now?" and whatever came into my head I wrote. I kept on writing to him all the time until the blackboard was covered with writing and my arm ached.

I emphasized words to his eye, and grouped them together on the board as I would have grouped them in utterance, leaving gaps here and there where one would naturally pause in speaking. In a word, *I tried to exhibit to his eye all the relations that would have met his ear, could he have heard my speech.*

I believed thoroughly in the principle announced by Dalgarno that *it is the frequency with which words are presented to the mind that impresses them upon the memory,* and hence aimed at much writing as the accompaniment of everything we did.

I followed up my blackboard conversation by a liberal use of pantomime, bearing always in mind the general principle that I had formulated for myself, viz., that *the use of pantomime is to illustrate language, not to take its place.* In carrying out this principle, therefore, I always wrote first and acted afterwards – avoiding the converse.

As an example of these impromptu exercises, I will give an imaginary conversation just as I might have written it upon the board:

Specimen of Impromptu Conversation.

Now George I wouldn't **whip** that poor horse if I were you.
You should be **kind** and **gentle** to it.
Please don't whip it any **more.**
You will be **naughty** if you go on whipping it like that.
You **mustn't** whip it any more.
Now be a **good boy** and give the poor horse **something** to **eat**
That's right. Kiss it.
You're a **good boy** to pat the horse so gently
Give the doll a ride on the horse's back.
Take care! — or the **doll** will **fall off!**

&c., ad libitum.

2. Regular sentence exercises. These exercises formed a regular daily game, which could be varied *ad libitum*. A number of directions were written upon the blackboard which were to be acted out. The game consisted in distinguishing one direction from another.

For example, the following sentences might have been written:

Walk very slowly to the window.

Give the doll a drink of water.

Run round the table.

Go and look out of the window.

Make the doll dance.

Put the doll to bed.

We would then act out the sentences, one by one, and afterwards I would take a pointer and indicate one of the sentences at random for him to act out without assistance. Of course he would make frequent mistakes. For instance, when I pointed to the sentence, "Run round the table," he might proceed to give the doll an imaginary drink of water! Under such circumstances I would laugh at him, and write somewhat as follows: "No, that's not right; you are giving the doll a drink of water!!" I would then point to the sentence, "Give the doll a drink of water," and write, "That's what you did," and make fun of him.

This exercise would be varied by George playing the master while I became his pupil.

I would test his knowledge by occasionally acting out the wrong sentence, and it gave him great delight to correct me.

In this way he learned very readily to distinguish about half a dozen different sentences, partly from their position on the board, partly by their differences in length, and partly by the recognition of individual words.

At first, however, the sentences were not recognized independently of their position on the board, and as a general rule, by next day he had forgotten their meaning, excepting when they had been left on the board over night, so that they occupied the same relative positions as before.

Writing

He was extremely fond of these sentence exercises; but when he played the master, he was not contented with merely pointing at sentences that I had written – he wished to write them himself! This desire was forced upon my attention one day in the following manner: he took the chalk and scribbled all over the board, and *then made signs for me to act that out*! After consideration of the subject, I came to the conclusion that this was a clear indication that the time had come to teach him to write. The great difficulty in the way of doing this lay in the fact that at this time he did not know a single letter of the alphabet – he recognized words and sentences only as wholes.

I determined to make the experiment of teaching him to write sentences as wholes, and the result was as surprising as it was gratifying.

I commenced by writing on the board some directions he wished me to act out. After partially erasing this, so as to leave the writing faintly visible I placed the chalk in his hand and allowed him to trace over what I had written.

It is true that his first attempts resulted in rather ludicrous caricatures of the originals; but *he never forgot the meaning of a sentence he had traced over in this way a few times*.

The attempt to imitate my writing forced him to observe minutiae that had hitherto escaped his attention, so that sentences began to be recognized quite independently of their position on the board, and were remembered from day to day.

His imitation of my writing improved with practice, and soon became quite legible. I observed also that his comprehension of my impromptu writing seemed to improve at the same time, and he evidently experienced a desire to use words in his communication with others. He had not progressed sufficiently to be able to write without tracing, but he would often come into the school-room out of school hours for the purpose of taking cards from the card-rack to give to servants or friends to make them understand what he wished.

Spelling

The moment he evinced the independent desire to communicate with others by written words, I felt that the time had come to give him a means of forming written words for himself by teaching him his letters and a manual alphabet.

For this purpose I adopted the plan, recommended by George Dalgarno, of writing the alphabet upon a glove. The arrangement of the alphabet I adopted is shown in the following diagram:

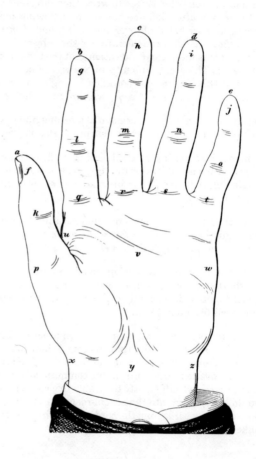

This glove I presented to him one morning as a new plaything. He put it on his left hand, and then went to the card-rack, as usual, and presented me with the word for some object he desired; we shall suppose the word "doll." I then covered up the word with the exception of the first letter, "d," and directed his attention to the glove. After a little searching he discovered the corresponding letter upon the glove. I then showed him the letter "o" on the card, and he soon found it on the glove; and so with the other letters.

After a little practice of this kind he became so familiar with the places of the letters that he no longer required to search, but pointed at once to the proper letter upon the glove. Every time he required a card from the card-rack I made his spell the word upon his fingers.

Occasionally I would test his memory by requiring him to spell the word while I held the card behind my back. When I became convinced that he knew the word by heart, I tore up the card.

In this way, one by one, all the cards disappeared from the rack. For a long time he was very proud of his glove, and was delighted to find that he could communicate with his parents and friends, and they with him, by simply pointing at the letters on his hand.

In communicating with me it was unnecessary for him to wear the glove, as we both remembered the places of the letters. I kept up the practice of writing to him, as before, but required him to spell the words upon his hand while I wrote them on the board. He soon became so expert that he could spell faster than I could write, and often finished his sentence by guessing what I was going to add before I had written more than two-thirds. When this stage had been reached I often used the manual alphabet with him, instead of writing. I took his hand in mine and touched the places of the letters upon his hand. He did not require to look; he could *feel* where he touched. He recognized the words in this way, however rapidly I spelled them upon his hand. As I had five fingers, I could touch five letters simultaneously, if I so desired, and a little practice enabled me to play upon his hand as one would play upon the keys of a piano, and quite as rapidly.

I could also give emphasis by pressure upon the fingers, and group the words together as they would be grouped in utterance, leaving pauses here and there, corresponding to the pauses made in actual speech.

The more I used with him this means of communciation, the more I rejoiced in the fact that I had decided to employ an alphabet addressed to the sense of touch, instead of sight. It left his eye free to observe the expression of my face and the actions and objects which formed the subject of our conversation.

The general principle upon which I was working was to speak to him by written words, as I would have spoken to a hearing child by speech, and I believe (with George Dalgarno) that he would in time come to understand written language by the same process that children learn to understand their mother tongue.

It seemed to me that hearing children, in acquiring their vernacular, derived great assistance from the free use of the eye as an interpreter of words addressed to the ear, and that therefore my pupil would derive similar assistance from his eye, as the interpreter of words addressed to the sense of touch.

In addition, therefore, to the "regular sentence exercises" and "impromptu written conversation," I would talk to him a great deal upon his hand.

We would go to the window and chat by the half hour at a time about what was going on in the street. At night also I would frequently visit him in his bed-room for the purpose of satisfying myself that I could communicate with him as readily in the dark as by day.

His progress now became very rapid, and he commenced to talk to me by words, instead of signs. I placed no other pressure upon him than my pretend difficulty in understanding his gestures, and allowed him to express himself in any way he chose.

From the moment we commenced to employ the manual alphabet I myself abstained from the use of any other gestures than those I would have employed in talking to a hearing child under the same circumstances. My pretended difficulty in understanding his signs increased from day to day, so as to force him more and more to attempt to express thoughts by English words. I would assist him in this by translating his signs for him from time to time and making him repeat the sentence independently upon his fingers.

In all our conversations I was careful to employ natural and complete sentences, but his first attempts at independent expression (like the first independent utterances of a hearing child) consisted of isolated words.

The use of the glove alphabet was so little noticeable that I could talk to him very freely in a crowd without attracting the attention of others. I took him to Barnum's museum and talked to him all the time the lions were being fed, and I am sure that no one among the spectators had the slightest suspicion that the boy was deaf.

From the moment he learned the alphabet I gave him regular writing sessions, so that he should form his letters properly and write with ease. I then made him keep writing materials about him, and encouraged him to use them constantly in communicating with friends.

Before six months had elapsed I frequently found the floor littered with scraps of paper that he had used in this way, and I am sorry that it did not occur to me at the time to preserve them for future reference. It was not until late in 1873 that I made the attempt to collect a few scraps of this description, and those that are preserved in my note-book possess great interest.

I shall conclude this paper by the following specimens of his composition, which will show that at little more than six years of age this congenitally deaf boy had acquired a vernacular knowledge of the English language sufficient to enable him to communicate by writing with hearing persons.

Specimens of Composition

1. July 1st, 1873. Scrap found upon the floor in his father's house in Haverhill:

Gordon is sick to Haverhill in the other Room in the sofa.

2. August 14th, 1873. Letter to his mother, written from Brantford, Canada:

Dear Mama,

The small cat loves the large cat. Mary will go to Haverhill. Grandma S----- will go to Haverhill. I will go home in the train and let I will sleep in the cars. Mama and Nat and I will drive in Haverhill. The many flags is in Haverhill. I will go upstairs in Haverhill to flags. Richards and John and nurse and I and Mr. Bell will go home. After breakfast I will go to see Freddy. is sleep. I will Eat fast. I love Gordon and auntie.

3. November 3rd, 1873. Scrap found upon the floor:

Are these mine? there to see the letters? if you please? Yes Dear Mr. Bell.

4. November 4th, 1873. Two scraps containing a conversation between George and myself:

First scrap

Mr. Bell. I think you are tired and *hot* now, so we will be *quiet* and *rest* now. What does "rest" mean?
George. "Rest" means stop.
Mr. Bell. Yes, dear. It means "stop" or "still".
George. Or "wait".
Mr. Bell. Yes.
George. Please may I put a your handkerchief and be like an old woman.

Note in my record-book: "After playing for a while he remembered that his grandmamma had made fun of him for pretending to be a woman, so he wrote:"

Second scrap

I am not put on my towel on my head and be like an old woman and Grandma said not now Grandma will be so very *sorry* now.

5. November 23d, 1873. Letter written by George to his mamma in Haverhill. No person saw this letter until it was finished. Everything in it, even to the emphasizing of certain words, is his own. The omission of capital letters can be traced to the too frequent use of the manual alphabet in place of writing:

"this is *sunday* to-day & to-morrow will be Monday. the people are going to *church*. Mary and Nat are grown by and bye. (Mary and Nat, his brother and sister, will grow up bye and bye.) *john* is not sick now. I *love* daniel now. I am going to *bed* bye and bye. the kitten is alive. (The kitten had been crushed behind a book-case and nearly killed.) *Mr. Bell* is *reading the book* but papa and mama are *not* coming to be glad and I matched the lamp on fire. I looked at my little watch from my ka. ("Ka" was the name for George's nurse.) we will not drive with Mr. Bell. I will say please may I be excused. (He had just been taught to use this expression when he wished to leave the dinner-table before others had finished.) grandpa is tired to drive very fast home. we are walk very fast and go to franks horse and drive the colt on wednesday to see the eggs and hens and the kitten and hay and cracker are on dog is not eat the kitten fall to die to the grave. and I am well and I think that Mr. Bell is sick to be tired and go to Boston to the house to go to bed to die to lie down on my pocket to put the pretty to keys. (This referred to some incident with which I was not acquainted. He went through a pantomime about it, showing there was some definite idea he wished to express, but no one could understand what he meant.) I looked at the kitten fast asleep on my straw. dan is going to the cow milk on Monday.

your loving

from George

6. December 14th, 1873. Another original letter from George to his mamma:

Salem
Sunday Dec. 14

"My Dear Mama

"I think that Mr. Bell is sorry that I wrote that to say My Dear Mama. (When George had written "Salem, Sunday, Dec. 14", he attracted my attention that I might see that he was going to write a letter. As he seemed in doubt to whom to address it, I suggested that he should begin "Dear Mr. Bell"; but he wrote "My Dear Mama". Upon which I looked very sorry, pretended to cry, and went out of the room, much to his amusement. When he was about half through his letter, I returned and read a book till he had finished.)

"I am sorry that papa and mama are not coming back now. I think that Dan is going to church on sunday with Ellen and Maggie now. By and bye Maggie will stay here with the house. Dan and I went out to the cow milked at the fair. It was dark and it is light. grandma is afraid but I will not go but tomorrow. Ellen is not afraid to see the cow too. I may not kick the cow with be sorry not glad to be still on sunday but bye and bye mary and nat is going to bed. Bye and bye Dan will cut. ("Will saw firewood.") but grandma is reading on Sunday. I think grandma has gone to church with Mr. Bell. Mr. Bell's beard is coming now. (George had seen me before I had shaved.) is like are the calendar. I am the deers in Boston. (He had been pretending to be a deer.) The snow is stopping. The rain is not well but rain is sick but the snow is well. Mr. Bell is reading too. Grandma is not reading but after dinner it is the sun too. Haverhill is very far away over here. are papa stay in Haverhill.

7. March 26th, 1874. Letter to Mrs. H-----, written without any assistance:

Salem, Mass
March 26th 1874

My Dear Grandma H------

I have been to the stable. I am very Glad that Mary will come back
tomorrow. I loves Grandma H------. I love Grandpa H------ too and I have
finished school before dinner. I have new wheel barrow and there is
Grandma's pig in the stable. Maggie is not going to church but maggie
is going to church on Sunday. Mr. Bell is writing to you, but I am busy
to write to you too. I have a new doll. The dolls are sitting in Mary's
chair here. Nat has a old bird and the new piano. (a toy bird and a toy
piano) Mr. Bell has a new piano in Boston and play with me and Lilly.
(Mr. Bell had a new piano in Boston *a long time ago* and played for
me and Lilly.) I am laughing at you. I am not laughing at Grandpa
H------. I have been the ladies last night and many days. (There were
a number of ladies here a few days ago.) I love Maggie. I love Maggie
dear pet. I must not go near the horse because the horse is large and
I may go near the cow. I slept in the train from Canada. but now I am
in Salem. I will go to Haverhill in a few days. Isa is upstairs sewing.
She is not finished sewing.

Your loving

George T. S-----."

Bell's debt to Dalgarno:

Young Alexander Graham Bell, having been ever alert to any and
all ideas relative to the teaching of English to deaf children, obviously found himself in debt to his ancient countryman, George
Dalgarno. It will be recalled how Dalgarno's work *Didascalocophus*
of 1680 had been lost and then retrieved in 1834. Through the interest and efforts of one Mr. Dugald Stewart it was republished by
the Maitland Club of Edinburgh. The essay then some 40 years
later found itself in the pages of the *American Annals of the Deaf*,
Vol. 9, pp. 14-64.

Dalgarno's concepts in application:

The essay, while fascinating because of its antiquity, was also a
meritorious piece of thinking. Bell perceived this fact and instead
of disregarding it because it was 192 years old decided to adopt it

and adapt it to the specific needs of his little pupil. Alexander Graham Bell's work with young George Sanders extended over a period of only three years; however, this point does accentuate the importance of *early* consistent and persistent visual exposure to and usage of *orthographic* language as essentials for the acquisition of that language.

Dr. Fay, in concluding his editor's note to Bell's presentation, wrote:

> Much of the method described is no less applicable to a class of pupils than to a single pupil; and we have no doubt that in the hands of capable and devoted teachers it would go far toward solving the great problem of the mastery of the English language by the congenitaly deaf.

(See Appendix 8.)

33

E. M. Gallaudet and His
Thoughts on English Acquisition
for the Deaf
1868-1876

The first 10 years of the National Deaf-Mute College were essentially experimental in terms of determining the nature and scope of collegiate learning to be given young deaf men. The students who were enrolled each fall were largely graduates of the various state residential schools for the deaf. The majority of the college's student population was adventitiously or postlingually deaf. These particular students, of course, had few problems relative to reading and assimilating printed text materials. Similarly, they were quite adept and often even superior at expressing themselves in written language. There were, obviously, few scholastic problems among them.

Prelingual deafness and its attendant problems:

That portion of the college's population, however, which was termed congenitally or prelingually deaf offered the faculty its greatest instructional problem. The problem, of course, was relative to receptive and expressive English usage. It was, indeed, so serious that Dr. E. M. Gallaudet and his colleagues gave a considerable portion of their time and thought to its possible resolution.

The intuitive theory of Vaisse, the French educator, who had taught at the New York Institution some 30 years previously, had made its mark on the minds of young progressive educators of that day. The theory, in practice, it will be recalled, emphasized the intuitive procedure of teaching language, i.e., teaching English through the use of English as opposed to the then accepted use of methodical signs.

Vaisse's procedure practiced:

David E. Bartlett, a proponent of Vaisse's procedure, had practiced it with considerable success in his Bartlett Family School through the 1850's.

Then, there was the phenomenal success of Dr. Samuel Gridley Howe in his work with the deaf-blind girl, Laura Bridgman. She had been led into learning through an exclusive English program of Braille and fingerspelling. Thus, with these various instructional precedents, their rationale, and their positive evidences, the direction for English acquisition for the deaf was clearly indicated to Gallaudet.

An additional problem was created, however, by the many schools for the deaf which were still bound by the "tried and true" instructional medium of sign language. Many of the graduates of these same schools were, as previously indicated, candidates for the National Deaf-Mute College and were arriving inadequately prepared in the all-essential area of basic English communication. E. M. Gallaudet, therefore, assumed the diplomatically "touchy" task of re-educating the institutions in what for most of them was a "new doctrine."

E. M. Gallaudet tackles the problem:

The opportunity to introduce the "English through the use of English" concept came in May, 1868. The occasion was the first meeting of the Conference of Principals to be held since the beginning of the "War between the States" in 1861. Gallaudet's presentation was entitled "The American System of Deaf-Mute Instruction – Its Incidental Defects and Their Remedies." In the course of his paper, he reviewed the educational developments of the past, both at home and abroad, and then abruptly dived "head first" into the subject of his concern.

Teachers and officers use signs far too freely; pupils are allowed to use them long after they might employ the finger alphabet in many of their communications.

In how many of our schools are teachers in the habit of communicating by manual spelling new facts, in the shape of miniature lectures, couched in language they are sure their pupils can comprehend? How often are pupils assembled in pleasant social gathering wherein all conversation is required to be in finger spelling? How general is the rule that all favors of the Principal, asked by pupils of over three years standing, must be asked in correctly spelled language or be denied? How often is the brake of dactylology applied to that well known ever moving propensity to talk in the school-room? Is it not true that in a great majority of cases, the actual use by the pupil of the forms of his vernacular is confined to the hours of school and study, and that even here signs are largely employed at times when they might be dispensed with? When speaking children are sent to French or German schools for the purpose of acquiring the languages spoken by the teachers of those schools, are they not expected after a short time, to make the new languages the media of communication with all around them? Why then should not the case be so with the deaf and dumb? In coming to our institutions the learning of the sign language, is not their most important task. Their lives are not in a majority of cases to be passed among deaf-mutes, but in association with speaking people, and their great object is to acquire a means of communicating accurately with the world in general. The failure to do this, manifest in too many of the graduates of our institutions, stands forth as the gravest practical defect of our system, and is largely attributable, in the opinion of the writer, to the cause just recited, which may so readily be removed. (Gallaudet, "American System," p. 155.)

While the general reaction of school administrators to Gallaudet's proposal was to receive it politely, it is conceivable that they did not want to create a professional hassle, in view of the amicable spirit which dominated this first united gathering of educators from the North and the South.

Two years later, in August, 1870, at the Convention of American Instructors of the Deaf in Indianapolis, Gallaudet extemporaneously voiced the same thoughts once again relative to the idea of schools for the deaf minimizing their use of sign language as an instructional mode.

. . . He even went so far as to say that, in his judgment, the sign language was a "dangerous thing" in an institution for deaf-mutes.

The announcement of this opinion called forth decided condemnation from several members of the Convention, who expressed their amazement at the suggestion of such an idea. One member, in particular, honored in his profession for a life long devotion to the cause of deaf-mute education, was especially earnest in his protest against the new doctrine. He was "astonished that a son of the father of deaf-mute education in America could call the sign language 'a nuisance' or claim that its use in the class-room was 'pernicious.' " (Editor's note to Gallaudet, "Sign Language," p. 26.)

Gallaudet was obviously taken aback and hurt by the reaction of his several colleagues, and he denied having used the words "a nuisance" or "pernicious" in reference to the sign language. ("Sign Language," p. 26.) Because his impromptu remarks had perhaps been misunderstood and had created such a furor in the Convention, Gallaudet determined to write an article for the *American Annals of the Deaf*, which would clearly state his idea relative to the language of signs.

E. M. Gallaudet's possible "inner conflicts":

In the January, 1871, issue of the *American Annals*, E. M. Gallaudet's position paper on the language of signs made its appearance under the title "Is the Sign Language Used to Excess in Teaching Deaf-Mutes?" In recalling Gallaudet's family background and upbringing, one may understand to some degree the inner conflict which he experienced between what he instinctively loved as an innate part of his heritage, the language of signs, as opposed to the cool and objective logic which resulted in his most reasonable objections to the instructional use of this mode. This inner conflict between emotion and reason was to place Gallaudet time and again in the equivocal position of being personally at odds with his own professional convictions.

Gallaudet holds his position:

In his *Annals* article, Gallaudet expresses his appreciation of the history of sign language and also his appreciation of its force, clearness, and beauty. For all of this, however, it is that

in the *abuse* of signs, and by this is meant their excessive use, may be found one of the gravest defects under which our national system of teaching the deaf is laboring. (*Ibid.*)

Gallaudet then quotes from an article written by the honored and revered Luzerne Rae, a long-time teacher and first editor of the *American Annals*. Rae had written back in 1853 that *"a too abundant and too constant use of signs to the neglect of dactylology and written language, is the grand practical error of the American institutions of the deaf and dumb."*

Strengthened with this precedent for the idea, Gallaudet writes,

> If the aphorism of Holy Writ, "By their fruits ye shall know them," may be properly applied to schools for the deaf and dumb; and if the main objective of such schools be to place their pupils in intelligent and free communciation with hearing and speaking persons through the medium of written language, then it must be admitted, that, with the great mass of so-called educated deaf-mutes, the great end of their school training is far from being attained.

> That this failure is, in large measure, attributable to the cause suggested, will, it is believed, be seen by any teacher who will trace the course of sign language in our institutions. (*Ibid.*, p. 29.)

Gallaudet thus places the onus for the linguistic predicament of prelingually deaf children upon the schools for the deaf. He then states:

> In the social intercourse of pupil and teacher, the sign language affords, probably, the easiest, and, certainly the laziest, means of communication. But would that English boy hope ever to master the French language, who should always speak English with his French teacher?

> In the mingling of deaf-mutes with each other, undoubtedly the sign language is the channel of thought expression, into which they most naturally glide. But would not the use of dactylology, even though it be at first under compulsion, and adopted reluctantly, tend to fit them better for those associations into which they must inevitably come after leaving the institution? (*Ibid.*, pp. 29-30.)

Re: The "natural order of thought":

Gallaudet also refers to the "natural order of thought" in sign language, which places modifiers after their nouns and the negatives *not* or *never* after positive statements to indicate negations. This reversal tendency represents his chief objection to the use of the "natural language of signs," which in this last quarter or so of the 20th Century has been popularly termed "American Sign Language" (ASL).

Referring to the average prelingually deaf person, Gallaudet writes,

> ... until the deaf-mute can think freely in conventional language and expresses his thoughts fluently and correctly in the same, *every instance of the use, by him or to him, of the language of signs in its natural order, impedes his progress toward the great end and object of his education.* (*Ibid.*, p. 30.)

(It is commonly observed even in this modern day some 100 years later that many prelingually hearing-impaired students and even their teachers, in their endeavors to use what is known as "Signed English," slip unconsciously into the omissions and reversals of natural sign language or ASL.)

In concluding his article "Is the Sign Language Used to Excess?" Gallaudet's answer is definitely in the affirmative. He then

> earnestly commends the subject to the readers of the *Annals*, and hopes that this imperfect presentation may elicit practical suggestions, and lead to practical results, which may be for the real advancement of the cause dear to us all. (*Ibid.*, p. 33.)

Gallaudet receives faculty support:

The request for a renewed emphasis upon English usage, reading, and writing, in schools for the deaf became a reocurring theme in the bulletins and articles on college preparation issued from the National Deaf-Mute College. One such article was written by a deaf member of the college faculty and alumnus, Professor Amos G. Draper. The piece appeared in the *American Annals* for April, 1876:

> "Preparation for the College Course"
>
> At the present time it may be said that no student can expect to enter the Freshman class who does not show himself fitted to cope with its difficulties.
>
> So rarely does a student come thus prepared that there is little danger of error in advising all to seek entrance to the *Advanced Preparatory* class, which is one year beneath the Freshman. No knowledge of Latin or of algebra is required for admission to this class. The student, therefore, in perfecting himself in the elementary branches – arithmetic, political and physical geography, the history of the United States, and the elements of natural philosophy – will gain time in which to extend his knowledge and command of English, the first requisite to success. Let him be persuaded to practice constantly in and out of the classroom, the art of putting his thoughts in connected language; as far as possible to banish signs, and express himself by speech, the pencil, or the manual alphabet. (*American Annals of the Deaf*, Vol. 19, p. 73.)

It was, of course, in this year 1876, the year of "Custer's Last Stand" and the year in which A. G. Bell received his telephone patent, that a little-known young man, Zenas Freeman Westervelt, resigned his position as a teacher of the New York School for the Deaf and moved to the city of Rochester, New York. Dr. E. M. Gallaudet's plea for improved English learning opportunities for the deaf had not been in vain. (See Appendix 9.)

Chapter Nine
New Directions in American Education of the Deaf

34

Westervelt and His
Rochester Method
1878-1917

Author's Note:

The following episode on "Westervelt and His Rochester Method" was written during the academic year 1939-1940, during this author's second year of teaching at the Rochester School for the Deaf. So impressed was he at that time with the school's comprehensive English learning environment for deaf children, that he set about to make a thorough study of Dr. Westervelt's personal notes and papers relative to his educational philosophy and instructional procedures. The result of this effort was eventually published in 1942 under the title *A Revaluation of the Rochester Method.* The material which follows originally appeared as the first chapter of that work.

The fact that Zenas Freeman Westervelt had possibly been influenced by educators of the deaf reaching back in time to Dalgarno, Braidwood, Bartlett, and a host of others did not occur at that time to the zealous, young educational writer in Rochester simply because he never heard of them. It may be said, however, that his *then* prevailing condition of youth and lack of knowledge was eventually remediated by time and considerable experience.

Interestingly enough, the piece which follows sets neatly into our historical framework as an integral part of the ever-evolving story of education of the deaf.

The observations and commentaries in the episode relative to the *then current* middle-20th-Century practices in education of the deaf may give one an interesting measure for determining the extent of our latter-day advances in educating hearing-impaired children.

THE COLUMBUS CONVENTION OF 1878

The Rochester Method as originally conceived is deserving of a reconsideration and revaluation in the light of educational progress made over the last 60 years. In 1878, when young Zenas Westervelt went to Columbus, Ohio, to attend the Convention of Educators of the Deaf, he carried in his briefcase a carefully prepared paper stating and defending a very new idea regarding the education of deaf children. There is no doubt but what he felt somewhat nervous at the idea of bringing his plan before the Convention. In that day it was generally supposed that only the gray and venerable masters of long experience were the ones sufficiently qualified to make proposals. Another reason why he may have felt a trifle uneasy was because his plan of instruction was exceedingly different from that which employed the sign language as its medium of instruction. As a matter of fact, his plan excluded the sign language altogether. He was not particularly sure how that would rest with the Convention, for the sign language was conceded to be the only sensible and logical means of teaching and communicating with the deaf. Of course, there were a few women up in New England who thought it possible to teach deaf children to speak, but that idea in itself was thought to be a little short of ridiculous. Even so, young Westervelt found himself sympathetic and quite interested in their efforts.

Finally, in Columbus at the Convention, all the programs moved along as scheduled. After an illuminating address on "The Legitimate Use of Pantomime in the Education of the Deaf," there followed a paper on "The Disuse of Signs" by Z. F. Westervelt of

Rochester, New York. Something new for the Convention! The "disuse of signs!" Imagine it! Zenas Westervelt stood up and proceeded to read his paper. The ears and eyes of the Convention were on him as he began.

> At the Western New York Institution, at Rochester, an experiment has been initiated, within the past year, that promises more satisfactory results than have hitherto been attained. At as early a day as the present habit of our pupils renders practicable, it is our purpose to require all conversation, all communication be carried on by means of proper English words, either spelled by the manual alphabet, or spoken, or written. The suppression of conventional signs which thus devolves upon us, has been zealously undertaken by teachers and pupils. . . . All that I shall attempt is to satisfy this Convention that the Institution which I represent acted with moderation and careful consideration which the importance of the change demanded.

> The majority of our profession, we concede, favor the use of the language of conventional signs, not only as a means of conversation, but as a medium of instruction and mental development. In this you are sustained by Dr. Fournie in his *Essai de Psychologie*. . . . ("Disuse of Signs," p. 165.)

Let us interrupt young Mr. Westervelt at this point and interpret his words in our present-day understanding. Regarding his last statement we can say that a great number in our profession do not object to the use of conventional signs in conversation but the majority do object to signs as a means of instruction except as a possible last resort to reach the mind of a very slow child. Going on:

> Opposed to this principle, various articles have appeared in favor of the "Natural method of teaching English." "If we would teach the deaf to write English." These articles have been from the pens of some of the ablest thinkers and most successful teachers engaged in our work. . . . *Their attention is given chiefly to school-room work, leaving the children to acquire what language habits they may outside of school.* [The italics are the present author's.] (*Ibid.*)

There are few educators of the deaf today who are not in complete agreement with the above. The italicized words are as true today as they were when first written. From four to six hours a day the average deaf child is held to expressing himself in English and the rest of the time he spends in violating every language principle he has ever learned. Some people would call this kind of education a waste of time.

Most of the points brought out in Westervelt's paper are refutations of the arguments in behalf of instruction through sign language. This, of course, is no longer considered a professional issue. The points do, however, contain sound reasons for the use of the manual alphabet as an acceptable means of instruction and communciation.

> The best political economists are generally agreed that there cannot be two standards of value at the same time. The baser currency introduced into circulation drives out the more valuable and becomes the sole standard of value and medium of exchange. It is equally true that two languages at the same time cannot be instruments of thought and the media of communication.

> It must be confessed that . . . we have ignored this fact, and have allowed signs to be the currency used for carrying on the commerce of ideas. By this the English language has been to too great an extent *retired* from circulation.

This apt analogy corroborates the idea of the preceding quotation.

> We admit that the English language has its difficulties for the deaf. We have tried to teach it as a dead language, by means of grammatical rules and exercises, and have practically failed. . . . The English language was meant to be spoken. Voice modulation, rhetorical pauses, accentuation, the grouping together of words that are connected in thought and uttering them as one, the rapidity or slowness of utterance varying with the nature of the thought to be expressed – all these, together with the appropriate facial expression, are as truly a part of our language as are the words and constructions which we employ. . . . English must be taught chiefly by means of manual alphabet. If our pupils are to master the language, we must carefully attend to every means which helps to give correct force to the words we use. In a word, we must cultivate elocution in spelling. The soul must speak as well as the lips or fingers. In order to gain control of this great engine of human thought, the English tongue, the deaf must learn to accompany every expression with its appropriate feeling, giving to the fingers every assistance that is given to voice. (*Ibid.*, p. 171.)

Young Mr. Westervelt thus concluded his paper on "The Disuse of Signs." He sat down satisfied, having expressed what he knew to be an innovation. After some discussion in which his idea was well trimmed by the "old guard," the following statement was kindly made by Dr. Isasc Lewis Peet.

> Mr. President, it seems to me that the last speaker has struck the keynote of this whole matter. [The previous speaker, Mr. Carroll, laid down a criterion by which new methods must be judged.] It seems to me we ought to feel very grateful to Mr. Westervelt for the kind of spirit in which he comes forward to make an experiment in behalf of the whole profession. If this experiment is a successful one, and by means of that we raise the deaf to a higher knowledge of language, it is our duty to thank him. It is now our duty to bid him Godspeed, and yet I know the man well enough to believe that if, at the end of a reasonable period, this experiment is not a successful one, he will return to his old method. (*Ibid.*, p. 182.)

This was the formal introduction of the Rochester Method to the educators of the deaf. It was, of course, in the beginning looked upon as nothing more than an interesting experiment.

THE BERKELEY CONVENTION OF 1886

After persistent effort on the part of the teachers and supervisors to bring the English language into its own right as the vernacular of the pupils, a report was made by Mr. Westervelt at the summer Convention in Berkeley, California. The year was 1886.

> At that time, the profession especially wanted testimony . . . of the experiment entered upon by the Rochester School eight years before, and to the method by which the result was accomplished. The Superintendent stated that English had practically become the only language used in the school. It might be occasionally a pupil would be sent to him because he had been seen to make a sign, as at this time every one who was seen to make a sign was sent to the Superintendent, though earlier in the development of the "experiment," it was only the persistent sign maker who was sent to the office. (Halpen, *Rochester School*, p. 9.)

This practice was continued over many years. The entire staff was inspired by their leader and worked accordingly for greater language accomplishment.

> The services of no teacher, officer, or employee who failed habitually to use good English with the pupils could be retained by the school. Everyone was expected to use English and the positiveness of this expectation and its persistency accomplished the object. English thus became the only language understood by a considerable portion of the pupils. (*Ibid.*, p. 10.)

THE MT. AIRY CONVENTION OF 1896

In 1896, the American Association to Promote the Teaching of Speech to the Deaf held its summer convention at Mt. Airy, Philadelphia, Pa. In the *Report of the Proceedings* under the title of "Some Notable Benefactors of the Deaf in America," there appeared the following:

> A method that may be styled the Rochester Method, from the Institution in which it has its rise, and in which it has been for twenty years persistently practiced, entirely discards the language of signs as being detrimental to deaf young in acquiring a knowledge of language and facility in its use. It insists upon the English language expressed by means of manual alphabet, writing and speech. To one who has been

accustomed to the vivacious and animated conversation carried on by the deaf through the medium of gesture expression, this would seem an uninteresting and insipid mode of procedure, but observation of the pupils of the Rochester School shows that they do not so regard it, they evince no desire for the sign language, finding the English language, whether spoken or spelled, quite sufficient for their requirements in the school room, social life, in the shops, the dining room, the debating society, the prayer meeting, on the street, in chapel, and on the playground. They have frequent opportunity of resorting to gesture expression if they feel so inclined, but they have no such desire, and pride themselves on using the language of their parents and friends, and regard with disdain one of their number who is betrayed into the use of signs. The officers of the Rochester School, several of whom have been connected with other institutions where the sign language was the method of instruction, are enthusiastic in their advocacy of this method of instructing the deaf, for which they claim the advantage and the credit of teaching English by the use of English. ("Some Notable Benefactors," p. 47.)

. . . The Rochester Method includes the teaching of speech to the deaf, which forms a very important factor in the work of the school room.

The Report continues,

Z. F. Westervelt, LL.D., is entitled to very great credit for the persistence with which he has clung to and insisted upon the use of this method in the Western New York Institution, of which school from its incipiency he has been the superintendent, and to him is due the credit of proposing and bringing to the attention of the profession this excellent method. (*Ibid.,* p. 48.)

The "experiment" of 1878 had succeeded. Interesting it is to compare the attitudes of the two conventions with 20 years intervening. The tribute to Dr. Westervelt was well deserved and his faith in the ability of deaf children justified.

DR. BELL'S ESTIMATE

A fact of considerable significance is that Dr. Alexander Graham Bell was a frequent visitor to the Rochester School and that he followed its growth and progress with great interest. The following newspaper account records Dr. Bell's first visit in 1887.

"Dr. Bell, what is the result of your examination of the system of instruction practiced in the School for the Deaf in Rochester?"

"Well, gentlemen, you should be proud of the fact, that in your fair city is one of the best disciplined and most admirably conducted institutions in the country. Superintendent Westervelt is a man thoroughly fitted for the work, and he has inaugurated the most effective system in existence, of training the deaf. One specific point that I did not examine was the conditions of the powers of articulation. In the majority of schools, the children are taught what is known as the sign language – that is, the language is made known to and signified by them through gestures." (*Union and Advertiser,* March 18, 1887, Rochester, N.Y.)

Although modern schools for the deaf do not use sign language as a general means of instruction, many of them do permit the use of sign language outside of the classrooms, thereby losing most valuable opportunities for natural language development.

This [signs] interferes with the progress of the child in the acquisition of the English language. In the oral schools, the English language is limited in its use because of the indistinctness of the movement of the lips, which does not give the young pupil as satisfactory a medium of communication as a gesture or sign language. I anticipated great results theoretically from the methods in operation at this Rochester institution, but I did not for a moment expect that the pupils had acquired such a knowledge of written English as they have shown themselves to possess. I selected five pupils, three boys and two girls, aged ten and nine years. I propounded to them questions in writing, to which they gave written answers which astounded me. Their replies were so mature and intelligent that I was fairly bewildered with amazement. I have traveled a great deal and have seen a great many schools for the deaf, but never in all my experience have I seen displayed such remarkable intelligence and such genuine precocity. . . . They gave such straightforward answers and easily understood replies to my questions that I am free to declare that the system of the entire and distinct use of the English language and the abolition of the sign language is the best method that can be used. My inquiries were mainly directed to children who were born deaf, and to this particular type of deaf person have I devoted my attention. I was especially pleased to see the application of the kindergarten system here, which I consider admirable in in its main features and arrangement. To Prof. Westervelt belongs the credit of introducing and practicing this system among the deaf.

Prof. Westervelt had made absolute demonstration of the fact that children who are born deaf can be taught the English language without the use of signs or gestures. This is particularly gratifying to me as well as to all others who are interested in this subject. I think the use of the sign language will go entirely out of existence very soon. (*Ibid.*)

We might interrupt Dr. Bell at this point in noting how far his prognostication of the fate of sign language went awry. The fact of the matter is that today sign language is as much the chief means of social intercourse among the deaf as it ever was. The use of English is the exception and not the rule. Because of this there is an insistence on the part of deaf leaders and certain educators of the deaf for a more careful and exact usage of signs. This is well enough, but it fails to further the cause of English for the deaf, which is the chief concern of both leaders and educators alike. Dr. Bell continuing:

> I think Prof. Westervelt deserves great credit for having established this peculiar method and having put it into practice, especially when he has such odds to contend against, nearly every teacher in the country having been opposed to his system. Prof. Westervelt has a complete mastery of the sign language and he deserves special credit for having overcome any temptation that might naturally have possessed him to resort to the use of gestures by reason of his perfect knowledge of them. (*Ibid.*)

DR. GILBERT O. FAY'S REPORT

For another early appraisal of the Rochester Method we may read the report of Dr. Gilbert O. Fay. In part he stated:

> The interest of such a report arises from the fact that the sign language is, and has been for ten years, wholly unused by officers and teachers, and nearly so by the pupils themselves. "The most important thing at school is that we must not make signs, but spell all the time, so that we may learn English as fast as we can. Those who make signs cannot learn English language and cannot be as smart as those who spell all the time" was the remark of a pupil in conversation with the examiner. The sentiment of the better class of pupils seemed to be that to make signs is to be ignorant, foreign and irreligious. The Principal informed me that twenty-five of the older pupils, who in vacation meet other deaf people educated elsewhere, are inclined upon occasion to use the sign language. But I saw no indication of it anywhere, nor did I see any consideralbe semi-signing, spelling fringed. All under twelve years of age carry their hands behind them in going to and returning from meals and school. The boys of all ages in going to and returning from their playground did not raise a hand except to spell, and during games both players and bystanders spelled out all they had to say. The severe punishment of a balking streetcar horse, lasting five minutes, was talked up by a group of girls wholly and only by spelling. Officers and employees, except when they spoke, which was not often, communicated with pupils by spelling universally and always. In chapel and in schoolroom, at the table, and in the evening study, in playrooms and out of doors, in all commands and explanations in all the small talk of the day, I saw, in the main, but one language – spelling. The suggested possibility of finger weariness elicited from a pupil a prompt denial, emphasized by an incredulous smile. Officers and teachers, however, frequently accompanied spelling with speech for the benefit of the speechreaders. I was impressed with the large vocabulary, the lengthy sentences, and the elevated diction of all the language in the chapel, in the schoolroom, and everywhere. All language was intelligible, and I saw no lack of comprehension. Expert spellers had about the pace of deliberate speech. At the Sunday school; at a subsequent meeting of the "Silent Workers;" at an evening prayer meeting; at the Lambda Phi Phi, a debating society of thirty members; at an evening

entertainment, when "The Courtship of Miles Standish" was elegantly dramatized before a crowded audience from the city, there was no
introduction whatever of the sign language. (Fay, "A Week at Rochester,"
p. 241.)

These reports of Dr. Bell and Dr. Fay enable one to see a picture
of the Rochester Method as it was viewed in its early days by two
well-known leaders in the field of education for the deaf.

J. HEIDSIEK ON THE ROCHESTER METHOD

Possibly one of the most outstanding educators of the deaf in the
latter part of the 19th Century and yet probably the least known
today is J. Heidsiek of the Breslau Institution of Prussia. Heidsiek
was a strong opponent of the German (Pure Oral) Method of instruction which dominated the schools of the Empire. Ardent in
his beliefs, he wrote articles condemning the educational practices
which were generally accepted throughout Germany. The argument
both for and against him took on international proportions, and
it was not long until the educators of the United States joined in
the fray.

Heidsiek's beliefs, in contrast with those held by the proponents
of the German Method, were well received in the United States by
a great number of American educators of the deaf. Heidsiek, interested in meeting this group which held ideas similar to his own,
came to the United States for a visit. He traveled throughout the
country and inspected a number of schools for the deaf. Among
those that he visited was the Rochester School, where he stayed
for a considerable time.

On returning to Germany, he wrote a paper entitled "Education
of the Deaf and Dumb in the United States." It is in this study,
translated by George Veditz, that we read a discussion of the
Rochester Method, which is then followed by a statement:

> These tenets of Dr. Westervelt's have given me much food for thought,
> and I do not hesitate openly to acknowledge that since my visit to the
> Rochester School, my position towards the sign language has undergone
> some modification. In my previous writings, it is not the relation of
> the deaf to the sign-language, but the relation of the sign-language
> to verbal language that I judged wrongly. (Heidsiek, "Education," Part
> 3, p. 203.)

Concerning his visit to the Rochester School, Heidsiek wrote:

> It was on a Sunday, at the hot hour of noon, that I visited the school.
> A deep stillness reigned everywhere, and my eye glanced about in vain
> for the pupils, of whom I expected to find about 170. Only when I was

conducted through the various apartments did I see little groups of pupils who had retired to the quietest corners, and were so absorbed in their reading that most of them failed to notice me. My conductor told me that the pupils of the intermediate and upper classes were required to read annually forty juvenile books, and to give the contents of some of them in epitome, either orally or in writing.

Those pupils who were taking the air in the garden impressed me by their sedate demeanor. In their conversation, I noticed no gestures, but communication was conducted and exclusively by means of the manual alphabet and in such an unobtrusive manner that only a quick professional eye would have noticed it.

The same means of communication with simultaneous use of speech was employed by Mr. Westervelt during chapel service. Mr. Westervelt is a virtuoso in the use of the finger-language, and in spite of the stifling heat that prevailed that day, and that was uncomfortably noticeable in the crowded chapel, the pupils followed the discourse of their master with rapt attention and visible enthusiasm. (*Ibid.*, p. 207.)

Heidsiek writes further:

The author of this report may likewise boast of having seen numerous schools at home and abroad, but even in the best of them he failed to meet results comparable with those seen in Rochester. It is not only the complete mastery of the English language that is so surprising here, but the amount of positive knowledge by which the pupils distinguish themselves is no less noteworthy. The pupils of the upper classes solved with equal accuracy and rapidity difficult problems in practical arithmetic, in interest and percentage, in calculations involving wages and prices, as well as in geometry. Questions in the domain of history, geography, and literature received answers that would have done honor to the pupils in the third class of our high schools. In general, these pupils were remarkable for their self-possessed bearing. . . . And it is precisely this training to independence and mental maturity that is a characteristic feature of the Rochester School. (*Ibid.*, p. 208.)

In concluding Part 3 of his study, Heidsiek states:

No other method is capable of theoretical justification like the above, nor can produce equal results. I therefore regard the Manual Alphabet or Rochester Method as the most perfect method of the present and the method of the future. (*Ibid.*, p. 455.)

It was with the Rochester Method in mind that he concluded his study with a list of seven principles for reform in the practices of education for the deaf in Germany. They are:

1. In order to bring the deaf to a mastery of verbal language in the shortest way, and to render sign-language superfluous, separate instruction in speech and language should be maintained.

2. The instruction in articulation and lip reading should begin on entering school and continue through the whole course.

3. Instruction in language should be based upon the manual alphabet and writing, and should precede instruction in speech.

4. The manual alphabet always should be used as a means of instruction and intercourse during the whole school life, but in the upper classes it should be retired more and more in favor of speech.

5. Pantomime, for purposes of illustration, should be used freely at all stages of the school course.

6. The conventional sign-language, however, should be rigorously excluded, and should neither be employed as a means of instruction nor tolerated as medium of intercourse.

7. Speech, finger-spelling, and writing are forms of verbal language, and all the same end in view, viz, to give the deaf-mute command of verbal language, and therefore we have but one name for this method — *The Verbal Language Method.* (Heidsiek, "Education," Part 4, p. 25.)

Regardless of the name, whether it be called the Manual Alphabet Method, the Verbal Language Method, or the Rochester Method, the underlying principles are the same. (See Appendix 10.)

A SURVEY OF AMERICAN SCHOOLS FOR THE DEAF

During the academic year of 1924 and 1925, a survey was made of the American schools for the deaf. This survey was sponsored by the National Research Council and was carried on by Professor Herbert E. Day and Professor Irving S. Fusfeld of Gallaudet College, and Professor Rudolf Pintner of Teachers College, Columbia University. Forty-two institutions, both residential and day-schools, were represented. Among this group of schools which came under the survey was the Rochester School for the Deaf.

At the date of this survey, the procedure of instruction remained in order, on the whole, just as it was at the death of Dr. Westervelt in 1918. In the publication of the survey under the Psychological Survey we read:

A plus difference indicates a better than usual educational achievement in terms of the mentality of the children; a minus difference indicates a poorer educational achievement in similar terms. The highest plus difference is 10.1 for R-20, (This symbol represents the Rochester School.) which indicates that this school is making better use of the mentality of its children than is usual among schools for the deaf. (Day, et al., *Survey*, p. 263.)

If this be true, then such a method as makes this possible should deserve the attention of every educator of the deaf.

Samuel Heinicke, Father of German Oralism. (1729-1790) Courtesy of the Volta Bureau.

Abbé Charles Michel de l'Epee, founder of the French National Institute for the Deaf. (1760)

Abbé Roche Ambroise Sicard, mentor of Thomas Hopkins Gallaudet. (1815)

Jean Massieu, one of Sicard's deaf master teachers. (1815)

Laurent Clerc, T. H. Gallaudet's deaf colleague, and first deaf teacher in the United States. (1817)

(Baker Collection print replications by Jan Afzelius. Made from the original at Gallaudet College. c. 1955)

Thomas Hopkins Gallaudet, founder of the American School for the Deaf at Hartford, Connecticut, April 15, 1817.

Samuel Gridley Howe and his deaf-blind pupil, Laura Bridgman. (1837) Courtesy of the Perkins School for the Blind.

Top: David E. Bartlett, head of the Bartlett Family School. (1852-1860) Courtesy of the American School for the Deaf.

Center: Edward Miner Gallaudet at the age of 20. (1857) Courtesy of the American School for the Deaf.

Bottom: Harriet B. Rogers, first teacher and principal of the Clarke School for the Deaf at Northampton. (1867) Courtesy of the Volta Bureau.

Alexander Graham Bell. (1872)

George Sanders, Bell's pupil. (1872)

Anne Sullivan and Helen Keller. (c. 1900) Courtesy of the Perkins School for the Blind.

Edith Fitzgerald, deaf teacher and author of *Straight Language for the Deaf.* (1926) Courtesy of the Volta Bureau.

Richard G. Brill, first superintendent
of the California School for the Deaf
at Riverside. (1951)

Marshall Hester, first to revive the
Rochester Method (fingerspelling
as a supplement to speech) at the
preparatory and primary school
levels. (1958)

Roy K. Holcomb, Father of Total Communication. (1967)

D. Robert Frisina, first director of the National Technical Institute for the Deaf at the Rochester Institute of Technology. (1968)

35

"Viva la parola!"
The International Convention
at Milan
1880

Dr. E. A. Fay, editor of the *American Annals of the Deaf,* in the January issue for 1880 wrote the following announcement in his "Miscellaneous" section:

> *The International Convention* – A private letter from Mr. Vaisse informs us that the International Convention this year will be held, not at Cosmos as at first proposed but at Milan. Its session will continue from the 6th to the 11th of September. While French will be the official language of the Convention, oral communications may be made by each member in his vernacular tongue. . . . Mr. Leon Vaisse, rue Gay-Lussac 49, Paris, France is the chairman. . . . Further particulars will be given in the next number of the *Annals.*

This rather inauspicious announcement was actually heralding one of the most significant conventions ever to be held. It was to impact not only on European education of the deaf but on American particularly.

Topics for discussion at Milan:

The *American Annals* for April, 1880, contained a second and more extensive article of invitations. More importantly, in it were listed a series of 32 questions which had been carefully selected by Mr. Vaisse, chairman of the Convention's Business Committee. These questions were to be the discussion subjects and are of current interest because they depict the educational concerns of that day.

PROGRAMME OF THE CONVENTION
ORGANIZATION OF SCHOOLS FOR THE DEAF AND DUMB.
Buildings. – Furniture.

1. Should the school receive boarders, or only day-scholars? (Point out the advantages and disadvantages of these two systems of education.)

2. A school for day-scholars refers only to the construction and arrangement of the class-rooms, according to certain hygienic rules, with a view to the preservation and improvement of the pupils' health, school furniture, the arrangement of blackboards, desks, seats, etc.

3. A boarding-school includes, besides class-rooms, the construction, 1st, of dormitories, according to hygienic conditions, allowing a large number of children to live in common; 2d, of a dining room; 3d, of a covered play-ground; 4th, of an infirmary; 5th, of one or more workshops, adapted to the object, whether the deaf and dumb learn a trade at school during the course of their studies, or enter as apprentices in private shops after leaving school; 6th, finally, a boarding-school requires large yards connected with the school, and provided with gymnastic apparatus.

Instruction.

1. What should be the number of pupils in a school for deaf and dumb?

2. What is the most favorable age for the admission of the deaf and dumb to school, whether the teaching is by articulation or by signs?

3. What should be the physical and intellectual condition of the deaf and dumb to receive a good education, and to acquire an intelligible pronunciation?

4. What should be the duration of the studies of the deaf and dumb, whether taught by the method of articulation or by that of signs?

5. Is it necessary to separate the congenitally deaf from those whose deafness is the result of disease?

6. What number of pupils can one teacher efficiently instruct, whether by the method of articulation or by that of signs?

7. Should the deaf and dumb, during the whole course of instruction, be committed to the same teacher, or should they change teachers after having acquired a certain degree of instruction?

8. Should the pupils habitually be seated or standing during the lessons? Should they habitually write on black-boards or on slates?

9. What should be the duration of a lesson? Should there be an interval between two lessons?

Methods.

1. Point out the advantages of the method of articulation over that of signs, and the reverse. (This should be considered principally with a view to instruction, without neglecting that which concerns social life.)

2. Explain in what the *purely oral* method, consists, showing the difference between this method and that called *combined.*

3. Determine exactly the limit which divides the signs called *methodical* from those called *natural.*

4. What are the most natural and efficient means by which the deaf and dumb may promptly acquire a knowledge of common language?

5. When and how should grammar be used in teaching language, whether the method of articulation or that of signs is used?

6. When should manuals or books be placed in the hands of pupils? In what branches of teaching should they be dispensed with?

7. Should not elementary free-hand drawing be made an essential part of the education of the deaf and dumb?

8. What is the amount of knowledge that the deaf and dumb may acquire in a given time, when taught, 1st, after the method of articulation; 2d, by means of signs?

9. By what systems can good discipline be secured in a school for the deaf and dumb?

Special Questions.

1. Is it a fact that the deaf and dumb, taught after the method of articulation, do forget, when out of school, most of the knowledge there acquired, and in their intercourse with speaking people prefer the sign-language to written language? If this evil does exist, what is the cause of it, and how can it be remedied?

2. Where and how can those whom deafness has prevented from following classical studies receive an education equivalent to that of the higher schools open to hearing and speaking students? Should it be in a higher department of the institutions for the deaf and dumb, or in a special institution? With special or with ordinary instructors?

3. What are the professions generally followed by the deaf and dumb? What do they follow most advantageously? May new careers be offered them?

4. Are there not certain diseases and accidents to which the deaf and dumb are more exposed than those who hear and speak? And is there not, owing to the peculiar constitution of the deaf and dumb, a certain hygiene to be followed by them, or a special therapeutic treatment to be applied to them?

5. According to the latest censuses taken in the countries of Europe, does the number of the deaf and dumb, compared with the general population of each country, increase or decrease? In either case, give the cause. ("Milan Convention Program," pp. 155-157.)

The National Deaf-Mute College contingent goes to Italy:

Thus with the program of the Convention laid out, the American representatives from the National Deaf-Mute College in Washington, D.C., knew precisely the tack they would have to take. The helmsman for the Milan venture was, naturally, Dr. Edward Miner Gallaudet, the highly regarded president of the college. His words which were so closely attended at home would unquestionably be attended abroad. Consequently, Gallaudet marshaled his thoughts and prepared his paper for the forthcoming debates which were certain to come in Milan.

Mr. Denison describes his impressions:

Once the Americans from the National College had arrived in the convention city, it was Mr. James Denison who subsequently provided a most extraordinary picture of his impressions of the Milan Convention Hall, the representatives in attendance, and the proceedings. Wrapped in the silence of his deafness and entering the Convention Hall, Denison was immediately struck by the ecclesiastical solemnity of the atmosphere because about three-fourths of the representatives were tonsured and cassocked in black. "I found it difficult to overcome the impression that I had stumbled into the wrong place." ("Impression," p. 41.)

The presiding officer, the President of the Assembly, was the Abba Giulio Tarra, an impressive-looking cleric who spoke with animation, enthusiasm, and conviction relative to the virtues of the pure oral method as opposed to the "abomination" of sign language.

> Amid the concurring applause of a majority of his hearers, the Abba
> Tarra stated as an undisputed fact the impossibility of conveying by
> signs any idea of the Divine Being but ideas gross, material, and untrue.
> But the gesture which he made in illustration was the unmeaning,
> if not misleading one, of pointing with the index finger to the ceiling.
> . . . On other occasions the gestures he employed to show the inferiority
> of signs in plainness and precision were only too well calculated to
> emphasize his remarks. (*Ibid.*, p. 42.)

This presentation along with others all followed in a similar vein.

> Those speakers at the Convention who argued in favor of the oral
> method of instructing deaf-mutes dwelt persistently, and, as far as
> concerned this class of individuals among their hearers, with evident
> effect, upon the unsuitableness, not to say the injuriousness, of signs
> as a means for conveying moral and intellectual ideas of an elevated
> kind. (*Ibid.*)

Obviously the delegates from the National Deaf-Mute College sat
in an atmosphere which was not exactly compatible with their
philosophy.

The Americans and their observations in Italy:

Just prior to the opening of the Convention, the Americans as well
as the other delegates had visited several schools for the deaf in
and around Milan. The Reverend Dr. Stoddard of the Board of
Directors of the New York Institution for the Deaf and Dumb, one
of the American delegates, wrote later in the New York *Observer*
of what he had seen in the Italian schools.

> The results are most gratifying, manifested not only in oral speech,
> but also in the deameanor and bearing of the youth, their lively interest
> in matters outside of their circle of deaf-mute associates, their
> intelligent comprehension of the language and thoughts of others, and
> their ability to take some fair place among their hearing and speaking
> fellow-men. (*Ibid.*, p. 50.)

Dr. Stoddard also wrote of an annual examination of the pupils
which he and his fellow delegates had observed at the Royal School
in Milan.

> The little ones were asked by their teachers a variety of questions.
> All these were oral questions, and the children read the lips with great
> accuracy and rapidity. Their answers were always intelligible, and were
> given promptly and pleasantly. No signs of any kind were used, and
> none are allowed in instruction and conversation, and the children
> talked orally with each other, with the members of the Council, and
> made pretty little impromptu speeches to the audience. It is said that
> the Italian language is peculiarly adapted to this vocalization, and the

> results are certainly marvellous, and show what personal instruction
> and continuous training can do even for the dumb. (*Ibid.*)

In a letter to the United States, another American delegate, the Reverend Thomas Gallaudet, a brother of Dr. E. M. Gallaudet, wrote from Milan.

> The Italian teachers have shown us some wonderful results here in this school, but they have comparatively few pupils and a much easier language to pronounce than ours. (*Ibid.*, p. 51.)

Both Dr. Stoddard and Mr. Gallaudet made the same significant observation relative to the simplicity of the Italian language in terms of "vocalization" or "pronunciation."

The Italians and their oral success:

Today we know that it is the dominance of vowels over the consonant elements in many Romance languages which renders them easier for prelingually deaf children to acquire orally. It is also this dominant vowel characteristic which makes these same languages easier to speechread.

In short, Italian is a *labial* language and consequently easier to see and imitate, whereas English is a *velar* or back-throat language, which must be to a large extent developed kinesthetically. It was this innate language difference factor which accounted for the high Italian speech quality observed by Stoddard and Gallaudet. Another important reason for the Italian oral success as noted by Mr. Gallaudet was that "they have comparatively few pupils." (See Appendix 11.)

The reactions of the National Deaf-Mute College delegates to what they saw in the demonstrations were positive, however, not sufficiently enough to dissuade them from their own ideas on the efficacy of sign language. While representing a definite minority in their support of signs, they did meet a group of French clerics, the Brothers of Saint Gabriel, who were philosophically in agreement with them. These teaching brothers knew and used many of the Sicard signs with which Denison and the other Americans were well familiar. These Brothers of St. Gabriel, like themselves, represented but a small minority of the Convention's assembly.

Dr. E. M. Gallaudet's presentation:

The program topic of "Buildings and Furniture" had been set aside at the beginning of the Convention in favor of the topics of "Instruction" and "Methods," which were of greater importance and urgency. In due time Dr. E. M. Gallaudet, speaking on behalf of the College delegation, delivered in French his address, entitled "Remarks on the Combined System."

First, Dr. Gallaudet acknowledged the earnestness and sincerity of the advocates of the pure oral method. He then defined the combined system as

> one which makes use of the language of natural signs to a limited degree as as an aid to instruction at every stage of the course, which employs the manual alphabet in the same manner, while articulation is attempted with all, and continued through the whole period of school training with such as give promise of attaining a reasonable degree of success in speech and lipreading. ("Remarks," p. 56.)

The phrase *to a limited degree* indicates the speaker's own and often expressed paradoxical reservations regarding the use of sign language as an instructional medium. This thinking will be elaborated upon subsequently. Gallaudet, continuing, treated the idea of speech as a blessing to mankind; however:

> The mere power of vocal utterance is not what has civilized the world.
>
> With speech, but without education, the common people even of Christian nations rested for centuries in a state of degradation, disenfranchisement, and practical slavery. And in our day we see thousands of millions expended every year in Europe and America that the masses who *have speech* already may be educated. . . .
>
> Shall we give speech to the deaf and dumb, and call them educated?
>
> It is because this question has been often answered in the affirmative that I venture to raise my voice against a method likely to mislead men by the almost miraculous character of its results, . . . a method which often brings its objects to the threshold of the temple of knowledge and leaves them there, with little hope of entering in. . . .
>
> And is there no danger that a method the beginning and end of which is to impart speech to the dumb will bring forth a generation of chatterers, with so little of real education that they must ever remain at the bottom of the social ladder? . . . [M]y observation does not lead me to believe that the mass of deaf-mutes can be taught to talk well. . . . [A] large portion fall so far short of success that the time spent in giving them the imperfect speech they acquire would be used to much greater advantage in the development of their minds, and increasing the store of knowledge to be gained by them during the period of their

continuance in school. And for those who can learn to speak well, natural signs and dactylology furnish too valuable an aid in the course of their education to make it right to throw them aside. (*Ibid.*, pp. 56-58.)

Gallaudet then predicted "The Combined System" to be the system of the future. He added, however,

That there will be schools where speech will be taught to all the pupils, and in which the processes of instruction will be mainly conducted through speech, no one will attempt to deny; and the in localities where the establishment of such schools is practicable, there will be classes and departments conducted in a similar manner. That there will also be schools and classes and departments in which no attempt will be made to give instruction in articulation is, in my opinion, equally certain. In all schools, the language of signs, the natural language of the dumb and the mother language of the world, will be accepted as a valuable and even indispensable adjunct at all stages in the course of instruction, while its excessive and injurious use will be carefully guarded against. (*Ibid.*, p. 59.)

A laudatory defense and a caveat:

This most laudatory defense of sign language, it will be noted, was concluded with the clear caveat relative to the sign language that "its excessive and injurious use will be carefully guarded against." (It might be observed that this warning reflected that previously mentioned deep-rooted philosophical conflict which E. M. Gallaudet bore with him all of his professional life. It was a conflict between loyalties to his heritage and loyalties to his own reason and experience.)

Gallaudet's presentation "Remarks on the Combined System" was concluded with his often repeated statement that this System will serve "the greatest good for the greatest number" and, once established, "the millennium of deaf-mute instruction will be entered upon."

While the Brothers of Saint Gabriel were observed by James Denison to be most attentive and interested in Dr. Gallaudet's remarks, the majority of delegates were polite in their response but most unenthusiastic. What was received by the National Deaf-Mute College contingent as being the most logical and appealing of Gallaudet's statements left the majority of the auditors wholly unimpressed. To be sure, Dr. Edward Miner Gallaudet was confronted with a general audience reaction the likes of which he had never before experienced.

Other presentations followed by Italian, French, and British educators of the deaf. Each of them lent an ever-strengthening support to the pure oral method. The Abba Tarra continued to wax enthusiastic and led the entire assembly in a pro-oral direction to the point that Denison referred to the International Convention as the In-*Tarra*-national Convention.

Support anticipated from the Brothers of Saint Gabriel:

According to Denison, a moment of high expectancy was reached on the part of the National Deaf-Mute College representatives when an elderly ascetic, a member of the Brothers of Saint Gabriel, made his way to the podium. The feeling of Gallaudet and his colleagues was one of relief, knowing that the good brother would give full support of his teaching order to their Combined System.

Once begun, the old brother's speech, rendered in French, was received with disbelief by Gallaudet and his friends because it extolled wholly and completely the innumerable virtues of the pure oral method over sign language as an instructional procedure. Such a turnabout was incomprehensible in light of the previously expressed thinking of the various members of the order. Gallaudet and his colleagues could but sit speechless and look at one another.

After the Abba Tarra's statement approving the Brothers' "conversion" to pure oralism, shouts of *"Viva la parola!"* ("Long live speech!") arose on all sides. Tarra then realized that the time for the introduction and discussion of Resolutions was at hand.

The Convention's "Resolutions":

Following a number of amicable discussions among the leaders, a set of eight Resolutions was formulated and presented to the Convention for a final discussion and vote.

RESOLUTIONS OF THE MILAN CONVENTION

1. The Convention, considering the incontestable superiority of articulation over signs in restoring the deaf-mute to society and giving him a fuller knowledge of language, declares that the oral method should be preferred to that of signs in the education and instruction of deaf-mutes.

2. The Convention, considering that the simultaneous use of articulation and signs has the disadvantage of injuring articulation and lip-reading and the precision of ideas, declares that the pure oral method should be preferred.

3. The Convention, considering that a large number of deaf-mutes do not receive the benefit of instruction, owing to the poverty of their families and of the institutions, expresses the earnest desire that governments shall make such provisions that all deaf-mutes may be instructed.

4. The Convention, considering that instruction of deaf speaking children by the pure oral method should follow as closely as possible the methods of instruction of hearing and speaking children, declares (1) that the most natural and efficacious means by which the deaf speaking child can acquire a knowledge of language is the intuitive method, which consists in indicating, first by articulation and then by writing, the objects and facts placed before the pupil; (2) that in the first period, called *maternal*, the deaf-mute should be brought to the observation of grammatical forms by means of examples and practical exercises, and that in the second period he should be aided to deduce from these examples the principles of grammar, which should be expressed as simply and clearly as possible; (3) that manuscript books, with the words and forms of language known by the pupil, may be placed in his hands at all times.

5. The Convention, considering the lack of very elementary books to aid in the gradual and progressive development of language, expresses the desire that teachers of the oral method shall publish special books of this kind.

6. The Convention, considering the results obtained by numerous experiments made upon deaf-mutes of all ages and conditions, who, a long time after they had left school, being questioned upon the most diverse subjects, replied correctly and with sufficient clearness of articulation, and read the lips of their interlocutors with the greatest facility, declares (1) that deaf-mutes taught by the pure oral method do not forget after leaving school the knowledge which they have there acquired, but rather increase it by conversation and reading which are rendered easier for them; (2) that in their conversation with speaking persons they use articulation exclusively; (3) that articulation and lip-reading: instead of being lost, are developed by practice.

7. The Convention, considering that the instruction of deaf-mutes by articulation has peculiar needs, and considering the almost unanimous testimony of instructors of deaf-mutes, declares (1) that the most favorable age at which the deaf-mute can be received in school is from eight to ten years; (2) that the term of instruction should be at least seven years, and still better eight years; (3) that the instructor cannot successfully teach more than ten pupils by the pure oral method.

8. The Convention, considering that the introduction of the pure oral method into institutions where it is not yet employed should be prudent, gradual, and progressive, in order to be successful, is of the opinion (1) that the new pupils ought to form a separate class, in which the instruction should be given by articulation; (2) that these pupils should be entirely separated from the other pupils who

are too far advanced to be instructed by articulation, and that the education of the latter should be completed by signs; (3) that each year a new class of articulation should be established in the school until all the old pupils taught by signs have finished their education (*Ibid.*, pp. 64-65.)

When President Tarra presented the foregoing Resolutions to the Convention for a vote, the results were an overwhelming 160 votes in favor and 4 opposed. It is not difficult to image who cast the negative votes.

Oralism, the instructional preference:

No longer was there any doubt as to the position of the European educators and their instructional preference. David Buxton, a British educator of the deaf, in his "Notes of Progress in Education of the Deaf" wrote, "I was officially present, when the 'pure oral' system was exemplified in its pupils, advocated by its teachers, and approved by the consensus of many nations and by a vote of 160 to 4. . . ." ("Notes of Progress," p. 42.) Further in his article Buxton wrote regarding a piece from the *London Times* for September 28, 1880.

No more representative body could have been collected than that which at Milan has declared for oral teaching of the deaf – and for nothing but oral teaching. . . . The resolution, it continues, was the act of representatives of countries which have countenanced the language of signs. The result [it adds] is a virtual unanimity of preference for oral teaching which might seem to overbear all possibility of opposition. (*Ibid.*, p. 43.)

At the close of the Convention, the National Deaf-Mute College delegation departed from Milan with considerably less than a sense of victory. Edward M. Gallaudet and his colleagues on shipboard ruminated, reviewed, and wondered at the amazing European mind which was so impervious to the obvious logic which had been set forth in the Combined System presentation.

Differences in perspectives:

The unfathomable position of the Europeans and their failure to grasp the obviousness of the Combined System stemmed actually not from what appeared to be stubborn ignorance and refusal to accept facts, but from a wholly different set of educational perspectives, objectives, and values.

The American view was unique to the Europeans because unlike their own view, the American political, social, and economic objectives were (and are) held equally attainable for all citizens, both hearing and deaf. These objectives could be secured only through increased educational opportunities. While speech achievement goals were important for American deaf people, their acquisition of knowledge through reading and writing were considered even more important. The American ideal, therefore, set a higher education as a possibility for every citizen, hearing or deaf, provided an individual had the intellectual wherewithal to handle it.

For Europeans, however, a higher education for the average hearing person was beyond all realistic expectations. Hence such considerations for a deaf person were impossible to consider. It was, therefore, natural that the most practical educational goal for European deaf children was to teach them how to talk in order to survive in whatever socio-economic class they might be born. In that a great depth or breadth of knowledge was not expected of any average European, there was obviously little or no reason to expect it from an average deaf European. Hence it was that the cry *"Viva la parola!"* carried the day at Milan.

E. M. Gallaudet's report on "The Milan Convention":

The differences in European goals as determinants in selecting an instructional philosophy went unperceived by Gallaudet. Instead, once at home, he gathered together what he conceived to be damning evidence that the Milan Convention had been "rigged" in favor of the "pure oralists." The result of his efforts was a report entitled "The Milan Convention."

Gallaudet's report began with a background review of the first International Convention of Educators of the Deaf, which was held in Paris in 1878. He stressed the fact that this gathering "was in the hands of the promotors of articulation," particularly the Pereire Society. This Society, he explained, was an organization which was founded to secure "the recognition of Pereire as the first teacher of deaf-mutes in France, and to bring about the general adoption of the oral method, which was practiced by Pereire." ("Milan Convention," p. 1.) This organization, according to Gallaudet, was financially backed by several of Pereire's great-grandsons who resided in Paris and managed a "very wealthy banking firm." These Pereires exerted considerable influence not only on the Paris Convention of 1878 but similarly on the Milan Convention which was to come.

When the Milan Convention was organized, Gallaudet pointed out, the board of officers was heavily loaded with oralists.

> . . . the head of one of the Milan schools, the Abba Tarra was made President, and the leading instructor in the other school Professor Fornari was made Secretary. Of the four Vice Presidents and four Vice Secretaries, seven were pronounced supporters of articulation. (*Ibid.*, p. 2.)

(Perhaps with such "a stacked deck" Gallaudet and his colleagues should have stayed at home.)

Throughout his account of the Milan Convention, Gallaudet was highly critical of the Italian, British, and French advocates of articulation. A high point in Gallaudet's exasperation with the Convention came with the inexplicable "conversion" of the Brothers of Saint Gabriel to "pure oralism."

> They took no part, however, in the debate until toward the close, when Frére Hubert, inspector of the schools under the direction of the Brothers, rose and announced his conversion to the "pure oral method," closing his little speech by giving thanks to M. Eugéne Pereire, through whose lberality the members of his brotherhood had been enabled to visit Milan and attend the Convention. And not a brother of St. Gabriel voted against the method of Pereire. (*Ibid.*, p. 8.)

E. M. Gallaudet's report, "The Milan Convention," was not exactly a document of diplomacy; consequently a concerted protest from numerous of his European colleagues resulted.

British reactions to Gallaudet's report:

A number of the British delegation responded with a firm objection which appeared in the *American Annals.*

> We the undersigned, English members of the International Congress of Milan, feel it incumbent upon us to record our most emphatic protest against the charges of unfairness in the constitution and management of the Congress made by Dr. E. M. Gallaudet in the last number of the *Annals.* (*Ibid.*, pp. 138-139.)

This statement was followed by the signatures of eight educators of the deaf, among whom were Mr. Arthur A. Kinsey and Dr. David Buxton, principal and secretary respectively of the British Training College for Teachers.

Miss Susanna E. Hull, one of the signers of the preceding British protest, wrote an additional brittle piece, "The International Congress, – A Reply," which also appeared in the April, 1881, issue of the *Annals*. In this reply Miss Hull critically pointed out what she saw in Dr. Gallaudet's article as inconsistencies and even misinterpretations of common terminology. She then brought into focus Gallaudet's thoughts on articulation and quoted his words, "Given ample funds, implying a large proportion of the teachers, ample time, and implying a long term of school training, the superiority of speech is admitted." In the face of this belief, Miss Hull found Dr. Gallaudet's opposition to the pure oral method incomprehensible and concluded her protest with the following impassioned statement:

> By the memory of his "sainted mother" and his honored father, we call upon him to revise his verdict, to lend his power, his influence, his knowledge, his great ability, to forward that which he acknowledges superior, and America's deaf shall yet rise up and bless him with their so long-withheld God-given *voices*.

Padre Marchio's "gentler protest":

A gentler protest featured in the *American Annals* came from Padre Marchio, an outstanding Italian teacher of the deaf. Marchio sought to clarify thinking relative to the vote of the Brothers of Saint Gabriel and their switch to the pure oral method. Their reason, he explained, was because they had been convinced through observation as was their leader, Brother Hubert, that the pure oral method was, indeed, better than their own former signing system.

The financial aid, Marchio continued, which the Brothers had received from Mr. Eugéne Pereire was to help two of their number attend the Congress. This assistance, they maintained, had no influence whatever on their vote. Actually in voting for the "pure oral" method, they were voting *against* the method of Pereire's great-grandfather. Pereire's method was actually "combined" and not "pure oral." (*Ibid.*, pp. 131-132.) This fact the American critic did not know.

Seeing the brouhaha which his "Milan Convention" report had caused, Gallaudet tried to clear up his apparently misunderstood purpose in writing the paper. In a letter to the Editor of the *Annals*, Dr. E. A. Fay, Gallaudet stressed that he had not

> intended to reflect on the honesty or pure intentions of those who had governed that body [the Milan Convention], or, indeed any supporters of the "oral method." (*Ibid.*, p. 135.)

The impact of "Viva la parola!":

After awhile the open resentments between the American Combined System advocates and the European Pure Oral supporters gradually subsided. An unfortunate schism, however, was rapidly evolving within the American establishment of education of the deaf, and long suppressed animosities began to surface. The result was a protracted and painful internecine conflict which the 20th-Century educator, Richard G. Brill, has aptly termed the "One Hundred Years War."

Despite, however, all of the differences which became apparent in 1880, the Oral movement began to make significant progress throughout the United States. The Milan cry of "Viva la parola" had indirectly made its impact on American teachers of the deaf and particularly upon the parents of deaf children. (See Appendix 12.)

36

"Make Way for the Ladies!"
1887

American higher education of the deaf was, indeed, a man's province from its beginning with the establishment of the National Deaf-Mute College in Washington, D.C., in 1864, and so it was to remain for the next 23 years. The intervening period, as it will be learned, was fraught with feminine anguish and frustration, because the historically unbending rule of male tradition was not about to give way. Ultimately, of course, the goal of higher education for deaf women was achieved. For the record, however, it should be known that the initial effort toward this goal was made by a young deaf woman, Miss Laura C. Sheridan of Indianapolis.

Laura C. Sheridan speaks her mind:

In the October, 1875, issue of the *American Annals of the Deaf,* Miss Sheridan's very eloquent statement for the extended educational rights of deaf women appeared as follows:

THE HIGHER EDUCATION OF DEAF-MUTE WOMEN

By Laura C. Sheridan, Indianapolis

Liberal provision for the dissemination of knowledge has been the source of the greatness of this nation, and the bulwark of our republican form of government. But not until recently did the country awake to the important fact that, to insure the greatest degree of progress, a high state of culture is as necessary for woman as for man – for the beings who must be mothers of our great men and mould the impressible years of childhood as for those who cast the ballot. So there has been much agitation of the question of the higher education of woman within the last few years, the result of which is that the doors of colleges and universities are opening to her everywhere.

But what have we heard of the question of the silent world? Nothing. Are deaf-mute women different in nature, mind, function, and influence from their hearing sisters? No. Has the National Deaf-Mute College, whose professed object is "to give to competent deaf-mutes and others, who by reason of deafness cannot be educated elsewhere, a thorough education in the studies usually pursued in American colleges," opened its doors to woman? It appears not; and that there is no plan under consideration among her friends to provide for her some similar institution.

Must we then conclude that in this enlightened age, when a state of culture is being acknowledged as the natural prerogative, the prime condition, of every healthy intellect, one-half of the "competent deaf-mutes" have been ignored? Hardly that. The National Deaf-Mute College was probably at first considered a doubtful experiment, even by many of its friends, and it was natural that the expediency and desirability of a higher education for girls also should not be taken into consideration until the wisdom of that experiment had been demonstrated. But this reason for silence or apathy on the part of the friends of deaf-mute women no longer exists, for that college is already a grand success. And is it not quite time that measures were being taken to provide for deaf girls the same advantages?

Deaf-mute girls cannot be expected to be the inaugurators of such a movement be they ever so earnest. They are not the independent beings their hearing sisters are, who through the ear and the press come in contact with every variety of mind in the world. All they know has been taught them, and what they read is often but imperfectly understood. They look to their instructors for advice and encouragement in all things, for their short school life has not prepared them for independent thought.

Yet we ask for them only the aid and hearty "God speed" already given their brothers. Judging by the ambition and progress of girls in the early school-room, can we believe they would pursue the higher education any less enthusiastic and successfully under the same favorable circumstances?

Miss Sheridan, continuing, then cited the outstanding academic achievement of a young hearing woman student at Indiana Asbury University who was one of four students to capture "first honors" out of a class of 33 and a student body numbering more then 400.

It was Miss Sheridan's contention that if a young hearing woman could attain such a record, certainly young deaf women could match it or at least approximate it. What follows in her article is a touchingly dramatic plea.

> The world has lost immensely by being so long in awakening to the importance of an equal education for woman. If her sphere is narrower, is it of less consequence?—is it less susceptible to the influence of a refined and exalted intelligence?
>
> While we deny it to be impossible for highly-educated deaf women to turn their superior knowledge to pecuniary advantage, that argument in behalf of such an education is regarded as an inferior one. It is the immortal soul and mind we are pleading for; the gratification of that yearning in the breast of every sentient being which demands something higher and better than what it recognizes within itself. Think you that this throbbing, restless, craving life never exists in the heart and brain of the deaf girl? Can you read the soul of the intelligent one? Silence sits around it, yet longing deep and unutterable. Her institution life has awakened within her a dim consciousness of her own powers. Perhaps she is one who out of utter darkness has emerged into the gray light of early mental morn. Mind is groping 'mid the shadows for the reality of grand truths but faintly traced there. She cannot grasp them, and turns with eager eyes to the paling east, where there is light—but not for her. Alas! her whole life is an early morn, burdened with that cry of the spirit that has issued from knowledge-seekers in all ages—"What is it?—where is it?—how shall I find it?"
>
> The deaf are more dependent upon a liberal education for happiness than any other class, and there is no reason to suppose that they would use it to less advantage to the world; therefore, both philanthropist and economist must perceive the importance of educating them thoroughly. The practical thinker, who recognizes that universal intelligence is the great lever on which the world is to rise to greatness and the race to perfection, cannot ignore the deaf-mute. Numerically, he is becoming an army; uneducated, he is so much lost force; and it is apparent that the deaf-mute boy or girl who has the necessary courage, patience, and powers of application to overcome the herculean difficulties of a college course possess the metal of which the men and women are made who make the world move. There are places for such in the world where they may better it, directly, as workers or thinkers, and indirectly as inspirers, leaders, and elevators of their class.
>
> Deaf mute instruction is yet in its infancy. Who can tell what wonders the future may bring forth, beside which the past may pale?

The young author then set forth a number of benefits to be reaped by deaf people generally through the inauguration of higher education for deaf women.

I. It would raise still higher the general standard of deaf mute intelligence. Who can doubt that the hope of entering college has already spurred to hard study in his primary school years many a boy who otherwise would have been incited to only ordinary application, and that the respect the gradutes of the National College are receiving from the world is raising the aspirations of all deaf-mutes for higher attainments?

II. It would hasten the establishment of high classes in all our institutions, and thus in another way elevate the standard of deaf-mute education. The masses always follow their leaders as nearly and rapidly as possible. These classes have been frequently recommended as the best places in which to prepare students for college; so the greater number of students there are to prepare for college, the greater the probability that these classes will be established.

III. It would hasten the time when the entire hearing world shall acknowledge the equality of the deaf. The greater the number of polished and highly-educated deaf-mutes sent out into business and social circles, the sooner will come this recognition so earnestly longed for by sensitive, high-minded deaf-mutes.

IV. It would supply our institutions with a greater number of deaf lady-teachers, who would also be much better qualified for their work than those employed at present. Teaching is an avocation in which woman has shown herself peculiarly successful, and in the hearing world she is fast monopolizing the profession. In this city there are 150 women teachers and less than twenty men; half the superintendents, and thirteen out of twenty principals, are women. Surely, when in proportion to their number more deaf than hearing women are forced to self support, and when by reason of their infirmity they are debarred from so many other fields of labor, they should be duly represented in deaf and dumb institutions. Yet out of 323 instructors of deaf-mutes in America, including superintendents and the faculty of the college, only 105 are deaf, and it is reasonable to suppose that the majority of the latter are gentlemen.

Miss Sheridan then concluded her article on the behalf of deaf women with a sincere request for support and, finally, a sensitive acknowledgement of her own personal need for higher learning.

Our plea is made, briefly and imperfectly to be sure, but with all earnestness of conviction and purpose. We hope that this matter will be taken into early and serious consideration by the friends of deaf women, and that, when this higher education is provided for them, there will be no effort made to lower the standard of the curriculum below that pursued by the other sex. Where this education shall be provided for them, and how, we leave to our friends, confident of their good-will and generosity. Knowledge is no longer a bug-bear to be held up to woman as something to obtain which she must sacrifice womanly feeling and delicacy, and we trust that much more able pens than ours will soon put in a plea for the higher education of deaf women.

The reader will readily perceive that the writer never received the higher education; but dreams, longings, and ambitions for it, buried in the cruel grave of misfortune and stern necessity, haunt her memory at times with a sadness inexpressible.

("Deaf-Mute Women," pp. 248-252.)

Responses to Miss Sheridan's article were not immediately forthcoming, probably because revolutionary ideas are almost never quickly nor easily assimilated. The young lady had, however, courageously planted a tiny but powerful seed of thought which was to grow, but not without opposition.

Dr. E. M. Gallaudet speaks his mind:

Unquestionably, Dr. Edward Miner Gallaudet, the president of the National Deaf-Mute College, had received letters from time to time regarding the advisability of enrolling young deaf women in the College. The thought of his replies to such letters may possibly be well reflected in his recorded answer to the principal of the Wisconsin School for the Deaf, Dr. William H. DeMotte, at the Fourth Conference of Superintendents and Principals held at the Clarke School in May, 1880. This exchange of ideas, it might be remembered, occurred some five years after Miss Sheridan's article on higher education for deaf women had appeared in the *Annals*.

Dr. DeMotte asked concerning the admission of young ladies to the College. He said there were some bright girls in Wisconsin who would like to see its benefits.

Dr. Gallaudet said there was no probability that the doors of the College would be open to young ladies at present. In his own mind it was an objection, that the bringing of deaf-mute young men and young women together in college would tend to increase the marriage of deaf-mutes with deaf-mutes, which is less desirable for them than marriage with hearing persons. If there is a demand for the higher education of deaf-mute young women, it should be met at some other point than at the young men's College at Washington.

("Women in College," p. 208.)

A discussion then began as to a suitable location for a women's college, whereupon Mr. Gillespie, superintendent of the Nebraska School, "suggested Omaha, Nebraska, as a desirable place for the college for young women, being the most central point in America." (*Ibid.*, pp. 208-209.) With this proposal falling flat, the discussion ended.

The noteworthy point of all of this was that the subject of higher education for deaf women was at least discussed. No one, however, was able to budge the topic's chief opponent, Dr. E. M. Gallaudet, and his biological rationale. Any objections to his argument appear to have been quietly swallowed out of deference to his name and position.

The genetic angle "soft peddled":

Curiously enough, three years later, in 1883, A. G. Bell advanced the *same* thinking in a scientifically conceived study entitled *Memoir upon the Formation of a Deaf Variety of the Human Race,* and accordingly stirred the animosity of deaf people across the nation. It was this vehement reaction against Bell which probably caused Gallaudet to "soft peddle" the genetic angle for not bringing young deaf men and women together on his campus. Instead he had to rely on the ultimate objection for that day, the possible moral endangerment to the sexes if they were permitted to commingle. This idea was so generally accepted in that Victorian period that common sense didn't have a chance. (This concept, incidentally, prevailed on Kendall Green even into the early 1940's.) After the Clarke School Conference, the issue of women attending the National Deaf-Mute College was laid to rest for another six years.

Georgia Elliott writes a letter:

The Eleventh Convention of American Instructors of the Deaf (1886), held in Berkeley, California, moved along smoothly without one thought to knit the brow, until Dr. Philip G. Gillett, superintendent of the Illinois School, arose and said, "Before I left home, one of the young ladies of our school wanted to know if she might write a letter to the convention. I told her I thought the members would listen to it, and if you will kindly accord with my quasi promise, I ask the Secretary to read the letter of this young lady." The secretary then read the following communication written by Georgia Elliott of Illinois:

> Kind Superintendents and Teachers:
>
> I ask the dear privilege of calling your attention to the young deaf and dumb ladies, who in all these years have seemed to be forgotten, while great attention is given to the higher education of the deaf and dumb gentlemen. Look at the excellent National Deaf Mute College, and its door which is always flung wide open to welcome the gentlemen, but not the ladies. I am deaf, but not dumb, and my great desire is to obtain a higher education, as many others of the young girls of the United States do. I have been attending school regularly at the noble institution of Illinois for the past few years, which has given me such fine advantages. From the primary grades I have been pushing steadily forward until now, having nearly completed the course, I am not content with my achievements, for I have but tasted of the fount—beyond lies the ocean of knowledge. Girls and boys are educated together in all common schools, in several colleges, and in all the institutions; why should they not be educated in the national colleges? Girls have in all schools as high a rank as boys; indeed, they generally rank higher in their studies than boys do. Thus, it is evident that they would improve their advantages at the college as well as the boys.
>
> Girls need a higher education as much as boys. Their influence upon society as women, as mothers, as sisters, is very great, and a thorough education will better fit them for all their duties. They exert the greatest influence on the active men that do the business of the world, and can use their strength for good or ill, as they like. As the civilization of any country advances, the scholars begin to inquire what the causes are that make it advance, and one of the greatest helps to improvement of every kind, has been learned are good women. They have the first years of all lives in their care, and can mold and direct them as they will. Among hearing persons, great attention is given to the higher education of women. Look at the many excellent academies, seminaries, and colleges: Wellesley, Nassar [sic], Smith, Mt. Holyoke, and a host of others. Look, too, at the opportunities given them by Harvard, Columbia, Amherst, Michigan, and other colleges for the pursuit of advanced studies. Is it not a reproach to our educators of the deaf and dumb, that in all these years they have provided no college for the deaf young women?
>
> The majority of teachers in our institutions are women, many of them deaf and dumb. How much better fitted they would be for such positions if they could go through a collegiate course. The girls of today are to be the women of tomorrow; and the country does well that looks after the education of its girls.
>
> What would the additional expense be to the United States Government when compared with the great benefits to the pupils? Could a few thousand dollars be spent to any better advantage?
>
> GEORGIA ELLIOTT

Leading the tremendous applause for the letter's contents and for its young author was a deaf woman teacher, Miss Laura C. Sheridan, who some 11 years previously had sounded the same call in an unheeded article published in the *American Annals of the Deaf.* At the risk of being maudlin, one might easily imagine that Miss Sheridan applauded not without tears.

The faculty of the college favor . . . .

Young Georgia Elliott's letter to the Convention had made an impact, because in the *29th Annual Report for the Columbia Institute for the Deaf and Dumb,* 1886, the following paragraphs made their appearance on page 9:

ADMISSION OF YOUNG WOMEN TO THE COLLEGE

Among the papers presented at the California Convention was a communication from a very bright deaf young lady, urging that the doors of our college be opened to those of her sex.

A communication on the same subject, and urging the same action, has been lately addressed to the president of the college by the Western Association of Collegiate Alumnae, meeting at Indianapolis on the 22d of May last. This latter communication urges with much force that deaf young women ought to be permitted to share in the advantages afforded by the bounty of Congress for higher education to the deaf young men of the country.

The faculty of the college favor the admission of young women, at least as an experiment.

Their presence in the college would entail no increased cost for instruction, which is the most considerable item of expense in carrying on the college.

The board of directors are disposed to take this subject into very serious consideration; and while they are not prepared to make a definite recommendation in this report, they respectfully ask the attention of Congress to the matter, as deserving of favorable action in the near future.

All of which is respectfully submitted, by order of the board of directors.

E. M. GALLAUDET
President

Hon. L. Q. C. Lamar
Secretary of the Interior

While the phrase "at least as an experiment" carried with it a scent of trepidation, we must appreciate the fact that many of the gentlemen with whom this great decision rested had little knowledge of the intelligence, courage, and perseverance with which they would soon be dealing. As one of them most likely said, "The die is cast."

Our "new departure":

In the spring of 1887 copies of the following letter were sent to the administrators of schools for the deaf across the country.

National Deaf-Mute College
Washington, March 17, 1887

To the Superintendents and Principals of
Schools for the Deaf in the United States:

Dear Friends:

By the same mail that carries this circular I send you copies of our new Announcement, in which full information as to the work of the College is given, except that no special mention is made of our "new departure," so-called, in admitting young women to the College.

It has been thought preferable to speak of this scheme in a special circular, since, by the action of the Directors of the College, it is to be an experiment, the success or failure of which will determine the future policy of the Board.

It is proposed to admit young women to the College next September on the same terms and conditions as have been heretofore applied to young men.

Suitable accommodations, and the care of a matron, will be provided for the young women in the residence of the President of the College.

They will be allowed to attend the regular recitations and public exercises of the College.

They will come under the general regulations of the College, with such additions thereto as may be deemed advisable by the Faculty.

It is considered of great importance that only such young women should seek admission to the College as are well prepared to enter the Introductory Class, and of still greater consequence that none should be recommended except such as are of the highest personal character, and are moved with an earnest desire for that intellectual and moral culture the College is designed to furnish.

In this connection attention is called to the fact that within the past two years altogether too large a proportion of the young men seeking admission to College have been unable to sustain the entrance examinations, some even failing to hold places in the High Class of the Kendall School.

It is believed to be easily possible, certainly in all the large schools for the deaf in the country, to prepare pupils for the Introductory Class of the College.

That many have failed to enter this class who expected to do so suggests certain serious questions which may be left to the intelligence of those to whom this circular is addressed.

The officers of the College are using their best endeavors to give to its students a training which, while it develops and strengthens their intellects, shall at the same time confirm their purposes of upright and moral living.

The success of these efforts depends, in large measure, on the preparation given in the schools to those who seek admission to the College, and on the character of those who are sent to it.

Relying on your thoroughly friendly interest in the College, and your desire to make its work what it should be, it is urged that you be careful to recommend for places in the college only those whose character and capabilities give strong promise of success, and that you take pains to see that those to whom the labor of preparing pupils for College is committed perform that duty in a faithful and intelligent manner.

The officers of the College desire to convey, through you, their sincere appreciation of the efforts of those instructors by whose faithful and intelligent training young men have been well prepared for College, and to assure these teachers that their work for their pupils has been, in its place, as important as any that has come after it.

Cordially yours,

E. M. GALLAUDET
President

("*New Departure*," pp. 128-129.)

The doors are opened:

In the fall of 1887 six young deaf ladies found their way to Kendall Green in northeast Washington and were immediately escorted to the home of the President, House #1. Dr. E. M. Gallaudet and his family had already vacated the premises and had moved to their home in Hartford. There they were to remain during what was determined to be a two-year experiment. The President was to divide his time between his family in Hartford and the College in Washington.

Miss Ellen Gordon, matron of the institution, who was to reside with the young ladies, greeted each of them as they arrived and helped each to get settled into the house and the college routine.

The young ladies were subsequently listed on the student roll by name and state, right along with the young gentlemen. These young ladies in the Introductory Class were:

> Georgia Elliott from Illinois
> Ella F. Black from Indiana
> Anna L. Kurtz from Indiana
> Alto M. Lowman from Maryland
> Margaret Ellen Rudd from Nebraska
> Hattie A. Leffler from Pennsylvania

The opportunity to try:

Of these six students beginning in the fall of 1887, only one was ultimately fortunate enough to complete the five-year course of study. The others probably succumbed to one of the age-old obstacles to collegiate progress: economic straits, family demands, change of interest, or, lastly, inadequate preparation. The important fact for them all, however, was that they had won *the opportunity to try.*

As to the graduation of that one young lady with the Class of 1892, it was recorded that

> in presenting the candidates for degrees the president of the college spoke . . . of the interesting fact that Miss Lowman, a candidate for the degree of bachelor of philosophy, was the first young lady who had completed a course of study meriting a degree. [Miss Lowman's oration was entitled "The Influence of Natural Scenery on Character."] ("First Woman Graduate," p. 8.)

In April of the following year, 1893, another young lady was graduated and the event was noted accordingly:

> He [the president of the college] also alluded to the interesting fact that Miss [Agatha] Mary Agnes Tiegel, of Western Pennsylvania, was the first young woman to receive the degree of B.A. from the college, and that in a class of twelve, the largest yet graduated. She outranked all of her classmates in scholarship. ("Second Woman Graduate," p. 7.)

The announced victory in scholarship was unfortunately discovered to be an administrative error and was coolly noted in the *Annual Report* as follows:

> The precedence in scholarship, which in April was given by the record to Miss Tiegel, was at the end of the college year in June accorded to Mr. DeLong. (*Ibid.,* p. 10.)

Considering the times, it might be fair to say that a few male egos probably drew quiet sighs of relief.

Nothing, however, could be taken from the significance and impact of young Miss Tiegel's commencement oration, entitled "The Intellect of Woman." After this singular presentation there was little doubt that women could "hold their own" on Kendall Green. With this, the efforts of Laura C. Sheridan and Georgia Elliott to open higher education to deaf women were, indeed, vindicated.

37

American Oralism Organizes
August 23-27, 1890

The twelfth gathering of the Convention of American Instructors of the Deaf (CAID) met on August 23-27, 1890, at the New York Institution for the Instruction of the Deaf and Dumb. Dr. Edward Allen Fay in his convention report for the *American Annals* wrote, "In the matter of papers the convention suffered an embarrassment of riches." While the papers were probably remarkably good, it was not for these that the Twelfth Convention was particularly noteworthy.

The one event at the convention which made it significant in the history of American education of the deaf was that a new, separate, and potentially influential organization was created. For many years teachers of articulation had met regularly at the CAID gatherings. While they were in the minority, they were nevertheless most zealous in expressing their views relative to speech instruction for deaf children and its tremendous importance.

"Growing pains" in the Articulation Section:

As Dr. Fay continued in his report on the convention, he wrote, "The value of articulation and speech reading is now so fully recognized by American teachers that it is no longer a subject of discussion." In other words, it had become an increasingly accepted approach for teaching the deaf. The oral endeavor, in fact, had outgrown its simple classification as the Articulation Section of the CAID and was now ready to assume an organizational identity of its own.

The teachers of articulation, therefore, in an assembly apart from the convention, discussed and voted for the establishment of a new and separate group which would nationally represent and promote the interests of oralism. The Executive Committee of the new body consisted of Miss Caroline Yale, Miss Ellen Barton, Miss Sarah Fuller, Mr. Greenberger, and Mr. E. L. Crouter. Mr. Zenas Freeman Westervelt was then chosen to act as the new organization's secretary.

A. G. Bell's gift:

At this point Dr. Alexander Graham Bell graciously announced his full support of the new association with a gift of $25,000 which would subsequently be presented. This financial support and sponsorship naturally did much to strengthen the zeal of the organization's members.

The new body then selected for itself the rather protracted name of American Association to Promote the Teaching of Speech to the Deaf (AAPTSD). This appellation brought a slight reaction of jaundiced amusement from those Convention members who were philosophically outside the oral camp. The name, certainly a mouthful, was generally thought not to be inappropriate for this zealous group of articulation advocates. The members of the new Association, however, having Dr. A. G. Bell's endorsement and his magnanimous gift, were quite impervious to the negative observations of their presumably less enlightened colleagues. Withal the oralists became even more determined than ever to have their infant organization, the AAPTSD, "stand on its own feet," and stand it did.

AAPTSD plans its first meeting:

Six months later the governing board of the AAPTSD met in New York City for two days for the purpose of considering the full scope of its mission and laying out plans for its first summer meeting independent of the Convention of American Instructors of the Deaf.

Following is the report of that board meeting:

AMERICAN ASSOCIATION TO PROMOTE THE
TEACHING OF SPEECH TO THE DEAF.

The first regular meeting of the Board of Directors of this Association was held at the Madison Avenue Hotel, in New York City, the 16th and 17th of February. Dr. Alexander Graham Bell presented to the Treasurer of this Association the gift of $25,000, announced at the Twelfth Convention in August last. This fund will be known as the Bell-Volta fund, and will be in the form of a permanent investment, the interest only to be used.

The Executive Committee were instructed by the Board of Directors to appoint a representative of the Association to visit schools with the view to promote the objects of the Association; and to conduct an institute during school time in any school that should so request, giving normal instruction and practical assistance to teachers in active work.

This Committee were also instructed to arrange for a summer meeting of the Association, and to publish bulletins or circulars of information at irregular times as material is furnished or can be secured.

In accordance with the resolutions of the Directors of the Association, Miss Mary H. True has been appointed representative or agent. During the past month she has visited the institutions at Cave Spring, Georgia; Talladega, Alabama; Jackson, Mississippi; Knoxville, Tennessee; Little Rock, Arkansas; Jacksonville, Illinois; Englewood (Chicago), Illinois; Milwaukee, Wisconsin.

The first circular of information is now in the printer's hands and will soon be issued, giving an account of the word-method or oral teaching pursued at Mr. Greenberger's school, Lexington Avenue, New York. The second bulletin will present illustrations and a description of the Phonetic Manual Alphabet devised by Mr. Edmund Lyon, of Rochester, New York.

Arrangements have been made for the Association to hold its first summer meeting at Lake George, New York at the Crosby Side Hotel, from the 26th of June to the 3rd of July. Because of interest in the object of the Association it has been arranged to open this hotel in advance of its regular season; the rates to members have been made from $1 to $1.50 per day. All teachers of the deaf and all persons interested in the education of the deaf are invited to attend, whether they have become members of the Association or not. All persons who expect to attend the meetings of the Association are requested to notify the Secretary as early as convenient. He will endeavor to answer all questions in regard to the summer meeting and to give necessary information in regard to arrangements with railways and the accommodation of members. Over two hundred teachers and others interested in the education of the deaf have united with the Association, and of these the larger number have expressed their desire and purpose to attend the meeting. All who have received notification from the

Secretary of their election may obtain their certificates of membership by remitting before June 1st next the annual assessment of two dollars to the Treasurer, Mr. Charles James Bell, 1437 Pennsylvania Avenue, Washington D.C.

The following is a program which suggests the line of work the Association intends to follow at the first summer meeting: In the forenoon of every day two or more lectures, of not more than forty minutes each, will be delivered, followed by questions asked with a view of obtaining information upon the subjects presented, occupying altogether three hours, from nine to twelve o'clock. Subjects:

1. History of the Education of the Deaf.
    Historical description of the –
    a) Sign or "Combined" Method;
    b) Manual Alphabet Method;
    c) Auricular Method;
    d) Oral Method.
2. Mechanism of speech.
3. The analytic method of teaching speech.
4. Speech-reading, or lip-reading.
5. The word-method of teaching speech.
6. Principles of elocution.
7. Day-schools for the deaf.
8. U.S. Census of 1890.
9. Visible speech and line writing illustrated by practical work.
10. The Lyon Manual.
11. Anatomy of the vocal organs, with models and drawings.
12. Anatomy of the ear, illustrated.

Papers will be expected from members upon the following subjects, among others not yet indicated:

    a) Personal recollections of older articulation teachers.
    b) The higher education of the deaf.
    c) Speech teaching in Southern institutions.
    d) Methods of the late Mr. Whipple, and the Whipple alphabet.
    e) Information concerning Grosselin's method.
    f) Apparatus useful to teachers; hearing tubes, hand mirrors, manipulators, etc.
    g) Objects of this Association and how best to accomplish the end.

Opportunity will be given during or at the close of the work of demonstration of such questions upon class-room work as are designed for information and are not in the nature of discussion.

Informational discussions will be held every evening, from eight until nine o'clock, upon such subjects as shall be arranged by the Executive Committee. No person to speak more than fifteen minutes. Two or more evenings will be devoted to informal social gatherings.

Teachers and schools and publishers are requested to send specimens of charts, text-books, or school apparatus be placed on exhibition during the meeting. Persons unable to be present are requested to send written papers.

A business meeting will be held during the session of the summer meeting of the Association.

Z. F. WESTERVELT,
Secretary

(Westervelt, "Minutes," pp. 222-224.)

In reviewing this first AAPTSD report, one is impressed with its liberality relative to the recognition and clarification of all methodologies and their historical backgrounds. The chief point of interest and emphasis, however, was on *speech* in schools for the deaf, regardless of the instructional methods which they may have espoused.

No deaf child in the United States was to be denied the opportunity for acquiring speech and speechreading. This worthy goal was now nationally in its ascendancy. (See Appendices 13-15.)

38

Teacher Education Comes
to Gallaudet College
1891

While A. G. Bell, before the United States Senate Budget Committee, took 45 minutes to discredit E. M. Gallaudet's proposed teacher training program for his College, the latter required but 13 minutes to give his arguments in support of the plan. (Boatner, *Voice of the Deaf,* p. 133.) Although Gallaudet had previously reassured Bell several times that there would be no deaf persons in the training program and that speech instruction would be mandatory, Bell persisted in failing to believe him. Bell saw the proposed Normal Department as creating an impenetrable stronghold by which oralism would be eternally blocked.

Senatorial support for Gallaudet:

Gallaudet, however, with his strong senatorial support was able to withstand Bell's verbal onslaught, and the Budget Committee voted in his favor. Hence it was, that the first class of the Gallaudet Normal Department was instituted in the fall of 1891.

It was this Normal Department issue that irreparably broke the cooperative spirit between A. G. Bell and E. M. Gallaudet and their respective factions. Although a surface agreement was eventually reached and the hatchet was said to have been buried, Gallaudet significantly remarked that he still knew where the weapon was hidden. (*Ibid.,* p. 136.) With this sentiment, an uneasy peace prevailed.

Ely and Hall, the leaders to be:

The first Normal Fellows, six in number, included a young Harvard graduate, Mr. Charles Ely, who was eventually to become a professor at Gallaudet and in later years Vice-President. One of Ely's greatest services rendered to the College was when he enthusiastically persuaded his Harvard classmate and close friend, Percival Hall, to join the second Normal Class which was then being organized for the fall of 1892.

Percival Hall was the son of Asaph Hall, an internationally known U.S. naval astronomer and discoverer of the moons of Mars. While Asaph Hall, to be sure, explored by telescope the "outer reaches of space," his son was fired by a newly found challenge, that of penetrating the inner space of human intellect isolated by silence. Young Hall's decision to join the Normal Class was indeed fortunate, for it was he who was eventually to become Gallaudet's successor as the second President of the College.

The Normal Department, its organization, and its program:

The new Normal Department at Gallaudet was effectively staffed with experienced educators of the deaf, among whom were three persons whose chief responsibility was to instruct the Normal Fellows or "Normals" in the method of teaching articulation. One of these instructors was Miss Kate H. Fish, who had trained at no less place than Clarke School. (*Ibid.,* p. 135.)

In addition to their receiving lectures on articulation, the Normals studied language instructional procedures as well as methods for teaching the common school subjects. Practicum, of course, was provided in The Kendall School, which served the deaf children of the District of Columbia. Along with these activities each Normal was to prepare a thesis on an approved subject in partial fulfillment of the requirements for a Master of Arts degree.

The Normal Department and its impact on education of the deaf:

The success of the Gallaudet Normal Training Department was

manifested within a few years through the upward mobility of its graduates into supervisory positions, principalships, and eventually superintendencies. Through the first half of the 20th Century the Gallaudet Normal Department was the chief source of administrators for American schools for the deaf. This reputation for preparing leaders came about through the joint efforts of Dr. Percival Hall, president of the College, and Dr. Sam B. Craig, a long-time principal of The Kendall School and director of the Normal Training program.

As a consequence, the Gallaudet Normal Department alumni became a close-knit and mutually supportive group which worked to preserve the personal and professional interests of its members in education of the deaf. To succeed as an educator in this field, a young man was made to understand that the *imprimatur* of Gallaudet College was for him, indeed, a professional necessity. Thus for nearly a century Gallaudet College came to direct the main course of American education of the deaf.

39

Anne Sullivan Discusses Her
Language Teaching Procedures
1892

In view of the fame of the Helen Keller–Anne Sullivan story there is little need to repeat it; however, a history of the education of the deaf would be seriously remiss in not giving some attention to some of the instructional philosophy and techniques employed by Miss Sullivan in bringing English to her little deaf-blind pupil.

Helen Keller as an educational challenge:

It must be remembered that the child, Helen Keller, was left deaf and blind at the age of 19 months. The trauma of her illness and its ensuing effects left the little girl devoid of any recollection of her infant speech. She remained in her dark silence for a period of 7 years until she reached out to touch the face of Anne Sullivan, a 21-year-old Irish girl, who had come to liberate her. Miss Sullivan's article "How Helen Keller Acquired Language" was written for a brochure entitled "Helen Keller – Souvenir of the First Summer Meeting of the American Association to Promote the Teaching of Speech to the Deaf" and first appeared in the *American Annals of the Deaf* for April, 1892.

HOW HELEN KELLER ACQUIRED LANGUAGE

In March, 1887, I first became Helen's teacher, and began work by putting her in possession of the use of the manual alphabet as rapidly as possible. Using any object that she could readily examine by the sense of touch, I would slowly spell its name with my fingers, while she held my hand and felt its motion; then I would aid her to repeat the word with her own fingers. She easily comprehended what I desired her to do, imitated the movements with careful precision, and seemed to understand that she was learning the names of the objects around her. In a few days she had mastered this entire alphabet, and could spell the names of numerous objects. Next I taught her words represented by action; she readily caught their meaning, and we were then enabled to form sentences. "Helen is in wardrobe," "Box is on table," Mildred is in crib," are specimens of sentences constructed by Helen in the month of April, 1887.

In these exercises, and in all my work with her previous to this time, I had followed the method adopted in teaching Laura Bridgman; but I found it was not sufficient for the needs of my little pupil. It became evident to me that it was not wise to confine myself strictly to the use of words of which she knew the full meaning, and I began to give her many words in my sentences without any further explanation concerning them than was conveyed to her by their connection with those words which she did know. I observed that she adopted their use, often without inquiry. After this I invariably gave her complete sentences in communicating with her, often long ones using many words of which she did not understand the meaning, but in connection with others of which she had full knowledge, and in such manner that she was able to comprehend the meaning I desired to convey. She thus became familiar with and in the daily use of, many words the full meaning of which had not been explained to her in detail; and, before I realized the importance to her of this practice, she was the possessor of a vocabulary which astonished me.

She learned with perfect ease the forms of the raised letters much as are used in printing books for the use of the blind, and we soon began to form sentences from words printed on separate slips of paper in raised letters; this exercise delighted her very much, and prepared the way for the writing lessons. It was not difficult for her to understand and make use of written language. On July 12, 1887, she wrote, without assistance, a correctly-spelled and legible letter to one of her cousins; this was a little more than a month after her first lesson in chirography. She now uses the "point," or what is termed the "Braille," system of writing; this she can read with her fingers. When writing for those who do not understand reading the point letters, she copies her work into the square writing in which some of her communications have appeared.

I am constantly asked, by persons familiar with teaching the deaf, how it is that Helen has acquired such a comprehensive command of language in so short a time. I think it is first, because she has, like many hearing persons, a natural aptitude for comprehending and making use of language as soon as it is acquired; and, second, because volumes of words have been placed in her possession by means of conversation, reading to her from books, and from her own constant use of books printed in raised letters. I have had no particular method of teaching, but have always regarded my pupil as a study, whose own spontaneous impulses must be my surest guide. I have never taught Helen to use signs such as have been employed in teaching the deaf, but confined myself to the use of the manual alphabet in communicating with her. I have always talked to her as I would to a seeing and hearing child, and have insisted that others should do the same. When a person asks me if she will understand this or that word, I reply, "Never mind whether she understands each separate word in a sentence; she will guess the meaning of the new words from their connection with others which are already intelligible to her." I am asked, "How did you teach her words expressive of intellectual and moral qualities?" It is difficult to tell just how she came to understand the meaning of abstract ideas, but I believe it was more through association and repetition than through any explanation of mine. This is especially true of her earlier lessons, when her knowlege of language was so slight as to make explanation well-nigh impossible. I have always made it a practice to use the words descriptive of emotions, of intellectual or moral qualities and actions, in connection with the circumstance which required their use. I began to use such words as "perhaps," "suppose," "expect," etc., when I thought she could understand their application. She was always anxious to learn the names of people we met in the horse-cars or elsewhere, where they were going, what they were to do, etc. The following illustrates her interest in those about her, and shows how these words were taught:

> HELEN. What is little boy's name?
> TEACHER. I do not know; he is a little strange boy; *perhaps* his name is Jack.
> HELEN. Where is he going?
> TEACHER. He *may* be going to the common to have fun with other boys.
> HELEN. What will he play?
> TEACHER. I *suppose* he will play ball.
> HELEN. What are boys doing now?
> TEACHER. *Perhaps* they are expecting Jack, and are waiting for him.

After the words became familiar to her she began to use them in composition. The following is an extract from a composition written by Helen in September, 1888:

> This morning teacher and I sat by the window, and we saw a little boy walking on the sidewalk. * * * I do not know how old he was, but *think* he *may have been* six years old. I do not know where he was going, because he was a little strange boy; but *perhaps* his mother sent him to a store to buy something for dinner. He had a bag in one hand. I *suppose* he was going to take it to his mother.

Her command of language has grown with her increase of experiences: while these were few and elementary, her vocabulary was more limited; as she learns more of the world about her, her judgment acquires accuracy, her reasoning powers become stronger, more active, and subtle, and the language by which she expresses this intellectual activity gains in fluency and logic.

I am convinced that the freedom and accuracy which characterize Helen's use of English are due quite as much to her familiarity with books as to her natural aptitude for learning language. I gave her books printed in raised letters long before she could read them, and she would amuse herself for hours each day in carefully passing her fingers over the words, searching for such as she knew, and would scream with delight whenever she found one. Many times she would inquire the meaning of some word she had not previously felt, and, having learned it, would go on with great eagerness to find its counterpart on other pages; she thus naturally became interested in the subject of which the words treated, and as books were placed in her hands suited to her age, she was soon reading simple stories. In selecting books for Helen to read, it has never occurred to me to choose them with reference to her misfortune. I have read to her such publications as other children of her age read and take delight in, and the same rule has been observed in placing in her hands books printed in raised letters. She has a great fondness for reading, grasps the ideas quickly, and has a faculty of embodying them in language often quite different from that used by the author; for instance, while reading to her from Dickens's "Child's History of England" I came to the sentence, "Still the spirit of the brave Britons was not broken." I asked here what she thought that meant; she replied "I think it means that the brave Britons were not discouraged because the Romans had won so many battles, and they wished all the more to drive them away." The very next lines are still more idiomatic: "When Suetonius left the country, they fell upon his troops and retook the island of Anglesea." This is her interpretation of the sentence: "It means, that when the Roman general had gone away, the Britons began to fight again; and because the Roman soldiers had no general to tell them what to do, they were overcome by the Britons, and lost the island they had captured." During the first year spent with Helen I read to her one day a pretty story called "Hyacinthus" which I found in a plant and flower-seed catalogue; it impressed her very much, and she made great use of it in her conversation and writing for some time after.

She commits to memory both prose and poetry in large measure, and many times suprises us by repeating pages from some favorite author, when we have not previously known that she had memorized any portion of the work. Sometimes it seems as if she absorbed the ideas and even the meaning, they lay dormant in her mind until some experience brought their application to her, when a comprehension of their meaning and significance flashed the language before her mental vision.

She is a great admirer of the writings of Dr. Oliver Wendell Holmes, and has committed to memory many of his poems. During the winter of 1889-90, which we spent at the Perkins Institution in South Boston, she was a member of a class in zoology. One day, the teacher, Miss Bennett, was explaining to the class the habit of the chambered nautilus; holding the shell of the mollusk in her hand, she minutely described it in detail. I sat by Helen's side, repeating the instruction to her with my fingers. When the shell was passed to her, in turn, for examination, she felt it over very carefully, rose to her feet, and, greatly to my surprise and astonishment, slowly repeated Dr. Holmes's beautiful poem on this subject, "The Chambered Nautilus."

During this winter (1891-92) I went with her into the yard while a light snow was falling, and let her feel the falling flakes. She appeared to enjoy it very much indeed. As we went in, she repeated these words: "Out of the cloud-folds of his garments Winter shakes the snow." I inquired of her where she had read this; she did not remember having read it, did not seem to know that she had learned it. As I did not remember ever hearing or reading it, I inquired of several of my friends if they recalled the words of description; no one seemed to remember it. The teachers at the Institution expressed the opinion that the description did not appear in any book in raised print in that library; but one lady, Miss Marrett, took upon herself the task of examining books of poems in ordinary type, and was rewarded by finding the following lines in one of Longfellow's minor poems, entitled "Snowflakes:"

> Out of the bosom of the air,
> Out of the cloud-folds of her garment shaken,
> Over the woodlands brown and bare,
> Over the harvest-fields forsaken,
> Silent, and soft, and slow
> Descends the snow.

It would seem that Helen had learned and treasured the memory of this expression of the poet, and this morning in the snow-storm had found its application.

As the two principal avenues of perception were hopelessly closed to Helen at the commencement of her education, and the manual alphabet appealed more directly and forcibly to her remaining sense of touch than any other known medium of communication, it was made the channel through which her ideas could flow. She became very proficient in its use; ordinary conversation could be communicated to her with comparative ease, and she could herself spell eighty common words in a minute. For three years the manual alphabet had been her only means of intercourse with the outside world; by its means she had acquired a comprehensive vocabulary, which enabled her to converse freely, read intelligently, and write good idiomatic English. Nevertheless, the impulse to utter audible sounds was strong within her, and the constant efforts I made to repress this instinctive tendency were of no avail. I considered that if she could learn to speak, her inability to watch the lips of others would be an insurmoutable obstacle in the way of her intelligent use of oral language.

During the winter of 1889-90 she became gradually conscious that her means of communication with others was different from that employed by her little friends and playmates at the Perkins Institution, and one day her thoughts found expression in the following questions: "How do the blind girls know what to say with their mouths?" "Why do you not teach me to talk like them?" "Do deaf children ever learn to speak?" I explained that there were schools where deaf children were taught to speak, but that they could see their teachers' mouths, and learn partly in that way. She interrupted me to say that she was sure she could *feel* my mouth very well. A short time after this conversation a lady came to see her, and told her about the deaf and blind Norwegian child, Ragnhild Kaata, who had been taught to speak, and to understand, by touching the lips of her teacher, what he said to her. Helen's joy over this good news can be better imagined than described. "I am so delighted," she said, "for now I know that I shall learn to speak too." I promised to take her to see a kind lady who knew all about teaching the deaf, and who would know if it would be possible for her to learn to speak. "Oh, yes, I can learn," was her eager reply; "I know I can, because Ragnhild has learned to speak." She did not mention the subject again that day, but it was evident that she thought of little else, and that night she was not able to sleep.

She began immediately to make sounds, which she called *speaking*, and I saw the necessity of correct instruction, since her heart was set upon learning to talk. Accordingly, I went with her to ask the advice and assistance of Miss Sarah Fuller, the principal of the Horace Mann School for the Deaf, on Newbury Street, Boston. Miss Fuller was much delighted with the child's earnestness and enthusiasm, and at once commenced to teach her. (Sullivan, "Helen Keller," p. 133.)

Pure oralism vs. oralism:

Helen's statement, "I shall learn to speak too," is of particular significance in terms of *pure oralism* as opposed to *oralism*. It will be recalled that in the former mode of oral instruction, the deaf child first learns to speak the word before he learns to read and write it. The rationale for this approach is that it follows the natural sequence of speech development.

In the latter mode, however, the child learns first to read and write the word and then he learns to speak it – the assumption being that the child, having some concepts clothed in English, is much more inclined to wish to speak. Having something to say, of course, has always been the prime motivation for anyone's speaking, wanting to speak, or wanting to learn how to speak. Thus Helen's motivation for speech evolved from her newly acquired ability to express her thoughts in English.

Continuing, Miss Sullivan writes,

It was just three years from the day when Helen became conscious that she could communicate her physical wants, her thoughts, and her impressions through the arbitrary language of the fingers, to the time when she received her first lesson in the more natural and universal instrument of human intercourse—oral language. She was not content at first to be drilled in single sounds, but was impatient to pronounce words and sentences. The length of the word or the difficulty of the arrangement of the letters never seemed to discourage her. When she had been talking for less than a week, she met her friend Mr. Rodocanachi, and immediately began to struggle with the pronunciation of his name; nor would she give it up until she was able to articulate the word distinctly. Her interest in this instruction never diminished for a moment, and in her eagerness to overcome the difficulties which beset her on all sides she taxed her powers to the utmost. In less than a month she was able to converse intelligibly in oral language. The child's own ecstacy of delight when she was first able to utter her thoughts in living and distinct speech was shared by all who witnessed the almost miraculous achievement. Her success was more complete and inspiring than even those had dreamed or expected who best knew her marvellous intelligence and great mental capacity.

She very much prefers to speak rather than to spell with her fingers, and makes rapid improvement in the art; she now uses speech almost exclusively, seldom employing her fingers in conversation except when she wishes to communicate a silent message, and is greatly pleased when told by strangers that they readily understand her articulation. She often reads aloud to the children at the Perkins Institution. I noted her, not many days since, reading and repeating from memory to them from Miss Alcott's story of "Little Women."

She can read somewhat from our lips by the sense of touch, and could, I think, become quite expert in this practice, did we devote any time to assist her; as it is, she often surprises us by catching at the meaning of words and phrases as we utter them. She has already read in this way words in foreign languages with which she was not acquainted. She understands the necessity of close observation, and carefully notes the slightest vibrations resulting from articulation.

ANNE M. SULLIVAN,
Teacher of Helen Keller

(*Ibid.*, pp. 133-134.)

Dr. Bell's possible reflections:

Dr. Alexander Graham Bell, upon reading Anne Sullivan's account of her instructional procedures, must certainly have reflected on the principles of George Dalgarno which he had himself applied so effectively some 20 years previously in the teaching of George Sanders. Similarly, he must have recalled the phenomenal language achievements of those deaf children whom he had recently observed at Zenas Freeman Westervelt's school in Rochester, New York. While all of these systems, including Miss Sullivan's, applied the common theory of "English through the use of English" in the instruction of deaf children, they were each notably dominated by Dalgarno's instructional watchword *diligence,* which has characterized the work of every successful teacher of the deaf from the beginning.

Dr. Bell, deeply interested in the Sullivan-Keller teaching-learning endeavor, wrote to Miss Sullivan for a more elaborate explanation of her work.

Washington, D.C., January 21, 1892

Miss A. M. Sullivan, Teacher of Helen Keller,
Perkins Institution for the Blind, South Boston.

Dear Miss Sullivan: Allow me to thank you for the privilege of reading your account of how you taught Helen Keller, which you have prepared for the second edition of the Souvenir issued by the Volta Bureau. Your paper is full interest to teachers of the deaf, and it contains many valuable and important suggestions.

I am particularly struck by your statement that you gave Helen books printed in raised letters *"long before she could read them,"* and that *"she would amuse herself for hours each day in carefully passing her fingers over the words, searching for such words as she knew,"* etc.

I consider that statement as of very great significance and importance when I try to account for her wonderful familiarity with idiomatic English. She is such an exceptional child that we are apt to attribute everything to her marvellous mind, and forget that language comes from without, and not from within. She could not intuitively arrive at a knowledge of idiomatic English expressions. It is absolutely certain that such expressions must have been *taught to her* before she could use them; and if you can show us how it was done, teachers of the deaf all over the world will owe you a debt of gratitude.

The great problem in the education of the deaf is the teaching of idiomatic language.

I am sure that instructors of the deaf will support me in urging you to tell us all you can as to the part played by books in the instruction of Helen Keller. We should like to form an idea of the quantity and quality of the reading-matter presented for her examination "long before she could read the books."

How much time did she devote to the examination of language which she could not understand, in her search for the words that she knew? I would suggest that you give us a list of the books she had read, arranging them, as well as you can, in the order of presentation.

Teachers of the deaf find great difficulty in selecting suitable books for their pupils; and I am sure they would thank you especially for the names of those books that have given Helen pleasure, and have proved most profitable in her instruction.

You say, "*I have always talked to Helen as I would to a hearing child, and have insisted that others should do the same*, etc. I presume you mean by this that you talked *with your fingers* instead of your mouth; that you spelled into her hand what you would have spoken to a seeing and hearing child. You say that you have "always" done this. Are we to understand that you pursued this method from the very beginning of her education, and that you spelled complete sentences and idiomatic expressions into her hand *before she was capable of understanding the language employed?* If this is so, I consider the point to be of so much importance that I would urge you to elaborate the statement, and make your meaning perfectly clear and unmistakable.

Yours very sincerely,

ALEXANDER GRAHAM BELL

(*Ibid.*, pp. 134-135.)

The foregoing letter enabled Miss Sullivan to focus on the particulars of Dr. Bell's interest, which were in fact the interests of all teachers of the deaf. It was, indeed, fortunate that he had the perception and the presence to draw from Miss Sullivan those perspectives and techniques which made the instruction of her pupil possible. In reply to Dr. Bell's letter Miss Sullivan wrote:

South Boston, Mass., January 26, 1892.

Dr. Alexander Graham Bell.

Dear Sir: Thanking you for your very complimentary mention of my paper prepared for the second edition of the Souvenir "Helen Keller," I will say that it gives me pleasure to reply to your inquiries; and I shall be much gratified if the teachers of the deaf can derive, from my experience with my interesting little pupil, any assistance and encouragement in imparting to deaf children a knowledge and command of idiomatic language.

The little deaf and blind child, Helen Keller, whom it was my good fortune to have placed under my care almost five years since, appealed to my woman's heart on account of her misfortune, with which in part I knew from experience how to sympathize, and at once won my affection by her sweet and loving nature. As soon as we were able to communicate with each other by means of the manual alphabet, I was enabled to become a substitute to her for sight and hearing. I

began talking to her with my fingers as soon as I could make her comprehend the *meaning* I wished to convey. Of course, at first we could
proceed but slowly; but as each sentence was an aid to the next one,
she gained rapidly in a knowledge of words, and by this means I was
soon able to give her a better acquaintance with her surroundings. I
talked to her almost incessantly in her waking hours; spelled in hand
a description of what was transpiring around us, what I saw, what I
was doing, what others were doing—any thing, every thing. Of course,
in doing this I used multitudes of words she did not at the time understand, and the exact definition of which I did not pause to explain; but
I never abbreviated or omitted words, but spelled all my sentences
carefully and correctly. I talked to this little girl with my fingers as
I should have talked to her with my mouth had she been a hearing
child; and no doubt I talked much more with my fingers, and more constantly, than I should have done with my mouth had she possessed the
use of sight and hearing, for, had she the full use of these senses, she
would have been less dependent on me for amusement and entertainment. When she had cards and books placed in her hands printed in
this style, they were at once an unfailing source of entertainment and
instruction to her.

(*Ibid.*, p. 136.)

Having established the manual alphabet as her sole medium of
communication with little Helen, Miss Sullivan endeavored to approximate for her the multiplicity of word exposures usually
directed toward the average hearing-sighted child. In addition to
this she talked to Helen (a) relating and describing almost "incessantly in her waking hours" the experience of the moment, (b)
using words which were not explained, (c) resorting neither to omissions nor to abbreviations, and, finally, (d) fingerspelling all
language "carefully and correctly" into sentences. These principles,
incidentally, bear a special significance in the language development of any child, be he hearing-impaired, deaf, or deaf-blind.

Miss Sullivan then continues her letter and discusses Dr. Bell's
special interest of reading.

You ask me to tell all I can "as to the part played by books in the instruction of Helen Keller." I do not know that I can describe to you the
importance and advantage that books have been to my pupil in acquiring a command of idiomatic English: the advantage has been in-
calculable. I am confident that Helen's remarkable command of
language is due to the fact that books printed in raised letters were
placed in her hands as soon as she knew the formation of the letters;
it at once became her delight to study these pages, with her sensitive
fingers, for many hours a day, not as a lesson, but as a pastime. I was
astonished at the rapidity with which she acquired the use of words
she had learned by first finding them on the printed page, inquired
of me their meaning, and applied them in constructing sentences. It

was not long before she would repeat to me a story she had read in her book; I mean, from the mass of words she had passed her fingers over, she would many times become possessed of the plot or basis of the tale, and recount it to me with her fingers, using any words by which she could make me understand her meaning, often the same used in the book for several sentences; the full meaning of many of these words she could not have understood but by their connection with others which she did know. Sometimes, in amusing herself in this way with her books, she would become completely puzzled, and come to me for help. I would then read to her (always spelling the words into her hand), when with great eagerness she would re-read it for herself with a bright and happy face, always expecting my sympathy and companionship to talk the story over with her, and participate in her appreciation of the author's portrayal of his subject. In doing this we naturally made use of many forms of expression not found in the book, and thus she readily discovered the meaning of words not previously understood. The more Helen used her books, the more she desired to do so, and much time was spent in the manner described.

In regard to the quantity and quality of books furnished Helen before she knew many words, I cannot give a list that will be of much value to teachers of the deaf, as, on account of Helen's double misfortune, she could not be supplied, as deaf children can who have the sense of sight, with a selection from the almost limitless number of beautifully printed and illustrated books for children of all ages which our bookstores so generously display.

I could only read to her with my fingers, and describe to her in the same manner the illustrations, from any of these interesting and attractive publications. The expense of printing books for the use of the blind is enormously greater in proportion than for ordinary printing. A book that one could purchase for from twenty-five to fifty cents for the use of a seeing child, would, if prepared for a blind child cost at least three dollars.

The only books which I had to place in Helen's hands at the beginning of my work with her were the Primer and a series of seven volumes of school readers such as are in use in the Primary Department at the Perkins Institution at South Boston; there eight volumes and a copy of "Our World" (a geography) constituted our entire library of books in raised print for many months. As to how much time was spent by this little girl in passing her fingers over the pages in these volumes, searching for such words as she knew, I cannot give you a definite estimate, any more than I could tell you how much time she gave to her doll or to her toys; but she preferred the books to either doll or toys, and spent much more time with them. Very many happy hours were devoted to this practice with her books every day; it often required special pleading to induce her to leave them. In March, 1888, Mr. Anagnos sent her a copy of a Geographical Reader in raised print. She was very much pleased with it, and took great delight in the discovery of many entirely new words to her on its pages. Not long after this she had two volumes of a series of readers termed "Youth's Libraries," selections in prose and poetry from various authors, and a child's book entitled "Heidi." When we came to Boston, in May of this year, she had access to a variety of literature in raised print at the library of the Institution. She read "Life and her Children," by Isabel Berkeley; "What Katy Did;" "Patsy;" "Story of a Short Life," etc. In the meantime I had been reading to her, by spelling the words into her hand, such books and selections as I had at command of the character that other children of her age enjoy. In August, 1888, I read to her in this way the popular story by Mrs. Burnett, "Little Lord Fauntleroy." Her delight in the book knew no bounds, and in response to her earnest entreaty Mr. Anagnos had this story put in raised print; since then she has re-read it many times for herself.

As I have never kept a record of the books Helen has read, or of the order in which I have read books to her, therefore it will be impossible for me to comply with your request in full; but among the books which Helen has read and enjoyed particularly, I recall "Most Celebrated Diamonds;" "Little Women;" "Tanglewood Tales;" "Wonder Book;" "In His Name;" "A Man without a Country;" "Bible Stories;" "Greek Heroes;" "Swiss Family Robinson;" "The Sleeping Sentinel;" "Stories by Hans Christian Andersen;" "The Queen of the Pirate Isles;" "Christmas Carol" (Dickens); "Child's History of England" (Dickens); "American Prose Selections;" "Birds' Christmas Dinner;" "Sara Crewe;" "Evangeline;" "Hiawatha," and many other of Longfellow's Poems; "Enoch Arden;" Holmes's Poems; Whittier's Poems; "Stories of American Progress," etc., etc.

In addition to the story by Mrs. Burnett before mentioned, the following are titles of books which I remember to have read to Helen since that date: "Queens at Home," "Triangular Society," "Donald and Dorothy," "Black Beauty," "Capt. January," three of Abbot's Rollo books (Rome, Germany, and Naples), "Little St. Elizabeth," "Stories from Roman History," "Stories from Shakespeare" (by Charles and Mary Lamb), "The Birds' Christmas Carol," "Veronica," etc.

Yours truly,

ANNE M. SULLIVAN.

(Ibid., pp. 136-139.)

It should be remembered that at the writing of this letter in January, 1892, Helen was but 11 years old and had been under instruction not quite 5 years. To be sure, she was a prodigy; however, had she had only one-half the intellectual receptivity, but the same degree of linguistic exposure and attention, she would probably still have been above the average of sighted-deaf children in achievement. At this point an apropos question might be, is the modern prelingually hearing-impaired child working to his full intellectual potentiality?

A reflection for the reader:

The reader might reflect on the idea that if deaf, mute, and blind Helen Keller, with her emotional disturbance, hyperactivity, and learning disability, had been born into the late 20th Century, what would her educational and social prognosis have been? Fortunately, however, she was born into a simpler time which recognized emotional disturbance, hyperactivity, and learning disabilities as natural problems inherent in *all* young hearing-impaired children. For Anne Sullivan the solution of little Helen's predicament lay, first, in the recognition of her pupil's basic need for English communication and, second, in the singular and diligent pursuit to fulfill that need; with that, all else followed.

40

Structured vs. Unstructured
Language Systems
in the 19th Century

Through the 19th Century educators of the deaf had struggled valiantly to devise systems which would bring order to the chaotic language structure of prelingually deaf children. Among the earliest of these was the Abbé Sicard of the Paris Institute, who through his "Theory of Ciphers" sought to objectify the elements of syntax by assigning each element a specific number. At the top of the blackboard was written a #1 to indicate the *nominative case*. Under this numeral all nouns and pronouns were listed. The next column to the right was labeled #2, beneath which were listed all of the *verbs*. Column #3, representing the *objective case*, was used for listing objective nouns and pronouns. Column #4 was designated for *prepositions*. The final column, #5, was given to the *objects of the preposition* with such elements being listed accordingly. (Taylor, "Sicard's Theory," p. 396.) Thus a kind of linguistic framework was provided upon which deaf children could place the abstract elements of language into aceptable syntax.

The Theory of Ciphers adapted to English:

Thomas Hopkins Gallaudet and his deaf colleague, Laurent Clerc, of course, had brought this language instructional system with them from France. They modified it to conform with English and introduced it into their American Asylum in 1817. It was also this American version of the Theory of Ciphers which was taught to all of the early teachers-in-training at Hartford. Consequently, upon the completion of their training they carried the System to their new places of employment in the various state institutions for the deaf. Thus it was the Theory of Ciphers became the prescribed structural procedure for teaching English to the deaf.

New movements in English instruction:

It will be recalled, however, that with the advent of the *Intuitive Method* of language development introduced by Vaisse at the New York Institute for the Deaf in 1823, a new movement in English instruction was commenced.

A number of years later in the middle of the Century, David Greenberger (Greene) aggressively espoused the *Natural Method* of language development at his New York Institute for the Improved Instruction of Deaf-Mutes.

Also during this period Rochester's Z. F. Westervelt placed heavy emphasis upon the practice of "English through the use of English." This approach, orally oriented, employed fingerspelling as a supplement and complement to speech and speechreading. In his Rochester Method, Westervelt had eclectically chosen and combined the principles of both the *intuitive* and *natural* methods.

All of these unstructured procedures were also largely unrestricted in terms of the sequence of language concepts to be taught. They were instead guided by the children's expressive and receptive needs to determine the direction of instruction. After some years had passed, Sicard's "Theory of Ciphers" was generally forgotten as an instructional mode, and the freer unstructured modes came to dominate language teaching for the deaf.

There were instructors, of course, who felt uncomfortable with the freedom accorded them by the intuitive or natural methods. Traditionally, Latin and English had been taught to hearing people through an analytical approach which provided the paradigms and specific rules for rhetoric. Having experienced this, many teachers of the deaf were more comfortable in teaching English to the deaf according to this more regulated and traditional manner. Consequently, English instruction for the deaf began to vary in its approaches from school to school and even from teacher to teacher.

Elements of language objectified:

It was Miss Katherine B. Barry, a teacher of the deaf in the Colorado School, who first sought to organize and objectify the elements of language in order that they might be more effectively taught.

In her thinking, Miss Barry saw the same logic and strategy perceived by the Abbé Sicard and consequently set about to designate the principal elements of the sentence just as he had done. This she did without knowing or ever having heard of the Abbé Sicard and his "Theory of Ciphers." This, of course, was very possible because of the passing of some 70 or more years.

"The Barry Five Slate System" was introduced in May, 1893, through the pages of an educational magazine entitled *The Educator*. (*Ibid*., p. 397.) Miss Barry's system originally involved the use of five separate columns headed from left to right with each of the following basic sentence elements: *subject, verb, object, preposition,* and *object of the preposition*. A sixth column was later added to accommodate the adverbial element which might shift in its position according to the requirement of the sentence.

In any event, Sicard's concept was once again revived, but under the new designation of "the five slates." The logic of Miss Barry's system appealed to many teachers, and the procedure was soon adopted by a number of American schools for the deaf.

George Wing and his contribution:

Another language approach which actually antedated Miss Barry's system was that of Mr. George Wing, a hearing-impaired teacher in the Minnesota School for the Deaf at Faribault. While Miss Barry's system is now generally defunct as far as modern education of the deaf is concerned, Mr. Wing's method continues to be used today in a few schools for the deaf. Hence the Wing Symbols are placed last in this consideration of systems.

Mr. Wing, a teacher of many years' experience, hit upon his symbol system in the middle 1870's. It was not, however, until 1884 that he, complying with the request of his superintendent, Dr. J. L. Noyes, wrote out his language system under the title "Function Symbols." In this paper he states,

> What we want is not a complicated machine in the hands of the teacher alone, but a simple tool in the hands of both teacher and pupil. This

has been kept in view in devising the method used in Minnesota. ("Function Symbols," p. 191.)

Mr. Wing then credits Dr. John S. Hart's *Language Lessons* for providing the "general plan" for his system. He then gives his "List of Symbols used in the Minnesota Method of teaching Language to Deaf-Mutes." These symbols were subsequently known as the "Wing Symbols."

Essentials, indicated by Letters:

Subject, ... s.
Verb, intransitive .... V⊃
Verb, transitive active .... V̄
Verb, transitive passive .... ⌐V
Object, ... o.
Complement, ... c.

Modifying Forms, indicated by Numbers:

Appositive, ... 1.
Possessive, ... 2.
Adjective, ... 3.
Preposition Phrase, ... 4.
Adverb and Adverbial Phrase, ... 5.
Infinitive, ... 6.

Special Symbols:

Auxiliary, ... +
Conjunction, ... ⊃⊂
Ellipsis, ... *

Modifications: The object and complement of the infinitive and participle are distinguished from those of the finite verb by lines over the symbols (ō. c̄.). Intransitive, active, and passive infinitives and participles may be distinguished by forward and backward strokes over the symbols, imitating like modifications in the verb symbol.

The above are all the symbols necessary to indicate the office of every word, phrase and clause in any English sentence. No additional symbols should be used until Grammar is taken up as a regular study. With advanced classes studying the rules of grammar a few further modifications may be introduced, *e.g.*

Nominative Absolute, Ⓢ; Nominative Independent, [S̲] .

Other convenient modifications may suggest themselves to the teacher; but he should remember that multiplication of symbols is a multiplication of the pupil's difficulties in comprehending them. (*Ibid.*, p. 192.)

Through the 19th Century there was a strong emphasis upon

the daily memorization of perfected sentences and paragraphs which pupils had written. They were then required to reproduce in writing the memorized materials on the following school day. The rationale for this was that with the memorization of corrected material, the pupils would have "built-in" models for their subsequent original composition efforts. The one essential for the success of this practice was that the material to be memorized first had to be *thoroughly understood.*

It was in this thinking, however, that George Wing had his strongest objections. It was his contention that actually too many pupils *failed* to understand fully the material which they memorized even though they had a great part in the composition of it. In turn it was this memorization of meaningless or partly meaningless material which caused the problem of "scrambled" language. (It might be observed that while modern practice generally spares prelingually deaf children from having to memorize much of anything, they still continue to be hobbled by the predicament of confused language.)

In his effort to combat the prelingually deaf child's language problem, Mr. Wing set forth the following objectives of his method:

First, to break up the habit of writing sentences with no guide but memory;

Second, to teach the essentials of the sentence – the subject and predicate – in such a manner that the pupils can comprehend them and intelligently use them;

Third, to teach the rational use of modifying forms, their offices and positions in the sentence, without burdening the pupils' minds with etymological distinctions before they are capable of appreciating them, and without confusing them with a multitude of symbols and diagram lines;

Fourth, to place in the hands of the teacher an instrument by means of which he can compel the attention of his pupils to his corrections and explanations.

It should be bourne in mind that the *forms, functions,* and *positions* of the parts of the sentence are all that we attempt to show; the etymology of words and the force and connection of words, phrases, and clauses are left to intelligent observation and persistent drill. The parts of speech and their various forms are taught by their names only; no symbols or manual signs are used to represent them. All grammatical symbols and arbitrary signs represent strictly the functions performed by words, phrases, and clauses in construction of sentences. (*Ibid.*, p. 193.)

Mr. Wing then provides his "four essential forms of declarative sentences," using his symbols to distinguish them.

S ⌒⊃
John walked.

S ⌒⊃ C
John was angry. (An angry boy.)

S ⌐‾   O
John struck a dog.

S __ ‾⌐
John was bitten.

Following "are some elliptical constructions which may be considered as combinations of these forms," e.g.,

S ⌐‾   O C S — ‾⌐ C
He made the dog angry. He was made angry.

In his presentation, Mr. Wing gives numerous other applied examples of his ingenious system which the interested reader is most certainly encouraged to investigate.

Probably the most outstanding modern proponent of the Wing Symbols was the late Miss Josephine Quinn, who served for 50 years as supervising teacher of the primary and intermediate departments at the Minnesota School for the Deaf. Totally convinced of the educability of deaf children, she demonstrated her love for them by not merely expecting an acceptable performance from her pupils, but by demanding it.

Wing's no-nonsense advice to teachers:

Through Miss Quinn's consistent application of the Wing Symbols throughout the school program and her providing an immense amount of usage reinforcement through "chalkboard" composition writing, her prelingually deaf pupils were able to acquire extraordinary levels of English achievement. This fact, of course, was demonstrated through the fine work of many of the Minnesota School alumni who subsequently attended Gallaudet College and were graduated from that institution. The preparation for these successes was accomplished through Miss Quinn's unequivocal adherence to George Wing's no-nonsense advice to teachers, " 'Fight it out on this line,' without yielding or compromise." With this thought, Dalgarno's word *diligence* comes to mind. (See Appendix 16.)

Chapter Ten
Early 20th-Century Advances in American Education of the Deaf

41

Dr. Max A. Goldstein
and the Acoustic Method
1914

The year 1914 brought to realization a dream which Dr. Max A. Goldstein, a St. Louis otologist, had entertained for a number of years. This was the establishment of a school which would emphasize the use of residual hearing in the education of hearing-impaired children. The school which he founded was, of course, the now well-known Central Institute for the Deaf (CID). All of this was a culmination of Dr. Goldstein's early graduate studies which he had pursued as a young physician under the direction of Dr. Victor Urbantschitsch, a Viennese otologist. Goldstein's observations of Urbantschitsch's work persuaded him conclusively that the aural avenue for teaching deaf children was, indeed, a valid one. Upon the completion of his studies, Goldstein enthusiastically returned to America to share what he had learned abroad.

Aural amplifications as an instructional mode:

While a few scattered attempts had been previously made in the United States to utilize the residual hearing of deaf children, the efforts were short-lived. From this there evolved among many educators of the deaf a certain skepticism which insulated them from any serious consideration of Goldstein's innovative thinking.

This negative reaction was quite likely the motivating reason which ultimately led to the establishment of the Central Institute.

It should be remembered that during the first several years at CID, the battery-operated individual hearing aid was a cumbersome device and still in its developmental stage. Goldstein, therefore, preferred the use of the speaking tube in his auditory work with children. The tube, he believed, was less inclined to distort the sounds of natural speech and was, consequently, a much more effective instructional device.

Over the next two decades, Goldstein put into effect his instructional ideas and confirmed through practice the efficacy of his theories.

In June, 1933, at the International Congress on the Education of the Deaf held at the New Jersey School for the Deaf at West Trenton, Dr. Goldstein had the opportunity to address the Congress on his acoustic method. Goldstein's work in the area of aural education had by this time been long known, but little understood. His presentation "The Acoustic Method," however, did much to clarify for school administrators generally the significance of what was being done at CID.

The Acoustic Method defined:

In his presentation Goldstein dealt first with nomenclature and endeavored to clarify specifically what he expected in aural education. For many years the *American Annals of the Deaf* had carried in each of its issues a page describing the various methodologies employed in the education of deaf children, i.e., oral method, manual method, combined method, and auricular method.

The definition of the auricular method approved by the Convention of American Instructors of the Deaf was of particular interest to Goldstein. The Convention statement read:

> The hearing of the semi-deaf pupils is utilized and developed to the greatest possible extent and, with or without the aid of artificial appliances, their education is carried on efficiently through the use of speech and hearing, togther with writing. The aim of the method is to graduate these pupils as hard-of-hearing, speaking pupils instead of deaf-mutes. (Goldstein, "Acoustic Method," p. 74.)

This definition, according to Goldstein, was too general and was consequently open to various interpretations. Its lack of specificity led to considerable uncertainty as to its proper implementation; hence, its chances for success were limited. In contrast, however,

Goldstein set forth the definition of his Acoustic Method, which in its conciseness left no question as to the "how" of its application.

> Stimulation of education of the hearing mechanism and its associated sense-organs by sound vibration as applied either by voice or any sonorous instrument.

> This definition is comprehensive enough to include:

> a. Voice and musical sounds directed through the physiological tract of the ear either to the peripheral or central auditory areas.
> b. Sound vibration as sensed by tactile impression to interpret pitch, rhythm, accent, volume.
> c. Analysis of speech-sounds by tactile differentiation.
> d. Synthesis and speech construction by tactile impression.
> e. Sound waves and their significance as appreciated by optical perception.

> An additional value of the inclusive expression "Acoustic Method" is to clear the atmosphere of a confusion of terms as "auricular training," "aural gymnastics," "aural method," and to embody all recent research, such as radio and telephone principles, inter-relation of the speical sense organs, and a wider appreciation of the physiology of hearing. (*Ibid.*)

Up to this period only those children who were recognized as hearing-impaired were afforded opportunities for sound amplification and auditory training. In keeping with the principles which he had acquired from Urbantschitsch, Goldstein stated:

> In planning our course of training by the Acoustic Method, we direct that every pupil shall receive daily systematic training of this character irrespective of the degree of deafness, the age of the pupil, or scholastic status. (*Ibid.*, p. 76.)

Goldstein then explained the reasons for the failure heretofore experienced in working with the residual hearing of deaf children.

> It is my sincere opinion that the principal reason for the unsuccessful attempts and the indifferent results in the use of the Acoustic Method are due to the desultory, aimless and unsystematic form of procedure which has discouraged teacher and pupil alike and which has given rise to so many misconceptious and misunderstandings about this particular special pedagogy. (*Ibid.*)

The clinical perspective in the education of the deaf.

Despite the imperfect auditory testing instruments of his day, with their intense vibrations which obscured the accuracy of tones,

Goldstein insisted on the importance of maintaining regular records on the hearing perception of each child. It was his belief that there should be "a clinical record of sound perception that might be considered as definite as a clinical record in which pulse, respiration and temperature indicate the course of progress or the physical status of a patient." This clinically oriented perspective of working with deaf children presented a new direction of thinking as compared to the teacher-classroom concept traditionally held by educators of the deaf. Many of them, however, were hesitant in accepting Goldstein's ideas simply because of their own limitiations for understanding what he was talking about. With references to *labyrinthitis circumscripta* and the *Cari end-organs*, he might as well have addressed them in Urdu.

High per capita cost, an objection:

One reasonable objection to the Acoustic Method which he recognized was its *per capita* cost, which would be obviously high because of the requirement for personal attention to be given to each individual pupil. To this possible criticism Goldstein answered,

> When actual speech appreciation through the ear can be developed, we obtain an even greater accomplishment, for in this group of cases we can make it possible for the pupil to receive practically all of his scholastic work directly through the ear. If such results can be produced – and they are produced – will Boards of Education and school authorities still cavil at the expense per capita of the development and splendid emancipation of the deaf child? (*Ibid.*)

Assistance from "outside" disciplines:

Aside from Goldstein's efforts for the reclamation and utilization of residual hearing in teaching deaf children, his perhaps greatest single contribution to modern education of the deaf was his welcoming the assistance of "outside" disciplines in the resolution of common problems. Goldstein stood as a pioneer in recognizing the need for new perspectives.

42

Dr. E. A. Fay's
"Progress in the Education
of the Deaf"
1915

The *Report of the Commissioner of Education* for the year ending June 30, 1915, was of particular interest to educators of the deaf. The *Report*, published by the United States Bureau of Education, contained a chapter entitled "Progress in the Education of the Deaf," whose author was the highly regarded Dr. Edward Allen Fay of Gallaudet College, and long-time editor of the *American Annals of the Deaf.*

Dr. Fay's unbiased and objective editorial policies made him a figure most acceptable, not only to the combined system advocates, but to the oralists as well. An illustration of this point was when he served for an extended time as the intermediary between Edward Miner Gallaudet and Alexander Graham Bell, during their "non-speaking" period. It was widely recognized that in any situation which called for fairness and objectivity, Dr. Fay could be depended upon to deliver. Thus it was that he was appointed to serve as the government spokesman on the state and status of education of the deaf in the United States.

Reflecting on the *then* prevailing philosophy of Gallaudet College, it is easy for one to understand and appreciate Dr. Fay's observations which he presented under several subheadings. The most revealing was:

A Constant Language Environment

While much reading of books gives the deaf child a repetition of words that corresponds in some respects to the repetition that the hearing child receives through the ears, it does not provide the same incentive to the use of language by the child himself, nor afford the same opportunity for practice in it. These essentials to the mastery of language are supplied as far as possible by the teacher in the classroom, who faithfully drills his pupils day after day and year after year in the use and practice of the English language, making all of his other instruction subsidiary to this. Much further than this few of the schools go. On the playground and in the general intercourse of daily life outside the schoolroom the children not yet having a sufficient command of the language of words to use it as a means of communication, resort to the easier and more intelligible language of signs. This is true not only of the combined-system schools, but also of the oral schools. The attempt to repress by severe measures the use of signs by little children who have as yet no other means of communication results in what is worse than the use of signs – no communication at all. The sign language thus is apt to keep its place in the mind of a congenitally deaf person as the natural medium of thought and expression in daily life, while written and spoken language are too often looked upon as something belonging exclusively to the classroom.

This great drawback to the mastery of language is probably most successfully overcome in the Western New York Institution for Deaf-Mutes at Rochester, N.Y., under the direction of Dr. Z. F. Westervelt. In that school the manual alphabet is used, to the exclusion of signs, as the ordinary means of communication, as well as of instruction from the very beginning of the child's education. The English language is so readily acquired by this method that the pupils become able to express their childish wants in it at an early stage of their instruction. In their hours of recreation they are under careful supervision, the persons in charge being always ready to address them in English rapidly spelled upon the fingers and to encourage and assist them in using English in the same way themselves. The children are thus provided with a constant environment of the English language, and the results, from a language point of view, are highly satisfactory.

Other American schools do not deem it wise to follow the Western New York Institution and its strict adherence to the manual alphabet method; some, because they regard the sign language as too valuable a factor in awakening and developing the mind of the deaf child and too convenient a means of addressing the pupils in the assembly to be wholly rejected; others, because they believe that speech, to the exclusion of the manual alphabet, should be the only medium of instruction and communication. But if they wish to achieve as good results in language as the Rochester school can show they must in some way provide an equally effective language environment for all the waking hours of the pupils. English spelled on the fingers, written, or spoken, must be the language used in the trade school and on the playground as well as in the classroom; and with the children there must be at all times, when they are not in school or shop, competent supervisors who will surround them with a constant atmosphere of good colloquial English. (Fay, "Constant Language Environment," pp. 496-498.)

Fay's move for unity in education of the deaf

Interesting for today's reader might be the fact that Dr. Fay's contribution to the *Report* was reprinted in the February, 1916, issue of *The Volta Review*, the journal for Bell's American Association to Promote the Teaching of Speech to the Deaf. This was done because Fay's article reflected so completely A. G. Bell's own educational philosophy. It thus became clear that many of the basic differences in the thinking of both Bell and Edward Miner Gallaudet had been to a large extent resolved. The "hold-outs" in both the oral and manual camps were composed mostly of persons in the small private oral school sector and in opposition to them some very articulate postlingually deaf people who curiously opposed speech for prelingually deaf children and were instead strongly in favor of sign language for them. A middle ground for these opposing forces was nonexistent and while each of the two sides mutually ignored each other, their antipathies remained. Despite these differences of a few, Edward Allan Fay's statements in "A Constant Language Environment" clarified the generally accepted standard and direction for American education of the deaf for the next five decades.

43

Day, Fusfeld, and Pintner's
Survey of Schools for the Deaf
1924-1925

The most outstanding piece of business to come out of the 1924
Conference of Superintendents and Principals of American Schools
for the Deaf at St. Augustine, Florida, was the move for a general
survey of their schools. This survey was to be a kind of institutional
self-examination, a report card which would tell the administrators
to what extent their various schools were succeeding. The big questions were, however, who was to survey whom and how. It was
therefore not without considerable discussion that the Conference
members finally agreed to invite the prestigious National Research
Council (NRC) of Washington, D.C., to assist with the planning and
conducting of the proposed study.

Education of the deaf as a "closed corporation":

For these school administrators to accrue a consensus among
themselves in favor of such an idea was, indeed, a historical feat.
Education of the deaf up to that time, it should be observed, and
for many years thereafter, was a "closed corporation" which recognized only trained teachers of the deaf as being qualified to act or
speak in the interests of deaf children. Those persons who were not
"in the work" or "in the field" were generally looked upon as interlopers. This, perhaps, *now-judged* peculiar perspective probably

originated as a sincere effort to protect deaf children from charlatans, soothsayers, and well-meaning do-gooders.

The proposed Survey and its organization:

The NRC subsequently accepted the invitation and set about to appoint a committee of specialists to administer the project. Needless to say, with the recommendation of the Conference, there were appointed to the committee some well-known educators of the deaf to make certain that the study stayed on the track. These were Dr. Percival Hall, president of Gallaudet College, and Dr. A. L. E. Crouter, superintendent of the Pennsylvania School at Mount Airy. Upon the latter's death, named to his place was Dr. Harris Taylor, principal and superintendent of the New York Institution for the Improved Instruction of Deaf-Mutes (Lexington).

Among the non-educators of the deaf on the NRC-appointed committee was Dr. Rudolf Pintner, a psychologist from Columbia University. Dr. Pintner later helped to author the final survey and eventually became an influential contributor to educational thought regarding deaf children.

The NRC placed the fact-gathering responsibility for the survey into the hands of Mr. Herbert E. Day, superintendent of the Missouri School and a former faculty member at Gallaudet College. Mr. Day was, therefore, to devote the academic year 1924-1925 to the task of visiting schools and collecting the necessary information. Professor Irving S. Fusfeld of Gallaudet College, editor of the *American Annals of the Deaf,* was appointed to assist him in this project.

The Survey outlined for the CAID:

The following year, at the 1925 CAID gathering at the Iowa School for the Deaf, it was with considerable interest and concern that word was received of the first genuinely scientific survey of American education of the deaf. The report, presented before the Iowa Convention by Prof. Fusfeld, was actually a preliminary document entitled "Purposes and Extent of the Survey of Schools for the Deaf."

For the present-day reader, Fusfeld's paper gives an interesting picture of the status of understanding relative to the testing of residual hearing, speech intelligibility, and educational achievement. After some introductory remarks, Prof. Fusfeld began:

It may be well to state here some of the problems that have been brought under scrutiny in the course of the year's investigation.

In the general educational field great studies have been made in reaching a scientific determination of what children actually accomplish in school work in relation to their natural ability. In our special field it is particularly important to us as teachers of the deaf to know what the school experience of deaf children means to them in the acquisition of media of communication and a foundation of knowledge. To meet this need, by means of a uniform and objective application of standardized tests on a comprehensive scale, is one of the aims of this survey. ("Purposes and Extent," p. 169.)

Those words and phrases which appear to be so trite and shop-worn today were in 1925 fresh, challenging, and even threatening for many teachers of the deaf.

Another problem. It is common knowledge among us that only a scant few of our children are totally deaf. Yet we have been plodding along these hundred years and a decade with the problem trailing behind us. One may point to sporadic efforts, with a few prophets declaiming in the wilderness, as proof that the problem has been receiving recognition. But these efforts have not met with the widespread acceptance they merit. There is a very evident reason for this in the fact that until recently we have had no means of readily determining with a fair degree of accuracy how much, or how far from normal, is the auditory power of our deaf children. It seems probable that the audiometric measurement of some thousands of children in the course of this survey may make it possible to obtain a clearer picture than we have had heretofore of the extent of residual hearing among our deaf children. (*Ibid.*, pp. 169-170.)

Having today scientifically confirmed through modern audiology what Fusfeld and others knew so many years ago as to the extensiveness of usable residual hearing among many so-called *deaf* children and youth, it is curious that through the 1970's there was evolving among many educators and teachers of the deaf an overt tendency to deal with such children and youth as though they were actually *deaf*, i.e., without usable hearing. The explanation for this phenomenon of perspective rests with the future. Fusfeld, continuing, stated:

Still another aspect of the general aims of the survey is to attempt to evaluate the results of the painstaking efforts of our schools in speech work, in the hope that suggestions for the betterment could be made. Here also, to carry out this purpose, a carefully devised standard measure was applied.

The survey has attempted to bring together data in regard to other important phases of our school activities, such as the course of study, the school plant, the training required of teachers, salaries of employees, pensions for worthy employees, the systems of management, control, and of financial support, custodial care of the children, and activities outside the schoolroom.

A definite program of examination was laid out to obtain adequate data for the purposes of the survey. It was thought best to include within its scope those schools that present typical phases of our work, taking into account such factors as:

1. Residence: Boarding and day-schools.
2. System of instruction: Oral, aural, manual, combined.
3. Location: City and country, industrial and agricultural centers.
4. Character of school population: Native born, foreign born, foreign born percentage.
5. Size: Large and small.
6. Support: Public and private.
7. School plants: Centralized institution and cottage plan.

The data gathered on these matters from a thorough study of over 40 schools representing a fair distribution as to type and geographic location should upon due analysis yield important information.

A brief resume reveals that the schools visited during the year by the agents of the National Research Council contain something like 8,400 deaf children. This is more than half the entire population of schools for the deaf in the United States and indicates the comprehensiveness of the study.

For the first time in the history of our work has a study been carried out on so extensive a basis. About 5,000 children have been tested with the audiometer in the hands of competent individuals, and to determine the intelligibility of speech and accuracy of lip reading approximately 1,000 children were examined. About 4,500 children were included in the mental and educational examinations, this being more than twice the number concerned in any previous attempt to establish norms for deaf children. Other data collected on a similar scale, including specific facts as to sex, age, cause of deafness, number of years in school, parentage, etc., make up a body of information of undoubted scientific value.

The collection of these data is the purpose of the survey. These investigators expect to analyze and prepare the information collected in such forms that it may be published and thus be made available and utilized by anyone interested in our field of education. It is not for this survey to attempt to draw conclusions. It is our earnest hope that we may collect and present such information as will provide a basis for future action, by the authorities of the schools for the deaf, that will be of enduring benefit in connection with the intricate work of educating deaf children. (*Ibid.*, p. 170.)

It is interesting to note that at the end of Fusfeld's presentation there were questions relative to the possibility of the survey committee drawing some conclusions regarding the information which had been collected. In reply, Prof. Fusfeld said, ". . . the field agents do not feel it within their province to enter into any particular judgment of the things they have seen. They hope by a careful examination and analysis of what has been selected, the data they have collected, to present it in such an impartial form that the results and conclusions will be self-evident." (*Ibid.*, p. 171.) In other words, the evidence revealed would speak for itself.

The Survey, practical, comprehensive, and comprehensible:

In the published survey, incidentally, the participating schools were identified by code in order to protect those which had less than favorable findings. Residential schools were designated as R-1, R-2, R-3, etc., whereas day-schools were identified by the symbols D-1, D-2, D-3, etc. Each administrator was informed of the designation of his particular school and thus he could see the rating of his institution in comparison with those of others.

While the survey was serialized in the *American Annals of the Deaf* through the years 1925-1926, the whole was published in 1928 by the National Research Council under the title of *A Survey of American Schools for the Deaf.* With this study by Herbert E. Day, Irving S. Fusfeld, and Rudolf Pintner, education of the deaf was introduced to its first scientific investigation. This work proved to be *practical* in content, *comprehensive* in scope, and *comprehensible* in style, three qualities which still determine the value of any research project involving deaf children or youth. It was, however, to be another 30 years before researchers generally discovered education of the deaf to be a broad, fertile, and lucrative field for their activities. (See Appendix 17.)

44

Edith Fitzgerald and
Straight Language for the Deaf
1926

At the CAID Convention in West Trenton, N.J., in 1933, Supt. Alvin Pope of the New Jersey School for the Deaf, and President of CAID, in the opening session relative to language instruction for the deaf said,

> Miss Fitzgerald, the inventor of the straight language device, has made a great contribution to the education of the deaf, greater I believe than any other teacher. Her method is developed more minutely and it serves as an outline throughout the grades. It is particularly helpful to slow pupils. ("Address of the President," p. 17.)

This well deserved tribute to Edith Fitzgerald was, indeed, a tribute to her remarkable depth of understanding regarding prelingually deaf children and their language predicament. She came by it well because such understanding as she had was born of her own deep-rooted personal experience.

Language beginnings and deafness:

Barely out of infancy as her rudiments of speech and language were being established, the child Edith Fitzgerald fell suddenly ill. It was not until after the little girl's convalescence that the mother became gradually aware of the child's possible hearing impairment. Kitchen noises, which had previously brought the toddler to her side to "help mommy," no longer attracted the little one. Finally, the validity of the mother's suspicions that her child might be deaf were subtantiated by Memphis physicians.

Accepting the diagnosis of deafness, however, not without the greatest anguish, Mrs. Fitzgerald set about to preserve the little girl's speech and language beginnings. If salvaged, these infant oral language attempts, she believed, would evolve into acceptable speech, just as they would in any normally hearing child. After many weeks the mother's determined interest and efforts to elicit speech from the child began to "pay off" in that the little girl's speech recollections were slowly revived and brought into use. This love and attention which was so effective in bringing the little girl into natural oral communication was, however, abruptly halted by the unspeakable fact of the mother's passing.

This tragedy for the young deaf child was manifested in the sudden disappearance of a beloved familiar face and the sudden appearance of several kindly but strange faces. The sad solemnity of her home was suddenly transformed into an atmosphere of very busy wordless activity. Two of the "kindly but strange faces," an aunt and uncle, had taken charge and filled the hours with busy preparations involving trunks and traveling bags. Soon little Edith, in their smiling and loving care, was aboard a "train of cars" which chugged out of Memphis and northward to a new home in Quincy, Illinois.

The aunt and uncle knew little of deafness, hence their newly acquired child was, indeed, an enigma. While the little girl would jabber away happily, they were not always able to understand. Nevertheless, she continued to jabber and before too long, not only could the aunt and uncle understand her, but the young cousins could as well. Actually, the children began to understand her almost from her first arrival.

Very early the little girl focused her attention naturally on her aunt's lips. Some natural prompting within had indicated to her that a person's mouth – the lips, teeth, and tongue – were together the mysterious and inexplicable source of human communication. By the time she was seven years of age she was a good speechreader, that is, within the scope of her young understanding.

The child appeared to have had that unique ability to synthesize movements, a kind of innate blessing which makes possible the achievement of all good speechreaders. Opposed to this, of course, is the tendency to analyze, a practice found almost invariably in poor speechreaders.

Educational development:

Little Edith was provided ample opportunities for oral communication through the child-chat of her lively cousins, who never ceased to find humor in her persistent efforts to speak. The children

> derided her one day, when she called a "yellow" cat "tan", yet a dress material of the same shade would be "tan", she argued. She had to think things out for herself, as any deaf child does, and inasmuch as language isn't always logical, she made some queer mistakes. (Hornaday, "Straight Language," p. 6.)

Unfortunately, there is a considerable hiatus in the records relative to Edith Fitzgerald's educational development through her elementary and high school years. It is known, however, that she attended grammar school with her hearing cousins and friends. In addition to being quite orally oriented, she possessed a particular penchant for reading and writing.

The first solid evidence of her early education *per se* appears at the Illinois School for the Deaf at Jacksonville. The date October 29, 1896, shows her to have enrolled there, but no dates relative to any previous educational training are extant. At some point during her high school program she learned of Gallaudet College, the National Deaf-Mute College in Washington, D.C. Once discovering this unique place, she "set her sights" accordingly.

Young Miss Edith Fitzgerald, states the record, was graduated in 1897, "Class #1 of the Oral Academic Department," with the grades of 90 in Lessons, 95 in Conduct, and 100 in Health. As quaint and as humorous as this probably seems to be a reader sitting comfortably at the nether-end of our rapidly disappearing 20th Century, it is, indeed, the record of a young woman destined to make a remarkable contribution.

Miss Fitzgerald goes to Gallaudet:

First on young Miss Fitzgerald's agenda of preparation for her future was Gallaudet College. This, of course, became a reality for her in the fall of 1901, when she entered the Gallaudet College Preparatory Class. While being a "RAT," the term for a first-year student, seemed most inappropriate for a serious young lady bent on an education, it was little enough for her to endure in order to reach her goal of becoming a teacher. Besides, Miss Elizabeth Peet of the College faculty maintained a strict standard of decorum for all of the young ladies and kept a close eye on each of them. Miss Peet, incidentally, had come to the College in 1900 at the personal request of Dr. E. M. Gallaudet. She, a third-generation Peet, was the daughter of Dr. Issac Lewis Peet and the granddaughter of Dr. Harvey Prindle Peet. Her students, she was always proud to say, were graduated ladies and gentlemen.

A career underway:

Edith Fitzgerald, upon graduation from Gallaudet in 1906, had some fairly clear ideas as to what she wished to do with her life. First and foremost, of course, was for her to bring learning to pre-lingually deaf children. This she set about doing her first day on the job as a teacher in the Wisconsin School at Delavan, a position which she was to hold for the next 17 years. While she had recollections of her own prelingually deaf childhood and memories of her classmates at the Illinois School, the sight of her first class of manual deaf children was, for her, overwhelming, because they were *her* responsibility.

Regarding the deaf teacher:

As a point of information, the word *manual* in that day and for many years thereafter referred only to the *manual alphabet* or *fingerspelling.* Every American state school for the deaf at that time was rapidly becoming oral with only a few manual classes. These were almost always taught by deaf teachers. Although some strongly oral school authorities objected to deaf teachers, they were, on the whole, highly valued by most administrators. A strong rationale for their employment, aside from their being effective teachers, was that they also served as effective role models. In this direction it was stated that:

> Most deaf teachers are proficient in finger spelling through having had considerable practice and they can present spelled English to the pupil who does not happen to make satisfactory progress through the use of spoken English. (Harris, "Value," p. 180.)

Edith Fitzgerald's perception of her pupils' English needs clearly set the course of her career as an educator. Her own childhood recollections of the sea of words rolling willy-nilly, meaningless and purposeless, clarified immediately for her what she must do. She was literally to bring order out of the chaos of language as seen through the eyes of a prelingually deaf child. This she could do as no hearing or postlingually deaf person could ever hope to do.

Straight Language, a summation of practical experience:

After a number of years of teaching English to prelingually deaf children, Miss Fitzgerald finally produced in 1926 her classic work *Straight Language for the Deaf.* To allow her to speak for herself is, indeed, the best way for one to get the trend of her educational philosophy and its application.

> I should like to emphasize three points to be kept in thought by every teacher of the deaf.
>
> 1. We must make sure that all language work states the child's own mental picture, that is, language he understands and which is clear to him.
>
> 2. The deaf child cannot lean upon his hearing sense in deciding how best to express his thoughts, for he has no hearing sense. He must have a substitute.
>
> 3. The child cannot be taught the English language as one would teach a foreigner.
>
> – – – – – – –
>
> 1. As to the first point, a fatal mistake is made by having the children memorize what they do not visualize. The deaf child's impression and mental picture are too often not clear-cut.
>
> In the beginning work, the class news is never ready to be studied until each child has been made to see clearly the "news" the others have given. This will often involve dramatization, and trips to the scene of the happening. Each child should see clearly the WHO or WHAT who did the thing, the verb or act involved, the WHERE (as a whole), and the WHEN. But before the children are permitted to memorize such an item of news as, "Ackley helped Mrs. Beard in the kitchen yesterday afternoon. He pared potatoes," a trip to the kitchen is necessary, and the children should be questioned so that the teacher may ascertain if they know that they are in the kitchen. Very often primary news is "fixed up" by the teacher, and because the child reads her lips, or her spelling, and memorizes what she has prepared (*her* language version of *her* mental picture) she thinks that he understands. We must have instead, the child's mental picture and help him put that picture into language. Of course we aim to have children get the thought of others through language but it is putting the cart before the horse to expect this phase of the work first. . . . It is true that hearing children often gain wrong impressions and make similar mistakes, but life holds

for them more varied experiences and their command of language is so much less limited than that of deaf children that they usually very soon clear up such misconceptions for themselves. The chances are that the deaf child's thought is soon clogged with hazy concepts, to say nothing of the number of things to which, mentally, he may be attaching the wrong names.

2. Do teachers of the deaf fully realize how dependent they are upon their hearing sense when it comes to expressing themselves easily and smoothly? In this hearing sense they have an excellent guide. The deaf child with whom we are dealing has no such guide. Why not supply him with a substitute? . . . We may correct and correct mistakes, but if the child is unable to see the reason for the changes we wish made, he can only resort to memory. Memory alone is a poor substitute for reason. A correction with the "why" of it stands an excellent chance of sticking and of helping in a similar instance in the future.

3. The third mentioned reason for some of our language disasters is that very often the teacher is trying to teach the deaf child as one would teach a foreigner who is learning English. The cases are vastly different. The foreigner has his own language to fall back upon and a clear understanding of what he is trying to express. He has a clear mental picture. The chances are that the deaf child has no mental picture, and the danger is that his language may be a jumble of memorized words, many or most of which are meaningless to him. (Fitzgerald, *Straight Language,* pp. 10-13.)

In her desire to bring form and order to the English language and to make it palpable to the deaf child, Miss Fitzgerald utilized certain Key words, which appeared across the top of the chalkboard as headings to six columns. These Key words, when used in various combinations, were designed to help the deaf children generate any one of several basic sentence patterns. The Key, never used in its entirety, reflected the pupils' current knowledge of sentence structure, and was expanded according to the needs and the progress of the children.

The use of the eventual six columns of the Key by older pupils for more complex sentence structure is somewhat reminiscent of Sicard's "Theory of Ciphers" and Miss Barry's "Slate System."

In addition to her Key words, Miss Fitzgerald developed some arbitrary symbols which represented the eight parts of speech plus the infinitive.

noun	——	adjective	⌐——⌐
pronoun	⊤	adverb	⊨——⊨
verb	══	connective	⌄——⌄
infinitive	══⇥	preposition	——⇥
participle	⇄══		

How far:
How often:
How long:
How much: When:

For . . . :
With: . . . :
How: Why:

                                    last year.

                                    Friday night.
                                    all day yesterday.

                                    last night.

                                    About ten o'clock

                                    for a long time this morning.

too.

either.

What: Whom:
( )   Whose:
Whom: What: Where:

a top.
a ball.
a tie.
brown eyes.
Ruth's cap.
bananas.
bananas,
honey,
honey,

in the closet.
in Dallas.

Who:
Whose:
What: =
        I see
        I saw
        I have
Emmitto has
Mary has on
        I like
James likes
        I do not care for
Bonnie does not care for
Mr. Murphy
        and
Mr. Scott are   kind.
Joan is   a good baby.
Miss Scaright was   my teacher
        It was   I.
Miss Holt's
        coat is
Betsy lives
The study hall looked   pretty
The sun shone
It is raining.
It lightninged
        and
        thundered
It is   very windy.

it became   cloudy.
It snowed

In the writing of News, should children have difficulty with the proper placement of words, they are automatically referred to the Key for assistance. The Key is consequently designed not only as an instructional system, but also as a self-corrective system as well.

Visible reasons in language development:

The onus for thinking is placed constantly upon the children. While this experience may go slowly at first, the teacher must remember that the objective is not so much to give her pupils concepts as it is to assist and insist that they *generate* their own. The challenge of intellectual stimulation sparks within them a genuine enthusiasm for thinking.

> Vocabulary books may be started at the discretion of the teacher. Before this, on a wall slate kept for that purpose, she has written in colored crayon the words WHO and WHAT, and the symbols ===== and ⌐—¬ . As the vocabulary grows, the children also sense the kind of word each new one is, and the word is written under its proper heading on this slate. On a certain day each week – once a month, perhaps, at first – this list is copied into the books by the children.
>
> The teacher herself should prepare the books, dividing up the pages so as to allow as many as she thinks will be needed for each kind of word, and should write the headings in ink – red if she wishes. Leave the first pages for the table of contents to be filled in by the children later on.
>
> If the pages are numbered, the first or index page may eventually be something like this:
>
> | | Page |
> | --- | --- |
> | Who | 2 |
> | What | 6 |
> | Who One – More than one | 10 |
> | What One – More than one | 12 |
> | Whose | 14 |
> | ===== (Verbs) | 16 |
> | === (Drill Verbs) | 20 |
> | Where | 22 |
> | When | 26 |
> | ⌐—¬ (Adjectives) | 30 |
> | —т— (Pronouns) | 32 |
> | Expressions | 34 |
>
> Under "Expressions" there would be "Come," "How do you do," "Thank you," "You are welcome," "Yes, _____ ," "No, _____ ," "Good Morning," "Good bye," etc., as they are taken up. Very soon the first of these expressions becomes, "Please come." The contents page adds vastly to the value of the book in the eyes of the child, and he soons learns how to consult it. (*Ibid.,* p. 25.)

Miss Fitzgerald provided innumerable such suggestions and aids to assist the teacher in her language instruction. Little wonder was it that the majority of the teacher-training facilities eventually adopted the Straight Language system as the common basis for their curricula, in both written and oral English.

National recognition for Straight Language for the Deaf:

Edith Fitzgerald's *Straight Language for the Deaf* both in philosophy and in application was quickly recognized by educators of the deaf to be a long-needed sequenced approach to the crucial problem of English instruction. The system insisted upon the teacher's first understanding the child's own mental picture or concept and then expressing it in such vocabulary and structure as were meaningful to the child. The system relied wholly upon *visible* reasons for its development. Consequently it had an obvious appeal to the intelligence of deaf children because it was concretely perceptible.

From 1927 on, Edith Fitzgerald was constantly in demand across the country to give workshops and lectures on her Straight Language system. By 1937 the majority of schools for the deaf, both residential and day, pure oral and combined, had adopted the Fitzgerald Key. Teacher education programs generally accepted Straight Language and its Key as the basic language system to be taught to all student teachers. Consequently young teachers-in-training or normal students, as they were often called, were thoroughly imbued not only with the practice of the Fitzgerald system, but also with its strongly fostered attitude of faith in the deaf child's ability to learn.

At the time of her death on June 26, 1940, Miss Fitzgerald's impact on American education of the deaf was inestimable. Certainly many present-day educators of the deaf and teachers of teachers would do well to acquaint themselves with the classic, *Straight Language for the Deaf* by Miss Edith Fitzgerald.

45

The Battle of the Nomenclatures
1930-1937

In the United States hearing-impaired children and youth had been variously referred to or classified as deaf-mutes, deaf and dumb, semi-mutes, semi-deaf, or mutes. Newspaper and magazine articles typically referred to hearing-impaired people as the deaf and dumb or as deaf-mutes. This writer recalls from many years ago a regular-line Omaha streetcar whose destination was announced in large letters on both the front and the side of the car, "Deaf and Dumb Institute." This grim legend having been well impressed on the minds of Omaha's population, over the years, made it exceedingly difficult to eradicate and to replace with the more acceptable appellation, "School for the Deaf." Because of such exposures, educated people across the United States referred to deaf people as the "deaf and dumb" despite numerous protests and not a few physical encounters on the part of deaf youths. One young boy in particular altered a note which had been written in reference to himself; he crossed out the offensive word *dumb* and wrote in a more appropriate substitute. His revision read, "deaf and *smart.*" For a long time, however, the battle of nomenclature seemed to be a losing one.

An attempt at definition:

In November, 1930, at the first White House Conference on Child Health and Protection (WHC), a decisive effort was made to establish a correct nomenclature for hearing-impaired youngsters. The idea to do so was an excellent one; however, the effort was to stir up the proverbial "hornets' nest," for the White House had neither sought nor asked for the modernly termed "input" of the Convention of American Instructors of the Deaf (CAID). Instead the Conference organizers supposed that the leaders of the American Association to Promote the Teaching of Speech to the Deaf (AAPTSD) were representation enough; needless to say, they weren't.

After considerable discussion among the Conference delegates in the section for Special Education, they arrived at what was presumed to be a suitable set of definitions for the various types of hearing impairment.

> The *deaf* are those who were born either totally deaf or sufficiently deaf to prevent the establishment of speech and natural language; those who became deaf in childhood before speech and language were established; or those who became deaf in childhood so soon after the natural establishment of speech and language that the ability to speak and understand speech and language has been practically lost to them. . . .

> The *hard of hearing* are those who established speech and ability to understand speech and language, and subsequently developed impairment of hearing. These children are sound conscious and have a normal attitude to the world of sound in which they live. ("Special Education–The Handicapped and Gifted," p. 277.)

The definitions challenged:

As might be expected the WHC definitions, when finally released in 1931, were greeted with a barrage of criticism. Letters on the subject were exchanged among the various members of the Conference of Executives of American Schools for the Deaf (CEASD) and the CAID.

For all of the dissatisfaction with the WHC definitions, it was not until the April, 1936, meeting of the CEASD at the Western Pennsylvania School for the Deaf that any constructive action was taken. This action, of course, was the appointment of a Committee on Nomenclature, the chairman of which was to be Elwood A. Stevenson, superintendent of the California School for the Deaf at

Berkeley. The other members of the committee were Ignatius Bjorlee, superintendent of the Maryland School; T. C. Forrester, superintendent of the Rochester School; Clarence D. O'Connor, superintendent of the Lexington School; and Irving S. Fusfeld, of the Gallaudet College faculty.

As to the work of this committee it was determined that the definitions relative to the types of hearing impairment should be "simple, clear-cut, scientifically correct and readily understood by the layman." With these rules the committee went to work in preparing its definitions.

The Conference definitions are introduced to CAID:

The following year, 1937, at the Thirtieth Meeting of CAID in New York City, Mr. Stevenson presented to the Conference of Executives business session the "Report of the Conference Committee on Nomenclature." First explaining the ground rules for writing the Committee's definitions, Stevenson then "opened up" on the White House Conference definitions relative to hearing impairment. He did, however, discreetly refrain from naming the source of what he saw as the offending definitions.

> The committee is very much concerned over the very evident effort of certain groups and individuals to classify the deaf and the hard of hearing, not from the true physical angle, but from the wholly false basis of ability to speak and use language. In other words there are many who are developing a new and most damaging terminology. They say that the deaf are those who are born without hearing or who lose it before the acquisition of speech. They go on to say that those who suffer a hearing loss after speech and language have been established are hard of hearing. They are very vague in their wording but the layman and the parent are left with the impression that the child who loses hearing after speech and language have been acquired (the adventitiously deaf) is hard of hearing. This is taking place in different parts of the country today and if continued and followed by teachers will prove a sad day for the deaf child's education and his future happiness. The committee desires to go on record, and begs the conference to do likewise, as condemning such misleading and erroneous terminology. (Stevenson, "Nomenclature," p. 203.)

Following this, Stevenson asked that all terms other than those expressly defined in the Committee's "Report" be excluded henceforth from any and all professional documents and journals. These terms included all of those previously stated as well as the term *deafened,* which had "been used to designate the hard of hearing."

Finally, the following committee definitions were proposed:

1. The deaf: Those in whom the sense of hearing is nonfunctional for the ordinary purposes of life.

   This group is made up of two classes based entirely on the time of the loss of hearing.
   (a) The congenitally deaf – those who were born deaf.
   (b) The adventitiously deaf – those who were born with normal hearing but in whom the sense of hearing became nonfunctional later through illness or accident.

2. The hard of hearing: Those in whom the sense of hearing, although defective, is functional with or without a hearing aid. (*Ibid.*, p. 204.)

Approval by the Conference of Executives was both moved and seconded, and Mr. Stevenson's report was unanimously accepted. The significance of this new CAID nomenclature was that it held for some 40 years. Meanwhile, the White House Conference definitions passed into oblivion.

46

An Assessment of American Education of the Deaf 1933

By 1933 educators of the deaf had settled into a routine of relative certainty as to the effectiveness of their various instructional procedures. There was a general agreement among them as to the educational priorities and objectives for deaf children. The disagreements which did exist lay largely in the area of procedure and of these differences little was said. No one was about to dig up E. M. Gallaudet's hatchet.

Perhaps the best and most authentic portrayal of education of the deaf and its status during this period was that given by Dr. Alvin E. Pope, superintendent of the New Jersey School for the Deaf in his "Address of the President of CAID" at the International Congress on Education of the Deaf, held at Trenton in the summer of 1933. Dr. Pope's remarks were directed specifically "to the laymen of our audience."

Prevailing perspectives:

In his paper, under a section entitled "Means of Communication," Dr. Pope set forth the prevailing attitudes and perspectives which were generally held by teachers of the deaf concerning their work at that time. Relative to communication, he said:

The sign language grew out of pantomime, but it has been thoroughly organized and now is very formal. Instead of following the English order, it follows the order in which things happen, somewhat as is seen in the silent moving pictures. The sign language has been abandoned as a means of education by almost every school for the deaf in this country and in foreign countries, particularly for the education of the smaller children. It interferes with their learning to use English, particularly the congenitally deaf. When the children have mastered the use of English and reach the age where they are entering social activities with the adult deaf, the sign language is almost always used.

Fingerspelling has no connection with either pantomime or the sign language. It is practically the same as writing on the blackboard and erasing it as fast as you write. Those who read finger spelling never see the separate letters any more than we do in reading a book; they catch words, phrases and whole sentences. When deaf children spell on their fingers, they practice the use of the English language. Some schools have this sign about their premises, "Use English – Spoken, Finger Spelled, or Written." Many schools are trying to substitute finger spelling for signing in outside activities, and one school has done this for many years.

The other methods are by speech and lip reading. The speech of the deaf is nearly always unnatural but it can be understood by their closest friends and relatives. Some of the semi-mutes (postlingually deaf) and hard of hearing speak very well and occasionally a congenitally deaf child speaks very well. Lipreading, of course, involves a considerable amount of guessing, as many words entirely different in sound look alike on the lips. Nevertheless, lip reading and speech offer a means of communication and a means of thought-exchange usable with the outside world. It is impossible for a small number of deaf people to hope to have the world remodeled for their benefit. If necessary they can always use pad and pencil. Some people object very much to the use of signs by the deaf, while others are very much jarred by their unnatural voices.

In addition to these we have auricular training which means the development of the residual hearing a deaf child may have. . . . The more hearing a child has, the easier it is to teach him by this method, and the more perfect the results achieved. Of course, hearing must be accompanied by intelligence. There is a high correlation between intelligence and hearing and favorable home conditions in the success of the auricular method.

In most of our schools the oral method predominates, accompanied by the auricular method, but on the playgrounds and in social activities, in many of our schools the children use signs. It is well to encourage speech, lip reading and the utilization of hearing, and to discourage the use of signs, but never to punish a child for signing as that is often the easiest and perhaps the only way for him to express himself, although every time an officer or a teacher signs to a deaf child, he robs him of an opportunity to learn English. (Pope, "Address of the President," pp. 28-29.)

A rationale empirically derived:

Thus Dr. Pope revealed the commitment of educators of the deaf to a simple but constructive rationale for teaching deaf children, which had slowly but logically evolved from the 19th Century. It was now firmly rooted as a viable set of instructional guidelines for the 20th Century. Understanding this perspective should prepare one to appreciate to some degree the historical turning points which were to come. (See Appendix 18.)

Chapter Eleven
Some New Perspectives and a Judgment

From this point on . . .

Author's Note:

    The reader, in considering the historical turning points from the 1940's on, should understand that this author has personally identified with each of the intervening decades into the 1980's. During all of these years he has not only been a fascinated onlooker but an enthusiastic participant as well. Therefore, if his sight of the trees occasionally intrudes to obscure his view of the forest, it is hoped that his critics will understand.

    The objective of this consideration of the latter portion of the 20th Century is to select certain occurrences in the education of the deaf through the 1940's and the subsequent decades which, in the author's *opinion,* may prove to be historically significant. Whether or not these selected events prove to be genuine "turning points" on the broad canvas of education of the deaf must be determined by some future historian who will see them in the light of a more appropriate time perspective. Until that time, however, one person's opinion will be as good as another's. After all, "crystal-balling" is not really within the purview of a historian.

47

The Ewings Come to Washington
1946

The fall of 1946 was to bring a significant effort to modify the contending attitudes of the "oralist" and the "combined system" factions. The place was Kendall Green and the occasion in point was to be announced to the Gallaudet faculty by Dr. Leonard M. Elstad, the new president of the College.

A joint invitation:

Dr. Elstad, himself a graduate of the Gallaudet Normal Department, interestingly enough had served at one time as principal of the once prestigious Wright Oral School in New York City. With this firsthand experience in the oral camp, which he had ably defended during his tenure at Wright Oral, and with his subsequent years as superintendent of the Minnesota School for the Deaf, a combined system school, Elstad was uniquely qualified to support either approach. No other Gallaudetian could have cooperated so fully with the American Association to Promote the Teaching of Speech to the Deaf. Together they extended a joint invitation to the renowned British oral advocates, Professor Alexander Ewing and his wife, Irene. The latter was a long-standing advocate and practitioner of early childhood education for the deaf.

The Ewings' early work and reputation:

As early as 1912 in Manchester, Mrs. Ewing, at that time Miss Irene R. Goldsack, became the first teacher in Britain's first infant school for deaf children. Some seven years later, in 1919, she established a teacher training program at Manchester University. (Bender, *Conquest,* p. 161.) This program centered on an acoustic approach with young children. Some years afterward, Miss Goldsack joined matrimonial forces with Mr. Alex Ewing and together they advanced the cause of aural-oral education. With their background, it was with considerable surprise that the Gallaudet faculty and alumni alike received Elstad's news of the Ewings' coming.

The Ewings come to America:

The couple's reputation as educators of the deaf would unquestionably draw to Washington oralists from all over the United States. Actually the Ewings had initially been invited to the U.S. in order for the Professor to present a paper before the American Otological Society. (Numbers, *My Words Fell,* p. 132.) This fact, however, became almost secondary on their agenda after a national audience of educators of the deaf had been offered to them on the Gallaudet campus.

Gallaudet's new perspective:

The occasion was to be particularly significant for Gallaudetians, because it would be the first time in some 50 years that oralists had set foot on Kendall Green. Although Dr. Elstad's action was not completely understood nor appreciated by the faculty, he obviously believed it was time for a change of attitude and took this first step to effect it. Bringing the Ewings to Gallaudet was, indeed, an administrative *coup*. In doing this, the President set forth the College as having a broad university-like perspective. The institution was henceforth to welcome and to entertain *all* schools of educational thought, a concept most new to traditional Gallaudetians.

   Immediately, plans went into gear for readying the campus for the honored guests. Chapel Hall, regularly the site of the Sunday evening and Wednesday morning services, was not only dusted, but varnished for the Ewings' forthcoming seminar and demonstration sessions.

The Ewings' arrival:

Finally on the appointed afternoon for the opening gathering, the visitors from across town at the Volta Bureau filed into Chapel Hall accompanied by their out-of-town guests. Representatives from all of the leading oral schools for the deaf in the United States soon found themselves seated under the steady portrait gaze of Edward Miner Gallaudet, Amos Kendall, and Thomas Hopkins Gallaudet. On one side of the Chapel, perched just beneath the tall blue and amber stained-glass windowns, were the plaster busts of the Abbé de l'Epee, the Abbé Sicard, and the Reverend Henry W. Syle. Beneath and along the walls around the Chapel were portraits of the departed worthies of Gallaudet College and of other early American educators of the deaf. Among the most outstanding of these were the bas-reliefs of Dean Elizabeth Peet's father, Issac Lewis Peet, and her grandfather, Harvey Prindle Peet. As might be expected, not one oralist was to be found commemorated in the entire Hall.

At long last Dr. Elstad and Miss Josephine Timberlake, executive secretary of the Volta Bureau, came into Chapel Hall accompanied by the honored guests, Professor Alex Ewing and his wife, Irene. Immediately, the audience arose with applause as the party mounted the dais. With some introductory remarks of welcome from President Elstad and Miss Timberlake, the Ewings introduced their opening observations on the exercise of residual hearing in young deaf children. The audience sat rapt.

Significance of the Ewing visit:

The innovations which the Ewings described that afternoon are today, of course, common knowledge to any well-trained teacher of the deaf. Actually, if the Ewings had not said a single word, history would still have been made. Nevertheless, another 20 years were to pass before the oralists and combined system people would gather, even figuratively, under the same tent. The Ewings' visit, however, was a start.

48

CAID Learns of the Tracy
Movement for Parent Education
1947

Occasionally a person's misfortune, and the manner in which the person handles it, turns the negative situation into a positive one. Such was to be the experience of a young wife and mother, Louise Tracy, as she faced alone for the first time the horrendous fact of discovering her two-year-old son's deafness. Her husband, a young actor, was at the time playing in a stock company and deeply occupied with his work. Consequently, she kept the sad news to herself until the child's predicament could be medically confirmed. It was to be some 20 years later that this mother was to describe, before a professional audience of teachers of the deaf, her problem and how she coped with it.

The occasion for this gathering of educators was the Thirty-Third Meeting of the Convention of American Instructors of the Deaf (CAID), held in 1947 at the Florida School for the Deaf and Blind at St. Augustine. This convention was a particularly lively one, because it marked the first gathering of teachers of the deaf since the four-year hiatus caused by World War II. No such national crisis had occured in education of the deaf since the "War Between the States," hence one may appreciate the festive air that prevailed at St. Augustine that summer of '47.

Mrs. Tracy's address on "The Role of Parents":

The Convention program was full and interesting with the whole to be topped off by an innovative topic entitled "The Role of Parents in Education of the Deaf." The speaker, of course, was to be Mrs. Spencer Tracy, the wife of the film star who had charmed millions of Americans with his clearly defined and rugged screen portrayals.

The uniqueness of Mrs. Tracy's situation as a speaker lay not in the fact that she had had a deaf child, but in the fact of what she ultimately did about the predicament created by her child's deafness. It must be said that many educators of the deaf of that day were not accustomed to *listening* to parents. On the contrary, if anyone was to do the listening, it was traditionally the parents.

At this time there were but two residential schools for the deaf which were engaged in early childhood education. These were the Lexington and Rochester schools. Most schools for the deaf at that time did not venture to accept children below the age of six. To begin the educational process at an earlier age was generally considered to be highly impractical, because such younger children were thought to be much too immature and distractable.

Professional advice vs. a personal decision:

Despite the contrary thoughts regarding parental input and early childhood education which were predominant in her audience, Mrs. Tracy launched her remarks by stating that over the previous five years she had addressed numerous groups. To each she had described the discovery of her little John's deafness through his having to be awakened from his nap by his mother's touch rather than by her voice. Mrs. Tracy then related how an otologist told her that he could do nothing to help the child. The best thing, he advised, was to keep the boy at home until he was, perhaps, six or seven and then place him in a state school for the deaf.

Wondering desperately what *she* could do to help her child, Mrs. Tracy hit on the idea of *talking* to the little fellow. Her husband, upon learning of his son's deafness, likewise joined in what appeared to be a futile activity, that is, talking to a child who obviously could not hear. In describing their efforts, Mrs. Tracy said,

> My husband happened to be playing in a stock company out in a little mid-western city and we did not know many people in the town and we had no one to ask questions. So we just pretended. We talked to him, I sang to him, I told him nursery rhymes. We acted just exactly as we

thought we would have done if John had heard. And, of course, that was just the thing we should have done. We learned that afterwards. ("Role of Parents," p. 238.)

It was not until many months later that a New York otologist informed the Tracys of their young child's potentialities which could be developed through lipreading. Mrs. Tracy, however, would have to do the teaching. Of this doctor, she said, "In three minutes he had changed the entire course of our lives." (*Ibid.*)

"On the right track":

Mrs. Tracy subsequently learned of a correspondence course for mothers of little deaf children published by a New York private school headed up by Mr. John Dutton Wright. She immediately availed herself of the course but found it to be like a very complicated cookbook and about as easy to follow. The one thing she did learn from the course, however, was that she was, indeed, "on the right track" in her practice of *talking constantly* to her child. Quite typically of little deaf children, John never focused on her lips; consequently all of her efforts appeared to be wasted. Nevertheless she pursued the practice with *diligence.*

After months of talking to her child, Mrs. Tracy one day found herself saying to herself the words, "Mama, mama, mama, mama." Suddenly she became aware that young John was *focusing* on her lips and he was imitating a soundless repetition of the word. (*Ibid.,* p. 239.) Being unsure of the procedure for evoking voice from her child, the young mother let slip a marvelous opportunity. She nevertheless continued to repeat the word "mama" again and again. Eventually one day the child volunteered the word "mama" himself, little understanding its love-freighted significance.

In her presentation Mrs. Tracy then related one of the many philosophical points gleaned from her experience in working with her child.

> In talking to him, when I would say a word I would give him the correct pattern and repeat it, feeding him plenty of encouragement and applause, giving him lots of experience to build up his language because, after all, we know that articulation is – well, almost a minor part of speech – that there is something to talk about, there is language with which to talk. There is a desire to talk, there are experiences to fit that language, there are many things besides that little business of articulation.
>
> I devoted myself to building up his experiences, to give him something to talk about, his language, and to try to keep him oral. We made him

> talk all the time. I would not say "made him;" there was no pressure
> exerted, but that was all he knew. And if he did not know a word, then
> he had no sound for it. (*Ibid.*)

Thus we see the importance which Mrs. Tracy placed upon the child's acquisition of an abundance of experience as a vital source for oral language. This, of course, would eventually become a source for written language as well.

Questions and a new responsibility:

Gradually Mrs. Tracy accrued more and more instructional ideas as she worked with her son. These ideas she quite willingly shared with other people. Finally one day, she was confronted by a very pertinent question, "Mrs. Tracy, why don't you do something for the deaf?" At first Mrs. Tracy protested, but other interested people pressed her and said, "You are in a position where you can help people." Mrs. Tracy was momentarily nonplused by the leadership role being urged upon her. More questions came, "Haven't you ever thought of doing anything? What would you like to do?" To this last question she replied, "Well, I would like to help parents. It seems to me there is an almost untouched field and it seems to me that is one of the greatest needs." (*Ibid.*, p. 240.)

In Mrs. Tracy's thinking "the die was cast," and shortly thereafter in the summer of 1942 she found herself with a group of 12 mothers. Together they talked, each reciting a list of family problems and heartaches, all of which stemmed from the fact of their having young deaf children. Almost every problem they offered had been personally confronted by Mrs. Tracy; hence the mothers found her to be a source of invaluable information as well as comfort. Frequently she had to say to a despairing and self-pitying parent, "Now, here, this is the way it is and it is no tragedy." Thus brought up short by one who "had been through the mill," the parent would acquire a new perspective of the problem.

A philosophy established:

Mrs. Tracy traced her inspiration to serve parents to a straight-forward piece of advice she had once received from Dr. Harvey Cushing, a well-known brain surgeon of Boston. Dr. Cushing, once a classmate of Mrs. Tracy's father, had examined little John and had found him to be neurally sound. He then gave Mrs. Tracy a

philosophy which she subsequently was to repeat as a matter of
policy for all parents coming under her influence:

> Yours can be an interesting life. It is up to you. Of course, you can go
> around all through life with your head down and feeling sorry for
> yourself and you can make yourself miserable and your family
> miserable and your friends miserable. You will not have friends long
> if you act that way. Or, you can treat this as an opportunity, as the
> gateway to a richer, fuller life. Maybe not the kind of life you thought
> you were going to live, but maybe a much happier one. (*Ibid.,* p. 241.)

Around the aforementioned nucleus of mothers and their young
deaf children, the clinic concept gradually evolved. The major thrust
of influence was not to be directed toward the children so much as
it was toward their parents. "You cannot do much about child
guidance until you do something about parent guidance." (*Ibid.,* p.
243.)

After the establishment of the parents' class, the University of
Southern California became genuinely interested in the project and
saw it as a movement toward the future. As a result, the University
in July, 1942, provided a cottage for the "mothers' study group."

The balance of Mrs. Tracy's remarks before the Florida
Convention in 1947 dealt with her work with John and with
answering questions raised relative to his then current educational
status and progress. By this time, of course, he was a young man
and had had two years at Pasadena College. While Mrs. Tracy's
initial concern was obviously relative to her own deaf child, it
expanded into a concern for everyone's young deaf child. At the
conclusion of her presentation, the professionals present little knew
of the impact her work would eventually have.

The John Tracy Clinic formally opened:

It was not until February, 1943, that the John Tracy Clinic was
formally opened.

> In that month the first parents were enrolled in its Correspondence
> Course, which was based on that of the Wright Oral School, permission
> to use and revise the Course having been given by the School.... Miss
> Mary New ... came from the Lexington School for the Deaf in New
> York City for the summer to set up this program and help to revise the
> Correspondence Course. (*John Tracy Clinic Bulletin,* Fall 1962, p. 2.)

Thus, it was from the beginnings described that a most phenomenal
program evolved on behalf of parents and their young deaf children.

For the first time parents were encouraged to become active in the educational process of their children.

In accordance with this encouragement, all of the services of the Clinic since the day of its inauguration have been regularly rendered without cost to the families of young hearing-impaired children regardless of their nationality, race, or creed. As a result of this magnanimous action, over the years more than 45,000 families in 120 different nations have been guided through the problems posed by deafness.

The Tracy Clinic as a turning point:

Mrs. Tracy's efforts have, indeed, created a significant turning point in the history of modern education of the deaf. The resulting major contributions have been the establishment and advancement of early childhood education and the development of parent education through the now generally known *demonstration home* concept. Today, these are both integral parts of the established educational process for hearing-impaired children.

49

The "New School" at Riverside
1951

In 1950 rumor had it that the State of California was planning a school for the deaf in the southern part of the state, probably at Riverside. There had not been a large residential school established since about 1912; hence interest ran high. When this word of the newly planned school was confirmed, numbers of teachers of the deaf began to dream about becoming a part of a lovely ultra-modern school bathed in sunshine and surrounded by palm trees.

The rumor substantiated:

The idea did not become a reality to most people until Dr. Herbert Stoltz, the deputy superintendent for special education for the California State Department of Education, began his search-interview trek across the United States. The object of his mission, of course, was to find a suitable person to take over the superintendency of the proposed institution.

Naturally, Dr. Stoltz's trip eventually brought him to the then Mecca of education of the deaf, Gallaudet College. In visiting with Mr. William McClure, a faculty member there, Dr. Stoltz spoke at length of his mission. In so doing, he revealed an amazing knowledge of the Rochester Method and its significance. The

California State Department of Education, which he represented, obviously had a clear and definite understanding of the philosophy which it wished to see implemented in its new school.

"The School of Tomorrow":

Aside from the literature which was available on the subject of the Rochester procedure at that time, another source of information was the Department's resource person in education of the deaf, Dr. Elwood A. Stevenson, superintendent of the school at Berkeley. Stevenson had long been interested in the Rochester Method, as indicated in his address entitled "The School of Tomorrow" which he gave at the CAID meeting in Fulton, Missouri, in the summer of 1941. Therefore, the advice which he gave the Department of Education at Sacramento probably reflected to a large degree those same thoughts which he had held for the future of education of the deaf.

An administrator selected:

With all of the considerations regarding educational theory completed, it was Dr. Stoltz's task to find a person who could conscientiously support the Rochester concept and who could be depended upon to implement it effectively. Stoltz's quest for such a person was ended when he interviewed an enthusiastic young educator of the deaf, Richard G. Brill, principal of the Bruce Street School in Newark, New Jersey.

Brill was from a family of educators of the deaf. He was a Rutgers man and a Gallaudet College Normal Department graduate. He had taught for E. A. Stevenson in the Berkeley school and was subsequently principal of the Virginia school in Staunton. During World War II he served commendably in the U.S. Navy as a PT boat commander, and when peace came he returned to education of the deaf, taking up his work as principal of the Bruce Street School.

By the time Dr. Stoltz was ready to interview him, Brill had completed his doctoral studies and was, indeed, a "natural" for the superintendency of the California school-to-be at Riverside. Most important, aside from Brill's experience and qualifications, was his personal commitment to the idea that deaf children could acquire English, if provided the proper around-the-clock environment for English mastery. To be sure, Brill got the position and the organization of the California School for the Deaf (Riverside) was underway. The new institution finally opened its doors for pupils in September, 1953.

An instructional philosophy to be introduced:

While the construction of the new school was of extreme importance, more important was the quality and supportiveness of the new faculty assembled to do the instructional task. Also to be determined was the curriculum and the strategy for its delivery to the children to be served. Indeed, the instructional procedure to be employed had already been determined by the State Department of Education, but the task of "selling" it to the faculty and to the public at large was the responsiblity of the school's administration.

Precedent for the use of fingerspelling as a supplement to speech and speechreading was strong, when it pertained to intermediate and advanced department children. With the primary and preschool echelons of the program, however, the general belief of the teachers held conservatively to the traditional oral approach *sans* fingerspelling.

This view had first evolved in the Rochester School for the Deaf shortly after the death of the school's founder, Zenas Freeman Westervelt, in 1917. The rationale for this unfortunate switch of policy was based on the unfounded fear and belief of a new school administration that fingerspelling would interfere with the establishment of speech in primary children. The introduction of visible English (fingerspelling) was, therefore, postponed to the intermediate and advanced department years. This change of policy, contrary to Westervelt's long years of success in providing deaf children with English reading and writing skills as well as speech and speechreading, became nationally accepted because of its place of origin, the Rochester School.

Consequently, some 30 years later, Brill found it extremely difficult to convince his primary teachers that visible English was indeed a practical instructional medium for young deaf children.

Visible English receives national acceptance:

Finally, after a number of years of effort on Brill's part, his primary supervising teacher was finally convinced that fingerspelling *per se* was not harmful to the speech and oral language development of young deaf children. By the time this was accomplished, however, the work of Marshall Hester in New Mexico (discussed in the next section) had been proving fascinating things in this area of early language development. Also at this period, the Louisiana School in Baton Rouge had been conducting a successful visible English program for five- and six-year-olds. Similar programs for young children were also underway in the Florida, Tennessee, and North Carolina schools as well.

A precursor of signs to come:

Through Dr. Brill's efforts at Riverside beginning in 1951 and with the support of several enthusiastic advocates, an entire movement was begun in the United States to introduce orthographical, syntactical English as a basis for reading, writing, and speech. Few suspected, however, that this national recognition of fingerspelling was in reality "the camel's nose under the tent" of organized English and speech instruction for deaf children. The "signs of the times" were yet to come. (See Appendices 19 and 20.)

50

Hester and the Santa Fe Innovation
1958

Superintendent Marshall Hester of the New Mexico School for the Deaf at Santa Fe had been long dissatisfied with the English reading and writing achievement scores of the pupils graduating from his school. In a paper presented to the International Congress on Education of the Deaf in 1963, he said:

> Year after year, about 20 percent of our school leavers were meeting only minimal requirements for adequate communication whether by hearing, by speech and lipreading, or by reading and writing. These graduates whether hard of hearing or profoundly deaf were generally above the average deaf with respect to intelligence. The other 80 percent of the product had inadequate ability to communicate either by speech, hearing, lipreading, or by pad and pencil, primarily because they had a severe deficiency in the language. This latter group was made up largely of those who were not hard of hearing, [but] those who were deaf from infancy, those who entered school at upper age levels and those who were lower in intelligence. ("Manual Communication," p. 212.)

A move to correct the problem:

After considerable thought on this problem, Hester finally decided that whatever had to be done to correct this situation would have to be done early in the deaf child's school experience. Therefore, in the fall of 1958 the idea of fingerspelling as a supplement and complement to speech was introduced to five-year-olds. The only other schools employing this mode at that time were the school at Rochester, New York, and the "new" school at Riverside, California. These two institutions, however, did not introduce fingerspelling until the elementary years on the unfounded fear that it would impede oral progress. Hester, however, had no such fear because of the rationale which he had formulated.

Early supporting research:

In support of his decision, Hester referred to Helen Johnson who in 1948 had written of her Illinois School for the Deaf study entitled "The Ability of Pupils in a School for the Deaf to Understand Various Methods of Communication." In this study Ms. Johnson wrote:

> When the pupils in this school for the deaf are communicated with as a group, there appear to be only two methods of communication which could be used with any reasonable degree of accuracy. Fingerspelling with a mean of 74 percent and reading with a mean of 72 percent of normal achievement afford fairly acceptable methods. The other media of communication tested cannot be considered acceptable for the group as a whole. . . . ("Ability," p. 300.)

Ms. Johnson completed her study with 26 concluding statements, two of which were:

> No. 18   Although fingerspelling as judged by the test scores can be considered only fairly accurate as a method of communication it is, for this group as a whole and for the separate manual and oral groups, the most satisfactory of any of the methods of communication tested. (*Ibid.*, p. 308.)

> No. 24   In as much as the ability of the oral pupils to understand language through lipreading is so inferior to their ability to understand fingerspelled language it might be advisable in the interest of increased academic achievement to replace lipreading with fingerspelling as the classroom method of communication for all those oral pupils without usable hearing acuity, a history of hearing experience, or high lipreading scores. (*Ibid.*, pp. 309-310.)

With Ms. Johnson's findings in support of his rationale and all of the past empirical evidences he had gathered, Hester moved ahead to introduce fingerspelling into his beginning classes. Of this action he wrote:

> The introduction of fingerspelling with small children at the New Mexico School for the Deaf brought numerous difficulties pertaining to teacher reluctance to depart from the traditional oral approach,

inability of teachers to fingerspell, and opposition by parents who wanted their children to have nothing to do with manual communication. Many of the opponents of fingerspelling thought that its use would inhibit or prevent the development of speech and lipreading. In spite of these difficulties, we continued fingerspelling with small children. ("Manual Communication," p. 213.)

Here, unique in the modern annals of education of the deaf, we witness an educator-administrator "laying his job on the line" for the sake of his deeply rooted faith in the learning ability of deaf children. And learn they did, as an answer to the patient and diligent English learning opportunity which was provided for them *both in and out of school.*

The Russian innovation:

During the next two years, 1959 and 1960, news of the work being conducted at the Russian Institute of Defectology in Moscow began to filter into the United States through observations of visiting Americans.

Among these were Dr. Samuel Kirk, director of the Institute for Research on Exceptional Children at the University of Illinois, and Dr. Boris Morkovin, a strict oralist from Los Angeles. According to these observers, the Russians were employing fingerspelling successfully with deaf children as young as two years of age. By the time the children were five or six years old they had accrued vocabularies "on the order of 2,000 words." Such news was, of course, received with considerable skepticism.

At this time Dr. Omar K. Moore of Yale University came to Gallaudet College and showed his films of little Russian deaf children communicating with their teachers through fingerspelling. While much was made of this achievement, little was said of Zenas Freeman Westervelt, the American, who had done substantially the same thing some 50 or 60 years previously.

Hester's survey of '61-'62:

Still concerned about the English reading and writing achievement of his "school leavers," Hester decided to make a survey of American schools for the deaf in order to see where his "leavers" stood in comparison with those of other schools. The survey which he designed was to tabulate the reading and writing achievement score averages of all 1961-1962 students graduating or leaving schools for the deaf across the country. Forty-two day classes and day schools plus 88 residential schools received the survey forms. Of these numbers 9 day schools responded, as did 55 of the residential schools.

These participating institutions reported 501 graduates for 1962 and 603 nongraduates, all of whom were 16 years of age or older. These numbers totaled 1,104 graduates and "leavers" in all. This number, prior to having left school, had also taken at least one of the following tests: the Stanford Achievement test, the Metropolitan test, and the California test. The graduates of the survey group showed in their total test grade equivalent scores a range from 3.1 to 12.8, with the median at 8.1. The nongraduates showed a range of 0.9 to 10.5, with the median of 4.7. Considering these findings, Hester wrote,

> . . . If we assume that these scores are reasonably accurate measurements of the achievement levels of the 1,104 school leavers in 1962, then we, as teachers of the deaf need to do something different. (*Ibid.*)

"Something different" was precisely what Hester was doing. By this time Hester's primary children had been exposed to a comprehensive English fingerspelling environment for a period of five years. The results of the Stanford and Metropolitan tests gave reason for Hester to write, ". . . the approach through simultaneous fingerspelling gives these youngsters a better command of language than we have been achieving for the average student in years gone by." (*Ibid.*, p. 219.)

Visitors come to observe:

As word relative to the New Mexico program began to circulate throughout the profession, visitors, several of whom were highly qualified, began to make their appearance at the school. Subsequently, letters stating their reactions to what they had observed were received. One of these dated March 28, 1963, was from Dr. Samuel Kirk who the previous year had visited Moscow's Institute of Defectology. Dr. Kirk, addressing Dr. Hester, wrote:

> The fingerspelling method you are using with your children was the first time I had observed its use by young children. From a theoretical point of view, it has some distinct possibilities. First, developmental psychology and biology have indicated to us that growth follows a mass action approach then individualization or differentiation and then integration of what has been learned. By starting your children with

global fingerspelling which they could partially imitate, later introducing the letters and integrating this form of habitual motor ideational expression into the total language, speech and reading processes, you are following sound developmental psychology.

Secondly, I am inclined to believe that the motor expression by fingerspelling and speech is using quite effectively the second signal system which should, if done properly, accelerate learning. Third, I noted considerable attention and motivation for this form of communication on the part of young children in the classes I observed. I am wondering whether the "success" in expression for these young children does not have something to do with attention and motivation. I hope that this variable, which is important for learning, will eventually be objectively evaluated. And fourth, if presented properly, I do not see why fingerspelling which should enhance language should necessarily interfere with the development of oral language, if simultaneous presentation and expression is required in the teacher's presence. (*Ibid.*, p. 217.)

Another letter of significance received was from Dr. Ralph Hoag, at that time Specialist, Educational Programs for the Deaf, Department of Health, Education, and Welfare, Washington D.C. Dr. Hoag wrote:

I would like to make a special comment regarding the simultaneous fingerspelling and speech experiment that you are conducting as a part of your program at the New Mexico School. The achievement level of these youngsters seems to be considerably nearer the goal of closing the gap in the educational lag of deaf students as compared to normal hearing children. That is, of course, what we have been striving [for] for such a long time. In comparison to deaf children of their age, the students in your experimental classes appeared to be above average in their performance of language, reading, vocabulary, and speech-reading. The speech of these children also appeared to flow more naturally than the speech of most deaf children at comparable ages. The intelligibility of speech, however, did not appear to be much better than that of other deaf children.

A direction to be reconsidered:

Through the 1960's the comprehensive English environment was continued at the New Mexico School until Marshall Hester's retirement in 1963. With the coming of a new administration and the advent of a new perspective as to what might be the best for deaf children, the advances made up to that time gradually became history. Nevertheless Hester's efforts in behalf of education of the deaf marked a distinct turning point, one that may once again influence positively the future of hearing-impaired children.

51

The National Leadership Training Program and Its Inception 1959

Through the 1950's there was a governmental agency in Washington, D.C., known as Rehabilitation Services, which operated under the auspices of the Federal Security Administration. Subsequently, under a new name, Office of Vocational Rehabilitation (OVR), it became an integral part of the Eisenhower administration's new creation, the Department of Health, Education, and Welfare. In the area of deafness OVR concerned itself primarily as an advisory agency for counseling, rehabilitation training, and job placement activities of the various state rehabilitation organizations.

OVR's expanding interest in the deaf:

It was not until the appointment of Miss Mary Switzer as Commissioner of OVR that the agency truly came to life on the behalf of handicapped people. This was particularly true in the counseling and job placement of adult deaf people. To spearhead the activities of this highly specialized field, Miss Switzer appointed a deeply motivated and professionally experienced postlingually deaf man, Mr. Boyce Williams. Williams, a Gallaudet graduate, had served both as a vocational teacher and as a vocational principal at the Indiana School for the Deaf. With this practical background, he was a solid addition to Miss Switzer's staff.

Today there is a quiet consensus that many of the innovations relative to the deaf which were generated by OVR were in fact the ideas of Boyce Williams. Credit due is nothing, if it isn't recognized. It was, of course, Miss Switzer who had the authority and the influence to bring the numerous good ideas into being. With this thought we can more clearly understand and appreciate not only Miss Switzer's genuine interest in deaf people, but also one of the prime sources of ideas which were presented on their behalf.

The need for a more progressive leadership:

In 1959, at a gathering of her Advisory Committee, Miss Switzer expressed her concern for the need of a more progressive leadership in the education and rehabilitation of the deaf. One of the committee members, Mrs. Spencer Tracy, had similarly perceived this need and immediately these two dynamic women began their conversations on the subject of leadership. With Miss Switzer's influence in the upper federal echelons of rehabilitation and Mrs. Tracy's heart interest and expertise in the oral education of the deaf, this sure-fire combination went into action.

Miss Switzer indicated that OVR could fund the leadership training project, if the Tracy Clinic in conjunction with the University of Southern California would sponsor it. Without further discussion an agreement was tentatively reached.

Boyce Williams, having for some time been on the national scene in education of the deaf, had had some negative experiences with educators of the deaf and felt that many of them were consistently inclined to "sell the deaf short." In this new leadership concept, upon which he had probably given considerable previous thought, Williams saw a marvelous opportunity for reshaping the attitudes of the whole of education of the deaf.

Calling a team together:

As Miss Switzer had called in Boyce Williams, her factotum, so Mrs. Tracy summoned Dr. Edgar Lowell, her administrator at the Clinic, to join the discussions in Washington, D.C. En route by plane, Lowell figured out an estimated cost for training one individual in a leadership program. He concluded that such a project would be cost-wise prohibitive. Upon his arrival in Washington, Lowell presented this observation to Mrs. Tracy and Miss Switzer. The latter's response was that the cost of educating a physician was considerably more. To her way of thinking, a person who was to direct the education and vocational preparation of young deaf people should be no less well prepared than a physician despite the cost.

At the behest of their superiors, Williams and Lowell went to work immediately to sketch in more detail a plan for the proposed leadership training program. Williams worked with an eye to the interests of rehabilitation and Lowell with the specific goals of education of the deaf in mind. Considering their backgrounds and professional interests, two more differently unique persons could not have been brought together as a team. With the leadership training proposal finally outlined, Miss Switzer moved for a one-year grant for the purpose of laying the groundwork.

A qualified director sought for the proposed program:

The immediate action due upon receiving the planning grant was, of course, the search for and the selection of a professionally qualified individual who would take over the project's administrative helm. Such a person immediately came to Mrs. Tracy's mind in the person of one Dr. Wayne F. McIntyre. Dr. McIntyre was, indeed, professionally qualified, being the chairman of the Department of School Administration and Supervision at California State University in Northridge (CSUN). More importantly, however, he was the parent of a deaf child with all of the heart interest and zeal such a responsibility could call forth. In addition, Dr. McIntyre was well acquainted with Mrs. Tracy and her oral program at the Clinic, for his daughter had received her introductory education under Mrs. Tracy's direction. Thoroughly imbued with the Clinic's philosophy and anxious to further the cause of education of the deaf, Dr. McIntyre accepted the directorship of the National Leadership Training Program (NLTP). The year was 1960.

To assist him in the planning and grant-writing phase of the project, the new director selected a faculty member from the CSUN Department of School Administration and Supervision, Dr. Ray L. Jones. While Dr. Jones had had no previous experience in education of the deaf, he did have a variety of school experiences ranging from that of a high school teacher to his services as a high school principal and, finally, he was a university professor in public school administration. Thus Dr. McIntyre and Dr. Jones, along with Dr. Lowell, devoted the balance of the planning year to putting the training program together and organizing the instructional staff.

"Dropping the pilot" and a new director:

In 1962, Dr. McIntyre, having developed the operating structure for the National Leadership Training Program, accepted a call to serve his church in Germany. At this surprising juncture Dr. Ray L. Jones took over the directorship of the program.

In a presentation given in Urbana, Illinois, in July, 1963, at the "Conference on the Training of Specialized Personnel to Work with Deaf People," Dr. Jones described the highlights of the NLTP as they had been developed up to that time.

I. *This is an Inter-Disciplinary Program.* The academic strengths and resources of a distinguished staff from the fields of psychology, sociology, health related services and educational administration are focused on the problems of habilitation and rehabilitation of the deaf. The whole-hearted involvement of this inter-disciplinary staff in regular planning and evaluation conferences has resulted in a program far superior to that which would be possible within any single discipline.

II. *The Leadership Training Program is "habilitation" and "rehabilitation" oriented.* Through extensive field visits to schools and agencies, and through internship assignments in community agencies and schools, participants in training gain a first-hand acquaintanceship with the network of community agencies and schools providing services for the deaf. Participants meet the distraught parents of a new-born deaf child coming to the John Tracy Clinic for diagnosis and counsel; work with pre-school and elementary school children at the Mary E. Bennett or Roosevelt School; attend the high school junior prom at the California School for the Deaf at Riverside; meet the deaf client making his first visit to the Vocational Rehabilitation Services; then interview a prospective employer on his behalf; and serve as teachers or interpreters in classes for the Adult Deaf.

III. *It is a cooperative program.* The San Fernando Valley State College shares with the profession the responsibility for the planning, instruction, and evaluation of the program. Numerous professional leaders in the area of the deaf were invited to assist in the initial planning. They and others continue to serve as instructors, as supervisors of the internship experiences, and as consultants. Among the Southern California leaders who have worked continuously with the program since its inception are: Dr. Richard Brill, Miss Alyce Thomas and Miss Grace Paxson from the California School for the Deaf at Riverside; Dr. Edgar Lowell and Miss Marguerite Stoner of the John Tracy Clinic; Dr. Ernest Willenberg, Mrs. Louise Barr and Mrs. Evelyn Stahlem of the Los Angeles City Schools; Mrs. Myra Jane Taylor of the Compton City Schools; Don Blyth, Zeb Gulledge and Harry Cook of the California State Rehabilitation Services; Allen Spett of the Los Angeles County Crippled Children Services; Dr. Victor Goodhill of the UCLA Otological Clinic.

IV. *The program utilizes new teaching methods and materials developed through extensive research studies in the fields of business and school administration.* "Sensitivity Training," first developed by Kurt Lewin and others at the Massachusetts Institute of Technology, and now utilized in the training of graduate students in Business Administration at Harvard University, Executive training programs at Arden House, New York, and in the School Executive Laboratories at Bethel, Maine is incorporated into the leadership training program. Through this training, participants gain an increased understanding of group processes basic to teamwork, and an increased awareness of their own effect on individuals and on group situations.

Extensive case studies, developed by experienced administrators from the field, form the basis of many of the seminar discussions in the classroom.

"Simulated situation" or "in-basket" training techniques and materials are utilized. These materials were first developed by Dr. Dan Griffin at Teachers College of Columbia University, to bring realism into the training of public school administrators. With the permission of the University Council for Educational Administration, these materials have been adapted to include problems encountered in administering and supervising classes for the deaf operating within a regular elementary school. Special "in-basket" problems have been drawn from the files of state residential schools, day schools, and speech and hearing centers to add *realism* and challenge to the training. With the support of the Captioned Films program, instructional films involving actual classroom teaching have been prepared. In a two-week workshop, participants will rub shoulders with public school administrators as each becomes "Marion Smith – Principal of the Whitman School" and works through the intricate and perplexing problems of administering a school which includes classes for the deaf. The Simulated Situation materials, as modified for use in this project, will also be utilized in September in an in-service workshop for administrators and supervisors in the special education division of the Los Angeles City Schools.

V. *It brings together future leaders from the various segments of the profession.* To date participants in this program have included teachers from state residential schools, day schools, and classes for the deaf; directors and workers in speech and hearing centers;

and vocational rehabilitation counselors. These participants represent programs from all sections of the United States and the Canal Zone. Students come to the program with different backgrounds of experience and training, and with differing philosophies and ideas about the education of the deaf. The program does not take sides in controversies involving philosophy or methodology, but attempts to focus upon all problems inherent in providing the best possible education or training for the deaf individual.

VI.   *The Leadership Training Program provides a laboratory within which participants are encouraged to explore leadership opportunities that will contribute to more effective habilitation or rehabilitation of the deaf.* Each participant is encouraged to develop a project or study which will make a professional contribution to the field. To date, such projects have included a bibliography of library materials related to the leadership training program; a handbook for supervisors; reports of conferences with the adult deaf, and the development of a number of 8mm "single concept" films for instructional use with the deaf.

During recent months, the entire leadership training class has participated in a cooperative pilot program of classes for the adult deaf. Working with the adult deaf from the First Baptist Church in Van Nuys, the trainees determined the interests of this group in adult education and the specific classes which might be desired. Based upon this information, a six-week pilot program of classes was planned with instruction offered in "Economics," "Law," "Insurance," "Child Growth and Development," "English," and "Politics (or Current Events)." One class was taught by a deaf instructor, four were taught by hearing instructors using oral and manual communication, two were taught by hearing instructors working though interpreters. Members of the leadership training class not only provided leadership in organizing the classes but also taught classes and served as interpreters.

Attendance at these weekly classes far exceeded original expectations – reaching a peak of 142 adults ranging in age from 19 to 77. Participants came from 35 Southern California communities, with several driving more than 160 miles each week to attend classes. Conferences with instructors and interpreters, and with the adult deaf students, have been held to evaluate the pilot program. Proceedings of these conferences are currently being prepared for publication by the Leadership Training participants.

On July 26th the project is sponsoring a conference on the theme "Increased Educational Opportunities for the Adult Deaf" which will, hopefully, lead to the establishment of a permanent adult education program in the Southern California area.

VII. *The Leadership Training Program attempts to give participants a vision of the opportunities and challenges that lie ahead in this profession and encouragement to contribute to its advancement.*

This new program made a direct appeal to the idealism of young educators and promised them a variety of experiences which would not only enrich their professional backgrounds but would specifically prepare them for leadership responsibilities. It was at this point in the early 1960's that Gallaudet College, long a dominating influence in directing the leadership of education of the deaf, began to relinquish its role to the "up and coming" San Fernando program.

A new dimension added:

During the first two years of the NLTP only hearing candidates were enrolled; however, in 1964 deaf candidates became eligible.

Since the time this oppportunity was first afforded them, many of the deaf NLTP graduates have distinguished themselves in the areas of rehabilitation and education of the deaf. As Dr. Jones was to say a few years later in an interview, "Accepting these deaf students into the training program added a new dimension we had not anticipated." ("Interview," p. 7.)

Upon the successful completion of its first five-year grant the NLTP was awarded a five-year extension. Now today as the NLTP has become federally anchored as a modern and progressive institution, some of its orally oriented critics wonderingly point to the program's once professed policy of non-participation in "controversies involving philosophy or methodology." This change of policy, when it came, was to mark yet another historical turning point in American education of the deaf.

52

The Council on Education of the Deaf 1960

Recalling the sharp philosophical differences between Edward Miner Gallaudet and Alexander Graham Bell in 1891 and their open conflict over Gallaudet's establishing a Normal Department, one might well have wondered at that time if "the twain" would ever meet. While a token peace was eventually established between the two, their respective followers were less inclined to show amiability toward each other. Hence the breach was such that anyone who might suggest bridging or closing it was suspect. Consequently, the 1946 effort of Gallaudet College's President Elstad to bring the camp of "combined" advocates into cooperation with "the oralists" through a meeting with the Ewings was, indeed, heroic, but without lasting effects.

Dr. Powrie Vaux Doctor, editor of the *American Annals of the Deaf,* after several years of conscientious work, successfully established himself and his publication as unbiased and cooperative communicators with the oralists and their A. G. Bell Association. Combined advocates on the whole, however, continued to be resistant to any efforts toward agreement. Nevertheless, Professor Doctor ("Doc") persisted in seeing the strong likenesses of the two groups rather than their differences, and he spoke accordingly.

A late-night conversation:

The concept of a cooperative alliance between the oral and combined advocates did not receive any genuinely serious attention until one evening in the pub room of a Virginia Beach hotel. The day, October 13, 1959, had been a long one devoted to a conference sponsored by the United States Office of Vocational Rehabilitation. The participants included a number of educators of the deaf who, as was their wont, gathered for some refreshments and a review of the day's proceedings. During their conversation, they discussed the 1958 Congressional action which had established the Media Services and Captioned Films for the Deaf program. It was noted that such a project's chances for acceptance by Congress would be considerably enhanced if *all* of the organizations which worked on the behalf of deaf children were to present an organized and cooperative united front in its support.

The American Association of the Blind, it was observed, had received federal support for its embossed book program and other projects for many years, simply because it spoke with *one* voice. Unquestionably the education of the deaf interests could do the same; provided, of course, they unified their efforts.

The idea immediately "clicked," and it was agreed that for too long American education of the deaf had been split into political ineffectiveness. With the federal coffers now opening to various national social needs, education of the deaf should organize itself and become a deserving recipient. It would, of course, require a total disregard of differences and a heavy emphasis on common needs. This same score being played in the same key would certainly have an appeal to the ears of Congress and the federal government. As the pub room lights flashed the time for closing, a tentative meeting date was hurriedly set for the first of the year.

An exploratory meeting:

On January 20, 1960, an exploratory meeting for the possibilities of a cooperative body was called in Washington, D.C. In addition to the original Virginia Beach "pub team," invitations had been extended to some people who were also to represent their respective organizations. Those to be in attendance were Dr. S. Richard Silverman, president of the Alexander Graham Bell Association (AGB); Dr. George Pratt of the Clarke School; Ms. Jeannette Johnson of the Volta Bureau; Dr. Richard G. Brill, president of the

Convention of American Instructors of the Deaf (CAID); Mr. Roy Stelle, superintendent of the Texas School; Mr. Lloyd Ambrosen of the Maryland School; Miss Frances Phillips of The Kendall School; Dr. Marshall Hester, president of the Conference of Executives of American Schools for the Deaf (CEASD); Dr. William J. McClure, superintendent of the Indiana School; Dr. Leonard M. Elstad, president of Gallaudet College; and Dr. Hugo Schunhoff, superintendent of the West Virginia School.

The neutral ground upon which these oralists and combined advocates were to meet was a conference room at the Statler Hilton. The prime business of this initial session "was to discuss the area of cooperation among the three organizations and the mechanics for making such cooperation effective." ("Initial Discussions," p. 222.)

Typical of such gatherings of school administrators, there was a period of intellectual sparing in an effort to get the discussion going. The temporary chairman went around the table gently prodding each of the representatives to initiate a discussion. After a number of noncommittal remarks from each, Dr. S. Richard Silverman was approached a second time for his thoughts. With some hesitation and seeming reluctance, Silverman went to the chalkboard and, with the typical incisiveness which all of his colleagues had come to expect from him, set down point by point an organizational outline for the proposed Council on Education of the Deaf (CED). Even after the two additional conference sessions which followed this first gathering, the organizational plan proposed by Silverman stood virtually as he had first presented it at that January meeting.

The next scheduled gathering was planned to coincide with the Conference of Executives meeting in Evanston, Illinois, in the spring. The objective of this gathering was to be specifically to complete the constitution for the new cooperative organization, CED.

A Constitution agreed upon:

On Sunday afternoon, April 3, 1960, the representatives of AGB, CAID, and CEASD met in Marshall Hester's suite at Evanston's North Shore Hotel. ("Constitutional Meeting," p. 140.) For this occasion the participating members were fewer, nine in all. This time the group included Alexander Graham Bell Association's representatives Dr. George Pratt; Mr. J. Donovan, a *parent*; and Dr.

Clarence O'Connor, superintendent of the Lexington School. CAID's representatives were Dr. Richard Brill, Mr. Lloyd Ambrosen, and Mr. David Mudgett, a *deaf* teacher from the Illinois School.

The CEASD's representatives were Dr. Marshall Hester, Dr. William J. McClure, and Dr. Hugo Schunhoff.

All of these representatives were most compatible as colleagues, and each had a high professional regard and respect for the other. Eminently qualified as educators of the deaf, they went to work to discuss the tentative constitution for the proposed CED.

> After a number of minor changes the proposed constitution was approved and adopted for submission to the three organizations with the recommendation that it be ratified. (*Ibid.*)

The body of the Constitution and By-Laws of the Council on Education of the Deaf read as follows:

Article I   NAME

This organization shall be known as the "Council on Education of the Deaf." (CED)

Article II   OBJECTIVES

Section 1. The objectives of this organization shall be to encourage and facilitate cooperation among the member organizations in such areas as the following:

A. Publication practices
B. Legislation
C. Meetings
D. Liaison with lay and peripheral groups
E. Mechanisms for receiving foreign groups
F. Teacher certification
G. Public information
H. Research

Section 2. The area of activity shall not be limited to those areas in Section 1, but may be added to by unanimous consent of member ogranizations.

Article III   MEMBERS

Section 1. Membership in this Council is by organizations.

Section 2. Original membership in this organization shall be composed of:

A. The Alexander Graham Bell Association for the Deaf
B. The Conference of Executives of American Schools for the Deaf
C. The Convention of American Instructors of the Deaf

Section 3. Subsequent members must be organizations which are primarily concerned with the education of the deaf.

Section 4. Each member organization shall retain its identity, autonomy and organization.

Article IV   THE EXECUTIVE BOARD

Section 1. The Executive Board shall consist of four representatives from each member organization as follows:

A. The president of each organization to serve during his term of office.
B. Three additional members to represent each organization.
C. The term of office of representation other than president shall be three years of until their successors are designated. Their terms shall be staggered to provide for termination of one of the three terms each year.
D. Each member organization shall determine the method by which it selects its representatives.
E. The first chosen representatives of each organization shall serve for one, two and three years respectively.
F. No representative shall serve more than six years consecutively exclusive of the term served as president of a member organization.

Section 2. A quorum shall consist of no fewer than two representatives of each organization.

Section 3. Voting shall be on a unit basis one vote for each organization.

Section 4. Each organization shall have the power of veto.

Article V   OFFICERS

Section 1. The Presidency of the Council shall be on a rotation basis by organization and in the alphabetical order of the name of the founding organizations as listed Article III, Section 2. Organizations that may become members later will follow three founders in chronological order according to the date of admission.

Section 2. An organization shall hold the presidency for two years, or until a successor is elected.

Section 3. All the delegates from the organization which is scheduled to assume the presidency shall be the nominees for the chairmanship and voting will be by all delegates present. In elections for officers of the Board the unit rule will not apply.

Section 4. There shall be a secretary and a treasurer elected from the Board by members of the Board with a term of office of two years or until their successors are elected.

Section 5. In the absence or disability of the President, the Secretary shall act as presiding officer. In the event the office of President is vacated the Secretary shall act as presiding officer until a successor to the President shall be elected at the next succeeding meeting of the council from the representatives of the appropriate member organization to serve out the unexpired term.

Section 6. All terms of office, both elective and appointive, shall begin on August first in the year in which they are selected.

Article VI   MEETINGS

Section 1. Unless otherwise ordered by the Executive Board, an annual meeting shall be held and may be coincident with the general meeting of one of the member organizations.

Section 2. At each annual meeting the date and place of the subsequent annual meeting shall be established.

Section 3. The annual meeting shall be for the purpose of electing officers, receiving reports of officers and committees, and for any other business that may arise.

Section 4. Special meetings may be called by the President or upon the written request of two representatives from each of two member organizations.

Article VII   FINANCIAL SUPPORT

Section 1. Financial support of the Council will be from member organizations. The Executive Board of the Council shall recommend to the member organizations the amount of support.

Article VIII   COMMITTEES

Section 1. Membership on committees is not restricted to representatives on the Executive Board. Only members of member organizations may be appointed to committees.

Article IX   PARLIAMENTARY AUTHORITY

Section 1. Except where otherwise specified in this constitution, *Robert's Rules of Order Revised* shall be the parliamentary authority.

Article X   AMENDMENTS

Section 1. This constitution may be amended by unanimous unit vote of the Executive Board, which action must be ratified by the affirmative vote of the board of directors of every member organization.

Article XI   ESTABLISHMENT

Section 1. This organization shall be formally established upon ratification of this constitution by the three member organizations.

Section 2. The first meeting of the Council on Education of the Deaf shall be called by the President of the Conference of Executives of American Schools for the Deaf. He shall serve as temporary Chairman until the first President shall be elected from the representatives of the Alexander Graham Bell Association for the Deaf.

(*Ibid.*, pp. 140-141.)

In accordance with the recommendation of the Evanston Committee, this most significant document, the CED constitution, was duly ratified by the three member organizations and thereby implemented. Upon the completion of this business, the first official gathering of the Council on Education of the Deaf was called to meet in Washington, D.C., on October 24-25, 1960.

The first CED assembly:

So it was in October that the CED delegates met in Washington for their first assembly. In keeping with the even-handed policy set forth in the new constitution, the two meetings sites were determined to be at Gallaudet College for the first day and at the Volta Bureau in Georgetown for the second.

On the first day at Kendall Green the delegates, obviously conscious of the significance of the occasion, filed into the Edward Miner Gallaudet Room of the Memorial Library. There they seated themselves under the fixed gaze of the incredibly lifelike portrait of E. M. Gallaudet rendered by the college's watchman-artist, Mr. Krum Mitakoff. While the portrait evinced no reaction, the spirit behind it must have looked on in amazement at the spectacle of oralists and combined advocates sitting down in harmony to work.

After the organization's preliminary business matters were concluded at the Gallaudet session, the meeting was adjourned with the announcement that the following day's deliberations and business would take place across town at the Volta Bureau in Northwest Washington. This final session was, of course, marked with the election of Dr. S. Richard Silverman as the first CED president, Dr. Richard G. Brill as the first secretary, and Dr. William J. McClure as the first treasurer.

A turning point was marked:

Thus it was that after generations, American education of the deaf had finally gathered itself together for some unified action on the behalf of deaf children. In all, the Council on Education of the Deaf proved that the philosophical and even practical differences of the oralists and combined advocates might be transcended once their common goals were discerned. The founding of the CED marked, perhaps, the most important turning point for education of the deaf in the 20th Century.

53

"Seeing Essential English" (S.E.E.)
1962

The lecture room on the second floor of Kendall Hall was packed with Gallaudet sophomores. They had sat there for the better part of an hour receiving their required exposure to the humanities. The topic was the philosophy of Bishop George Berkeley, an 18th-Century Irish philosopher.

Berkeley, it will be recalled, taught that concrete objects are not in themselves things of substance, but merely sensory perceptions of whosoever observes them. Objects, consequently, do not exist independently of the mind which perceives them. The world is, therefore, in fact completely subjective and exists only as perceptions in the minds of its beholders.

The instructor, this writer, in his concluding remarks on Berkeley, presented the well-known limerick which epitomized the philosophy of the good Bishop. The final flip sheet in large bold lettering read:

> There was once a man who said, "God
> Must find it exceedingly odd,
>   If he finds that this tree
>   Continues to be
> When there's no one about in the Quad."

With this and a final explanation, the class was dismissed and the students pushed their way out of the lecture room.

One student, however, came forward to speak to the instructor. In a modulated voice and a distinct British accent, he suggested politely that he could recite a sequel to the limerick which had just been given to the class. The instructor's curiosity stirred and the student was encouraged to recite. Neatly and from memory, the young fellow responded orally:

> Dear Sir,
>   Your astonishment's odd:
> I'm always about in the Quad,
>   And that's why the tree
>   Will continue to be —
> Since observed by
>
>   Yours faithfully,
>   God.

The instructor, amazed at this clever contribution to his Berkeley notes, savored that rare moment of contacting a genuine student intellect and urged the young man to write out the piece for him. Little did the instructor know that this student, David Anthony, a graduate of Britain's well-known Mary Hare School, would one day become a significant innovator in American education of the deaf. His interest was to become instructional communication.

Re: The dominant modes of instruction:

Through a little more than the first half of the 20th Century, the predominant modes of instruction had been all or in part pure oral. A less heralded approach was the oral with sign language. This combination was frequently used unofficially or even surreptitiously in the advanced departments of many schools. It will be recalled that the Rochester Method had been introduced into the new California School at Riverside in all areas of its program excepting the primary department. This was followed in 1958 with Marshall Hester applying the Rochester concept and giving his beginning classes fingerspelling. In addition to these efforts, the Russian experiments in the use of dactylology as a supplement and complement to speech created a great American interest in an old topic under the new name of *neo-oralism*. This increased emphasis and interest in fingerspelling was welcomed by adult deaf organizations. Consequently, the contending camps of instructional methodology were at long last finding a possible common ground for agreement in fingerspelling as a supplement and complement to speech, speechreading, and aural amplification.

The past revived:

In 1962, however, Mr. David Anthony, a deaf teacher of the deaf, employed to instruct a class of retarded deaf youngsters at the Michigan State Institution at Lapeer, found himself frustrated in his teaching efforts. Pondering on his problem, he hit upon the idea of modifying sign language to conform to English structure and through it leading his pupils into effective English reading and writing. Actually, this idea had been buried for so long that when it was rediscovered, it shimmered in the light of possibilities.

Rather than using signs haphazardly to suggest concepts to his pupils, Anthony decided in favor of formulating a specific gestural vocabulary. His criterion in this task was the Basic English system of 850 words devised by the semanticists C. K. Ogden and S. A. Richards. The good teacher that he was, Anthony enlisted the thinking of his pupils in helping him to determine the appropriate signs to be included in the new system. Likewise, he enlisted the thinking of his colleagues in putting together the system which he eventually called Seeing Essential English (S.E.E.). Unquestionably, the spirits of the Abbés de l'Epee and Sicard looking over the golden bar of Heaven must have rejoiced. With the basic principles of S.E.E. established, Anthony and his supporters had but to develop further new signs to accommodate the requirements of English.

The evolution of S.E.E.:

In a presentation describing the evolution of S.E.E., Mr. Anthony wrote:

> Our first step was to make a list of all possible expressions. Our second step was to put each word and each of the expansions (variations) on a card – one word, one card. We had much more than 850 cards! The step after that was the teaching of these words.
>
> By this time, most of the boys and girls had knowledge of the 26 English letters, "A" to "Z". Our first words were simple ones: CAT, DOG, EYE, EAR, MILK, BREAD, SCHOOL, HOUSE, and so on.
>
> We saw that several of the basic words (FRUIT, WIRE, SUCH, THE, to give a few examples) and all measurement words (INCH, FOOT, YARD, MILE, OUNCE, POUND, TON, PINT, QUART, GALLON) had no sign. These words we put to one side. Keep in mind that we are taking signs from Sign [Language].
>
> One day we had the word GLASS, and for this we gave the three common uses of that word – window glass, drinking glass, eye glasses

– each with a different sign. One boy said this was not so: a glass is a glass is a glass. The teacher sent him back to his seat and made him be quiet. A few days after that, this same boy came up to the teacher and gave a new and "better sign" for GLASS. . . .

With the "better sign" for GLASS, we come to the first stage in the development of S.E.E. and its first rule: one word, one sign, never mind the sense of the word. After all, a word itself has no sense till it is put with other words to make a statement.

The second stage in this direction, which took us from one sign for all the forms of TO BE (AM, IS, ARE, WAS, WERE, BEING, BEEN, which one sign also represents EXIST, TRUE, SURE, FACT, REAL, and all their inflections) to a separate sign for each form, is but an expansion of the first rule.

The *Basic English Word List* was put up on the board. Seeing the number of times -MENT and -TION was in print the boys and girls said that we had to have a sign for these parts of words. Other questions and requests came: a sign for -ED, for -ING, for -ER, for -LY, and for others. For the third stage, where a word or an affix had no sign, we made up a sign. And so S.E.E. took root. . . . (Anthony, *Recent Developments,* pp. 14-15.)

New experts and new conflicts in the new camp:

From this beginning there eventually evolved a complete system for rendering English words into signs. Rules for formulating signs were determined to circumvent the peculiarities of American Sign Language (ASL) which stressed concepts only. After a couple of years,

Some of the members of Anthony's group had some philosophical differences and started another system under the leadership of Gerilee Gustason and have entitled their system Signing Exact English (S.E.E.-2). (Brill, *Education of the Deaf,* p. 271.)

Still other authorities began to appear, with each creating a somewhat different sign mode. Aside from ASL, S.E.E.-1, and S.E.E.-2, there also came into being Visual English, Siglish, Ameslish, and Signed English. There was created, consequently, a fascinating Tower of Babel or more appropriately a Tower of Signals, all of which contributed to a growing confusion in modern American education of the deaf. For all of this, it should still be remembered that the ultimate instructional goal for hearing-impaired children was to provide them with the skills to meet the basic communication demands of the hearing workaday world – English reading, writing, and speech.

54

The "Babbidge Report" 1965

Through the early 1960's Gallaudet College became a target of criticism for a number of administrators of schools for the deaf. The criticism was centered largely on the expanding liberal arts curriculum of the college and its administration. Along with this was an internal criticism by a few of the faculty who identified with what was viewed as the traditional Gallaudet. Actually, it was on their part a conflict of loyalties between what had been and what was to be.

From the middle 1950's on there had been an expansion in the liberal arts areas of the humanities and social studies. There was also a much needed additional emphasis on reading, writing, and vocabulary. This idea was excellent, but an apparent lack of appreciation of the deaf language problem on the part of the implementors created unnecessary difficulties. Consequently, Gallaudet students, particularly those in the lower division, i.e., freshman and sophomore classes, found numbers of themselves inundated with the classics of ancient Greece and Rome.

Increasing problems from student complaints:

Before too long complaints began to find their way in letters to the desks of several superintendents and principals. These administrators became aware that many of their graduates, now

317

at Gallaudet, were "in over their heads." These students who found themselves in academic straits had been for the most part the star pupils and beloved "shining lights" of their various state residential schools. Their superintendents, traditionally father figures and revered as such, began to accumulate a certain umbrage in regard to what was being done to their "boys and girls" at Gallaudet College.

"Signing deaf" vs. "oral deaf":

In the expanding Gallaudet student population, however, there was a considerable number of young people who were academically succeeding in their studies of Plato's *Trial and Death of Socrates*, the tragedies of Euripides, and Virgil's *Aeneid.* For the most part, these more fortunate students were not graduates of the various state residential schools for the deaf, but instead were graduates of hearing high schools in urban systems which supported programs for the hearing-impaired. These particular youngsters, having been raised in hearing milieus, found themselves comfortable with the speech and speechreading expected of them in communicating with their hearing instructors. Many of the instructors at Gallaudet during this period were still new to the deaf and were themselves inept at signing. Obviously, they would have a better rapport with those students who could communicate orally. Such rapport, however, was almost impossible for those students who were graduates of the more sign-oriented schools. As a result, the college student population began to find itself divided into the "signing deaf" and the "oral deaf." The latter group learned sign language out of self-defense or, more accurately, for social acceptance. Incidentally, at this time there were no organized classes in sign language for oral students. They were expected to learn the medium through association with their classmates. This period of college growth and change was not easy for either of these two groups of students.

Communication increased among those residential school administrators who were highly concerned regarding the "Gallaudet problem." One of their prime fears appeared to be that Gallaudet College was no longer for the deaf but for the hard-of-hearing. This idea was confirmed by their occasional visits to the college, their observations of students speaking orally to one another, and finally their notice of the growing use of hearing aids among the students. These facts confirmed in their minds that Gallaudet had changed, but not for the better.

A *"summit meeting"* at Gallaudet:

Finally in the fall of 1961 a kind of summit meeting of the College administration with the leaders of several residential schools was called. The representatives gathered in the new Edward Miner Gallaudet Memorial Library for the purpose of discussing and hopefully resolving concerns regarding the curriculum and the problem of faculty-student communication.

One of the rather "touchy" points of the discussion was to be relative to the Dean, Dr. George Detmold, a Shakespearean scholar and a Columbia University graduate in college administration. The complaint was that he had no background in education of the deaf. Consequently, it was believed by some administrators that the Dean was wholly unprepared to understand the needs of deaf students and to cope with their difficulties. An Elstad appointee, Dr. Detmold had the full support of the administration, which was all he needed. While efforts had been made to orient Detmold to "the field," he responded negatively, because he viewed the Gallaudet traditionalists as being academically closed-minded and a general drag on progress. In all, the summit gathering of the Gallaudet and residential school administrators ended in a chilly impasse.

The school administrators look to HEW:

The next phase of the Gallaudet – school administrators' squabble occurred in 1964 when the administrators, feeling a sense of crisis, prevailed upon the United States Department of Health, Education, and Welfare to underwrite an investigation relative to Gallaudet College and its difficulties as they perceived them.

The Gallaudet administration graciously accepted the possibilities of submitting itself and the College to scrutiny. The federal authorities, however, were judiciously reminded that those college students who were suffering from limitations in the area of English – speech, reading, and writing – were, indeed, products of the residential schools. Therefore, for a comprehensive understanding of the Gallaudet situation, if there was one, it might be wise to include *all* of the residential schools in the study. These schools were, after all, the sources upon which the College depended for its supply of students. Thus with this suggestion and the resultant action, the responsibility was placed not on Gallaudet College as originally intended, but more specifically upon the schools for the deaf and particularly upon those administrators who proposed the investigation in the first place.

A National Advisory Committee appointed:

In March, 1964, a National Advisory Committee was named by the Secretary of HEW, Anthony J. Celebrezze, Jr., with its chairman being Dr. Homer D. Babbidge, president of the University of Connecticut. In addition to the chairman, there were 10 committee members, two of whom were deaf, one orally oriented and one non-oral. Also on the committee were two oral educators of the deaf and one audiologist. The remaining five members were from university settings wholly unrelated to education of the deaf *per se*.

The Advisory Committee was assisted by a project staff headed up by Mr. Ralph E. Spear, Washington Representative of the Public Service Administration. The staff consisted of six additional people representing various geographical parts of the nation. None of them was involved in any way with the education of the deaf. At first thought, this selection of people might have been viewed as unwise. Actually, however, their lack of experience with deaf children probably served to guarantee their objectivity. After a general orientation to the subjects of deafness and the deaf, the six staff members fanned out across the United States to commence their interviews.

This author, at the time, principal of the Louisiana State School for the Deaf in Baton Rouge, was interviewed by a pleasant, efficient, and perceptive young woman, an Advisory Committee staff member. Questions were plied to him relative to every aspect of the school and student life. Similarly queried was almost every school for the deaf administrator in the United States. The final result of this tremendous interviewing effort was, of course, the now famous "Babbidge Report" published and released in February, 1965.

The "Babbidge Report" summation:

If "confession is good for the soul," certainly American education of the deaf must have felt considerably better for having revealed its all in the "Babbidge Report." Under the rubric "Summary and Recommendations" we read,

> The American people have no reason to be satisfied with their limited success in educating deaf children and preparing them for full participation in our society.
>
> Less than half of the deaf children needing specialized preschool instruction are receiving it.
>
> The average graduate of a public residential school for the deaf – the closest we have to generally available "high schools" for the deaf – has an eighth grade education.
>
> Seniors at Gallaudet College, the nation's only college for the deaf, rank close to the bottom in performance on the Graduate Record Examination.
>
> Five-sixths of our deaf adults work in manual jobs, as contrasted to only one-half of our hearing population.
>
> This unsatisfactory state of education of the deaf cannot be attributed to any lack of dedication of those who teach and work with the deaf. The basic explanation lies in our failure to launch an aggressive assault on some of the basic problems of language learning of the deaf through experience or well-planned and adequately supported research, and in our failure to develop more systematic and adequate programs for the deaf at all levels.
>
> Today, the problem of teaching the deaf is further complicated by the fact that a greater proportion of our deaf young poeple were born deaf, or were deafened before language had been acquired, than was the case 25 years ago. But while the problem of teaching the deaf has become more difficult, economic and scientific advances are requiring higher levels of educational preparation of young people entering the world of work. (Babbidge, *Advisory Committee*, p. XV.)

While the foregoing statements did not come as big news to American educators of the deaf, the item relative to "our failure to launch an aggressive assault on some of the basic problems of language learning of the deaf"was received by some as a rather wry observation in view of the valiant work and little heralded achievements made by a number of outstanding educators.

One genuinely significant statement recognized the increase over the previous 25 years of young people who "were born deaf, or were deafened before language had been acquired. . . ."

One wonders, however, why no mention was made of the equally important fact that over the same period there had been a marked *drop* in the number of postlingually deaf as well. As an aside, this decrease was due to the advent of antibiotics and the resultant suppression of the nerve-destroying high fevers which characterized many of the theretofore more serious diseases.

Need for improvements cited:

After the "Summary and Recommendations" there followed a section entitled "Needed Improvements":

> Our responsibility in the education of the deaf is the same as it is for all our youth – to assist them in developing their talents fully, to prepare them to be responsible citizens, and to offer them stimulus and opportunity for cultural enrichment of their lives.

> To meet that responsibility, we must move promptly and vigorously on several fronts. Of prime importance, we must expand and improve our programs of *early attention* to the deaf child. Without such early attention the deaf child's difficulties in acquiring language, the indispensable tool of learning, are greatly increased.

> The infant with a hearing defect or a potential hearing defect should have a better chance of being identified in the early months of life and put in touch with better and more generally available clinical facilities and multidisciplinary services for diagnosis and evaluation. Parents of deaf children need more readily available counsel, guidance, and instruction. Programs designed to facilitate language and speech preparation for very young deaf children as well as programs to make maximum use of residual hearing should also be more generally available.

> Significantly improved education of the deaf is also unlikely without a *new research effort* to extend our knowledge about the deaf and how they learn. For many years, the field has been characterized by a lively "methods" controversy. On the one hand, there are those who feel strongly that only oral methods should be employed. On the other, there are those who feel that the deaf will never really be happy with only oral communication, preferring to adopt at an early age forms of manual communication which are easier for both pupil and teacher. The majority of educators in the field appear to favor a combination of methods that permits use of both oral and manual communciation. Also, there has been controversy between those who favor educating the deaf in residential schools and those who favor day schools for such education. Because of these controversies, some have said that for 100 years emotion has been accepted as a substitute for research in the education of the deaf.

> In 1964, only a fraction of one per cent of the cost of educating the deaf was devoted to finding better ways of educating them. This, we believe, is too little and is a major shortcoming of our present efforts. There is no reason to believe that we have reached the limit of human potential in educating the deaf. The longer we delay in supporting

substantial, well-planned programs of research into more effective ways of teaching language and into a variety of other areas which offer promise of improvement, the more we waste the potential talents and skills of those maturing young people whose only difference is that they cannot hear.

Special emphasis on early diagnosis and on new knowledge through research must also be accompanied by attention to other important specific deficiencies in education of the deaf.

For example, deaf young people whose learning problems are complicated by the presence of one or more additional handicaps require special attention. The education of the multiply handicapped deaf person is an almost untouched field.

Of more general concern, any deaf child with the desire and requisite ability should have the opportunity to complete a true high school program. Yet, there are probably no more than a half-dozen true high school programs for the deaf in this country. The changing occupational outlook for all young people requires a better foundation in English, science, and mathematics, subjects in which the language and speech problems of the deaf continue to create special difficulties.

There is a particular danger that the deaf may be early victims of a changing occupational outlook. While in the past vocational education programs for the deaf have been successful at the mechanical and operative level, recent and anticipated future developments are and will be creating a need for more sophisticated occupational education for the deaf, realistically geared to the more complex demands of the future.

Post-secondary educational opportunities for deaf young people are, with the exception of the liberal arts program at Gallaudet College, extremely limited. The deaf should have access to a full range of post-secondary occupational and adult education available to the general population and be prepared to benefit thereby.

While marked improvements have been made at Gallaudet College during the past decade, its role needs sharper definition, and certain aspects of curriculum and faculty preparation need strengthening. In addition, certain features of its governance would benefit from changes.

There is a general lack of systematic approach to the education of the deaf. With few exceptions, state programs are aggregations of program elements (e.g., some preschool classes, a few day classes, or a day school, a state public residential school, etc.), rather than planned and coordinated systems.

All states could profit from a careful appraisal of the extent to which they provide comprehensive programs. In those states with too few deaf children to warrant complete systems, two or more states should join their efforts to assure adequate programs.

A satisfactory system for the education of the deaf requires the availability of many medical, audiological, psychological, social service, and other diagnostic services not routinely associated with education. Such services are, however, commonly accepted as necessary adjuncts to the field of special education, of which the education of the deaf is a part. As its name suggests, special education requires particular attention to the needs, capabilities, and limitations of the individual child. Educators of the deaf should recognize that important new services and facilities now being brought to bear on the whole field of special education offer promise of alleviating some old problems persistently encountered in the education of the deaf.

In summary, there is an urgent need to raise the level of hopes and expectations in the education of the deaf. Deaf individuals and their teachers should not accept a severely limited goal in life for the deaf. A look at the history of the field makes it clear that there have been important advances in the past. There is no reason to conclude that the future is without opportunity for further similar advances. (*Ibid.*, pp. XVI-XVIII.)

Obviously the "Babbidge Report" had a rather traumatic effect on the field of education of the deaf, in that its shortcomings like soiled linen were publicly run up the mast. Nothing, however, was actually revealed of which the majority of educators were not already aware.

Some positive and negative results of the "Babbidge Report":

The problem, in most instances of deficiency, was that the financial wherewithal necessary for making improvements was not forthcoming. There were barely sufficient funds to sustain current programs, much less to expand early childhood education, secondary education, and research. All of these had been proposed and developed to certain degrees, only to fail for the lack of funds. Bringing such inadequacies to the fore provided the educators with an effective but embarrassing lever with which to boost the federal government and state legislatures into action.

One negative feature which resulted from the Report was that the credibility of educators of the deaf was put into question. Consequently, a few administrators, who naturally wished to look good in the eyes of their alumni and state associations of the deaf, felt compelled to make changes in their school programs in order to meet the demands for improvement. Tritely put, in a number of such instances "the baby was tossed out with the bath water."

Following the release of the "Babbidge Report" there came, as might have been expected, panaceas aplenty.

Chapter Twelve
Old Differences Revived
and
A Thrust to the Future

55

The Advent of
"Total Communication"
1967

With the release of the "Babbidge Report" in 1965, educators of the deaf were sufficiently stimulated into action to consider any and all possibilities for a "new look." The year 1962 has seen the advent of David Anthony's "Seeing Essential English," a quasi-English / sign language system. The consensus toward signs, however, had long been and continued to be that reflected in the statement of Gallaudet's president, Dr. Leonard M. Elstad, "The use of sign language in classrooms is discouraged in all schools." (Frampton and Gall, *Special Education*, p. 160.) He was, of course, stating a recognized fact; hence no administrator was about to "upset the apple cart" in his school by inaugurating S.E.E. as an instructional approach.

The Indiana School for the Deaf under the leadership of Dr. William J. McClure was in the process of gradually adopting the Rochester Method as its instructional mode. Thus fingerspelling as a supplement to speech was encouraged by the school's administration. The faculty was generally agreed that this approach was considerably more effective than the traditional oral mode, particularly in the primary and elementary years. Upon Dr. McClure's finally moving, however, to the Florida School for the Deaf and the Blind, his ideas relative to the use of fingerspelling went with him.

A concept in the making:

Along in 1967 Mr. Roy K. Holcomb, a deaf teacher in the Indiana School, became absorbed with an idea which had been taking shape in his mind. If fingerspelling were an acceptable supplementary medium to speech, would not the entire manual package including sign language be possibly even more acceptable? Would not a completely manual (fingerspelling and sign language) mode supplemented with speech, speechreading, and aural amplification effect a more receptive medium of communication for deaf children than speechreading alone or even speechreading supplemented with fingerspelling? Unburdened by the history of instructional evolution, Holcomb seized upon an idea which had been long used by many advanced department teachers. From it he formulated a procedure of instruction which would involve *all* manual, oral, and aural modes. Thus the rationale was that if a child were deficient in one medium of communication, another simultaneously rendered would be available to him. Consequently comprehension would always be guaranteed to him. Such an innovative procedure, of course, would require a suitable name.

Being aware of the need for an all-inclusive and descriptive appellation for his new procedure, Holcomb hit on the "untoppable" designation, *Total Communication*. As he later wrote, he was inspired by "a supermarket slogan advertising 'Total Discounts.' " From this he derived the name "Total Communication" (TC). ("Three Years," p. 524.) In the future his detractors were agreed that perhaps the supermarket slogan should have been adopted without modification, for in TC they saw a variety of "discounts." Such negative observations, however, were to have little effect.

Northridge support for TC:

In 1967 Holcomb matriculated in the Leadership Training Program in the Area of the Deaf (LTP) at California State University in Northridge. After some discussions with Dr. Ray Jones and Dr. Lloyd Johns, members of the training faculty, Holcomb was convinced that with TC and its objectives he was on the right track. In "Total Communication" both Jones and Johns recognized a new thrust which might possibly correct some of the ills of American education of the deaf as depicted in the "Babbidge Report."

Dissatisfaction in Santa Ana:

Before the academic year at Northridge was completed the Santa Ana Unified School District had created a new position, that of area supervisor for its education of the deaf program. The District, having employed the oral method for 20 years, had found a rising dissatisfaction with its pupil achievement levels. Futhermore, the District's negative findings reflected to a large extent those mentioned in the "Babbidge Report"; the officials at Santa Ana were open to suggestions.

The Riverside School with its oral/fingerspelling (Rochester Method) approach seemed a likely direction. At any rate, to implement a new program of any kind at Santa Ana, an area supervisor for education of the hearing-impaired would be required. The only logical place to seek out a progressive and innovative candidate for such a position was at the Leadership Training Program at Northridge.

A likely candidate:

The most likely candidate for the new position was Mr. Roy Holcomb, a natural for the job. Aside from being a fully qualified teacher of the deaf with a number of years of experience, he was also hearing-impaired and had intelligible speech and acceptable English. Momentarily he was in the process of completing his graduate work in the area of administration of programs for the deaf. Indeed, he was the man for the position.

Philosophically Holcomb was a pragmatist; he advocated not only fingerspelling as a supplement to speech and speechreading but sign language as well. Mr. Holcomb's "Total Approach" or "Total Communication" would most certainly cover all of the communication bases and leave no child "outside the pale" of understanding.

As for the sign language aspect of TC, it would be presented in David Anthony's system, "Seeing Essential English." This system according to its very title epitomized the prime goal in education of deaf, *English.* Speech, speechreading, reading, and writing would naturally follow suit for the simple reason that all of these modes were integral parts of the TC procedure.

"What is TC?" A continuing question:

One of the most persuasive arguments that Santa Ana parents and all subsequent audiences faced relative to TC may be summed up in Mr. Holcomb's presentation before the Indianapolis Convention of American Instructors of the Deaf in 1973.

> In my opinion one of the most important right things at the earliest age is Total (full) Communication. Hearing children are exposed to full communication in their home, school, and life. In fact, they expect and demand it in their daily lives. Is it not then wrong to give our deaf children anything less than full communication? How are these people, who want full communication for themselves, but deny the same right to their less fortunate fellowmen – the deaf, going to answer for their sins of omission? Can these people truly say that they thought part communication was good enough for the deaf while they demanded full communication for themselves? So I repeat, full communication must be given to our children from the beginning in very much the same manner it is given to hearing children, except, that the deaf must depend more upon their vision to obtain communication. In other words, they must have opportunities to see what hearing people hear. ("Total Communication," p. 324.)

It is interesting and curious to note that after having had two American Instructors of the Deaf conventions (1971 and 1973) consider in open discussion the subject of "Total Communication" and its ramifications, there was still a debate as to whether TC was a philosophy or a method. Although Mr. Holcomb observed that "most people are in agreement that it (TC) is a philosophy," others felt the need for a sharper definition.

This author in a 1972 article entitled "Total Communication in a New Perspective" volunteered the following statement of definition:

> Total Communication is a prescriptive philosophy based on the individual communication-needs of children. Accordingly speech, fingerspelling, and lipreading may be recommended for one child in a particular class, while speech and sign language may be suggested for another youngster in the same class. Still a third classmate may be slated for speech, lipreading, and the acoustic approach. A fourth child in the group being postlingually hard of hearing will require only the aural amplification of his teacher's speech. A fifth less perceptually endowed youngster will be recommended for sign language only. The remaining four children in the class will each glean what he can according to the medium or media of his choice as rendered by his teacher.

Under Total Communication the teacher of the aforementioned class will be an expert in sign language, fingerspelling, and speech. She will, as nearly as possible, employ all three of the different media simultaneously. Each child will theoretically focus on his particular medium being used by the teacher and accordingly be instructed. The point of emphasis, of course, is that communication is clearly established between each individual child and the teacher.

The rationale is that with education in a class or school with such opportunities for total communication, the child's chances for learning will be enormously increased. In addition psychologists cite improved achievement scores for many sign-oriented children as a definite plus for Total Communication. (Scouten, "New Perspective," p. 1.)

The debate as to whether "Total Communication" was a method or a philosophy continued for another four years until May, 1976, when a "definition committee" appointed by the Conference of Executives of American Schools for the Deaf finally pinned down an official definition. The committee's effort reads:

Total Communication is a philosophy requiring the incorporation of appropriate aural, manual and oral modes of communication in order to ensure effective communication with and among hearing-impaired persons. ("Total Communication Definition," p. 3.)

Before TC was defined or even completely understood, many schools had already adopted it. The chief reason was apparently that a number of these schools had been for many years pursuing variations of this procedure in their advanced departments, but had never had an appropriate name for what they were doing. Publicly committed now as these schools were to "Total Communication," it was with relief that they finally had the system defined, even though in most instances they differed in its application.

56

NTID-"A Dream and a Possibility" Realized
1968

As early as 1888 Mr. D. S. Rogers, an instructor in the South Carolina School for the Deaf, presented his thoughts on advanced technical education for the deaf in a short article entitled "A Plea for a Polytechnic Institute." This piece published in the *American Annals of the Deaf* set forth Mr. Rogers' rationale for such a school and concluded with the words:

> There are theological, law, medical, surgical and other colleges and polytechnic institutes for hearing persons to get a practical education, but not a single establishment for deaf-mutes, excepting the industrial departments connected with the institutions, and these are too often regarded as secondary importance.
>
> As this nation is becoming more and more practical, is it not time to establish an independent institute for deaf-mutes where arts may be taught so as to enable them to engage in certain higher occupations without disadvantage from deafness?
>
> The appropriate name for this institute would be Polytechnic Institute for Deaf-Mutes, and it should be at Washington. ("Plea," p. 185.)

While Mr. Rogers' idealistic proposal had received but one response, and that devastatingly negative, his thought was destined to take root. (See Appendix 21.) Actually, four years were to pass before the idea of a technical institute for the deaf was again to make its appearance.

Advanced technical education officially considered:

In August, 1892, the subject was introduced at the Colorado Springs Conference of Superintendents and Principals by Mr. F. D. Clarke, superintendent of the Arkansas School. Mr. Clarke's concept was similar to that earlier one presented by Rogers; however, Clarke specifically advocated "a *National* technical school for the deaf."

The Conference, after some discussion, was favorably disposed to the idea and moved for the selection of a committee to investigate the possibilities and ramifications of higher technical education for the deaf. Accordingly, a study committee was organized with Mr. Clarke as chairman, along with Dr. E. M. Gallaudet and three other school administrators as members.

A national technical school reported impracticable:

On July 24, 1893, the Conference was called to a special meeting in Chicago. It was on this occasion that the technical education committee presented the following report:

> WHEREAS a committee appointed by the conference of principals at Colorado Springs in 1892 has had the subject of the technical and manual training of the deaf under consideration the past year, and has reported that the establishment of a separate school for this purpose at this time is impracticable, and that there does seem to be a chance to get a sufficient appropriation from Congress to establish a department in the National Deaf-Mute College for the higher technical education of the deaf: Therefore
>
> RESOLVED, That the establishment of a department for the technical education of the deaf at the National Deaf-Mute College is very much to be desired for the good of all the deaf in America.
>
> RESOLVED, That this conference earnestly request the directors and faculty of the college to establish a technical department, and to apply to Congress for a sufficient appropriation to meet the expense of such a department.
>
> RESOLVED, That we pledge ourselves to aid in the establishment of this department in every way we can.
>
> RESOLVED, That the secretary of this conference be requested to send a copy of these resolutions to the college authorities.
>
> ("Resolution for Higher Technical Education," p. 12.)

The Conference responded by unanimously adopting the resolutions with the following motion made by Dr. J. L. Noyes, superintendent of the Minnesota School. It was voted:

> That the secretary be requested to send a copy of the above resolutions to all the superintendents and principals of schools for the deaf in the United States, and that they communicate with their Senators and Representatives in Congress upon this important matter. (*Ibid.*)

With the idea of a national technical *school* having been set aside by the Conference, the onus was now clearly upon the National Deaf-Mute College to assume the responsibility of higher technical education. Subsequently, the subject was examined and discussed thoroughly by the College faculty which, after a time, voted unanimously in favor of the establishment of such a department. The issue of technical education for the deaf was, consequently, resolved for the better part of a century.

The national technical school concept resurfaces in 1930:

While certainly the concept of a national school of technical education for the deaf continued to be discussed in numerous private conversations over the years, it was not until 1930 that the idea surfaced publicly once again in an article by Mr. Peter N. Peterson, a deaf vocational teacher in the Minnesota School at Faribault. Mr. Peterson's piece entitled "A Dream and a Possibility" appeared in *The Vocational Teacher,* a short-lived journal edited by Mr. Tom Anderson, a deaf man and vocational principal of the Iowa School for the Deaf at Council Bluffs.

The article reviewed the industrial arts activities of the 1929 CAID gathering at Faribault. The intriguing aspect of this piece was Peterson's clairvoyance in the words:

> Ideal industrial education for all the deaf is a long way off, although much can be done, and is being done by schools that have generous legislatures and industrially minded superintendents. But day schools and residential schools that have very limited appropriations are necessarily handicapped.

> A National Technical Institute for the Deaf, located at the center of population in a large manufacturing city, is what deaf young America needs more than anything else. It would be a complement to Gallaudet College, and on a par with it in usefulness and influence. It would give all the deaf who wanted it a practical education that would lead to bread with butter spread thick upon it. ("Dream," p. 8.)

The "stuff of dreams":

The chief difference between Peterson's proposed National Technical Institute for the Deaf (NTID) and the institute ultimately realized some 38 years later was that the former was to be subsidized by private money, with Mr. Henry Ford being considered as the likely philanthropist. As it developed the latter evolved under the financial auspices of the United States government. In Peterson's day government support for such a project was "the stuff of dreams," and inveigling Mr. Ford or any other philanthropist to release $10 million on the behalf of industrial education for deaf youth was the same "stuff." Peterson's ideas, consequently, sank into oblivion along with Tom Anderson's defunct journal, another tiny but courageous victim of the Great Depression.

The Barnes proposal in 1941:

The next proposal for higher technical education for the deaf was made 11 years later by a genuine idealist, Mr. Harvey Barnes, principal of the vocational department at the Illinois School for the Deaf in Jacksonville. The occasion for his presentation was the Fulton, Missouri, Convention of American Instructors of the Deaf in June, 1941. Barnes' paper was entitled "How a National School of Trades, Agriculture and Technical Training Would Solve Our Problems."

On the day just previous to Barnes' presentation, the Vocational Teachers Section of the Convention had met and he had suggested "that the resolutions committee take into consideration that there is a need for more advanced vocational training and the fulfillment of this need." Mr. Barnes' request for such a resolution and his success in gaining it naturally buoyed his hopes for his idea's ultimate acceptance by the Convention and eventually perhaps by the federal government. Thus success seemed fairly certain for the proposal Mr. Barnes was about to make.

Because of this happy turn of events, i.e., the quick acceptance of his suggested resolution on the behalf of advanced technical educational training for the deaf, Barnes had to revise his presentation somewhat in order to assure support for his idea from the whole Convention. He therefore, early in his presentation, gave a list of current problem questions relative to the vocational education of deaf children and youth. The questions, well-known and frequently experienced by vocational teachers, were actually directed to the school administrators and academic teachers of the Convention, i.e., those whose understanding and support were of especial importance.

Mr. Barnes then listed 12 possible solutions to the problems which he had cited. These he led off with the one solution in which he was the most interested.

1. Establishment of a national school of trades, agriculture and technical training for the deaf, as proposed in the *Illinois Advance*, February 1940, and since further described.
2. Continuation of present haphazard, poorly planned, opportunistic practices, mingling industrial arts and vocational education and practice.
3. Persuade our State universities to take over the job of advanced vocational education of the deaf.
4. Each State school for the deaf independently to offer a complete variety of vocational training opportunities.
5. Establishment of separate vocational schools by each State.
6. Establishment of sectional vocational schools.
7. Depending on the rehabilitation departments of each State, if any.
8. Combine services of State and Federal rehabilitation departments.
9. Establishment of complete high-grade training in one or two vocations by presently established schools, then exchange pupils.
10. Persuade Gallaudet College to expand to provide for all needs in the field of advanced education.
11. Move Gallaudet College to some industrial city.
12. Establish summer sessions to permit postgraduate students to return to the State schools and take advantage of their (very limited) facilities in order to correct or supplement the training which we now give.

The times not yet ready:

For all of Harvey Barnes' efforts and enthusiasm, however, the times were not as yet ready. A number of factors tended to mark the idea of advanced technical education as being highly visionary and impractical. One strongly opposing factor was the consensus that Gallaudet College in Washington, D.C., with its graphic arts program taught by Mr. Frank Smith, its agricultural theory course taught by Prof. Harley Drake, and a required freshman mechanical drawing course taught by Miss Margaret Yoder, was sufficient to meet the needs and aspirations of technically oriented students. These programs had successfully served and satisfied the needs of generations of students; consequently there was no genuine demand for an expanded technical program. This perspective, it should be remembered, was not limited to education of the deaf only, but was actually a reflection of our national attitude of self-satisfaction as a whole. It was, of course, to be changed abruptly six months later, come December 7.

In a moment, however, the dream of Harvey Barnes of Illinois joined those of D. S. Rogers and P. N. Peterson. Actually the first generation destined to be served by their idea was not yet even born; consequently the dream of advanced technical education for the deaf rested another quarter of a century and awaited its moment.

The kindling of federal interest:

It will be recalled that in March, 1964, Secretary Anthony J. Celebrezze of the Department of Health, Education, and Welfare (HEW) brought together his Advisory Committee on Education of the Deaf. The purpose of the Committee was to render a report on the status of American education of the deaf. This was, of course, to become known as the "Babbidge Report."

The assembling of this federally supported Committee was common knowledge to most school administrators; consequently, when the Conference of Executives of American Schools for the Deaf (CEASD) met at the Riverside School in April, 1964, there was high curiosity as to the federal government's blossoming interest in education of the deaf. With this new government concern for their problems, the members of the Conference discussed extensively the issue of vocational education.

Growing federal support and a CEASD resolution:

Closely involved in these discussions were two Department of Health, Education, and Welfare representatives. One was Dr. Ralph Hoag, a man with Gallaudet credentials, plenty of professional experience, and a heart interest in the deaf. The other was Mrs. Patria Winalski (now Forsythe), an attractive, outgoing mother of a deaf child, who along with a persuasive manner also possessed considerable political "savvy." Dr. Hoag, a specialist in educational programs for the deaf, and Mrs. Winalski, an assistant to the Congressional Liaison Officer for HEW, came to Riverside primed with an important idea, that of a National Technical Institute for the Deaf. With the full support of HEW's Office of Education, these two representatives pushed the NTID concept. While there were a number of educators who supported the idea of regional institutions, the consensus among the administrators was clearly in favor of a national technical facility.

Despite the efforts of the pro-regional school supporters, the strongest of whom was Mr. Roy Parks, superintendent of the Arkansas School at Little Rock, Dr. Hoag and Mrs. Winalski firmly maintained that federal aid could never be expected for the support of regional schools. On the other hand, such aid might be much more easily raised by Congress on the behalf of a National Technical facility. The majority of the Conference members concurred.

Consequently at the encouraging behest of HEW's Dr. Ralph Hoag and his colleague, Mrs. Patria Winalski, the Conference of Executives passed the initial resolution in support of Congressional action for the establishment of an NTID project. This adopted resolution read as follows:

> WHEREAS, there is an immediate and imperative need for technical and vocational training to enable the deaf youth of this country to meet the challenge of our rapidly advancing technology which is greatly accentuating the demand for specialized training, and,
>
> WHEREAS, the deaf have the ability to master technical and vocational skills to a high degree, and,
>
> WHEREAS, the full utilization of such abilities and skills is in the best interest of the entire nation as well as of deaf persons themselves, and,
>
> WHEREAS, there are few special technical training facilities for the deaf, and the vocational training which the great majority of schools for the deaf are able to provide is vastly inadequate and the schools cannot meet this vital need of the deaf,
>
> THEREFORE, be it resolved that the Conference of Executives of American Schools for the Deaf meeting in Riverside, California on April 16, 1964, does, by vote, urgently request the Congress of the United States to make provision for the establishment of technical and vocational facilities for the deaf as may be deemed necessary to prepare deaf youth to utilize fully their abilities and skills in the increasingly complex world to make their rightful contribution to the nation. ("Resolution for the Establishment of NTID," pp. 245-246.)

The National Workshop on Improved Opportunities:

Events were moving fast in favor of some kind of decisive action on behalf of the economic betterment of deaf people because in the week of October 18-22, 1964, a government-sponsored National

Workshop on Improved Opportunities for the Deaf met in Knoxville, Tennessee. This gathering was attended not only by educators of the deaf but by representatives of general education, industry, and the federal government as well.

While this particular workshop covered many aspects of possible opportunities for the deaf, the one most germane to this story was the topic which related specifically to the improvement and expansion of vocational and technical education for the deaf. As previously mentioned, the concept of a national technical institution for the deaf had some months earlier been very well received by the Conference of Executives with the result that a strong resolution was passed in its favor. Thus, the possibility for a national technical facility was high on the workshop agenda.

The *Workshop Proceedings* for the Knoxville meeting which were released some months later disconcertingly veiled the identity of one of its most significant contributors by referring to him as a "discussant"! Thus, this author through a dint of sleuthing discovered the "discussant" not to be the non-entity indicated in the *Proceedings*, but a very live and creative person in the form again of Dr. Ralph Hoag of the U.S. Office of Education. It was he, of course, who had introduced the NTID concept at the CEASD meeting at Riverside six months previously.

A projection of "things to come":

In what appeared to be a spontaneous presentation, but obviously the result of some solid "homework," Hoag made the following statements:

> In view of the problem of providing adequate opportunities for deaf people to prepare for and make satisfying adjustments to the changing world of work, there should be established a comprehensive, multi-purpose vocational and technical institute for the deaf. A residence institute is proposed. The following functions are suggested:
>
> 1. Offer an extensive array of vocational and technical programs in response to the wide range of aptitudes, interests, previous educational attainments, and realistic occupational aspirations of deaf youth and adults.
>
> 2. Provide a comprehensive program of vocational counseling, basic educational remediation, occupational training and retraining, placement and follow-up, school-job coordination and other ancillary services required to ensure occupational preparation and adjustment.

3. Serve as a major laboratory for research with reference to the many problems of occupational preparation and adjustment of deaf individuals.

4. Develop curricula, instructional media and teaching methods required to improve occupational training programs for deaf students in other schools throughout the country.

5. Provide realistic laboratory experience as an integral phase of the preparation of vocational teachers, administrators, counselors, rehabilitation specialists and other professional personnel required to staff vocational departments of schools for the deaf.

The unique functions of the institute envisaged here strongly suggest that it be attached to a major university which meets the following criteria:

1. Located within or near a major labor market area.

2. Having outstanding research and instructional programs in such fields as: special education, speech and audiology, medical and health sciences, vocational and technical education, sociology, psychology, social work, labor and industrial relations and rehabilitation counseling.

3. Possessing a long history of cooperative working relationships with various agencies whose services will be essential to successful pursuit of the functions of the proposed institute.

4. Expressing interest in making a long-range commitment to the development and support of a comprehensive institute along the lines suggested herein. (Hoag, "Proposal," pp. 21-22.)

With such a grasp of the NTID concept, one may easily understand how Dr. Hoag eventually came to be named NTID Project Staff Director, a key job for bringing all of the planning elements together.

Unity essential for action:

The National Workshop at Knoxville had succeeded at last in unifying the various interests and forces of educators of the deaf, rehabilitation workers, and representatives of several state associations of the deaf into a concerted body on behalf of a national facility for the technical education of young deaf people. Seven more months, however, were required to translate the abstraction into a "green-go" reality.

. . . on April 1, 1965, three identical bills for the establishment of a National Technical Institute for the Deaf were introduced in both houses of Congress. They were introduced in the Senate by Senator

Lister Hill of Alabama and in the House by Congressman John Fogarty of Rhode Island and Congressman Hugh Carey of New York.

The House legislative timetable permitted it to act first. A hearing was held by the Special Subcommittee on Labor of the Committee on Education and Labor on April 27, 1965. Departmental representatives who participated in the hearings included Mr. Philip H. Des Marais, deputy assistant secretary for legislation, Mrs. Patria Winalski, legislative assistant, Dr. Marvin Wirtz, director of the Division of Handicapped Children and Youth of the Office of Education and Dr. Ralph L. Hoag, coordinator of Programs for the Deaf. Others who testified included Dr. Leonard Elstad, president of Gallaudet College in Washington, D.C.; Dr. S. Richard Silverman, director of the Central Institute for the Deaf, St. Louis, Missouri; Monsignor John Hourihan, director of the Mount Carmel Guild Speech-Hearing Center, Newark, New Jersey; and Congressman John Fogarty of Rhode Island. At the conclusion of the hearing, the subcommittee reported the bill to the full committee. On May 6, 1965, the full committee reported the bill to the House of Representatives. On May 17, Congressman Carey's bill (H.R. 7031) was considered and passed by the House of Representatives.

The Senate, on May 17, the same day that the bill passed the House, held hearings on the companion bill, S. 1650. Testifying for the Department of Health, Education, and Welfare were Under Secretary Wilbur J. Cohen and Commissioner Mary Switzer of the Vocational Rehabilitation Administration. Additional witnesses and statements were presented representing the Council for Exceptional Children, the Mount Carmel Guild, the Central Institute for the Deaf and Gallaudet College.

Supporting statements were presented by representatives of numerous schools and associations for the deaf, some of whom were the National Fraternal Society of the Deaf, the Georgia Association of the Deaf, the Illinois Association of the Deaf, the Nebraska Association of the Deaf, the Council on Education of the Deaf and its three constituent organizations: the Alexander Graham Bell Association for the Deaf, the Conference of Executives of American Schools for the Deaf, and the American Instructors of the Deaf. Statements from the administrators of schools for the deaf supporting the legislation included in the report came from West Virginia, Pennsylvania, New Hampshire, North Dakota, Washington, New York, Nebraska, Arizona, Hawaii, Idaho, and Maine.

The bill accompanied by its report was introduced on the floor of the Senate on May 26 and was passed.

On June 8, 1965, President Johnson signed into law the National Technical Institute for the Deaf Act. The record shows that this legislation received strong bipartisan support in both the House and the Senate. (NTID, *Report of First Year Ending Dec. 20, 1967*, pp. 6-7.)

The NTID Act and its authorizations:

This Act, designated as Public Law 89-36, authorized the Secretary of Health, Education, and Welfare, following consultations with his National Advisory Board, "to enter into an agreement with an institution of higher education for the establishment and operation, including construction and equipment, of a residential facility for post-secondary technical training and education for persons who are deaf." (*Ibid.*, p. 8.)

The next task was to select a sponsoring institution for the proposed technical education facility for the deaf. Bids were consequently called for from various universities across the United States. While numbers of institutions responded to the National Advisory Board's request with letters of recommendation, supporting documents, proposed plans of operation, and curricula, each stressed the advantages of its own geographical site. The rationales and evidences of each were carefully studied by the Advisory Board, which finally pinpointed one as being the final choice. This, of course, was the Rochester Institute of Technology (RIT), located in the upstate center of industry, Rochester, New York. This choice was announced in the National Advisory Board's DHEW Report for October 1, 1966. In this document were the words, "We consider that Rochester Institute of Technology represents the best combination to carry out the intent of the legislation now and in the future." (*Ibid.*, p. 11.)

Purposes and Objectives determined for NTID:

Subsequently in conjunction with the Secretary of Health, Education, and Welfare's National Advisory Board and the newly designated sponsoring institution, the Rochester Institute of Technology, the following primary "Purposes and Objectives of NTID" were agreed upon. These objectives were particularly significant because they clearly set forth the intent and direction which the new facility was to take. They were slated as follows:

1. To provide, for post-secondary deaf students, the opportunity to prepare for and to pursue semi-professional and professional level educational programs in science, technology and applied arts that lead to successful employment in business, education, government and industry.

2. To provide special support services, within an institution of higher learning, which facilitate and encourage deaf students to achieve a high degree of personal, social, and cultural development.

3. To encourage qualified deaf students to pursue graduate studies at RIT or elsewhere.

4. To conduct research into the occupational and the employment related aspects of deafness.

5. To develop and evaluate new imaginative instructional technology for application in the education of deaf students.

6. To conduct training programs, seminars, and short courses relating to deafness for RIT personnel, for graduate students preparing to work professionally with the deaf, and for other special groups.

7. To disseminate information regarding current NTID practices concerning curriculum, courses of study, special services, and research findings related to those offering programs for deaf children and to the RIT educational community.

8. To develop and modify the educational specifications, to design and construct the facilities, to procure the equipment, and to develop and maintain the staff necessary to meet the objectives of NTID. (*Ibid.*, pp. 8-9.)

A leader sought and found:

With the site selection completed and the guiding principles determined, the next major step was to begin the search for a professionally qualified person to head up and implement the entire National Technical Institute for the Deaf program and make it a reality. Such an individual had to evince some very special qualifications in addition to those of a specifically professional nature.

While there were a number of applicants for the new Institute's directorship, the one best qualified was a man whose professional background, experience, and temperament appeared to have precisely cast him for the task. On January 13, 1967, the name of this man, Dr. D. Robert Frisina, was announced as the newly appointed RIT Vice-President for the National Technical Institute for the Deaf.

Frisina, an energetic, innovative, and inspiring educator of the deaf, upon the completion of his initial professional preparation at Gallaudet College in 1950, taught deaf children and youth at the Missouri School for the Deaf at Fulton. Subsequently he returned to Gallaudet College, where he joined the faculty of The Kendall School and served as a demonstration teacher.

Frisina then pursued graduate studies at Northwestern University in the area of audiology and took his doctorate in this field in 1955. Eventually he returned to Gallaudet and became the director of the Hearing and Speech Center at that institution. In 1964 Frisina was appointed dean of the Gallaudet College Graduate School. Thus with such a background and experience, Dr. Frisina brought to the emerging NTID an energy and a perspective which were soon to be reflected throughout the new institution as it evolved.

Among Dr. Frisina's many responsibilities which had to be borne in his new capacity as vice-president for NTID was the all-important mission of recruiting faculty and staff. The extensiveness of this task alone made obvious Frisina's need for an assistant to whom he could delegate many of the ongoing responsibilities.

The pace-setters:

For the position of Assistant to the Vice-President and Director of Instructional Affairs, Dr. Frisina wisely selected a man of proven academic and administrative ability, Dr. William E. Castle. Prior to his coming to NTID, Castle had served as the associate secretary of Research and Scientific Affairs for the American Speech and Hearing Association (ASHA). Obviously his presence as assistant to Frisina added to the credibility of NTID as a research-oriented institution. It was, of course, in this area of research that the new facility was committed by law.

A masterstroke in recruitment (and there were many) was the selection of Mr. Robert F. Panara, an outstanding postlingually deaf man and a much beloved associate professor of English literature and drama at Gallaudet College. Panara had served in this instructional capacity for a number of years at Gallaudet and had accordingly earned for himself a national reputation as one of the foremost advocates and promoters of culture in the American deaf community. Now his presence on the NTID scene as the first teaching member of the faculty set a high standard and a quick pace for all those faculty members, hearing and deaf, who were to follow. Equally important, as a deaf person Panara would set a solid role-model for all the deaf students to come. On his shoulders also rested the all-important NTID English program which was to be established.

Readying the team:

In a relatively short time a nucleus faculty, a training cadre, was assembled. Through the efforts of this body a program of orientation and training was inaugurated for the academic year 1967-1968. The objectives for the program were indicated as follows:

1. to prepare a receptive climate for NTID students entering the freshman class in September, 1968 through an orientation of RIT faculty and students.

2. to train RIT faculty and staff who will have key roles in providing direct academic and student personnel services to incoming NTID students.

3. in both orientation and training programs to instill an enthusiasm for continuing to develop skills of special significance in relating to NTID students. (*Ibid.,* p. 85.)

The keynote of the NTID thrust in faculty training and orientation was succinctly epitomized in the topic of a December, 1967, dinner meeting: "The instructor's role in helping the deaf student in an integrated academic setting." (*Ibid.,* p. 89.)

The following statement laconically describes the training and orientation program conducted during the spring and summer of 1968:

> During February and March of 1968, 105 RIT student leaders were given a training and orientation program by NTID. In the spring of 1968, 57 community representatives from business, industry, education, and the general public participated in an evening program series dealing with communication and deafness. An intensive six-weeks full-time Summer Institute for 50 new and existing RIT and NTID faculty and staff was offered in June and July 1968 by NTID to ready RIT for the enrollment of a pilot group of deaf students in September 1968. A 55 clock-hour orientation program for 34 RIT residence hall advisors was conducted in September. During the month of September 65 non-teaching RIT staff members attended an NTID orientation training series dealing with the communication and educational aspects of deafness. (NTID, *Report of Second Year Ending Dec. 31, 1968,* p. 2.)

Thus may be observed the actual effort made to familiarize a number of publics with the subjects of deafness, deaf people, and their modes of communication.

NTID opens its doors:

In September, 1968, the scene was set and the NTID administration, faculty, and staff, along with the rest of the RIT community, with a touch of trepidation, awaited the arrival of the first contingent of 70 deaf students. Arriving were 44 young men and 26 young women, the youngest being 16 and the oldest 34. The reception they received was a warm and exciting experience. At long last the National Technical Institute for the Deaf was now "A Dream and a Possibility" realized.

57

The A. G. Bell Association Meets "Total Communication" 1972

By 1971 a considerable number of residential schools with their traditional combined system, i.e., oralism through primary and elementary grades with the simultaneous method in the advanced department, had changed over to Total Communication (TC). In the vanguard of this TC movement figured a Maryland psychologist, Dr. McCay Vernon. Vernon's nonpareil interest in deaf people along with his no-nonsense stand in support of their educational and social rights had won him national attention and praise from the deaf community. Holcomb's TC concept had struck a receptive chord in Vernon's logic, and therefore the idea needed no other champion.

Dr. Vernon's position as editor of the *American Annals of the Deaf* gave him a particular position of vantage from the standpoint of reaching the profession of educators of the deaf. Consequently this very important journal became a sounding board for any and all thoughts relative to Total Communication and its advocates.

Through the year 1971 those educators who tended to disagree with the TC concept were awed at the rapid dissemination and implementation of the idea even though no one as yet was able to agree upon a definition of it. An inexplicable educational phenomenon appeared to have taken hold. Opponents of the TC movement began to organize under the leadership of the Alexander Graham Bell Association (AGB), formerly the American Association to Promote the Teaching of Speech to the Deaf.

The AGB Association faces up to TC:

The Association officials after considerable deliberation determined that rather than continuing the sniping at TC by means of letters and articles in the Association journal, *The Volta Review,* it would be much wiser to sponsor an open discussion with TC proponents at the upcoming A. G. Bell national convention, which was scheduled for Chicago in the latter part of June, 1972. At such a meeting both the TC advocates and the oral advocates could "lay their cards on the table" in order that their respective positions, values, and goals for the education of deaf children could be objectively considered.

TC's first proponent:

The representative speakers for the contending TC and oral positions were well selected, because each was deeply committed and dedicated to his or her respective philosophy. The first of these to address the Association was Dr. McCay Vernon, professor of psychology at Western Maryland College, who spoke as a proponent of Total Communication.

> It is an historic and progressive step forward for the Bell Association to open its convention and journal to views on educational methodology different from its own. Dr. Northcott, this year's program chairman, deserves the major credit for this. Lest the thought be given that this is a thoroughly open meeting in which all viewpoints are given equal opportunity, it should be noted that tomorrow's program includes a critique on "total communication" by a prominent oralist. He will be speaking unopposed. Furthermore, his presentation follows these presentations on "total communication." This kind of an advantage is not designed to provide the fairest and most open exchange of ideas. Despite this, Dr. Northcott and the A. G. Bell Association are to be commended for leading the way from what has been historically a one-sided convention to a convention in which both sides are given some platform. It will be of special interest to see if *The Volta Review* is as open as the convention and publishes both Dr. Simmons-Martin's paper and this paper.
>
> What follows is an examination of some of the rationale for "total communication." Of necessity this rationale must look in detail at the options to "total communication" and evaluate them. One is oralism. Let us first consider a common sense reason for "total communication." (Vernon, "Mind over Mouth," p. 529.)

Dr. Vernon's first supporting reason for advocating Total Communication centered on the deaf community and its united support of the procedure.

> The point to be made is that deaf people as a group stand solidly behind "total communication" despite the fact that most of them were educated orally. In fact, some of the leading supporters of "total communciation" in the National Association of the Deaf and the National Fraternal Society are graduates of the citadels of oralism. Educators, and especially parents, interested in deciding on the relative merits of the two educational methods should make a point of talking privately to deaf adults when other educators and other parents are not present. Unfortunately, parents and professionals of the Bell Association generally are only exposed to deaf members of ODAS who could not have joined this group unless they agreed to support oralism. However, there are a number of non-ODAS members who are on this afternoon's panel on black deaf persons. I personally urge everyone here to try to attend the panel and to talk to the deaf participants. (*Ibid.*, p. 530.)

The speaker then took up the second reason for supporting Total Communication which he represented in the inadequacies of speechreading as a receptive mode.

> What could be more ridiculous or cruel than for us to force deaf children to learn and to communicate through a modality as invisible and ambiguous as speechreading? It is in a very real sense a violation of fundamental human rights of deaf children.
>
> By contrast, "total communication" supplements speechreading with fingerspelling and sign language. Consequently, in "total communication" the deaf child is taught and is given the opportunity to communicate through a system no more ambiguous to him than the spoken word is to us.
>
> "Total communication" is a constructive coping with the reality of the limitations of speechreading. Oralism evades this reality, forcing the deaf child and his family to pay a huge educational and psychological price. (*Ibid.*, p. 531.)

Dr. Vernon then moved into aural amplification and endeavored to show that

> ... those who imply that amplification is the answer for deaf children are talking about a very tiny minority of "hearing-impaired" children and ignoring the other 90%. By contrast, "total communication" provides a clear, understandable means of communication for all children in programs for the "hearing-impaired," not for just the 5-10% who have enough hearing to learn language through amplification. It provides all deaf and hard of hearing children with the identical benefits of amplification, speech and speechreading which are present in a restriction to just oralism. (*Ibid.*, pp. 531-532.)

The crux of the educational problem, language development, and its resolution through Total Communication was next discussed.

> Language development is the key to the deaf child's hope for education and communication. Without a command of language he cannot hope to read, to integrate with hearing people, or to be an equal in the family and culture into which he is born. "Total communication" provides the deaf child a language environment of symbols he can see and learn to understand. Homes in which "total communication" is used involve a situation in which the deaf child sees language continually and learns it incidentally as hearing children do.
>
> By contrast, oralism assumes that a deaf child can learn language with an exposure to it consisting of the brief periods in the course of a day when people's mouths are facing him free of cigars, mustaches, protruding teeth, food, and all the other common blocks to lipreading. It assumes he can learn language this way, even though under ideal circumstances two-thirds of what is said is either invisible on the lips or else looks just like some other sound. The 100-year failure of oral education is testimony to the folly of this kind of approach.
>
> Speechreading plus whatever gross sounds some deaf children may get from amplification leave the deaf child unable to perceive language for other than fleeting moments. This kind of a minutia of exposure is insufficient. Few of us here today would have learned language this way and neither will deaf children.
>
> Another obvious but often overlooked fact is that in oralism the deaf child is limited in his expressive language to the words he knows how to pronounce. Because of the enormous difficulty deaf children have in articulating, this represents an overwhelming type of constriction which compounds the language problems due to speechreading and leaves the deaf child cheated in both his receptive and expressive opportunity for language.
>
> Perhaps the most compelling of all arguments is that "total communication" is oralism and amplification plus much more. In other words, it is speech, speechreading, amplification, writing, sign language, and fingerspelling. Furthermore, there is ample research evidence to show that the addition of manual communication helps, does not hinder the development of other communication skills. Thus, among other things, "total communication" facilitates integration of the deaf child and maximizes his adjustment to hearing people. (*Ibid.*, pp. 532-533.)

The advantages of Total Communication were then given as reflected through research. "These investigations have been done at the leading institutions of higher learning. . . ." (Table references are omitted.)

> 1. "Total communication" improves language skills rather than impairing them, as oralists used to claim would happen if deaf children used manual communication.

2. "Total communication" improves academic performance to the point of doubling reading gains in several of the studies.

3. "Total communication" does not impair speech or speechreading skills. In fact, some studies report speechreading skills were better with "total communication."

4. With preschoolers "total communication" produced lasting gains in language and education achievement. By contrast, deaf children who had extensive oral preschool training obtained no lasting academic or communication benefits. In other words, children with extensive oral preschool did no better than those who had absolutely no preschool at all. (*Ibid.,* pp. 533-534.)

Dr. Vernon then related how difficult it was to conduct research on Total Communication because of the refusal of oral programs to cooperate. This section was concluded with the statement:

Although you may hear eloquent criticism of the research comparing "total communication" with oralism, several points need to be remembered. First, there is no research in professional journals comparing oralism to "total communication" which yields results supporting oralism. In the absence of supporting research findings, oralists use a lot of testimonials. Unfortunately, testimonials are as poor at pleading the value of oralism as they are at pleading the curative powers of patent medicines.

Thus, what we see from research is that there are a large number of studies which find that the results of "total communication" when tested under the most difficult of conditions yield academic and linguistic achievement gains often double those of just oralism. There is no professionally published research comparing oralism to "total communication" which supports oralism. (*Ibid.,* pp. 535-536.)

Under the heading *psychological development,* Dr. Vernon clarified his perspective of oralism:

It is in the area of psychological developments that oralism is most destructive. The gross deprivation of the opportunity to communicate openly with one's parents and family which the ambiguity of oralism/auralism entails is irreversibly crippling psychologically (Grinker, 1969). It denies deaf children the basic information and civilized interaction necessary for normal human development. Blowing feathers, pointing out which is the ball, the fish, or the boat, and clapping or jumping to some ancient record in auditory training class have been the hallmark of oralism for a hundred years. With parents beginning to see the kind of communication that can occur between themselves and their child with "total communication", oralists are being forced to acknowledge the limitations of what they have historically done, and they have been forced to promise more. Promises based on a hundred years of failure which contradict existing research findings are very hollow promises. (*Ibid.,* p. 536.)

The summary statement of Dr. Vernon's presentation was a thoroughgoing catharsis which must have certainly relieved him considerably, as he said,

> In sum, there is a wealth of data showing the value of "total communication" and an absence of scientific evidence favoring oralism. Equally compelling is the logic and common sense of providing deaf children with a non-ambiguous, non-invisible means of communication they can see when compared to arguments supporting primary dependence on the ambiguous sounds that are heard through fragmented auditory perception.

> Finally, how can we as educators, parents, and psychologists continue to be so utterly presumptuous as to ignore the overwhelming support of deaf people for "total communication"? Even Alexander Graham Bell said: ". . . spoken language I would not have used as a means of communication with the pupils in the earliest stages of the education . . . because it is not clear to the eye, and requires a knowledge of the language to unravel the ambiguities. In that case, I would have the teacher use written language and I do not think that the manual alphabet differs from written language excepting in this, *that it is better and more expeditious*" [author's emphasis] (DeLand, 1923, p. 37). In years past when over half of the deaf children lost their hearing after learning language, oralism did not do so much harm. Today, when 95% of deaf children are prelingually deafened, oralism is untenable (Vernon, 1968).

> The tragic irony of this debate from the point of view of deaf children and their families is that the oral-only approach is given the status of being an issue deserving debate.

> This statement today and some of the other things that have been said to you, a group that has been kind enough to invite me here to speak, sounds rude and it sounds ungrateful. In many ways it is. However, what is at stake is the right of deaf children to a decent education, to a workable means of communication, and to a fair chance in life. Under such circumstances, manners and protocol rightly take a back seat to honesty and to directness. Thank you. (*Ibid.*, p. 538.)

Bell's statement, a clarification:

With all pros and cons aside, an observation must be made regarding Dr. Vernon's reference to Alexander Graham Bell's memorable statement, ". . . I do not think that the manual alphabet differs from written language excepting in this, *that it is better and more expeditious.*" Dr. Bell, it should be understood, was not referring to Total Communication and he was certainly not referring to sign language. His statement dealt exclusively with the orthographic and syntactic mode of Visible English (fingerspelling), which he advocated for the teaching of prelingually deaf youngsters as a basis for their subsequent instruction in speech. His rationale was that a child who has something to say in English is more motivated to learn to speak than one who has nothing to say. This vital concept was somehow forgotten by many speech advocates after Bell's demise in 1922. Dr. Vernon's use of the quotation, however, does not seem particularly germane to the context of his conclusion.

At the close of Dr. Vernon's address the Association had a clear understanding of Total Communication and also Dr. Vernon's ideas on speech, speechreading, and aural amplification.

The oral-aural proponent:

The next speaker, representing the oral-aural position, was Dr. Audrey Simmons-Martin, an associate professor in the Teacher Education Program of Washington University (St. Louis). She was also the director of the Early Education Program at Central Institute for the Deaf at St. Louis. In introducing her presentation, the speaker said,

> I want to rationalize the system of communication that I endorse for the education of hearing-impaired children. It is based, I believe, on pertinent facts resulting from scientific inquiry in acoustics, physiology, and linguistics. I hope to relate these findings to sound instructional procedures leading to the development of a functional aural/oral system of communication. It is the constructive collaboration of disciplined investigators and conscientious teachers that I hope I reflect. I do not plan to debate the methods of communication for hearing-impaired children nor engage in a polemic where sober analysis is obscured by moral outrage. ("Oral/Aural Procedure," p. 541.)

Four classifications of hearing loss:

Dr. Simmons-Martin then began an analysis of the hearing-impaired child population. She indicated one of the great and unfortunate situations which has held consistently from the early 19th Century into the present day. This was the educating of "a disproportionate number of children with residual hearing" as though they were deaf. It was her belief that to classify all hearing-impaired children into one "undifferentiated monolithic group" was to do them a "great disservice." The four classifications of hearing loss, *mild, moderate, severe,* and *profound,* as determined by audiometric tests must be determined as the first basis for grouping pupils.

In that 48% of Gentile's 1970-1971 survey of the hearing-impaired child population fell within the mild, moderate, and severe categories, educators could not think of denying them "the grand spectrum of opportunities our society affords."

> To think that parents, teachers, and associates must learn a foreign system of communication to "talk" to the children in the mild category who have losses of less than 40 dB seems unbelievable. Yet, this group comprises 8.8% of the enrollment in special programs according to the Gentile survey. Surely it is obvious that the route for these children is aural.
>
> Is a circumscribed life the outlook for children with moderate losses from 40 to 65 dB? While these children do need assistance, and they represent 15.2% of those in programs in the United States, anyone would admit that they have hearing which would benefit greatly from training. Really, these children shouldn't require much special schooling; yet we find them, in this proportion, up to 18 years of age. I am curious about how these children, who are capable of using the telephone, communicate manually over it.
>
> Severely deaf children have losses in the 65-90 dB range. In this study, Gentile used 85 dB, however, as the cutoff and found 24.4% in that group. While they need help, must they have to learn to live apart from the mainstream of society? Are they forever going to be "deaf" because they were so diagnosed? Surely, for these I don't have to make a case for sustained effort to train their hearing and speech.
>
> It is interesting that of the children enrolled in special programs only 51.5% are classified as profoundly deaf (Gentile, 1971), where losses in the three speech frequencies exceed 85 dB. If 250 Hz had been included in Gentile's survey, there would have been a smaller percentage yet. (*Ibid.*, pp. 541-542.)

Traditionally the profoundly deaf category was seldom, if ever, considered for aural amplification. Simmons-Martin, however, thought differently.

> It is on the last group with profound losses that I would especially like to focus my attention. Obviously, we don't need to rationalize the use of hearing and speech for the others.
>
> I base my remarks on my experience at Central Institute for the Deaf where our distribution differs from the national norm. In our "read out" from the Gentile data, it was shown that we had 78.5% in the profoundly deaf category according to their classification. Now I would like to look at this group more closely.

Elliott (1967) studied 177 children at CID and, at the time of her study, found only three children who gave no response to sound at the 130 dB hearing level. When she used a cutoff level of 110 dB, she found that 94% of the children responded. Even though classified as profoundly deaf, 94% responded to sound. There is potential there if we use it. (*Ibid.*, pp. 542-543.)

Early introduction to acoustic training essential:

Dr. Simmons-Martin went on to stress the fact that "in order for children to understand the signals being delivered, they must have experience and training." As she said, "There is potential there if we use it."

In order to get the maximum effectiveness from acoustic training, children must be launched into such programs as early as possible. Should a child, however, not have the advantage of early acoustic intervention, "he still benefits from the aural-oral approach." Dr. Simmons-Martin stated that her own observations and study "suggest strongly that these children develop the language code in the same order as hearing children but at a slower rate."

Re: Code learning:

Relative to *code learning* the speaker revealed that:

Code learning, rather than sounds, words, or even phrases, should be our concern in teaching the hearing-impaired child to speak. Since sounds, words, phrases, and sentences follow each other in accordance with the structure of the language, the listener familiar with the code will be able to anticipate at any point in the sequence what elements are most likely to come next. His ability, it must be stressed, is entirely dependent upon his experience with communication; and this knowledge is so important that it probably carries much more weight than the sounds of speech themselves.

If the child applies the knowledge of the code to information, imperfectly received, he should be able to supply those absent linguistic elements. For example, he might hear:

u bi baw ol dow u ee.

If he knows the code, he could fill in:

The big ball rolled down the street.

The strength of our knowledge of possible speech sequences helps us fill in any gaps in a stream of words we hear. For example, an English nursery rhyme can be understood with one-third of the letters missing. Omitting some consonants, you still can fill in what is meant.

M*R* H*D * L*TTL* L*MB H*R FL**C* W*S WH*T* *S SN*W

TH* S*N *S N*T SH*N*NG T*D**

S*M* W**DS *R* EA*I*R T* U*D*R*T*N* T*A* *T*E*S

The great importance of knowing the code and being able to guess what is said or is to be said can be demonstrated with another example from Denes and Pinson (1968). The experimenter chose a sentence and, without giving any hint as to its nature, asked the subject to guess the sequence of sounds that make up the sentence. In the sentence, *Speech is an important human activity*, three fourths of the letters were guessed correctly on the first try, even though the person who was doing the guessing had no preliminary information of what the sentence was about or how it was constructed. . . .

The listener with normal hearing is guessing a good deal of the time; and when reception becomes difficult because of noise, the proportion of guessing increases. Significantly, the hearing listener has the pattern of speech to which to match the received signals or pieces of code. What is important for the hearing-impaired listener is the demonstration of how much can be "guessed" in the absence of a large portion of a message. Code interpretation that is possible with a small amount of residual hearing, and with proper amplification, is appreciable. In order to accumulate the knowledge of the linguistic code, however, the hearing-impaired child needs as much, *not less*, listening to the code as does the normally hearing child. (*Ibid.*, pp. 546-547.)

In *code learning* educators of the deaf in the Association audience recognized the revelation of a new language instructional direction which utilized not only the child's residual hearing, but also his intuitive sense for grasping "absent linguistic elements."

Re: The phonologic code:

Dr. Simmons-Martin then continued with a discussion of the *phonologic code*, another aspect of the new aural-oral approach.

While I have illustrated with examples of the linguistic code requiring phonemes, words, and structure information, language contains speech nuances or prosodic factors that convey meaning regardless of the particular phoneme or word. Let me illustrate – suppose the topic is Nixon and, in talking to you in nonsense words, I say, *Dududdu* (no intonation). You could predict exactly how I will vote. On the other hand, the meaning you derive when I say *Dududdu* (with fluctuating intonation), is quite different.

Language is deriving *meaning* from talk and conveying meaning through talk. The meaning, to be certain, can be transmitted by words, but the way we say them may alter the interpretation altogether. The same words in the same order,

Nixon is a great president.

can be said by either a Republican or a Democrat, yet may have two distinctly different meanings.

The message is embedded in the nuances or prosody of speech, e.g., the rhythm, duration, stress, accent, and pitch. These features are the very ones missing in the speech of many hearing-impaired children who are denied amplification (Calvert, 1962).

We use intonation to indicate grammar. It tells the kind of sentence we employ:

dudududu–statement   *dudududu?*–question
dudududu!–command

We used it to convey feelings and attitudes. This time-stress envelope is important for conveying affective meanings. It is interesting that the deaf have been reported to have difficulty describing feelings. In normal conversation, affective attitude is transmitted through intonation using duration changes, pitch, and stress. I can express fatigue, pleasure, sarcasm, sadness, and contentment, to mention a few, using the same word order, e.g., *Oh my.*

While spectral information, i.e., information about the frequencies of speech sounds, is important, Erber (1972) has demonstrated that the perception of the patterns of speech can aid lipreading. When only the time-intensity envelope is perceived, the child's comprehension of oral language increases. Furthermore, perception of stress patterns also can help the child achieve better rhythm and voice quality in his own speech.

Recently Ross (1971) has demonstrated that the speaker's emotional state can be received through a low pass transmission system. The implication, then, is that hearing-impaired children have the potential for appreciating these distinctions, also.

As Silverman (1971) pointed out, vocabulary, particularly words with auditory associations, may be enriched through the use of amplification. Words such as *cry, roar, growl, scream, whistle, murmur, ring, shout,* etc., have auditory connotations. If the child has been deprived of acoustic input, these words may mean little to him. On the other hand, these sounds heard over an amplifying system, even though not perceived precisely, should enrich the meanings. (*Ibid.*, pp. 547-548.)

Good reading skills determine overall academic success:

Relative to academic achievement, the speaker stated that there is little or no experimental evidence to show that acoustic training improved academic achievement levels; however, it was a fact that those hearing-impaired children who do well in reading similarly do well in all reading subjects. Those, however, who were poor in language ability were usually also poor in reading and this obviously had a negative effect on their academic achievement as well. (*Ibid.*, p. 548.)

Concluding her presentation, Dr. Simmons-Martin stated:

> In summary, it is imperative that hearing-impaired children learn the language code in order to achieve academically, socially, emotionally and, in short, to become a member of our society. Components of the language code of our society are auditory – vocal. This being the case, it is necessary that these components be made available to the children by whatever means are at our disposal: auditory, visual, vibrotactile. Auditory experiences supplemented by other sensible modalities are the most effective routes to helping the child develop the language code. If I may borrow a term my colleagues, the "total" use of residual hearing must be begun as early as possible and should continue remittently; and that training should be related to speech.

> We must recognize that this places great demands on the teacher. She must energetically apply in the classroom the principles I have talked about. And, very importantly, she must communicate their validity and, if you will, their "worthwhileness" to all who come in contact with the child – his siblings, friends, and, above all, his parents. (*Ibid.*, p. 550.)

In discussing *code learning* and the *phonologic code*, Dr. Audrey Simmons-Martin had introduced an innovative procedure for speech and language development for hearing-impaired children.

The first reactor speaks:

The first reactor to the presentations of Dr. McCay Vernon and Dr. Audrey Simmons-Martin was Dr. Patricia Sherer, director of the Diagnostic Center for Hearing-Impaired Children at Northwestern University.

> Since I am a teacher of the deaf by profession, consistency is one of my basic principles of education. Therefore, if I am going to stand up here and talk about "total communication," I have decided that it is necessary to use it myself. As there is no way for a short person like me to stand

in back of a podium and use "total communication" and be seen, I must thank the media man who was kind enough to obtain a lavalier mike which permits me to stand clearly visible before you.

I want to make just a few general comments about this morning's presentations. It seems apparent to me that there are very few people sitting in this room who do not have something to offer to the area of education of the deaf. And yet, we come to meetings like this, and we continue to hear this methodology argument. However, it seems we never *really* hear each other. If we support "total communication", we don't hear the good points Dr. Simmons-Martin makes. If we call ourselves "oralists", we're not really listening to Dr. Vernon. We sit and seem to listen, but we think our own thoughts: and we find it very difficult ever to make constructive change. I know how difficult the process of change can be because I have experienced change. In making this change, I have retained the same commitment I always had to helping deaf children: although my primary goal is the acquisiton of language, I am keenly aware of the importance of developing good oral skills in speechreading and speech. Many of my goals have not changed, but I believe I have learned a better way to attain them. Before clarifying this statement, I want to take just a minute to comment on some issues raised this morning in the presentations.

I know that hearing loss is based on a continuum. I know that losses differ and affect children in varied ways. As a teacher of the deaf, I am very interested in these variations. I also want to know what amplification will do for each hearing-impaired child with whom I come into contact. However, this morning we saw a visual and an auditory presentation of partial information. We were asked to synthesize this incomplete information into a complete message. We could do this easily because we knew the code. We had a language base, and that language system made the essential difference. Therefore, this analogy cannot be used to describe the process the deaf child uses when he is trying to learn language for the first time.

Language, we all agree, serves as the basis for the feeding of information to the mind. Since I arrived here, I have heard again and again that the early years of the child's life are so important – that this is the time when children learn at the fastest rate. This statement appears to be accepted by everyone, and I am in complete agreement. That's why I say I cannot wait; the young deaf child must have a functional language system. It is one of the most essential needs in his life. We must give him functional language while he is a baby so that his mind receives the stimulation that is necessary for total development.

I prefer to call "total communication" a diagnostic approach to teaching because it is based on the concept that children differ. For years, most of us have given lip service to the idea that we are diagnostic teachers; and yet, in presenting language we offered only one alternative to all deaf children. Research studies indicate that if any single approach is applied indiscriminately to all children, the results generally end in failure. A rigid approach, therefore, cannot be classified as diagnostic training.

I like to present "total communciation" for deaf children as the English language on the hands, on the lips, supported by residual hearing, supported by everything that is needed to assure the communicator that he sends a clear message to the receiver. During this act of communication, the child is observed and he tells you how he needs to learn language. You must then respond to him in the channel or the way that is best suited to meet his particular and specific needs.

Also needed is a warm home and school environment that is conducive to learning – an environment which communicates totally with the child and provides him a pathway or road to successful, total, and complete development. (Sherer, "Reaction," pp. 552-553.)

The second reactor speaks:

The second reactor was Dr. Daniel Ling, an associate professor in the School of Human Communication at McGill University in Montreal. Dr. Ling initially trained with the Ewings at Manchester University.

Ladies and gentlemen, it's my job this morning to react to the two presentations that preceded me. The first point that I want to make is that oralism as Audrey Simmons-Martin has shown us this morning is certainly not widespread. And it certainly has not been in use for a hundred years as Dr. Vernon has claimed. I think that one of the points that hasn't been made very well, perhaps not at all this morning other than from Dr. Sherer, is the fact that no one system can cater to all deaf children. And I think that holds true for oralism. I don't know any oralist worthy of the name who would claim that it did. There is a proportion who can't benefit. (Ling, "Reaction," p. 553.)

Dr. Ling then followed this up with the idea of tossing both fingerspelling and the Rochester Method into the same bag with sign language! Whereupon A. G. Bell and Z. F. Westervelt, probably both, "turned over twice and simultaneously" – unbeknownst, of course, to either the speaker or the audience. Dr. Ling then went ably to work on the vocabulary limitations of sign language as compared to English. Following this he proceeded to dismantle Dr. Vernon's research references.

Dr. Vernon claimed in his presentation that a lot of research supports "total communication." Now, I deny that. I think that the research has been reported in a very selective and biased way so that it appears to support it; but that is not supported by the research itself. Dr. Vernon quoted, for example, higher institutes of learning. I am a researcher in a higher institute of learning at McGill, which is a very famous school. Now, I can assure you that not all of the research that goes on at McGill is good research. When he quoted one particular thing, a statement about the University of Edinburgh, he was referring to the great work of Montgomery, which he claims supports the fact that if children sign it doesn't affect their oral skills. When Montgomery made this statement, he based it on a very poor statistical treatment of his data and a very poorly designed experiment, as many of these experiments were that he quotes. In the sample he studied, Montgomery found that 71% of the kids could fingerspell and sign fluently, whereas only 7% could communicate orally. I think that indicates the sort of standard of comment that is required to dispel notions that some of the research Dr. Vernon quotes is valid, reliable, or indicates anything. (*Ibid.*, pp. 553-554.)

It was obvious that Dr. Ling, as an oralist, was a fair match for Dr. Vernon. The members of the Association audience, usually the cool and calm recipients of scientific facts and figures, sat pop-eyed in wonderment at their champion and wondered altogether what he would deliver next. Politely they restrained their enthusiasm and awaited the speaker's next point.

What about the other point – that children taught by "total communication" do not fall behind educationally and learn high-level language skills? That is garbage. And the reason that it's garbage is evident from research, also. For example, a recent study by Klopping compared three groups: one who'd been taught orally, one who'd been taught manually, and one who'd been taught by "total communication." Let me tell you that one-third of the children, regardless of the methodology used, were unable to use language meaningfully. Now, surely the point here is that what we've got to face is that poor standards are not necessarily due to the communication mode at all, but to damn poor teaching. (If you clap too long, you're cutting down on my allotted time.) Let me say, then, that one of the things that none of these speakers has mentioned, and it's pretty important, is that 40% of the people who are dealing with our children in these schools today have no professional training in teaching deaf children; and that is ghastly. And, let me add that a lot of the teachers who have this training have very little experience, and some of their training isn't worth that much.

So let's look at some of these points in relation to teacher training and "total communication." Now, how do we train teachers not only to be good auditorily, to be good orally, to be good everywhere, to be good scientists, to be good teachers, and everything else? This is quite a problem in view of the fact that we haven't yet got good teachers anywhere, you know, as a general rule. It's a big problem. (*Ibid.*, p. 554.)

Shifting the focus:

Dr. Ling's shifting the focus of attention from the long harried topic of communication as being the cause of poor educational standards to the simple fact of "damn poor teaching" came as a bittersweet shock to the Association members; nevertheless, they recognized its possible truth and responded accordingly. With this, Ling followed through on the immensity of the task of training good teachers and concluded his point with the observation, "It's a big problem."

Ling's speaking time had not yet run out and the audience settled back and waited with confidence. A few, of course, were probably a bit uncomfortable.

> Why, though, "total communication"? Why has it got appeal? Because, I'm telling you all, it's a simple solution, apparently, to a very complex problem; and it has that sort of superficial surface appeal. And because it has that sort of appeal it will spread. But I must say I believe that Dr. Vernon is one of its worst advocates because he distorts the problems through selective and biased reporting and by being extreme. The support he will receive for it will not be on its merit but will be because it's a cheaper form of education than oralism. Oral education, to be good, is a darned expensive process. For most, it is superior in the long run, and I think there's a lot of evidence that it is. We need research and we've got to have research, but let's not have this sort of reporting that makes garbage of research. Let's not talk so much about method; let's talk about the child and his needs and the method in relation to the child. Perhaps we'll get somewhere. (*Ibid.*, pp. 554-555.)

Despite his rather heavy eloquence, Daniel Ling had introduced a new and possibly significant reason for the modern inadequacies in the education of deaf children. As he said in his conclusion, "Let's talk about the child and his needs and the method in relation to the child." Dalgarno would have added, "Let us then be *diligent* in our teaching."

The third reactor:

The third reactor to the presentations of Dr. Vernon and Dr. Simmons-Martin was child psychiatrist Dr. Eugene D. Mindel of the Michael Reese Hospital in Chicago. Dr. Mindel had a long interest in deaf education stemming from his medical student days as an assistant in the Gallaudet College Health Department. Dr. Mindel, in referring to the previous speaker, began by saying, "That is a hard *act* to follow." This, of course, was in reference to Dr. Ling's "hammer and tongs" approach to Dr. Vernon's presentation. Dr. Mindel asked, "How really representative is this meeting to be? Judging by the program it will be decided in the corridors, not in meeting rooms."

Dr. Mindel then explained that Dr. Vernon's experience with deaf children and adults had generated in him "a total sense of disbelief and outrage." Learning of the facts relative to deaf people, Dr.

Mindel had been moved to the same sense of outrage. Thus, with their outrages mutually established, they collaborated on a book entitled *They Grow in Silence: The Deaf Child and His Family.*

A broader perspective:

Dr. Mindel then characterized Dr. Simmons-Martin's presentation as being a kind of "future vision of oral success."

> A young deaf college girl, smiling and nodding agreeably as one of her mentors – preferably before television cameras – asks her a few questions. She will answer in a voice that those of us who have worked with deaf people will immediately recognize, and we will think of the time wasted on the production. Most do not see the childhood that has been sacrificed behind that voice.
>
> It has been my orientation as a child psychiatrist to look at educational methodologies in a broader perspective. It is the grim inheritance of all children that they must live in the world structured by adults. It is a world that readily infringes upon their right to be childlike. In some parts of the world this life centers around the quest for a crust of bread or the struggle against disease. In America it centers around a struggle to avoid pollution of the mind and the body. Just a flip of the switch in the morning, and while the child is eating his breakfast the television set displays 10 different ways to jeopardize the life of his enemies. Or, in the evening with his family, on the news he watches the violent actualization of his fantasies, killing for keeps in the Far East. Our arguments over methodologies are dwarfed by that world outside. (Mindel, "Reaction," p. 556.)

The speaker then concludes his statement with a quotation by a linguist, Ursula Bellugi. She indicated that after two years of research, she found that sign language, while not having any counterpart in English, does have "grammatical properties." She also said that "we can suggest that while the surface structure of sign(s) and speech vary widely, the language learning process is the same." She observed that "what it [sign language] lacks in comparison with spoken English, it amply compensates for in other ways." From this study it was suggested that insights might also be gained "into the structure of language and the universality of communication."

The right to be childlike:

Dr. Mindel's quotation of Bellugi appears to have been a bit far afield relative to the educational objective of giving prelingually deaf children reading, writing, and speech. For him, however, this apparently was not the objective, but as a psychiatrist he saw the goal to be preserved as being that of the deaf child's "right to be childlike."

The "grim inheritance of all children" to which Dr. Mindel referred must of necessity include for deaf children the adult reality of the hearing workaday world. It might suggest that *this* is the reality for which teachers of the deaf are realistically endeavoring to prepare their children.

The fourth reactor:

The fourth and final reactor was Dr. Joseph Rosenstein, director of the division of Research, Development and Evaluation at Model Secondary School for the Deaf at Gallaudet College. He was, incidentally, trained at Washington University in St. Louis, which explains his unique perspective despite his Gallaudet affiliation.

Dr. Rosenstein began by complimenting the A. G. Bell Association for opening its forum to the "pros and cons" of Total Communication. "If an issue or topic purports to have some kind of merit, we *should* examine it and look at it." After this statement he said,

> We have heard reference made to the linguists who indicate that sign language has a structure and has a grammar. They also point out that sign language does not follow the structure and grammar of English. As an educator of the deaf, I firmly believe that it is my responsibility to equip and help a deaf child to learn the structure of English language as spoken by the community at large in order that he may interact with that community to the maximum extent possible. In order to realize this goal, we must teach him in that language system. (Rosenstein, "Reaction," p. 557.)

Speech tempo and fingerspelling:

The speaker than considered the speed of rendering a statement in fingerspelling with that of one given in spoken English. Unknowledgeably, he lumped fingerspelling (Visible English) with signs in the statement, "Fingerspelling and signed messages take time."

Dr. Rosenstein apparently did not realize that in fingerspelling the tempo of its rendition depends on the tempo of its accompanying speech and not vice versa. Sign language, however, with its naturally laconic structure, can frequently convey a complete message before the average oral speaker can clear his throat. This, of course, was not the kind of language that Dr. Rosenstein advocated. The speaker continued:

> A further word about the language of silence. We have not been told by Dr. Vernon just what forms of sign language or manual communication he would use, in what combinations, and with what fingerspelled additions. American Sign Language, as is signed by native speakers — that is, born deaf of deaf parents — is the form used by the children in the Bellugi studies and in some of the other studies Dr. Vernon mentioned. Deaf children of deaf parents constitute approximately 8 or 9% of the total school-age deaf population. In sign language, there are many structures in English that are omitted or, if included, do not appear unambiguously. For example, we say in sign language, "Mother here?" instead of "Is your mother here?" And the signed answer would be, "Mother here" (Mother is here). English language structure is missing. In order that I am not misinterpreted by some colleagues, I do not wish to say that *communication* cannot or does not take place; I am saying that my goal as an educator, to help a child learn the structure of English language, is not being realized. (*Ibid.*, pp. 557-558.)

A *constructive contribution:*

Relative to Dr. Simmons-Martin's presentation, Dr. Rosenstein made the following observation.

> The central problem in the education of the deaf is the acquisition of language. Dr. Simmons-Martin has demonstrated the tremendous possibilities inherent in the acquisition of oral language through early identification, early amplification, and effective parent education. To establish the rhythm and flow basic to oral language, every child must have proper, consistent, meaningful, and pervasive auditory input of the desired language system. Will this happen in every "total communication" classroom? (*Ibid.*, p. 558.)

That a constructive contribution to education of the deaf had been made by Dr. Simmons-Martin was thus duly recognized. Dr. Rosenstein then concluded his reaction statement with the words,

> I submit that every deaf child should be given the opportunity to benefit from the new approaches in early amplification as identified by Dr. Simmons-Martin before we look to alternatives which may prove necessary and appropriate later in his educational experience. (*Ibid.*, p. 559.)

While the four reactors had opportunities for second statements, their presentations confirmed fairly well their previous positions.

With this the Chicago Convention wound down, but not without a final statement, however, from a representative oral deaf person.

A *deaf man's adjustment and solution:*

After a brief introduction, Mr. Philip R. Drumm, a deaf New York public relations consultant and writer, went to the podium and orally delivered his paper, " 'Total Communication' – Fraud or Reality?" The major thrust of Mr. Drumm's presentation was obviously in favor of oral and aural opportunities for hearing-impaired children. His most significant remarks, however, were "on 'total communication' as a combination of signs and speech."

In the following brief passage of an extended speech, Mr. Drumm revealed his own adjustment and solution to the question of communication.

> Personally, choosing the language to fit the person I am communicating with is all-important. If he understands English speech best, foreign and sign languages are out. If he understands signs best, I *sign*. If he likes both at the same time, so okay, both. ("Fraud or Reality," p. 565.)

Although brief as this statement was and obscured by the plethora of ideas which followed, it remained one of the most significant made by Mr. Drumm. In it he acknowledged his concern for the communication right of each deaf person and adjusted himself accordingly to accommodate that right. Context, however, indicated that he had reference to deaf *adults* only, not children. In any event the idea fell as it had arisen, unnoticed by the contenders on either side, probably because the audience was weary of the word *communication*. Perhaps, too, Dan Ling's piquant phrase had taken its place. Subsequently, the Association convention for 1972 was adjourned *sine die*. The gathering had, indeed, marked a turning point, only no one was quite sure in what direction. Before the decade was out, however, everyone knew.

58

Public Law 94-142
Makes History
1975

Among the controversial movements to come to the fore during the 1970's was the "mainstreaming" of hearing-impaired children and youth into the public hearing school milieu. While the mainstreaming or integration of deaf children with hearing children had occurred sporadically in the United States over the previous 100 years, the general reaction of educators of the deaf appeared to be in opposition to it.

Mainstreaming in the past:

As may be recalled, David E. Bartlett had in the 1850's attempted what is now called "reverse mainstreaming"; i.e., he brought the hearing siblings of his deaf pupils into his school program. Alexander Graham Bell at his Scott Circle experimental school in Washington, D.C., also brought hearing children into the learning situation of his deaf pupils.

Day schools and day classes from their beginning had, of course, stressed as advantageous the fact that their pupils had the full opportunity of living at home in the hearing environments of their families and friends. Also the graduates of Clarke School at Northampton and the Central Institute at St. Louis had traditionally moved on to high schools and subsequently to colleges for the hearing. It may be added that the majority of these young people met with considerable success. Thus it may be seen that the integration or mainstreaming of deaf youngsters into the hearing academic world was not a particularly new idea. Nevertheless, it had always been unpopular among the majority of educators of the deaf, particularly those affiliated with state residential schools. The mainstreaming of deaf children had, therefore, been no great concern, because educators and the public alike saw the schools for the deaf as the only logical place for the education of deaf children, and there the matter rested.

Mainstreaming as a public issue:

Interestingly enough, when the subject of mainstreaming was finally raised as a public issue, it came from an unexpected quarter.

> In 1971, the Pennsylvania Association for Retarded Children brought action against the Commonwealth of Pennsylvania for the state's failure to provide access to a free public education for all retarded children (PARC v. Commonwealth, 1971). A U.S. District Court ruled that the state could not delay, terminate, or deny mentally retarded children access to a publicly supported education. The decree asserted that it was highly desirable to educate these children in an environment most like that offered to nonhandicapped children.
>
> In the same year, parents brought action against the Board of Education in Washington, D.C. (Mills v. Board of Education, 1971), charging failure to provide all children with a publicly supported education. A U.S. District Court reaffirmed the constitutional right of all children, regardless of any exceptional condition of handicap, to a publicly supported education and indicated that any policies or practices which excluded children without provisions for adequate and immediate alternative services and without prior hearing and review of placement procedures are in violation of the rights of due process and equal protection of the law. The Court further added that the District of Columbia's interest in educating the excluded children must outweigh its interest in preserving its financial resources. Legislation and new regulations responsive to these rulings soon followed in a number of states, e.g., Massachusetts and Tennessee in 1972. (Bishop, *Mainstreaming*, p. 21.)

In line with these legal decisions which required equal educational opportunities for retarded children was the strong supporting policy statement of the Council for Exceptional Children (CEC). This organization espoused full educational opportunities for *all* handicapped children, including the hearing-impaired.

Congressional action for mainstreaming:

With the full force of judiciary action along with the concurrence and support of the influential CEC, mainstreaming was obviously soon to become a legal reality under a Congressional mandate. This was, indeed, guaranteed under the 14th Amendment of the United States Constitution, which provides all people with equal rights and protection under the law.

As in many matters of human rights it had been a long time coming. The new law read:

> It is the purpose of this Act to assure that all handicapped children have available to them . . . a free appropriate public education which emphasizes special education and related services designed to meet their unique needs, to assure that the rights of handicapped children and their parents or guardians are protected, to assist States and localities to provide for the education of all handicapped children, and to assess and assure the effectiveness of efforts to educate handicapped children.

The United States Congress:
The Education for All Handicapped
Children Act of 1975. P.L. 94-142

It is interesting to note that this legislative action, so important to the education of deaf children, was planned and inaugurated independently of any consultation or supportive action by either the Convention of American Instructors of the Deaf or the Conference of Executives of American Schools for the Deaf. Without the input of these two longstanding professional organizations being sought in the planning and writing of P.L. 94-142, one may surmise the slightly jaundiced eye with which many of their members viewed the legislation.

From P.L. 94-142, however, the concept of mainstreaming hearing-impaired children received its greatest impetus. Educators of the deaf had to readjust their thinking accordingly.

Mainstreaming, a prescriptive placement plan:

Mainstreaming *per se* was not, of course, to be a wholesale funneling of hearing-impaired children into hearing public school systems, but it was to come through a careful selecting of those individual children who could most successfully benefit from such an educational relocation. Nor was mainstreaming conceived as solely a one-way movement of pupils into a set public school mold. There had evolved over the years three variations of the mainstreaming concept. According to Dr. Grant Bitter, an authority on the topic of mainstreaming, each of the three provided a somewhat different opportunity for interaction between the deaf and hearing pupils within a given school environment. These are listed as follows:

> *Standard mainstreaming* is the approach whereby hearing-impaired children are instructed for all or part of the school day in the regular classroom with hearing peers under the direction of a regular classroom teacher.
>
> *Cross-mainstreaming* is a teaching arrangement similar to a team-teaching concept which involves the regular classroom teacher and the teacher of the hearing-impaired, or resource room teacher. However, in cross-mainstreaming, the teachers do not occupy the same room. The regular classroom teacher may take one or more of the members of the special class into her room for a period or periods of instruction. As a reciprocal measure, the teacher of the hearing-impaired includes one or more children from the regular class in one or more periods of instruction in his/her classroom with hearing-impaired children.
>
> *Reverse mainstreaming* refers to the strategy of bringing one or more hearing children into the classroom with the hearing-impaired for one or more periods of instruction each day. (Nix, *Mainstream Education*, p. 13, with author's and publisher's permission.)

According to Bitter, the resource room might be an integral part for each of the above type programs. The resource room, in this context, is designed to serve as a center to which the hearing-impaired pupils may go to receive special assistance in any of the subject areas in which they may require additional attention.

While the mainstreaming of selected individual pupils into public school systems was a question of interest and concern, a number of schools by 1975 had already met the concept of integration "head-on" by developing cooperative educational programs with their local public school districts. Dr. William N. Craig and Mr. James Salem of the Western Pennsylvania School for the Deaf, in the summary of their study "Partial Integration of Deaf with Hearing Students: Residential School Perspectives," wrote:

> Residential school faculties have become increasingly aware of the possibilities for integrating deaf with hearing students. Potentially, deaf students who spend part of the day with hearing students should improve in such areas as communication capabilities, social awareness, academic skills and vocational competency. The development of partial integration in twenty-two residential schools, and the interest shown by seventeen additional residential schools, strongly suggest that at

least some of these objectives are being met. Of the 410 students known to be participating in some program of part-time integration, only thirty-seven students are considered as questionable when continued integration is anticipated. However, it should be noted that integrative experiences are not proposed for all students and that those participating are individually selected.

Though support for the concept of partial integration of deaf with hearing students has evolved into operating programs in one third of the residential schools for the deaf in the United States, the programs have taken many forms. Residential school size, availability of neighboring schools, and local conditions influence the development of these programs. The variety of integrative experiences must certainly represent an accommodation of these factors with the more general concept of integration. The abstracts from the reports of visits to the residential schools certainly indicate the diversity of approaches that are possible. Certainly integrative programs must be viewed as a part of the residential school program and not an alternative to the specialized instructional approach used in these residential facilities. In fact, to be successful, very careful preparation for and support of the deaf students' integrative experiences is indicated both in the survey data and the narrative abstracts of selected programs. However, with careful organization, thoughtful selection of the cooperating school, and sensitive encouragement of deaf students, partial integration can serve as a valuable extension of the residential school program for deaf students. ("Partial Integration," pp. 35-36.)

Individualized education program (IEP):

With the plan for mainstreaming handicapped children into regular public school environments, there was recognized the need for a more exact system of administrative accountability for the academic evaluation, placement, and progress of these pupils. In keeping with this need, another aspect of P.L. 94-142 set forth the very important and progressive concept of an individualized education program (IEP) as a requirement to be met on the behalf of every handicapped child attending school. October 1, 1977, was specified in the law as the date upon which the IEP regulation would go into effect. It was also indicated that the pupil evaluation process would be repeated annually for every handicapped child.

Parental participation in pupil-program planning:

A revolutionary element was also provided in P.L. 94-142 for the individualized educational planning process, and that was *parental participation.* Traditionally, educational programs had been written (and not always that) by professionals, and parents generally accepted what had been ordered for their child. Now, under the law, parents were encouraged to express their preferences as to their child's curriculum, how he should be taught, and what his ultimate academic goals for any given year should be. For educators of the deaf, of course, this was, indeed, something new!

According to the law, there were five points in the process which were to be carefully studied, prepared, and complied with by a panel of professionals along with the parents of the child under consideration. The program upon completion would consist of:

    (a) a statement of the child's present levels of educational performance;

    (b) a statement of annual goals, including short-term instructional objectives;

    (c) a statement of the specific special education and related services to be provided to the child, and the extent to which the child will be able to participate in regular educational programs;

    (d) the projected dates for initiation of services and the anticipated duration of the services; and

    (e) appropriate objective criteria and evaluation procedures and schedules for determining, on at least an annual basis, whether the short-term instructional objectives are being achieved.

While there could be no promise that the instructional objectives would be fulfilled, the school would, of course, make every effort to attain them. Should a child's parents, however, be of the opinion that the school had not put forth sufficient effort or had mismanaged, they might according to the law have recourse to "due process." That is, they might rely upon the courts to protect whatever of their rights or those of their child which they feel might have been violated.

Theory vs. practice:

Thus P.L. 94-142 had ushered in a new era for education of the deaf. Under it the hearing-impaired child and his problems were no longer the concern of any one group of professionals, but the concern of all. The IEP aspect of the law was, indeed, a genuinely constructive contribution. Mainstreaming, however, while excellent in theory, required certain realistic constraints particularly as it dealt with prelingually deaf children. Dr. Richard G. Brill, in writing his opinion on the subject, at the same time included an indirect caveat:

> We seem to be in an era of simplistic solutions to complex problems. The less one knows about the details of a situation the easier it is to generalize and pronounce panaceas. Unfortunately, jurists, lawyers, legislators, general educators, and strangely enough, parents of many deaf children, know little about the actual educational problems facing deaf children. ("Format or Quality," p. 377.)

Mainstreaming today is taking many prelingually deaf children from the highly structured educational environments provided for them by residential schools for the deaf and moving them into the hearing school milieu. It remains, however, for history to determine the psychological and social impact of this experience upon these young deaf people as they graduate into the adult hearing society and the hearing world of work.

Epilogue

EPILOGUE

In the long history of education of the deaf, the recorded successes in teaching deaf children have suggested that the most common element present in these successes has been a diligent instructional pursuit of verbal language, the key to all academic and advanced technical learning. Such a pursuit, it has been observed, requires an unremitting discipline and a concentrated effort on the part of both teachers and pupils for the latter to achieve a sufficient level of *verbal* language to serve them as a functioning tool of thought and communication.

It is the acquisition of verbal language in all its aspects, *reading, writing, speech, and aural amplification,* that provides deaf children their passage from the microcosm of the deaf to the broad reality of the hearing world and its innumerable opportunities. To achieve this passage has long been and should continue to be the objective of education of the deaf.

While history concerns the past, it still may provide perceptive educators with some realistic directions for their future in the instruction of deaf children.

Appendices

Appendix 1

For those readers who have historical interests in speech and language development, the following additional material from Herodotus provides for them the first recorded example of practical research.

In an effort to determine the antiquity of his people and nation, Psammetichus, the king of Egypt, set about to discover this fact through an intriguing experiment.

> He took two children of the common sort, and gave them over to a herdsman to bring up at his folds, strictly charging him to let no one utter a word in their presence, but to keep them in a sequestered cottage, and from time to time introduce goats to their apartment, see that they got their fill of milk, and in all other respects look after them. His object herein was to know, after the indistinct babblings of infancy were over, what word they would first articulate. It happened as he had anticipated. The herdsman obeyed his orders for two years, and at the end of that time, on his one day opening the door of their room and going in, the children both ran up to him with outstretched arms, and distinctly said *Becos*. When this first happened the herdsman took no notice; but afterwards when he observed, on coming often to see after them that the word was constantly in their mouths, he informed his lord, and by his command brought the children into his presence. Psammetichus then himself heard them say the word, upon which he proceeded to make inquiry what people there was who called anything *becos*, and hereupon he learnt that *becos* was the Phrygian name for *bread*. In consideration of this circumstance the Egyptians yielded their claims and admitted the greater antiquity of the Phrygians. (*Persian Wars*, Book II, pp. 116-117.)

As naive as Psammetichus' solution to the question of his nation's antiquity was, the story as related clearly shows the high significance placed upon speech and language acquisition in early society.

One might also facetiously surmise today, that for "kids" whose only communicating associates were goats, the word "be-e-e-cos" coming from them should have, perhaps, not been too great a surprise.

Appendix 2

While the medieval St. John of Beverley figures most prominently in his efforts on the educational behalf of the deaf, another much later religious of equal note is St. Francis de Sales.

Francis was born near Geneva, Switzerland, in 1567. Studying for the priesthood, he was ordained in 1593. Almost immediately young de Sales was identified with the poor of his parish and through his efforts to help them.

It was not, however, until after his consecration as Bishop of Geneva that Francis de Sales' interest in the deaf began to develop. This interest centered on one particular deaf man named Martin.

Martin was congenitally deaf and consequently without speech or language. Being wholly uneducated, he was obliged to work at various odd domestic jobs to sustain himself. Martin and his plight touched the heart of Bishop Francis, and the deaf man was added to the Bishop's household staff. The Bishop observed Martin as he conscientiously pursued his tasks. It was then that Bishop Francis was determined to help the man's limited spiritual state.

> Martin had never received religious instructions, so Francis, with great patience, began to teach him through natural sign language and Martin made his first communion and was confirmed. His instructions continued and Martin became known as the very holy deaf man who worked for Bishop Francis. ("St. Francis.")

Forty-five years after his death in 1622, Bishop Francis was canonized and thus he became Saint Francis de Sales. Through his great interest and work on behalf of Martin, the deaf man, Francis de Sales was eventually designated as the patron saint of deaf and hearing-impaired people.

Appendix 3

Re: Oral and pure oral distinctions:

Frequently today people use the terms *pure oralism* and *oralism* interchangeably without understanding that the two designations are distinctly different in their denotations. The distinction between the two terms is clarified in a statement by the father of American oralism, Alexander Graham Bell, who stated:

> In many of our oral schools the principle is adopted that no word shall be presented in writing until after the child can read it from the mouth. That is what is meant by the pure oral method in our country.

> The plan that I would advocate is where the written word is always presented in the earlier stages with speech. (De Land, "Memorial," pp. 38-39.)

Appendix 4

The Braidwood family:

The Reverend H. W. Syle of Philadelphia and the editor of the *Annals*, in connection with their work on the *Annals* Index, have lately had occasion to look up the genealogy of the members of the Braidwood family who were engaged in teaching the deaf, which, so far as it can be gathered from the materials at their command, is *here* put on record for the benefit of future historians:

1. *Thomas Braidwood* opened his school in Edinburgh in the year 1760 and removed it to Hackney, near London, in 1783. He died in 1806.

2. After Thomas Braidwood's death the school at Hackney was carried on by his widow and his son, *John Braidwood*, and after the death of both of these, by *John's widow*.

3. John had two sons, one of whom *Thomas Braidwood*, named after his grandfather, the original teacher; he opened a school at Edgbaston, near Birmingham, in 1814, and remained there until his death in 1825. This was the Mr. Braidwood to whom Dr. T. H. Gallaudet applied in 1815 for the release of Mr. Kinniburgh, of Edinburgh, from his obligation not to reveal the art of instruction, and who, after consultation with his mother at Hackney and with other friends, refused the request.

4. John's other son, named *John Braidwood* after his father, took charge of the Edinburgh Institution in 1810, but in 1812 came to America with the view of instructing the deaf-mute children of a Virginia gentleman named *Bowling* or Bolling. He endeavored to establish schools in Maryland, New York, and Virginia, but being of dissolute habits failed in all of these enterprises, and finally died a victim to intemperance.

5. *Joseph Watson*, LL.D., the first master of the London Asylum, which was begun at Bermondsey and afterwards removed to its present location at the Old Ken Road, was a nephew of the first Thomas Braidwood. The principalship of the the London Asylum is still held by a member of the Watson family.

(Syle, "Braidwood Family," pp. 64-65.)

Appendix 5

Thomas Carlyle, in producing his classic history of the French Revolution, encountered a staggering setback during its composition. John Stewart Mill, the British philosopher and a friend of Carlyle, borrowed the precious manuscript to review the work which had been done.

Mill's housekeeper, a zealous foe of untidiness, seeing what appeared to be a pile of messy papers on Mr. Mill's library table, scooped the entire stack into the roaring fireplace to be consumed.

Carlyle, without sorrow or anger, received the bad news and went heroically back to work to rewrite what was to become his *magnum opus*. He completed his work in the early part of 1837.

Appendix 6

A note of interest relative to Dr. Samuel Gridley Howe is that his wife was the famous Julia Ward Howe, author of the soul-stirring "Battle Hymn of the Republic" which excited the hearts and strengthened the resolution of Northerners during the War Between the States.

Appendix 7

A Socratic exchange:

David E. Bartlett's skill as a teacher was demonstrated through his enthusiastic efforts to draw concepts from his pupils through the intuitive process. This is most clearly evidenced in a Socratic exchange between him and his 10-year-old postlingually deaf pupil Henry W. Syle.

At the conclusion of a conversation Mr. Bartlett asked the boy, "What is *anything*?" The child replied, "*Anything* is the pivot on which the bar which separates *something* from *nothing* turns."

(Davidson, "Henry Winter Syle.")

Appendix 8

While this volume is concerned with *turning points in the education of deaf people*, the author thought it would be of interest for the reader to consider a turning point which might have been.

The following letter was made available through the kindness of Mr. Kendall Litchfield, superintendent of the New York School for the Deaf at White Plains.

The principals concerned in the document are the writer, a young Scot named Mr. Alexander Graham Bell, and the recipient, Mr. Isaac Lewis Peet, superintendent of the New York Institution for the Deaf and Dumb.

18 Harrington Square.
N.W. London
May 10, 1870

Dear Sir:

In the Report for 1867 of the New York Institution for the Instruction of the Deaf and Dumb, I find you use the following words:

> "The Committee of Instruction, at its meeting in September, authorized me to confer with some intelligent young man who had received a thorough medical education, with a view to his becoming a professor of articulation in the Institution XXXX I have taken steps in the direction indicated by the Committee, but have not yet succeeded in finding a man qualified for this important post."

Perhaps you have by this time been successful; but if *not*, I should like you to know that I am peculiarly fitted for the work required, having been specially trained in this department, for the purpose of correcting defects of Speech. I have been engaged in teaching Articulation for the last six years. My age is twenty-three.

My name, I believe, is not unknown to you. I am a son of Mr. A. Melville Bell, Professor of Vocal Physiology, and author of "Visible Speech," who had the pleasure of making your acquaintance in 1868.

I have recently superintended the progress of four deaf-and-dumb children who have been taught Articulation by means of Visible Speech; and I have become so much interested in the work, that I should be willing to devote myself entirely to the teaching of the Deaf-and-Dumb if a suitable field presented itself.

I am told by those who have had an opportunity of hearing my pupils, that they already articulate better than the majority of those who have been otherwise instructed for a much longer period. Two of the little girls are congenitally deaf.

In regard to Medical Education, I may say that I am a student of Medicine and Science – an undergraduate of the London University.

I had contemplated graduating only in Science; but, if a medical degree would render me more eligible for the Professorship of Articulation in the New York Institution, I should, in view of a satisfactory arrangement, continue my medical studies, and pay particular attention to Aural Surgery.

Requesting the favour of a reply at your earliest convenience.

I am, dear Sir,

Yours very truly,

A. Graham Bell

I. L. Peet Esq. M.A.

Appendix 9

At the Fourth Conference of Principals of American Institutions for the Deaf and Dumb held at the Clarke Institute in May, 1880, Dr. Edward Miner Gallaudet, President of the National Deaf-Mute College, presented his remarks on "Preparation for the College Course."

> ... I need hardly say that in a literary point of view the matter of greatest importance is, that the applicant for admission to the College should be able to use verbal language readily. I imagine that sometimes the heads of institutions, and even teachers themselves, do not appreciate fully how often it is the case that boys of bright minds, and who have made very respectable attainments in study, are deficient in this respect. We are rather apt to refer to such deficiencies to those who are of rather weak minds. But this is not always the case. Sometimes bright young men come to us very imperfect in the use of verbal language, and I would suggest that in all institutions (of course, the suggestion is not needed in some institutions, because verbal language is constantly there, but in other institutions) where signs are very considerably used, that their disuse be made very marked during the last years of the course of study. I do not mean to underrate the value of signs at certain points; but when it is known that the boys are preparing to enter college, special efforts should be made to secure for them the greatest possible facility in the use of verbal language, and to give them the power, and form in them the habit of thinking in words. When we consider that textbooks are necessarily used, and that verbal language must be employed at every point of the College course, in recitation and examination, the importance of this will be readily understood. . . .
> We must compel our young men to fall back on their own resources, and when a question is asked in intelligible English, they ought to be able to respond to that question without assistance from any quarter.

("Preparation," pp. 201-202.)

Appendix 10

J. Heidsiek:

J. Heidsiek of Breslau, in his efforts to break the hold of pure oralism in the German schools for the deaf, continued to write extensively on the subject after his visit to America. Unwisely he involved the names of some German schools' administrators and as a result found himself with a libel suit. To compound his predicament he was also without sufficient funds to provide an attorney for his own defense.

Through the efforts of his American friends and colleagues, the sum of $127.55 was raised in his behalf. ("Heidsiek's Legal Problem," p. 174.) For all of Heidsiek's struggle, however, oralism continued to prevail in Germany and has so continued well into our 20th Century.

Appendix 11

1. The Reverend Thomas Gallaudet, an ordained Episcopal priest, became the first missionary for deaf people. He is also credited with founding Saint Anne's Church in New York City, the first Episcopal church established exclusively for deaf people.

2. The Reverend Thomas Gallaudet and his younger brother, Edward Miner Gallaudet, although both were raised in the same household in which deafness was a central interest and concern, appear to have disagreed in their perspectives of that disability. Thomas Gallaudet viewed deaf people, as he once said, as a "peculiar people." ("Peculiar People," pp. 131-133.) His brother Edward, on the contrary, devoted his life to proving their normality.

Appendix 12

The *American Annals of the Deaf* for July, 1880, carried the following under "Institution Items."

> The exercises of Presentation Day were held in the presence of a large audience, including the President of the United States and many other prominent officers of the Government, on the first Wednesday of April.

... Mr. Goodman's admirable oral delivery of his (valedictory) oration was a pleasing feature of the exercises. Mr. A. Graham Bell gave an interesting exposition of Visible Speech, at the close of which he was surprised with the honorary degree of Doctor of Philosophy conferred by the Corporation in recognition of valuable services he has rendered to the art of articulation teaching. . . . ("Bell's Honorary Degree," p. 224.)

Appendix 13

Mrs. A. G. Bell on speechreading:

Down through the years, the efficacy of speechreading as an instructional medium for prelingually deaf children has been brought into question by numbers of critics of the pure oral approach. One of the most notable of these was Mrs. Alexander Graham Bell (Mabel Hubbard Bell), who was herself postlingually deafened at the age of five as the result of scarlet fever.

Mrs. Bell in her classic article "The Subtile Art of Speech-Reading" stated that:

> There must always be, first, an intimate knowledge of the English language, especially in its vernacular form, so that a speech-reader shall have at command a large stock from which to select the right word used by a speaker. Thus one with the requsite knowledge of English would not make the mistake of supposing that he was asked to wipe his feet on a "man," while one without this knowledge would happen on the right word only by accident. "Man" and "mat" look alike to the eye. ("Subtile Art," p. 112.)

This is a concept which modern pure oralists might reinvestigate as to its validity and practicability in terms of English development in prelingually hearing-impaired children.

Appendix 14

Dr. A. G. Bell on language and speechreading:

> A knowledge of language will teach speech-reading, but speech-reading will not teach a knowledge of language, so that, I think, that every means we can employ to make the English language familiar to the pupil should be adopted before we cause him to rely exclusively upon the mouth. (De Land, "Memorial," p. 38.)

Appendix 15

In the spring of 1947, Dr. George Morris McClure, editor emeritus of *The Kentucky Standard* and a long-time teacher in the Kentucky School for the Deaf, was the Kendall Green guest of his grandson, William J. McClure, principal of the The Kendall School. This charming old gentleman, who incidentally lived to be 105 years of age, related the following anecdote which he subsequently recorded as follows in an article entitled "Dr. E. M. Gallaudet as I Remember Him."

> There came a day when Dr. Gallaudet, too, indulged in a bit of satire. At a meeting of the (1895) Convention held at Flint, Mich., he read a paper in the course of which he mentioned the name of Dr. Bell's pet project, "The American Association to Promote the Teaching of Speech to the Deaf." Using a slow Southern drawl he strung out the name, while the interpreter, Superintendent John E. Ray, then of the Kentucky School, put the drawl into a manual alphabet by starting at one end of the long platform and walking slowly to the other, spelling laboriously, "T-h-e A-m-e-r-i-c-a-n A-s-s-o-c-i-a-t-i-o-n t-o P-r-o-m-o-t-e t-h-e T-e-a-c-h-i-n-g o-f S-p-e-e-c-h t-o t-h-e D-e-a-f." Every one was smiling by the time the spelling was finished, – that is everyone but Dr. Bell, sitting a few feet away. But I have not space to describe that historic clash that followed. On motion of the Convention peacemaker, Dr. Robert Mathieson, of Belleville, Canada, the Convention passed a resolution asking the two men to shake hands and forget their differences. After a long moment they exchanged a frigid handshake, but never again did they meet in amity.
>
> (McClure, "Gallaudet," pp. 1-2.)

Appendix 16

Mr. Frank W. Booth, principal of the Mt. Airy School for the Deaf manual department and subsequently superintendent of the Volta Bureau, summarized before the Chicago 1893 World Congress of Instructors of the Deaf the place of English acquisition in the educational development of deaf children.

> The great work of educating the deaf is the great work of giving the English language. Much else should be given and is given; but English is essential, and, if given, practically all is given, for all else is contained and may be contained by it. . . .
>
> A language is not learned by talking about it, even in its own terms, much less by talking about it in another. A language is best learned, not by talking about it, but by talking *in* it, – about anything and everything that may interest the reader.

Appendix 17

Rudolf Pintner:

Professor Rudolph Pintner of Columbia University was the senior investigator in the now historical *Survey of American Schools for the Deaf.* In subsequent years his research impressed upon him the seriousness of the language problem of prelingually hearing-impaired children.

Like many persons, however, whose theoretical knowledge exceeds their practical, he determined the language problem of deaf children to be practically insurmountable. As a consequence, he hit upon a solution which recommended circumventing the problem rather than attempting to solve it.

Eventually in collaboration with his Columbia colleagues Eisenson and Stanton, Pintner wrote a book entitled *Psychology of the Physically Handicapped*, published in 1941. In his chapter on deafness, Pintner wrote the following rationale and proposal:

> The motor and mechanical ability and the concrete intelligence of the deaf are their great assets. Their abstract verbal intelligence, their academic achievement, are their great liabilities. This being so, is not the time ripe to reorient the whole education of the deaf? For most deaf children the emphasis should be upon the motor, the mechanical, the concrete. Make the core of their education center around the concrete and the mechanical. Make the learning of language subsidiary and ancillary to making, building and doing. Only for a few should the academic curriculum be followed. Shop work, home economics, trade training of all kinds, dramatics, gardening, and the like, these would be the main "subjects," and reading and writing and arithmetic would be subsidiary and incidental aspects of the main "course." Some bold and wise educator of the deaf has a great opportunity here. (Pintner, "Education of the Deaf," pp. 178-179.)

Two unfortunate occurrences evolved which precluded any substantial rebuttal to Pintner's negativistic approach. First, he died, and second, World War II began. With the confusion and concerns brought on by the latter event, scholarly debates were set aside and Pintner's idea had to wait.

After the war, however, a "bold and wise educator of the deaf" did step forth in the person of a young New Jersey vocational teacher named Charles M. Jochem. Jochem was named superintendent of the New Jersey School for the Deaf in West Trenton. With the "Pintnerian" thesis in mind Jochem set about to organize one of the finest vocational schools for the deaf in the United States.

True to Pintner's idea, language learning was made "subsidiary and ancillary to making, building and doing." For all the emphasis placed upon vocational education, however, pupil and parental demands alike brought back a renewed emphasis on academic learning, specifically that of English reading and writing. With this Pintner's idea was laid to rest.

Appendix 18

Dr. Percival Hall on "Instructional Communication at Gallaudet College":

> As the students of the college come each year from over 30 different states and from schools employing somewhat different methods, and as good results in educational progress are aimed at, rather than exploitation of any method, the combined system of instruction is employed. The basis of our work, of course, is the English language. Manual spelling and writing constitute the chief method of communication. A great deal of speech is used, interpreted in most cases by the eye, but in some cases by the ear. Manual spelling is particularly efficient and necessary in the teaching of French, Latin and other foreign languages. Teachers do not hesitate to use a gesture or sign when such use adds to the understanding of a confused or slow pupil. The aim of the college in all of its work is to make the vehicle of communciation subordinate to the educational progress which must be had by any student to be promoted from class to class and finally graduate. ("Instructional Communication," p. 16.)

Appendix 19

"A Combination That Works in a Preschool Program for Deaf Children" (by Richard G. Brill, Ed.D., and Joan Fahey, B.S.):

> While many educators of deaf persons have subscribed to the philosophy that methods should be adjusted to the child rather than the child to the method, not many have practiced this with young children. Most schools for the deaf have had exclusively oral primary departments for younger children, even when providing a combination of oral and manual communication for older children.
>
> The rationale for this discrimination with younger deaf children has been that every deaf child should be given the opportunity to learn to talk and to speechread, and that only after the child has shown that he failed at this method should other communication systems be

allowed. It has also been assumed or claimed that any manual communication would interfere with a child's learning oral communication.

. . . Postponing utilizing manual communication in a deaf child's educational program until he is old enough to have failed at oral communication can seriously inhibit the child's ability to communicate, and can thus affect the development of his personality.

At the California School for the Deaf in Riverside, which includes grades one through 12, the Rochester Method of using manual communication and fingerspelling combined with oral speech and speechreading has been utilized with all children regularly enrolled in the school for some years. We have mounting evidence that this is raising the achievement level, the language level and the communication abilities of these children much more rapidly than when only single methods are used.

With this record of success, we felt a similar approach would be effective with children of preschool age. Earlier, we had tried a program using manual fingerspelling combined with oral presentations. This was not very successful in terms of words the children of this age learned, and we concluded that children under five are not usually mature enough to learn the abstract symbols of spelled words.

Thus in September, 1969, we decided to institute a program for preschool deaf children utilizing signs and oral communication simultaneously. Sixteen children, eight boys and eight girls, were enrolled for the first session. Their ages ranged from three to five years. Eleven of the children were deaf as a result of rubella, one from meningitis and four from unknown causes.

The mothers of these children were asked to attend one class session with their child each week, so that they could learn to communicate with and work with their child at home. When attending class the mothers were shown the new sign vocabulary, speech and speechreading vocabulary which their children had learned that week. They were asked to work on these new words with the children at home. They were also asked to make picture scrapbooks of the new vocabulary, so the child would have concrete visual reinforcement in using the words they had learned.

The children were able to learn signs at the rate of 10 to 20 words or more a week. At the end of the session, they had learned 350 words in signs, including 276 nouns, 35 verbs, 32 adjectives, five prepositions and six question forms. They also learned such expressions as, "Good morning," and "Happy birthday." In utilizing this vocabulary, the children learned to distinguish between various picture descriptions such as, "The boy is eating ice cream."

Since sight is the deaf child's main vehicle for learning, we utilized many visual aids for instruction. We had films such as "Little Red Riding Hood," and the stories were told in signs and speech. The children also did various typical preschool activities such as easel painting, finger painting, coloring, cutting, water painting outside, and they worked with educational toys.

While giving the children freedom of expression through sign language, we simultaneously emphasized the development of speech. Individual speech and speechreading work was done with each child, and each had his own speech books. With the concepts already learned from signs, the children had a clearer understanding of purpose of speech and they were better prepared to transfer sign to spoken words.

All of the children learned to imitate almost all of the elements. Some also learned to recognize the written form of these elements. The number of words learned by each in exact speech varied with the age of the child, the amount of hearing and the length of time the child had been in school. Some could say only four words in understandable speech, while others had a speech vocabulary of around 50 words and began doing simple sentences.

We found that the use of signs did not hinder the development of speech, but actually helped by making the children more willing and more cooperative in all activities. They had already learned to associate symbols (signs) with objects, and they were better prepared to associate the abstract speech word with the object. With both systems of communication available for their use, the children would use words spontaneously, sometimes with the sign and sometimes without it.

Since it is much easier to teach sign language to deaf children than it is to teach speech, combined programs of learning must be very conscientious in stressing the development of speech. The sign language comes naturally, and it can be used as a very important foundation for building a good speaking vocabulary, if the proper instruction is given.

Speechreading must be equally emphasized. The children in our program learned to speechread from six to at least 100 words. Only one child did not learn to speechread at all, and she was later diagnosed as emotionally disturbed. As in speech work, we found that the use of signs was a help, not a hindrance, in teaching children to speechread. We also found that children in this program were just as adequate in speechreading, if not better, than children in previous classes were when signs were not used.

As a result of our combined approach of signs, speechreading and oral communication, many important developments were manifested with this group of children. Perhaps the most important was the increased social adjustment of each of the children. They all seemed to enjoy thoroughly the progam, and they learned to play well together. Using signs they were able to communicate with adults and with each other. The children were involved in their work, looked forward to learning new words and concepts and approached the learning process with intelligence and optimism.

The behavior of the children was quite good. Very few showed any signs of temper tantrums, and almost none showed signs of frustration, as is often evidenced in strictly oral approach. They took their excitement in learning home and began to communicate with their families, other adults and friends.

Another advantage of using the combined method applied particularly to our children who were rubella victims. These children tend to be hyperactive, and their attention span is very short. Such children cannot concentrate long enough to see a spoken word. However, they were able to make the association quickly through signs with objects and pictures, and as they learned they became calmer and more attentive. Having already grasped the concept of associating a symbol with an object or picture, the children had only to learn to recognize the speechreading word which went with the symbol, and this simplified the process of learning to speechread.

The results of this experimental program indicated conclusively to us the success in using a combination of oral and manual methods simultaneously in teaching communication to preschool deaf children. After only one year, the children in this program had developed an understanding and communicating ability of over 350 concepts. This is in contrast with children in most totally oral programs who have very limited numbers of concepts after just one year.

The speech and speechreading abilities are better in children who experience the combined system than with restriction to oral methods, and the social adjustment as demonstrated by behavior is far better. As a result, the child's familial relationships, as well as his school ones, are appreciably smoother and more rewarding.

The language of signs enables young children to begin cognitive growth at a very early age, thus making it possible for them to utilize the various thinking processes which result from having a symbol system. Once the symbol system is established, speech and speechreading can be fitted into the cognitive pattern. An ability to communicate through one system—sign language—frees the child from tension and enables him to progress to the more difficult systems of speech.

Sign language can be the missing key the preschooler so desperately needs to adapt himself to the hearing world, and in our programs, we do not feel we can deny him this important link.

(Brill and Fahey, "Combination," pp. 17-19.)

As indicated, in 1971 the Riverside School for the Deaf administration found through practical experimentation a valid use for sign language on the *preschool level.* Improvement in the area of concept development was, indeed, established among the preschool children at Riverside. Having concepts established, they generally moved without frustration into speech and speechreading.

The two remaining questions for future educators of the deaf to resolve are:

1. How is the transition from a child's growing dependency on the language of signs to an acceptance of orthographic English (reading and writing) to be effected?

2. At what level in the educational program should such a transition be commenced?

Appendix 20

As indicated in the text, it was during the 1960's that the Rochester (Visible English) Method was revived *in toto* at the Louisiana School for the Deaf at Baton Rouge as a practical alternative to traditional oralism. From the instructional experiences gleaned over a five-year period (1962-1967) a set of principles relative to the Rochester Method, its implementation, and its practice was formulated and published as follows in this author's *American Annals* article on the method, pp. 51-55.

> For parents, teachers, and school administrators in this latter half of the twentieth century who are interested in the Rochester Method as it is functioning in the Louisiana State School for the Deaf in Baton Rouge, this approach may be defined as an oral multi-sensory procedure for instructing deaf children. It is predicated upon the following operational guidelines:
>
> I
>
> A knowledge of the English language, both in reading and writing is essential to academic achievement, to complete social adjustment, and to adequate vocational placement.
>
> II
>
> The English language which is normally acquired through hearing must be made *visually perceptible* for the prelingual deaf child. This may be done easily through the use of writing and fingerspelling. The latter medium is more practical in most social and instructional situations because it may serve as a simultaneous supplement to the non-grammatical receptive medium of speechreading.
>
> III
>
> Speechreading is recognized as a non-grammatical receptive medium because it presents to the eye of the prelingual deaf child only key-words or broken syntactical patterns. Repetitious and persistent exposure to such incomplete language forms as are seen on the lips serves to reinforce the child's tendency toward the use of similar elliptical forms in both his written and oral language. In short, he imitates and learns only what he sees. The result is commonly termed "deaf language." Consequently, speechreading unsupplemented by a visible English medium is most unsatisfactory in an instructional or social situation.
>
> Mrs. Mabel Hubbard Bell in her classic article "The Subtile Art of Speech-Reading" recognized this fact in effect when she wrote:
>
>> There must also be an intimate knowledge of the English language, especially in its vernacular form, so that a speech-reader shall have at command a large stock of words from which to select the right word used by a speaker. (Bell, Mabel H., "The Subtile Art of Speech-Reading," *The Volta Review*, Vol. 19, p. 112.)

IV

The natural language of any child is that language to which he is consistently and persistently exposed from birth through the first five years of his life. For the prelingual deaf child the language exposure must be *visual*. The child's written and oral language will always tend to reflect what he sees or fails to see. The environment, therefore, of both home and school must be dedicated to the objective of making English *visually perceptible*. Without accurate perception of language there can be no accurate learning of language.

V

The point of emphasis in all language instruction for the prelingual deaf child should be upon the development of concepts through syntax rather than vocabulary. This is particularly important during the first five-year period of instruction. The reason is to compensate for the language deficit created during the first five years of life which are normally the "linguistic years" for the hearing child. Too often undue emphasis has been placed upon the acquisition of vocabulary. The language problem does not lie in the area of vocabulary, but in the area of syntax.

Many young deaf people having faithfully lived with their dictionaries possess extensive vocabularies. They cannot, however, set five words in correct sequence for a simple sentence. If syntax is not a functioning aspect of a prelingual deaf child's expressive language after his first five years of schooling, it is likely never to be.

VI

The beginning prelingual deaf child should first come to know visible English or fingerspelling as a receptive medium. Always should the child's focus of attention be upon a speaker's lips, *never upon the hand*. The hand is to be perceived only through the peripheral vision as a supplement to the lip movements. Westervelt stressed specifically the face as the center of focus:

> One proficient in dactylology is not in the habit of keeping his eye upon the hand of the speller, but watches the play of expression upon his face while, at the same time, the eye takes in the spelled language. (Scouten, *A Revaluation of the Rochester Method*, Dr. Bell's Estimate, RSD Alumni Assn., Rochester School for the Deaf, 1942, pp. 14-16.)

The beginning deaf child is not taught the manual alphabet in its a, b, c sequence: nor is he expected to use fingerspelling during his first months of schooling. Only after weeks and months of exposure to the visible English of fingerspelling as a supplement to speechreading will he gradually begin to imitate fingerspelling and to approximate words. There will be observed after a time a marked and ever-increasing effort on the part of the child to use expressive English. Relative to the use of fingerspelling with congenital or prelingual deaf children, Dr. Alexander Graham Bell made the following statement:

> Spoken language I would have used by the pupil from the commencement of his education to the end of it; but spoken language I would not have used as a means of communication

with pupils in the earliest stages of education of the congenitally deaf, because it is not clear to the eye, and requires a knowledge of the language to unravel the ambiguities. In that case I would have the teacher use written language, and I do not think that the manual language [fingerspelling] differs from written language excepting in this, that it is better and more expeditious. (De Land, Fred, "An Ever-Continuing Memorial," *The Volta Review*, Vol. 25, p. 37.)

Hearing persons in supplementing their speech with fingerspelling must remember not to *name the letters* as they fingerspell words. The names of letters, for example see-aye-tee (cat), present to the eye of the deaf child three separate and distinct words, which of themselves are meaningless. The speaker must always *orally pronounce* words, giving the full phoenetic values of letters rather than their alphabetic names; thus, comprehension through speechreading is greatly facilitated for the child. More important, however, is the fact that the total pattern of oral language is made clearly perceptible.

VII

While oral articulation or speech is a vital objective in the education of the deaf, it must not be confused with the more fundamental objective, *language acquisition*. Speech is the physical result of the integrated and coordinated interactions of lips, teeth, tongue and innumerable refined muscles over and through which breath is passed. Closely considered, speech development is a very precise type of physical training. Because of the tediousness and the monotony of the required physical exercises and drills necessary for the development of and combining of speech elements, *motivation* is of primary importance.

VIII

In that a prelingual deaf child's progress in speech development is dependent upon motivation it is first contingent upon a state of readiness—*speech readiness*. In this direction it has been observed that the early and consistent introduction of *visible* English concepts, syntax and vocabulary, quickly fill the child's vacuum of personal need for a communicative medium. The intellectual press of concepts clothed in English serve the child as a strong factor for speech readiness.

The most classic example of early and consistent language instruction serving as a motivating force for speech is summed up in the determined announcement of the deaf-blind and *mute* child, Helen Keller, when she fingerspelled to her teacher in simple and correct English, "I must speak." It was then that Miss Sarah Fuller was contacted to teach little Helen how to talk. (Fuller, Sarah, "How Helen Keller Learned to Speak," *American Annals of the Deaf*, Vol. 37, No. 1, January, 1891, p. 24.) The motivation for speech and speech development comes only through having something to say. Hence *visible* English, receptive and expressive, should be encouraged to blossom and to flourish as an incentive for oral expression. Speech instruction should move along at its own measured pace; but, at no time, should it ever be permitted to impede the progress of education. The Helen Keller reference, incidentally, refutes the idea that fingerspelling detracts from or is a deterrent to speech instruction.

IX

The objective to be achieved in the physical speech performance of a prelingual deaf child is not normality of production, but *intelligibility*. Normality is an unrealistic goal in view of the impossibility of the deaf child to monitor himself adequately. The true test of the intelligibility of deaf speech is the aural understanding of an unsophisticated listener unaided by speechreading.

If, after three years of careful speech training supplemented by aural amplification, a child fails to respond, does so poorly, or does so with a half-hearted interest, he should be encouraged to participate in oral language activities which allow for speech approximations and stress language precision.

X

No foreign language, including the language of signs and the unsupplemented lip movements of speechreading, has a place in the home or school environment of a prelingual deaf child. The employment of any language or symbol system other than that of visible English is detrimental to the child's acquisition of correct English. Such other languages deny the child the all-essential exposure necessary for English mastery. They likewise reinforce syntactical habits which result in "deaf language."

If the mastery of receptive and expressive English is to be the prime academic goal, an unequivocal and unyielding adherence to a total visible English atmosphere must be the rule.

XI

The role of auditory amplification is of particular importance. First, a maximal use of residual hearing through amplification serves to bring the child closer to the world of sound and to his identification with it. This is of positive psychological value even if it places the child but a mite closer to the reality of a dog's bark. Second, and equally important, whatever residual hearing exists will serve well in the physical development of speech. Therefore, every prelingual deaf child should be administered a thorough auditory test to determine specifically his areas of residual hearing. The child should be encouraged to use his aid in all instructional situations and with maturity in all social situations.

XII

Parents must be made aware of the great educational responsibility they share with teachers in maintaining the "visible English front" at home on holidays, weekends, and during the long three months of summer vacation. Parents must realize the vital significance of a simple explanation, a little chat, an occasional loving word in *visible* English—fingerspelling supplementing speech. Such a communicative experience will do more to bring the child into the reality of family life than any other kind of effort.

Parents would not deny the orthopedic child his leg braces, nor the blind child his Braille. Logic similarly dictates that the prelingual deaf child should not be denied his right to *see* the total of English syntax by whatever means that will enable him to imitate and to learn it. This right to be realized, however, must be unequivocally supported by his parents as well as his teachers.

Conclusion

While these principles for action have not yet received the imprimatur of scientific research, they are based upon an aggregate of more than ninety years of empirically established evidence. As a consequence, our lending the deaf child a hand through the Rochester Method is considerably more than a metaphor; it is a demonstrable fact that makes a more complete language mastery for the child not just an ideal, but a natural and reasonable goal.

Appendix 21

Re: A polytechnic institute (Mr. Rogers' plea):

> There is a danger that a great central institution endowed by the wealth of a nation, might overdo the subject and substitute the fanciful for the useful, spoiling good artisans to make poor artists. ("Re: A Polytechnic Institute," p. 285.)

This proves that a genuinely strong idea can crawl out from beneath the wettest blanket.

Bibliography

BIBLIOGRAPHY

Amman, John Conrad. *Surdus Loquens* (The Talking Deaf Man). London: Howkins, 1692.

_____. *Dissertation on Speech*. 1700. Reprint. London: S. Low, Marston, Low and Searle, 1873.

Anthony, David. *Recent Developments in Manual English*. Washington, D.C.: Gallaudet College Press, 1973.

Babbidge, Homer. *Report on the Advisory Committee on Education of the Deaf*. Washington, D.C.: U.S. Government Printing Office, 1965.

Barnes, Harvey. "How a National School of Trades, Agriculture and Technical Training Would Solve Our Problems," *Proceedings of the 32nd Meeting of the Convention of American Instructors of the Deaf*. Fulton, Mo.: U.S. Government Printing Office, 1941.

Barry, Katherine. *The Five Slate Method: A System of Objective Language Teaching*. Philadelphia: Sherman and Company, 1899.

Bartlett, David E. "The Acquisition of Language." *American Annals of the Deaf*, Vol. 3, No. 2, 1851.

_____. "Family Education for Young Deaf-Mute Children." *American Annals of the Deaf*, Vol. 5, No. 1, 1852.

_____. "Mr. Bartlett's Family School for Young Deaf-Mute Children." *American Annals of the Deaf*, Vol. 24, No. 4, 1879.

Bede, the Venerable. *The Ecclesiastical History of the English Nation.* London: J. M. Dent, 1903.

Bell, Alexander Graham. *Memoir upon the Formation of a Deaf Variety of the Human Race.* Washington, D.C.: National Academy of Science, 1883.

_____. "Upon a Method of Teaching Language to a Very Young Congenitally Deaf Child." *American Annals of the Deaf,* Vol. 28, 1883.

Bell, Mabel Hubbard. "The Subtile Art of Speech-Reading." *Volta Review,* March, 1917.

"Bell's Honorary Degree." *American Annals of the Deaf,* Vol. 25, No. 3, 1880.

Bender, Ruth. *The Conquest of Deafness* (3rd edition). Danville, Ill.: The Interstate Printers & Publishers, Inc., 1981.

Bishop, Milo (editor). *Mainstreaming: Practical Ideas for Educating Hearing-Impaired Students.* Washington, D.C.: The Alexander Graham Bell Association for the Deaf, 1979.

Boatner, Maxine Tull. *Edward Miner Gallaudet: The Voice of the Deaf.* Washington, D.C.: Public Affairs Press, 1959.

Bonet, Juan Pablo. *Simplification of the Letters of the Alphabet and Method of Teaching Deaf-Mutes to Speak.* Madrid: Francisco, 1620.

Booth, Frank W. "English Acquisition for Deaf Children," *Proceedings of the World Congress of Instructors of the Deaf.* Chicago: 1893.

Brill, Richard G. *The Education of the Deaf: Administrative and Professional Developments.* Washington, D.C.: Gallaudet College Press, 1974.

_____. "Mainstreaming: Format or Quality." *American Annals of the Deaf,* Vol. 120, No. 4, 1975.

_____. *Mainstreaming the Prelingually Deaf Child.* Washington, D.C.: Gallaudet College Press, 1978.

Brill, Richard G., and Fahey, Joan. "A Combination That Works in a Preschool Program for Deaf Children." *Hearing & Speech News,* Vol. 39, No. 4, 1971.

Bruce, Robert V. *Bell: Alexander Graham Bell and the Conquest of Solitude.* Boston: Little, Brown & Co., 1973.

Bulwer, John. *Chirologia; or The Natural Language of the Hand.* London: H. Moseley, 1644.

_____. *Philocophus* (The Deaf Man's Friend). London: H. Moseley, 1648.

Buxton, David. "Notes of Progress in Education of the Deaf." *American Annals of the Deaf*, Vol. 28, 1883.

Carlyle, Thomas. *The French Revolution*. New York: Random House, Modern Library, n.d.

"Constitutional Meeting of CED." *Volta Review*, March, 1961.

Craig, William N., and Salem, James. "Partial Integration of Deaf with Hearing Students: Residential School Perspectives." *American Annals of the Deaf*, Vol. 120, No. 1, 1975.

Dale, D. M. C. *Language Development in Deaf and Partially Hearing Children*. Springfield, Ill.: Charles C Thomas, Publisher, 1974.

Dalgarno, George. *Ars Signorum* (The Art of Signs). Oxford: Timothy Halton, 1661.

_____. *Didascalocophus* (The Deaf and Dumb Man's Tutor). Oxford: Timothy Halton, 1680. (*American Annals of the Deaf*, Vol. 9, 1857.)

Davidson, S. G. "Henry Winter Syle." *American Annals of the Deaf*, Vol. 35, No. 2, 1890.

Day, Herbert E.; Fusfeld, Irving S.; and Pintner, Rudolf. *A Survey of American Schools for the Deaf*, 1924-1925. Washington, D.C.: National Research Council, 1925.

Deaf-Mute Education in Massachusetts: Report of the Joint Special Committee of the Legislature of 1867 with an Appendix. Boston: 1867.

Defoe, Daniel. *The Life and Adventures of Duncan Campbell*. London: 1720.

De Land, Fred. "An Ever-Continuing Memorial." *Volta Review*, Vol. 25, 1923.

_____. *The Story of Lip Reading*. 1931. Reprint. Washington, D.C.: The Alexander Graham Bell Association for the Deaf, 1968.

De l'Epee, Charles Michel. *The True Manner of Instructing the Deaf and Dumb, Confirmed by Long Experience*. Paris: Chez Nyon l'Aine, 1789.

Denison, James. "Impression of the Milan Convention." *American Annals of the Deaf*, Vol. 26, No. 1, 1881.

Doctor, P. V. (editor). "Founding of the Council on Education of the Deaf." *American Annals of the Deaf*, Vol. 105, No. 2, 1960.

Draper, Amos. "Preparation for the College Course." *American Annals of the Deaf*, Vol. 19, 1876.

Drumm, Philip R. "Total Communication – Fraud or Reality?" *Volta Review*, Vol. 74, No. 9, 1972.

Farrar, Abraham. *Arnold's Education of the Deaf* (updated). London: Francis Carter, 1901.

Fay, Edward Allen. "A Day School in Chicago." *American Annals of the Deaf*, Vol. 16, No. 3, 1871.

———————————. "Institution for the Improved Instruction." *American Annals of the Deaf*, Vol. 16, No. 4, 1871.

———————————."Changes and New Appointments." *American Annals of the Deaf*, Vol. 18, No. 3, 1873.

———————————. *Histories of American Schools for the Deaf.* Washington, D.C.: Volta Bureau, 1893.

———————————. "New York Institution for Improved Instruction." *American Annals of the Deaf*, Vol. 42, No. 6, 1897.

———————————. "A Constant Language Environment." *Volta Review*, February, 1916.

Fay, Gilbert O. "A Week at Rochester." *American Annals of the Deaf*, Vol. 34, No. 4, 1889.

"The First Woman Graduate." *35th Annual Report of the Columbia Institute for the Deaf and Dumb*, 1892.

Fitzgerald, Edith. *Straight Language for the Deaf*. Staunton, Va.: McClure Company, 1926.

Fourgon, Fernand. *Historique de la Pedagogie des Sourds-Muets*, Vols. 1 and 2. Paris: 1957.

Frampton, Merle E., and Gall, Elena D. *Special Education for the Exceptional*, Vol. 2. Boston: Porter Sargent Publishers, Inc., 1960.

Fusfeld, Irving S. "Purposes and Extent of the Survey of Schools for the Deaf," *Proceedings of the 24th Meeting of CAID*. Washington, D.C.: U.S. Government Printing Office, 1925.

———————————. *A Handbook of Readings in Education of the Deaf and Postschool Implications*. Springfield, Ill.: Charles C Thomas, Publisher, 1967.

Gallaudet, Edward Miner. "The American System of Deaf-Mute Instruction – Its Incidental Defects and Their Remedies." *American Annals of the Deaf*, Vol. 13, No. 3, 1868.

———————————. "Is the Sign Language Used to Excess in

Teaching Deaf-Mutes?" *American Annals of the Deaf*, Vol. 16, No. 1, 1871.

_____. "Preparation for the College Course." *American Annals of the Deaf*, Vol. 25, No. 3, 1880.

_____. "The Milan Convention." *American Annals of the Deaf*, Vol. 26, No. 1, 1881.

_____. "Remarks on the Combined System." *American Annals of the Deaf*, Vol. 26, No. 1, 1881.

_____. "Admission of Young Women to the College." *29th Annual Report of the Columbia Institute for the Deaf and Dumb*, 1886.

_____. "Letter re: The 'New Departure'. " *American Annals of the Deaf*, Vol. 32, April, 1887.

Gallaudet, Thomas. "A Peculiar People." *Proceedings of the 9th Convention of Instructors of the Deaf and Dumb*, 1878.

Goldstein, Max A. "The Acoustic Method." *Proceedings of the International Congress on the Education of the Deaf*, 1933.

Gordon, Joseph C. "Re: J. J. Valade-Gabel." *American Annals of the Deaf*, Vol. 30, No. 2, 1885.

Greenberger, David. "The Natural Method." *American Annals of the Deaf*, Vol. 23, No. 2, 1878.

_____. "The Natural Method II." *American Annals of the Deaf*, Vol. 24, No. 1, 1879.

_____. "The Word Method" (review by E. A. Fay). *American Annals of the Deaf*, Vol. 36, No. 4, 1891.

Green, Francis. *Vox Oculus Subjecta* (Voice Made Visible). London: 1783.

Griffith, Jerry. *Persons with Hearing Loss*. Springfield, Ill.: Charles C Thomas, Publisher, 1969.

Groht, Mildred. *Natural Language for Deaf Children*. Washington, D.C.: The Alexander Graham Bell Association for the Deaf, 1958.

Hall, Percival. "Instructional Communication at Gallaudet College," *Percival Hall's Collected Papers*. Washington, D.C.: Gallaudet College Press, c. 1941.

Halpen, Rosa. *Historical Sketch of the Rochester School for the Deaf*. Rochester, N.Y.: R.S.D., 1936.

Harris, G. I. "The Value of the Deaf Teacher." *Proceedings of the International Congress on the Education of the Deaf*, 1933.

Heidsiek, J. "Education of the Deaf and Dumb in the United States" (Part 3). *American Annals of the Deaf,* Vol. 44, No. 3, 1899.

_____. "Education of the Deaf and Dumb in the United States" (Part 4). *American Annals of the Deaf,* Vol. 45, 1899.

"Heidsiek's Legal Problem." *American Annals of the Deaf,* Vol. 38, No. 1, 1893.

Herodotus. *The Persian Wars.* New York: Random House, Modern Library, 1947.

Hester, Marshall. "Manual Communication," *Proceedings of the International Congress on Education of the Deaf.* Washington, D.C.: Government Printing Office, 1964.

Hoag, Ralph. "Proposal for a Comprehensive, Multipurpose Vocational and Technical Institute for the Deaf," *Proceedings of a National Workshop on Improved Opportunities for the Deaf.* Washington, D.C.: 1964.

_____. "Remarks Relative to a Proposed NTID," *Proceedings of a National Workshop on Improved Opportunities for the Deaf.* Washington, D.C.: 1964.

Hodgson, Kenneth W. *The Deaf and Their Problems.* New York: Philosophical Library, 1954.

Holcomb, Roy K. "Three Years of Total Approach, 1968-1971." *Proceedings of the 45th CAID Meeting,* 1971.

_____. "The Total Approach," *Proceedings of the International Congress on Education of the Deaf – Stockholm, 1970,* Vol. 1. Stockholm: Swedish Teachers Association, 1972.

_____. "Total Communication Is a Must." *Proceedings of the 46th CAID Meeting,* 1973.

Holder, William. *Elements of Speech &. with an Appendix Concerning Persons Deaf and Dumb.* London: Printed by Thomas J. Martyn, Printers of the Royal Society, 1669.

Hornaday, Mary. "Straight Language." *Christian Science Monitor,* October 31, 1933.

Howe, Samuel Gridley. "Education of Laura Bridgman." *American Annals of the Deaf,* Vol. 20, No. 2, 1875.

"Initial Discussions for a CED." *American Annals of the Deaf,* Vol. 105, No. 2, 1960.

Johnson, Helen. "The Ability of Pupils in a School for the Deaf to Understand Various Methods of Communication." *American Annals of the Deaf,* Vol. 93, Nos. 2, 3, 1948.

John Tracy Clinic Bulletin, Fall 1962. Los Angeles: John Tracy Clinic, 1962.

Jones, Ray L. "The National Leadership Training Program," *Proceedings of the Conference on the Training of Specialized Personnel to Work with Deaf People.* Urbana, Ill.: 1963.

_____. "An Interview." *Audiology and Hearing Education,* June/July, 1976.

Lane, Harlan. *The Wild Boy of Aveyron.* Cambridge, Mass.: Harvard University Press, 1976.

Lash, Joseph P. *Helen and Teacher.* New York: Delacorte Press / Seymour Lawrence, 1980.

Ling, Daniel. "A Reaction." *Volta Review,* Vol. 74, No. 9, 1972.

McClure, George Morris. "Dr. E. M. Gallaudet as I Remember Him." *The Kentucky Standard,* Vol. 77, February, 1950.

"Milan Convention Program." *American Annals of the Deaf,* Vol. 25, No. 2, 1880.

Mindel, Eugene D. "A Reaction." *Volta Review,* Vol. 74, No. 9, 1972.

Mindel, Eugene D., and Vernon, McCay. *They Grow in Silence: The Deaf Child and His Family.* Silver Spring, Md.: National Association of the the Deaf, 1971.

Moores, Donald F. *Educating the Deaf: Psychology, Principles and Practices.* Boston: Houghton Mifflin Co., 1978.

Morel, Edward. "Morel's Biographical Sketch of DeGerando." Translated by Edward Peet. *American Annals of the Deaf,* Vol. 4, No. 3, 1852.

_____. "Biographical Sketch of Dr. Itard." Translated by Edward Peet. *American Annals of the Deaf,* Vol. 5, No. 1, 1852.

Nix, Gary W. (editor). *Mainstream Education for Hearing Impaired Children and Youth.* New York: Grune & Stratton, 1976.

NTID. *Report of First Year Ending Dec. 20, 1967.*

NTID. *Report of Second Year Ending Dec. 31, 1968.*

Numbers, Mary E. *My Words Fell on Deaf Ears.* Washington, D.C.: The Alexander Graham Bell Association for the Deaf, 1974.

Peet, Harvey Prindle. *On the Legal Rights and Responsibilities of the Deaf and Dumb.* New York: Steam Power Presses, 1857.

Peterson, Peter N. "A Dream and a Possibility." *The Vocational Teacher,* Vol. 1, No. 1, 1930.

Pintner, Rudolf. "Education of the Deaf." Chapter 5 in *Psychology of the Physically Handicapped*, edited by Eisenson and Stanton. New York: Columbia University Press, 1941.

Pope, Alvin. "Address of the President," *Proceedings of the International Congress on the Education of the Deaf.* Washington, D.C.: U.S. Government Printing Office, 1933.

Rae, Luzerne. "The Great Peril of Sicard." *American Annals of the Deaf,* Vol. 1, No. 1, 1847.

_____. "Dr. Peet's European Tour." *American Annals of the Deaf,* Vol. 4, No. 4, 1852.

"Re: A Polytechnic Institute (Mr. Rogers' Plea)." *American Annals of the Deaf,* Vol. 33, No. 4, 1888.

"Report of the Committee on Technical and Manual Training of the Deaf." *36th Annual Report of the Columbia Institute for the Deaf and Dumb,* 1893.

"A Resolution for Higher Technical Education for the Deaf." *36th Annual Report of the Columbia Institute for the the Deaf and Dumb,* 1893.

"A Resolution for the Establishment of a National Technical Institute for the Deaf (NTID)," *Proceedings of the Conference of Executives of American Schools for the Deaf.* Riverside, Cal.: 1964.

Rogers, D. S. "A Plea for a Polytechnic Institute." *American Annals of the Deaf,* Vol. 33, No. 3, 1888.

Rosenstein, Joseph. "A Reaction." *Volta Review,* Vol. 74, No. 9, 1972.

"St. Francis de Sales." *Listening,* Vol. 2, No. 1, 1979.

Scouten, Edward L. *A Revaluation of the Rochester Method.* Rochester, N.Y.: Rochester School for the Deaf (Lawyers Co-Operative Publishing Company), 1942.

_____. "The Rochester Method, An Oral Multisensory Approach for Instructing Prelingually Deaf Children." *American Annals of the Deaf,* Vol. 112, No. 2, 1967.

_____. "Total Communication in a New Perspective." *The Pelican,* Louisiana School for the Deaf, Vol. 92, No. 5, 1972.

"The Second Woman Graduate." *36th Annual Report of the Columbia Institute for the Deaf and Dumb,* 1893.

Sherer, Patricia. "A Reaction." *Volta Review,* Vol. 74, No. 9, 1972.

Sheridan, Laura C. "The Higher Education of Deaf-Mute Women." *American Annals of the Deaf,* Vol. 20, No. 4, 1875.

Simmons-Martin, Audrey. "The Oral/Aural Procedure: Theoretical

Basis and Rationale." *Volta Review*, Vol. 74, No. 9, 1972.

"Some Notable Benefactors of the Deaf in America." *Proceedings of the 5th Summer Meeting of the American Association to Promote the Teaching of Speech to the Deaf*, 1896.

"Special Education – The Handicapped and Gifted," *White House Conference on Child Health and Protection*. Washington, D.C.: 1931.

Stevenson, E. A. "Report of the Conference Committee on Nomenclature," *Proceedings of the 30th Meeting of the CAID.* Washington, D.C.: U.S. Government Printing Office, 1937.

_____. "The School of Tomorrow," *Proceedings of the 32nd Meeting of the Convention of American Instructors of the Deaf.* Washington, D.C.: U.S. Government Printing Office, 1941.

Sullivan, Anne. "How Helen Keller Acquired Language." *American Annals of the Deaf*, Vol. 37, No. 2, 1892.

Syle, Henry Winter. "A Summary of the Recorded Researches and Opinions of Harvey Prindle Peet." *American Annals of the Deaf*, Vol. 18, No. 3, 1873.

_____. "The Braidwood Family." *American Annals of the Deaf*, Vol. 23, No. 1, 1878.

Taylor, Harris. "Re: Abbé Sicard's Theory of Ciphers." *American Annals of the Deaf*, Vol. 61, No. 5, 1916.

"Total Communication Definition Committee Report," *Proceedings of the Conference of Executives of American Schools for the Deaf.* Rochester, N.Y.: 1976.

Tracy, Louise. "The Role of Parents in Education of the Deaf," *Proceedings of the 33rd Meeting of the Convention of American Instructors of the Deaf.* St. Augustine, Fla.: U.S. Government Printing Office, 1947.

Vaisse, Leon. "Practical Suggestions Relative to the Instruction of the Deaf and Dumb." *American Annals of the Deaf*, Vol. 19, No. 1, 1874.

Valade-Gabel, Jean Jacques. "The Institutions of the Deaf and Dumb in France." *American Annals of the Deaf,* Vol. 24, No. 4, 1879.

Vernon, McCay. "Mind over Mouth: A Rationale for Total Communication." *Volta Review,* Vol. 74, No. 9, 1972.

Wallis, John. *Grammar of English for Foreigners with an Essay on Speech or the Formulation of Sounds* (6th edition). Lugduni, Batavorum: Apud Jo. Arn. Langerak, 1653.

_____. "A Defence of the Royal Society &., in Answer to the Cavils of Dr. W. Holder 1678." *Supplement to the Philosophical Transactions*, 1678.

Walther, Eduard. *History of Deaf-Mute Instruction in German Speaking Countries* (review by E. A. Fay). *American Annals of the Deaf*, Vol. 28, No. 4, 1883.

Westervelt, Zenas F. "The Disuse of Signs." *Proceedings of the 9th CAID Meeting*, August, 1878.

_____. "Minutes for the First Planning Meeting of the AAPTSD." *American Annals of the Deaf*, Vol. 36, 1891.

Wing, George. "Function Symbols." *American Annals of the Deaf*, Vol. 30, No. 3, 1885.

"Women in College." *American Annals of the Deaf*, Vol. 25, No. 3, 1880.

Wright, David. *Deafness*. New York: Stein and Day, 1969.

Yale, Caroline. *Years of Building*. New York: The Dial Press, 1932.

Index

INDEX